Bi Parchamaan, The Flagless Ones

An Iranian Refugee Family's Story

by

Hassan H. Faramarz

A-Argus Better Book Publishers LLC
North Carolina***New Jersey

Bi Parchamaan, The Flagless Ones

A-Argus Better Book Publishers, LLC

For information:
A-Argus Better Book Publishers, LLC
Post Office Box 914
Kernersville, North Carolina 27285
www.a-argusbooks.com

ISBN: 0-9846348-3-5
ISBN: 978-0-9846348-3-5

Book Cover designed by Dubya

Printed in the United States of America

INTRODUCTION

A few words with the readers

In 1979, we, the people of Iran, decided to free ourselves from dictatorship. We flooded the streets throughout the country and revolted against the government, calling for our basic human rights. Our efforts seemed to be bearing fruit; we overthrew the Shah and tasted freedom; it tasted sweet!

Unfortunately, this didn't last long. Within a few months, while we were still heady with the feeling of victory, religious extremists, similar to the Taliban in Afghanistan, suddenly 'hijacked' our revolution.

For the past thirty years, severely deprived from their basic human rights, the people of Iran have ceaselessly fought against a government that calls itself the 'representative of God on earth' and is doing all it can to not only convert the entire nation to Shiite Islam but also to export that religion all over the world. During this time, no countries have paid particular attention to Iran until lately when the nuclear energy issue has come under attack.

The first time I thought of writing a book was in the early eighties when, as a schoolboy, I, in fear and despair, witnessed how the people of my village were brutally suppressed for their political ideals. Among them were four of my brothers.

At the suggestion of a close relative, I started a diary. In the beginning, I wasn't thinking of keeping track of what was going on in the country, I was just making notes of the events in my own family, how I felt being the only child left and all my brothers scattered. But our village was small, everybody knew everybody else by name and even knew which animals belonged to whom. Most everybody was somehow related, if not directly, then by marriage, and if not by marriage, then by the cooperation formed by mutual property boundaries. So my diary evolved to include others:

Friday...'Today, the third victim of the war arrived in a box and the school authorities took us out again to the local cemetery to accompany the other villagers in the burial ceremony'.

Wednesday...'Last night, the Islamic government forces secretly buried Behdad in one corner of the cemetery. He was executed for supporting the Mojahedin. At dawn, when these forces returned to their base, a group of unknown people attacked and killed one of them in what is said to be a retaliatory operation'.

Sunday...'This morning as I was leaving for the local bakery to buy bread, I found a 'night letter' on the stairs of our veranda. In the paper, distributed by the Mojahedin organization, I read that Darius, my oldest brother, along with eight others, was killed in an ambush set up by the Islamic Revolutionary Guards. I cried all the way to my uncle's bakery'.

My diary disappeared one day but the idea of writing a book persisted. During university years, I started writing the book, but although I knew how to begin it, I was not so sure how to end it or which language to write it in, English or Persian. If Persian, where could I publish it, then? How many people would get the chance to read it? I chose English but my English skills weren't up to such a herculean task. I put it aside and didn't pick it up again until I was living in China.

The idea of my story stayed on a back burner for years. I no longer remember how I came to discuss my writing with a student, but she, on hearing my life story, shifted her initial goal of learning Persian, and 'chose' to be part of my history. Together, we worked on this project, meeting several times a week on internet for over two years, writing, revising and editing. It was through her 'unperturbed and persistent interrogation' process that I was 'encouraged' to remember and put in words as much information about my past as I felt free to divulge. Without her, this book would never have reached you. She has my eternal gratitude.

In this book, except when I felt the need to intervene in order to give the readers a glimpse of my own attitudes, I have honestly reflected the events around me on my long journey. I know well in advance that such openness may upset certain groups of people. For those who feel offended, I refer you to a Persian poem that says, 'Do not break the mirror if you don't like what you see in it; break yourself'. As long as there are people who damage the greenery of nature which belongs to everybody to make temples for a few, as long as selfish dictators consider themselves the sole owners of their nations and as long as the leaders of the free world continue compromising with dictators, tension will threaten the peace and security of the globe.

We may need to remind ourselves that regardless of our belief systems, ethnicity, color, geographical locations or capabilities, we all have one thing in common: our equal share of this planet on which we are living. If there is anything sacred in life, it is life itself; it is this home, it is the people living here and it is the equal rights among the residents of this house.

The names of certain people and the descriptions of certain places have been changed for their protection, and some issues are not discussed in depth due to their sensitive nature. Any quotes are used for their beauty or their relationship to the story and not because I subscribe to the authors' ideologies.

Hassan H. Faramarz
Friday, 15 May 2009

Prologue

Either write something worth reading or do something worth writing!
.............Benjamin Franklin

My longest day—One

I have been pedalling for some time under the early morning sun and sweat has begun to trickle down my face. I want to stop and wipe my eyes, but knowing I will shortly arrive at the familiar building along the highway, which is my destination, I push on.

A gated fence surrounding a courtyard protects the entrance. I park my bicycle just outside the gate, light a cigarette and watch the cars come and go. People with papers in their hands are also walking into or coming out of the front door, hope, relief or frustration lining in their faces. I entertain myself with fantasies about them while smoking and cooling off a bit. My cigarette finished, "Excuse me!" I call to a young lady who is walking through my patch of shade, "What time is it?"

"Almost nine," she replies, looking at her watch.

It is time. With reluctance, my mind uncertain about the outcome of this day, I get up and join the crowd heading into the building. The structure is of concrete, and it is degrees cooler inside than out; cement stairs lead me to the second floor, where hundreds of people have lined up in various long queues. I make my way through the throng, finally joining the few other foreigners who are facing a short and wide cement wall at the end of the hall serving as the police officers' table. The wall curves around the large hall like a halved oval, with a staircase centered in it. Officers are sitting at different points behind the wall with people forming lines in front of them.

As the people in my line stand waiting their turn, a young man greets me. We begin to chat and I learn he is a reporter from Spain whose passport and perhaps other documents have been seized. He tells me he has been here in this line every day for about a week, trying to convince the authorities to return his papers.

A short time later, one of the staff, a woman sitting across the table, calls to my new friend who is then given his documents and asked to respect the laws of the country in the future. From the sound of it, he has had visa overstay problems. Smiling, he puts his documents in his bag and waves goodbye. I am next.

"Yes?" The same young lady calls to me.

"I am here to meet Mr. Lee."

"May I have your name, please?"

"Hassan."

"Nationality?"

"Iranian."

She asks me to wait for a moment and picks up the phone. Not long after that, I see Mr. Lee and a few of his friends, all dressed in military-style uniforms, walking towards me. I begin moving forward as well, and we meet near a door. Mr. Lee approaches me with a big smile on his face, and shakes hands with me warmly.

"Good morning."

"Morning."

"How are you?"

"Fine, thank you."

"How is the family?"

"They are fine."

"He has three lovely children," he says, turning to his colleagues.

"Yes, I know," answers one of his friends, "I have their pictures."

Our children, ages 4, 6 and 8

They spend the next few minutes talking about my kids.

"The oldest child was less than a year old when I first saw him." Mr. Lee tells his friends. "With long blond curls falling around his bright face, he was very beautiful, as beautiful as a girl."

We all smile and I follow them through the doorway and into the main part of the building. From there we descend to the first floor and enter a room. Everyone sits and one of them brings me a glass of water. An ashtray is set beside me and another young officer offers me a cigarette.

"Mr. Fu is very angry with what you did, Hassan," Mr. Lee begins in his Chinese-flavoured English. "Other people don't like your actions, too."

"I am sorry for making them upset," I try to explain. "It wasn't my intent to make trouble for you."

"I know," he admits, "but you did. Our government also doesn't like it at all. We all want to quickly resolve these issues. I asked you to come here today because we need to review your life story again."

"But you already know everything."

"This time is different," he answers. "We plan to send your case to the government authorities here in Beijing."

"Why?"

"Because we want to find a solution. We are trying to help you. I don't promise anything, but let's see what we can do." Pausing for a moment, he continues, "Now tell me your story again, in detail, nothing left out."

I agree, and begin a tale still raw and painful for me, a tale of deceit, betrayal, bloodshed, disillusionment and homelessness. The police officers meticulously write everything down, filling paper after paper with the events through which I have lived for what seems like a lifetime.

Bi Parchamaan, The Flagless Ones

In the beginning was light,
And the light gave life to the earth,
And the earth hosted man.
But man in his folly was selfish,
And blood was shed,
Thus tension replaced peace.
Hassan H Faramarz

One

This land could have been my paradise

In the Middle East, there is a country called Iran. On the very northern edge of this country is a huge landlocked body of water known as the Caspian Sea. A country road, like a long, skinny and lazy snake leaves the sea and, heading south about six kilometres, begins to climb towards the high Alborz Mountain Range. Nestled somewhere near the stomach of the snake, is a verdant village surrounded by vast flat rice lands on one side and tea fields on the other. Farms are large and houses far apart. Fruit trees, hardwoods and flowers lead eventually to rainforest.

In spring, the natural perfumes of flowers and orange blooms burst out to fill the land. At night, the moon transforms a clear and peaceful sky into an observatory lighting entire galaxies to the awestruck spectator below. The symphony of frogs accompanied by the comforting whistles of night birds and the relaxing sound of water streams with their gentle sway of willow trees, break the silence with their soothing murmurs. This season is the beginning of work for farmers after a restful winter break. Rice fields have to be readied and the seedlings transplanted from their nursery. Irrigation channels are scooped out. Wild boars begin to attack the land and become the object of hunting for those farmers who own shotguns. Lumber mills are busy as trees are sacrificed for lumber to build houses and make boxes to be used during orange harvest.

Reaping crops in summer brings everybody outdoors to help under the hot, humid sun. Horses rush around, galloping to carry the gathered crops from the fields before the rain comes. Tempers flare. Children spend their time in the river keeping cool. Evenings, workers from the fields shoulder a bundle of grass to take home to their animals. Mosquitoes fill the night air. Once the crops are in, large groups of young boys use the empty rice fields to play soccer and people gather at night to wrestle to loud music with crowds of fans cheering them on; these games herald the end of summer.

Warm winds, or Garmesh as we call them in Gilan, blow the last of the fruit, seeds and leaves to the ground. Hundreds of children, both boys and girls, head out to school, books in hand. Men have time to crowd into teahouses to chat and smoke. Women visit with each other over the fence catching up on the news, or gathering together to make pomegranate and quince preserves as well as tomato paste.

The green of the village turns into a kaleidoscope of colours as leaves get ready to fall. Overhead, flocks of migrating birds pass on their way further south. Fresh snow covers the peaks of the Alborz, a signal that autumn is giving way to winter.

Soon the long country road will be invisible under the snow.

~ * ~

The farmhouse – A deserted monument

The road approaches a weather-beaten house from the sea before heading towards the Alborz. This house belongs to a peasant farmer. Behind it on the north, there are both a small garden and a rice factory one after the other flanking the road. A

2

yard sits alongside the front of the house with a second garden beyond it.

This old house is in the shape of an elongated rectangle starting from the road and ending at a neighbour's orchard on the east. A small barn followed by the kitchen, living room, and a couple of other rooms make up the first floor of the rectangle from west to east, all connected by a large open veranda made of mud, where children play whenever the weather is not good enough for outdoor activities. The farmer's wife also makes fires on its far west side for cooking. The veranda is built above yard level and several long wooden pillars in front connect it either to the upstairs veranda or to the roof.

Mom and dad on the lower veranda near the stairs leading to the upper veranda

Except for the kitchen, each room has a small window through which the road and most of the surrounding areas to the north can be seen. In the middle of the veranda and in front of the living room, the steps of a wooden ladder lead to a smaller wooden veranda on the second floor. There are two rooms on the upper eastern part of the house. During spring and summer, the family always sleeps on this veranda, listening to the rhythmic drumming of heavy rain on the metal rooftop of the house, a sound that once a person has heard it, he will always treasure.

The western part of the house – the barn, the kitchen, and the living room – was constructed several centuries ago at the time of the farmer's great grandfather. The farmer himself built the eastern part soon after moving his bride here. The barn, where some of the animals were kept in earlier days, nearly butts up against the road and has its own separate loft, under the metal rooftop, which serves as a warehouse. The front yard is spacious and dotted with fruit and shade trees; a pear tree right in front of the barn, has cows tied to it during spring and summer.

Up a short steep bank from the road, a gnarled old walnut tree shades the right side of the yard and stands guard over a row of bamboo. Pomegranate, hazelnut, pear, apple, fig, peach, plum, quince, willow, orange and lemon trees along with grape and kiwi arbores are scattered everywhere. An enclosure formed by fence posts with branches woven among them surrounds the entire area and gives access to the road by a gate. Juxtaposed to the neighbour's garden, a small pool for washing laundry rests beside a well under the shadow of fruit and willow trees. Water from the well is used for the animals, trees and gardens; drinking water is brought from a spring near the riverbank.

Detached from the house on the south-eastern side of the yard, sits a proud new barn; since it was built, the animals make their home here. Between this barn and the well, a pyramid-shaped room, called a kanduj in our local language, perched atop four pillars, stores newly harvested rice, to one side of it in the middle of the yard is an outhouse. Beyond this stand two other homesteads, through which children usually take a shortcut to reach the east side of the upper village where they play. Adults, however, use the narrow, unpaved road which branches off the main road and heads east, passing by the far southern edge of the front garden.

One of dad's last pictures taken exclusively for his children
abroad. The kanduj is on the right behind him.

~ * ~

Start from somewhere; anywhere will do

It is the summer of 1969. Four boys, ranging in age from two
to eight, are playing noiselessly in the front yard of this farm. The
voices of a few women can be heard from inside. In his worn-out
soiled clothes, the farmer who owns the house, impatient and
nervous, is sitting under a pomegranate tree, keeping himself busy
with his old sickle. A couple of men squat near him, exchanging
clipped words and phrases. Women rush around. The deep and
distressed voice of a woman fills the air.

"What the Hell is going on in there?" the farmer asks.
Nobody bothers to answer him. He keeps on murmuring to
himself. Moments of unease, nervousness, and anticipation pass.
"Somebody tell me what is happening. I need to get back to
work." It is the short farmer speaking again.

Suddenly the loud voice of a child is heard. "The child is
born!" somebody shouts. Then, there are more whispers.

"A boy!"
"Another boy?"
"Who dares to tell him?"

"Since losing his oldest child, he has been waiting for another girl all this time."

"Now, here comes his fifth son!"

One of the women, the child's second youngest aunt, strikes the baby on his back and leaves the room in tears of anger and frustration. Even she has been hoping for a girl this time. There is no need to tell the farmer; he knows he has another boy. He walks to the veranda and starts grumbling, "Just my luck; other women give birth to girls all the time and my wife cannot produce even one. What is she good for then?"

People try to calm him down. The poor woman is weeping inside the living room where she has just given birth to her fifth boy in a row. Murmurs and whispers continue. Nobody knows how to deal with the farmer and his disappointment.

"Stop it, stop it, stop it!" a woman screams abruptly. "Why is it always the woman's fault? Why didn't you put a girl in her belly? She just carried what you gave her."

The woman who delivers this tirade in an effort to get the farmer's attention is his sister. "What is wrong with this boy anyway?" she continues. "Look at him. I am sure you will love this one more than all your other kids. Go back to your work and stop being angry with this poor woman."

Everybody stands mutely as the farmer, head hanging and a baffled look on his face, walks back to his work.

"Now, let's give him a name," she exclaims emphatically.

"Call him Hassan," says my mother, "in honor of an uncle of mine who died at a young age."

Thus my life started; I have heard it told from various family members tens of times. So many times, in fact, that I have the feeling I was an eyewitness to these events.

~ * ~

I wish I could bring a change

Some three or four years pass.

It is mid spring and the weather is not as warm as it should be at this time of year. Several women are singing folk songs while they plant a rice field.

"Take care of Hassan," my mother tells my aunt - the one who slapped me on the day of my birth - who is living with us now

6

and loves me very much. "If something happens to him, his father will kill me."

"He is fine," comes the reply from my aunt, "he is playing over there by the tree. He cannot go anywhere."

One end of a rope is tied to my right leg; the other end is knotted to the tree. It is true, I cannot go anywhere. This was a common and safe way for farmers to take care of their children in those days. Because of the hard work, nobody had time or energy to tend to children.

For me, Nature is one gigantic toyshop. I am entertaining myself with worms, ants, frogs, dragonflies, butterflies, and any other creatures I can reach, when loud voices draw my attention. The planters are tense. I keep a watch on them as they walk one of the women from the rice land and sit her under the tree where I am secured. I see it is my mother. She is trembling. My aunt is crying.

"Give me something to eat," my mother pleads, her breathing rapid and shallow, "I feel very cold."

A man, probably the farm owner, makes a fire. The women gather around her with bread and tea and begin to talk among themselves.

"We should tell her husband to take her to a doctor," one of them says to the others.

"Don't say anything," requests my mother. "I don't want him to get angry. He is too busy during this season to take me to a doctor, besides a doctor is expensive; I will be fine soon."

* * *

Later in the evening, my mother and I are still sitting under the same tree. The other women are back at work but nobody is singing anymore. My mother is deadly silent. Something is wrong. I am terrified. In my heart, I wish I were a doctor.

~ * ~

The fruit I picked for my aunt's guests

"Come here, Hassan." My aunt calls to me. "Take this basket and pick some fruit from the trees in the garden; we have guests."

Picking fruit is one of my favorite things to do. Usually, I climb the trees with a wooden knife under the belt of my long shorts, imagining I am Tarzan. Today I scale several trees and pick as much fruit as I can carry. The pear tree is tougher to climb than the others; instead of trying to climb it, I throw a stick into the tree and the pears fall one after another. We keep our cows under one side of this tree and cow pies are piled under it on the other, to be used for fertilizer. Some of the falling pears land in the dung; I pick them up and clean them on my hip. Then with a feeling of happiness, I take the basket to my mother.

"My Goodness, what a clever boy!" one of the visitors says.

"He is much bigger than when I last saw him," adds an old woman.

"Hassan is almost six now," says my mother, "and a big help to me." She then coaches me to offer fruit to our guests. I walk around the room, offering the basket. They each pick out one or two pieces and praise me warmly for listening to my mother.

One of the women, with a bite of pear in her mouth, starts talking. "I know this girl has been a big help for your family since your wife became disabled," she is saying to my father. "But you realize that she is grown up now and needs to start her own life. I will take care of her as if she were one of my own children."

My aunt has gone outside the room. I go to where she is sitting on the veranda. Taking me in her arms, she bursts into tears and kissing my face and hands, says, "I will miss you, Hassan."

My mother calls her in. She joins the guests and I follow her.

"I am the one who raised this girl," my mother explains. "Our parents died when she was very young. Now I put her hands into yours. Please take good care of her."

* * *

What I remember of the wedding is getting to ride in the back of a large Dodge pickup truck up steep winding mountain roads to the home of the bridegroom. Sitting in the back of the pickup, we sing and clap and generally celebrate the occasion.

My aunt, who for a long time has been closer to me than my own mother, and knowing she will be putting life with us behind her, cries throughout the ceremony and the rest of the day and wants to accompany us when we are ready to leave for home.

The following day, her mother-in-law shows up at our house and tells my mother how depressed and homesick my aunt is; the two women decide that I should go stay with her for a while.

I love being in the Alborz Mountains which I have been watching from our house all my life! My aunt's new household is self-sufficient, growing their own fruit, vegetables and raising milk and beef cows. Every morning I wake up early to the smell of bread baking in an oven dug into the ground. Once the bread is ready, we spread it with homemade butter and cheese, eat it and wash it down with milk fresh from the cows.

Surprise! We have just finished breakfast one day when I hear my father's voice calling out for me. There is my father with his friends, heading into the hills for firewood. Early in the afternoon, when the men return by the same route, they stop by for a cup of hot tea.

After about two weeks, my aunt is adjusting, and I return to my own home.[1]

----

[1]Unfortunately, the marriage was short-lived, as my aunt's husband became ill and died a few years after they had their second child. From then on, she dedicated her life to taking care of her children and I rarely saw her.

~ * ~

Babysitting

One spring day, one of our relatives takes me, along with his wife and child, to a weekly bazaar in a nearby town. In those days, the outdoor traditional bazaar at the Caspian beach was gorgeous; hundreds of local vendors would come from across the province, chanting happily to advertise their wares. The bazaar set up in a different town on each day of the week and came to our area on Thursdays. Vendors offered a wide variety of local vegetables, fruit, eggs, chickens, ducks, geese, fish, clothing, shoes, home appliances, tools, ropes, saddles, mosquito net and anything else you could desire. Behind the market was a large field where people traded lambs, cows and horses.

The shopping finished, "Choose something for yourself," my uncle encourages me.

"I want this nail cutter."

"Ok, but why a nail cutter?"

"Any time our nails grow, my father cuts them with his sickle," I mumble with my head down. "Sometimes, he cuts our nails with a kitchen knife."

Both he and his wife laugh while my face grows red, but I soon forget about it. We stay at the market enjoying ourselves until evening.

"How was the bazaar, Hassan?" asks my aunt on the way back home.

"Super!"

"You know, Hassan," she continues, "we are farmers and spring means work for us. From tomorrow on, your uncle and I will work the rice lands and you will come to our home to take care of little Amir while we are out in the fields. He is a good boy, just like you. As a reward, we will take you to this bazaar again in the summer."

"We have talked to your father already," adds my uncle.

Starting the next day, my mother gives me my breakfast early and sends me to our relatives' house. I take care of Amir in his house until he begins to fuss and cry and I know he is getting hungry. Then, if the fields are close, I carry him on my back and run to look for his mother to breastfeed him; other days, she prepares his milk in bottles.

When the weather is fine, she lets us stay and play on the ground nearby. On days when it rains, the narrow paths in the fields become very slippery and Amir and I fall down several times so that when I reach the planters in the fields, both of us are totally covered with water and mud, making the women laugh aloud. If this happens, my aunt has to leave work and take us back home to get us dry clothes, washing our dirty ones in a hurry and hanging them on their veranda to dry.

On the days we don't join the workers for lunch, Amir's mother returns at noon and prepares food for us. She has only a few minutes, and we have to gulp down our food quickly. Although Amir is almost two years old, it is his habit to poop his pants at lunch. His mother then washes him in a big basin by pouring water on the child's backside from a small jar. Placing Amir on a blanket, she washes her hands by pouring water on them and rubbing them together before rinsing out the basin and setting it aside. Without drying them, she uses these very same hands to put rice on my plate. I imagine every single spoonful I put in my mouth is tainted. She insists that I have to finish my food in order to keep up my strength. Sometimes in spite of all my efforts to contain myself, I lose control and vomit up my lunch. On many occasions, once Amir's mother leaves the veranda to feed the chickens, ducks and geese behind their house, I throw the rest of my food into the front garden.

Days are long and my job is hard. My face grows paler day by day; people comment that I look sick but I am too shy to complain. During this time, one thing takes my mind from my miserable baby-sitting chore – the joy of waiting for my brothers who usually pass by Amir's house on their way to and from our tea farms. Almost every evening I take Amir to the narrow path they use, and wait for them there. I feel elated when my brothers appear on the path where it reaches the horizon and feel terribly sad on days nobody shows up.

Finally, the long spring is over and one evening my relatives decide I can go home. I hurry out of their house and run to tell everybody in our family that I am free from the next morning on. It is hard to hide my feelings of giddiness; my old friends and I can go back to playing with each other as we used to.

One day the next summer, while playing with my friends, I see that same uncle carrying his child in his arms. The young Amir wandered away from the tea farms where his parents were working and is later found in the river, caught by the current in a hollow under a rock. When in tears I relate to my mother what has happened to Amir, she reminds me how instrumental I was in keeping him safe while he was in my care.

Amir's death puts more limitations on the rest of us. During summer, we used to swim in the nearby river most afternoons. Now our parents will no longer let us do that although we continue swimming without their permission whenever they are not around. My father punishes us severely if he happens to find out about our water activities.

~ * ~

Children and their brilliant ideas - ignored!

In autumn, there is not much farm work to do. Some adults, my father among them, ride their horses to the mountainous areas to gather wood to be used for fuel in winter. Many farmers, who do not have any work on the farm after the harvest season, spend their free time in one of several teahouses in the old market.

One day as I was in the habit of doing, I wake up before dawn to watch my father and his friends prepare for their forage to the forest. His friends have already arrived, and I look on while my father saddles our horse, wishing I could go along. He puts one foot in the stirrup and swings the other over the back of the animal to ride after his friends, asking me to bring him his ax and sickle before he rides away. The horses leave the yard and I walk after them as far as our wooden gate leading to the road, the road the men will take to the woods, and watch them until they disappear from sight.

I turn at my mother's voice asking me to help her take the dirty dishes out to the veranda where she will wash them; that done, she sends me to the well with our dirty clothes. I pull up several buckets of water and fill the pans for her so she can wash the laundry piece by piece. After that long ago day when she felt so cold in the rice fields, for the rest of her life, my mother is unable to stand straight and has numbness in her legs and feet in spite of visits to many specialists and prescriptions; still, she manages to do the majority of the housework herself.

Today, like every morning, when my brothers are in school and my father has left to cut wood, the village is pretty quiet. I am entertaining myself at home, but soon run out of games and find the dominating silence around the house very boring. I sit at the top of the stairs which connect our first floor to the second. From that viewpoint, I can clearly see the massive Alborz Mountains that face the front of our house. The peaks are white-tipped with fresh early snow, below which the entire body of the mountain range is a canopy of beautiful orange, red and yellow autumn leaves beginning to die. My glance moves on to a group of sparrows ambushing the fig trees in our yard and boisterously eating the leftover fruit on the partially leafless branches through which the sun makes moving shadows on the ground where the autumn chicks are scratching in search of food. The weather is cool and the air bright and clear as glass.

While I am watching this whole landscape, what I think is a brilliant idea suddenly pops into my head. It has been my recurring dream to go to school like my brothers. To me, anything they do is fascinating; I like the way they do their homework, the way they debate with each other on any particular issue, and even the way they fight with one another occasionally.

Overwhelmed by my new scheme, I start looking through my brothers' clothes and books. Minutes later, I have donned a large shirt, long pants and a huge coat, and grabbing a few books, I wrap them in a long piece of elastic tubing like my brothers do. In those days, there were not many schoolbags available and even if there were some in the market, most families could not afford them. Although all the villagers had lands and animals, the majority of them did not have cash. Besides, the 'bag culture' society hadn't arrived yet.

With the pile of books under my arm, I soundlessly leave the yard and walk down the road, my mother's attention focused on the laundry. Our village school is about a hundred meters away, just behind our home. It was established around 1925 and was called Khayyam Primary School, after Omar Khayyam[1]. The building is old and large enough to accommodate a lot of students from neighboring villages that don't have their own schools. Every morning I can hear the students clearly when they sing songs in chorus. Sometimes I watch as they raise the flag and sing the national anthem.

Walking along, I daydream of raising the flag in front of the Shah and his wife Farah, whose picture I have seen in my brothers' books. I see the Queen, in her glorious clothing, saying kind words to me, putting her hands on my head and smiling. How I love this vision!

When I sneak into the schoolyard through the old iron gate, the students are returning to their classes after a break. Having no idea about choosing a class, I join those who are close to my age and walk into a classroom, silently taking a seat among the other students. Nobody says anything to me and I sit hunched over, trying not to be spotted among the four or five students on the same bench.

The first class over, a noisy bell clangs and it's break time; the teacher still has not noticed my presence there. As the students start to leave for the yard, not sure I can find the same classroom again, I grab my books and holding them tightly under my arm, walk out. Soon the bell sounds once more and we line up for another class. This time the school's principal, who is one of our neighbors, sees me. He is a noticeably big man in the village, both physically and socially, and there is authority in his voice. We fear him a lot even outside the school. Whenever he walks in the village, all of his students hide immediately. He, as well as the teachers, can punish students for any reason, especially when he sees them playing outside, even during national holidays and Fridays, which are our weekend.

From his place at the top of the stairs, in a very commanding tone that nails me to the spot, the principal yells, "What the heck are you doing here?"

All the lined-up students turn around to look and see a small boy in huge clothes standing behind the youngest children. Suddenly all of them are fainting with laughter, as we say in Persian. The principal's words terrify and intimidate me and I feel the world burst and fall on my head. Not knowing what else to do, I run to the main gate; it is closed. As hard as I try, I am not strong enough to open the latch. The more I struggle with the gate, the louder the students laugh. Seeing me helpless and humiliated, Kaveh, one of my brothers, runs and opens the gate for me. I scurry away in morbid fear and never look back - the loud laughter of students still rattling in my brain after I get home.

* * *

Later that day my brothers, explaining how embarrassed they were because of what I did at their school, tell me that if I will be patient, in one more year I can go to school like they do.

_____

'Omar Khayyam (1048 - 1131) - Neyshabur/Nishapur, Khorasan province, Iran. A Persian mathematician, astronomer, and poet, renowned in his own country and time for his scientific achievements but chiefly known to English-speaking readers through the translation of a collection of his roba'iyat ("quatrains") in The Rubáiyát of Omar Khayyám (1859), by the English writer Edward FitzGerald (Source: Britanica). Khayyam also compiled the Khayyam Persian Calendar, which is still in use today. After the 1979 revolution in Iran, many of his poems were regarded as examples of absurdity by the Islamic government and people were gradually discouraged from extolling him.

~ * ~

A peaceful village life

Since I am the youngest in the family and because my mother's condition limits her, it is my job to take care of many chores at home.

Cats, cows and pigeons, a horse, a dog, a few lambs and a large number of beautiful chickens make life on our farm colorfully animated. We keep our horse and the cows in the new barn on the far south-eastern side of our front garden. In its loft, we store hay for our animals to eat during the winter. Most of our chickens lay eggs inside the hay without our knowing where, and once every few days, my mother sends me looking for them. When the hens are ready to brood, she asks me to leave the eggs where I find them and gives me additional ones to put under the setting hens who have too few. Then after about 20 days, there is the choral whispering of young chicks filling the air. Some of the older hens will have about fifteen chicks, while the less experienced ones, who don't know how to keep all the eggs warm, usually hatch only five or six. After the new chicks are born, I climb happily up the creaky wooden ladder to the loft, put them in a basket and bring it down with me; at night, these chicks will be housed in crates or cardboard boxes to protect them from weasels and other predators.

Mornings, I wake up early, when the weather is still dark, to watch my father milk the cows. Milking fascinates me and I listen very carefully to his instructions. When he is in the mood, my father lets me try my hand and eventually I become good at milking.

At daybreak, I help my father prepare food for our animals. Once the cows and lambs are fed, I scatter grain for the chickens here and there under the trees in the yard and they push one another to reach it first. Then I head for the little chicks waking up noisily. Opening their boxes, I sit down and they scurry out in a big rush, crawling and jumping all over me, searching for the grain I have taught them to eat from the palms of my hands.

Evenings, I take the chickens, my favorite animals, to their nests; some sleep on the branches of the pear and hazelnut trees and others rest in the barn loft.

In winter, we build a fire in the open fireplace in our living room, to be used for both cooking and heating purposes. The fire keeps the room filled with heavy smoke all winter long, and because of this, the walls have become as black and thick as asphalt on a street.

My father hangs newly harvested rice on the wooden bars just under the high ceiling. The rice remains drying over our heads for a couple of months and then we take it down and have it cleaned in a factory. The smoked rice is unbelievably tasty when we cook it later.

We all sleep together in this room and my mother, who, when she arises to start breakfast, does not want to disturb us children by turning on lights, works by the only light in the room, a flame that burns slowly at dawn. Every so often, she stirs the coals and the big dried branches inside the soot-blackened fireplace give off sparks like fireflies. While she is busy boiling the milk, the fire projects her shadow on the wall of the darkened room. I spend quite some time in silence watching my mother busily stirring the milk to keep it from scorching. As I watch her shadow on the wall, I notice how it moves lighter and faster than she does; I find myself wishing she were like she used to be before becoming ill, moving as effortlessly and freely as her shadow does. I even wish the shadow could be my mother, then she would be relieved from her suffering and I would have a healthy mother like my friends.

On weekend mornings when my brothers do not wake up at her calls, my mother asks me to go for hot bread from our local bakery. We dip the fresh bread in hot milk and together with homemade quince, fig or blackberry jams, we eat our breakfast while my brothers and I ceaselessly banter with one another, ignoring dad's admonition that we mustn't speak at meals. The rest of the milk goes into the foods my mother is so talented at making: yogurt and cheese.

I watched her doing this for so many years that I can still make superb yogurt in a jar, which will not fall out even if you turn it upside down.

~ * ~

Stories take root when shepherds have long days ahead

One spring, knowing I will be home in the afternoons after classes to take care of them, several neighbors bring their lambs and goats to us to be stabled. A few of my friends and I take the lambs, goats and horses to pasture every day. To get there, we head south until we are just under the Alborz range.

When two of our older horses die, my father buys another horse which is more than half-wild. Since he hasn't been broken in and my father is afraid I will be thrown, I am forbidden to ride him, so to get to the grazing grounds, I have to take hold of his bridle and run alongside him. My friends ride their horses in front, while the lambs and goats, which number fourteen or more by this time, move as a small flock between them and me, while I trail along behind. Not being able to keep up with my friends, everyone else is already playing when the flock and I finally arrive.

We leave the animals to enjoy the green grass while we pass our time under the shadow of Alborz, playing or telling stories we have heard from our brothers and sisters. Most of the time, I lead the group in storytelling since, in addition to be talkative by nature, I am the only one with older brothers who read a lot and pass many compelling tales from their books along to me. If I happen to run out of stories, I make up new yarns, improvising as I go along. I once tell a long story in which Bruce Lee is traversing a huge jungle while being attacked by lions, wolves and elephants. He fights bravely and knocks the animals down one after another with kung fu chops. While I am telling the story, I clumsily attempt karate slashes and kicks in the air to show my friends how the hero killed those wild animals – 'Like this! Like this! Like this!' I make the tale end sadly though, with one of the wolves killing Bruce Lee. My friends, who sit mesmerized as I tell this tale, remain silent for a long time afterward.

As we grow older, they come to realize that I made up many of the episodes, and, even now, will remind me of what they call 'those stupid stories' with which I entertained them and which kept us occupied on so many of our long days at the pasture.

Getting bored with these activities, we start riding each other's horses and competing with one another on a narrow country road. I long to ride my own horse since I believe mine is stronger and faster than those of my friends. This idea makes me try my wild horse occasionally; taking him to the river, I make him stay in the water up to his belly. This way, the animal cannot move fast and I won't get hurt. When I feel he is obedient, I ride him out of the water and urge him on slowly. He is fine for several steps, then suddenly he begins his wild behavior again and throws me off his back. This hurts a lot, both physically and psychologically. Whenever he makes me very angry, I beat him with narrow branches of trees then try again. I have warned my friends not to say anything to my father about me riding the wild horse because I know how seriously angry he will get, and I fear he will punish me in the same way I punish my horse, beating me with a stick.

We keep that untamed stallion a year or so longer, then my father sells it and replaces it with another. The new steed is white, tame, and I love him, but he gets bitten by a snake while grazing in pastures in the Alborz Mountains, and dies. Later on, we buy another, younger pony. He is physically small and my brothers aren't interested in spending too much time with him, so I start training him myself, all on my own. Soon this little red colt, with whom I share my daily life, becomes one of my best friends[1].

* * *

I remember one harvest season when, instead of one of my brothers, I arrive at my neighbor's farm on horseback for the very first time. He looks at me and decides I am too young, insisting that I go home and send one of my brothers to him, but I keep pushing that I can ride faster than my brothers. The neighbor finally agrees to let me try once. Overjoyed, I ride to near where he is working, dismount with a jump and help him load the horse with bundles of rice plants. Unloading the rice at his house, I leap back on my horse and pitico, pitico, pitico, I gallop to the fields again, before the next load is ready. Satisfied, he lets me stay and work for the rest of the harvest season. Although getting up, leaving home early and being gone until dusk everyday is physically taxing for me, I really love this job.

My final years with the little red horse - a friend and I are loading him with bundles of rice plants. After military service, I never saw my pony again.

'During my first days in China, I once dreamed I was riding my little red colt when we arrived at the Great Wall. The wall was huge, like a giant mountain and there was no way ahead. Suddenly I kicked the haunches of my horse with both my legs and he started galloping. He jumped and we seemed to be flying, my heart in my throat. I held my breath until we landed safely in soft sand on the other side.

~ * ~

20

Forgotten traditions

On Yalda, the longest night of the year, during the evening we gather at each other's houses to feast on watermelon, pomegranates, quince, oranges and tangerines, dried pumpkin, sunflower and melon seeds, pickled pear, crab apples, and cookies, and play local games until late into the night. One of my favorites is 'gol ya pooch', a type of shell game with two teams competing for points. Our parents tell stories about their ancestors, their youth and how they met and married their spouses. Grandparents tell us cultural traditions and myths, passed down from generation to generation, while we warm ourselves around the fireplace. A king named Houshang, for example, they say, accidentally discovered fire. On horseback when a snake struck, he jumped down, grabbed a stone and threw it at the viper. Instead of hitting the snake, his stone hit another stone, a spark flew and the snake slithered away. Curious, he tried again to produce the spark, and after several tries, he succeeded; that was the birth of fire.

Another tradition, Char Shanbeh Suri, is dedicated to the last Wednesday of the year, when early in the evening large groups of people swarm onto different parts of the village, heaping bushes and bundles of dry hay into long lines for bonfires. When these piles are ready, we play around and wait impatiently for sunset. As darkness falls, we ignite the piles. Dozens of boys and girls and their parents run, one after another, jumping the fires. While we do this, we sing a song to the fire, 'sorkhi ye tow az man, zardi ye man az tow', meaning, 'Take away my yellowness and give me redness.'

Historically, Iranians have respected fire as a means of cleansing. Yellowness is the symbol of weakness while red proves good health and life. We play and laugh and sing until far after midnight when, exhausted but content, we walk back home.

* * *

Mehregan, the harvest festival, celebrates the day when, according to Ferdowsi's Epic of the Kings, Fereydoon and Kaveh, the symbols of light in our traditional myths, defeated Zahak, the symbol of darkness. Among all holidays, Iranians consider Mehregan second in importance only to Norouz, although, sadly, these days we don't celebrate it much anymore.

As the New Year gets closer, we start a game we call jij or egg fighting. Taking some eggs from home, first we hit them against our front teeth to test the strength of their shells and choose the ones we believe are most resistant to breakage. Eggs in hands or pockets, we rush to the middle of the village to join others who have the same arsenal. Clumps of villagers are scattered all over the area, either busy playing jij or shouting and cheering the players on. The rules of the game are simple: if you can break your competitor's egg on its two ends without breaking both your own, you are the winner and the loser has to give his broken egg to you. To make the game more exciting, we bargain awhile for a few additional rules. This game goes on for two weeks, during which we keep a check under the rooftops of our barns, hoping to find more ammunition; by this time, even weak-shelled eggs are welcome. Since it is New Year's Eve, parents have no objections to wasting eggs and, in fact, they usually take part in such entertainments.

New Year's, or Norooz, means 'the new day' in Persian and starts on the first day of the spring equinox. In preparation for welcoming it, my brothers and I help our parents clean the house, whitewash the walls, scrub all the rugs and carpets and make a type of cookie called kolucheh. Relatives and neighbors get together, taking hours to mix the dough by hand and shaping the sweets with a spoon, fork or just using fingers.

The night before Norooz we go to our public bathhouse, or hammam, located on the northern edge of the market in the lower village. Since the majority of the villagers do not have showers at home in these days, it is always crowded and we chat with each other for hours, waiting our turn to bathe.

The next morning, we set up a tablecloth, or sofreh, on floor in the living room and place seasonal snacks and cookies on it. Candles and a mirror, dyed eggs, coins, a jar of small goldfish, sabzeh, or a plate of grass sprouts which we grow at home, sib, or apples, ground sumac, samanu, a type of pudding, senjed, the fruit of the lotus tree, sir, or garlic, and serkeh, or vinegar are placed on the cloth. Each of these items starts with the letter 'sin' or 's', giving the name 'haft seen' or 'seven Ss' to this display. Candles alight in front of a mirror are a symbol of fire, eggs represent fertility, garlic wards off bad omens and evil, coins are for prosperity.

Minutes before the New Year arrives, one of my brothers leaves the house, while the rest of us remain inside. The one who leaves stays out in the yard until we hear, seconds before the New Year, the ticking of the countdown and a 'boom', then a voice saying, 'the year 25361 has officially started' and folk music pours from the radio, TV, and the loudspeakers of the mosque, then we call him back in. He enters the house, in one hand carrying the Quran, on which he has placed flowers and green branches from our trees, and a jar of clean water in the other. He passes through all the rooms of the house, one after another, pouring a little water into an inside corner of each. Then the small jar of water, the Holy Book and the flowers go on the tablecloth. These things, too, are symbols, the green branches symbolize life, water represents brightness and the flow of life, and the Quran is the word of God on the New Year's sacred sofreh. We kiss each other in celebration and the younger children accept gifts from their parents.

After our family festivities, we start the New Year out by visiting our older relatives then going to the houses of our neighbors, spending a few minutes at each house. Children usually receive money or token gifts, the best of which are eggs for our games of jij. The visiting of friends and relatives lasts about two weeks.

The New Year holiday is officially over after the thirteenth of the month. On that day, my brothers and I, like the majority of the villagers, spend the entire day away from home, scrambling through the foothills of the Alborz with a large group of our friends. Towards evening, we pick up thirteen small stones and throw them, along with the grass shoots which we have brought with us from the 'haft seen', one by one into a flowing river, make wishes for the New Year, pack up and return home. Our ancestors, whose superstitions were happiness oriented, believed that our actions on this day would bring us good fortune and prosperity for the rest of the year, breaking the bad omen traditionally associated with the number 13. So people spend the day entertaining themselves on sizdah bedar, or the 13th of the first month of the year, going to the seashore, mountains, movies or even picnicking under their own trees.

* * *

According to ancient calendars and books, Iranian culture originally focused on happy occasions. Celebrations marked harvest season, Sadeh, or the occasion of the discovery of fire, mid-winter and passing into spring and summer. Sharing wine together made Iranians happy, and they avoided fasting, because being hungry made a person useless to society.

When Islam stepped in, gradually what was valuable lost its value, and what had no value became important. In this reversal, mourning gradually replaced happy occasions. It is probably due to these old traditions that Iranians today, even though the majority may not observe Ramadan or daily prayers, take part in public religious ceremonies, turning them to their benefit. During these times, young girls and boys take advantage of freedom from parental eyes to seek out one another, some of the older ones gather to drink or smoke opium together, and visiting gives the elderly release from tensions.

_____

¹The year 2536 dates from the Persian dynasties and corresponds to 1978. After the 1979 revolution, this 'symbol of tyranny' was replaced with the Islamic calendar.

~ * ~

Education is the most powerful weapon which you can use to change the world
........................Nelson Mandela

Two

Respected through simplicity, protected by immunity

Almost every week, my mother asks me to catch one of our young roosters to be slaughtered for meals. I sit in the yard and call the chickens; they gather round and with the concert of their jik jik jiks and ghod ghod ghods, jump on my head and shoulders. I grab one and shoo the others away, since my mother doesn't want any other animals to see one of their own killed. She is of the opinion that animals are like humans and feel bad when we kill their companions. As soon as the others are scattered, I call for my father, who then reaches for his sickle or a kitchen knife and joins me in the yard. After giving the rooster water, he calls God's name several times and offers his prayers to Him before putting his sharp weapon against my rooster's neck. When the animal is bled, I take it to the kitchen, where my mother stuffs it with vegetables and spices and makes rice and stew to accompany it.

At the noon mealtime, she asks me to call the teacher for lunch. I climb the stairs to the veranda on the second floor, which leads to two rooms, the rooms of my older brothers, Darius and Davood. The teacher is a clergyman who visits our house once a week to teach my brothers the Quran. We, like other villagers, pay for these classes, and have a lot of respect for the teacher, even though he is very strict and punishes his students mercilessly. In my father's day, Quranic classes were used to teach literacy and my father, who is himself a strict man, believes in education so strongly he allows us to endure the teacher's chastisement.

Usually when I get upstairs, and close enough to knock on the door, I can hear my brothers crying inside the room we use as the mullah's classroom. They quit crying when I rap, and the teacher calls out to know who is knocking.

"My mother says the food is ready," I tell him.

"Ok," he answers, asking me to go back downstairs. Soon my brothers appear on the veranda, some trying to hide their still flowing tears. They know, as do I, that their father will punish them even more if he finds out they have angered the religion teacher for any reason. He gives the mullah branches from our pomegranate or quince trees to be used to whip my brothers if they fail in answering questions during the Quranic classes. These branches are flexible and sting sharply when beat against the bare feet of a student whom the mullah believes deserves punishment. His beatings go on and on until his anger is sated. Distracting the teacher for any possible reason, turning the pages without his permission, talking to each other even if it is related to the class, not being able to find the page or the sentence the mullah is talking about, are all subject to severe punishment.

My brothers meet me in the kitchen and wait for the food to be handed to them. Our mother, who is very particular about the appearance of the dishes, keeps all of the food separate, and carefully wipes each platter along the edges with a piece of cloth before serving. She then passes the platters of food to me one by one, and I in turn hand them to my brothers who take the dishes upstairs to the teacher. We leave the food and the homemade desserts in front of the mullah on a small sofreh spread on the carpet.

Traditionally, we do not have meals at the table, but lay a sofreh on the carpet, set the dishes on it, and the whole family sits on the floor together sharing their meal.

After putting the platters before the mullah, we leave the room, closing the door to let him partake of the food in peace. We wait downstairs silently until he finishes eating and calls us to clear his dirty dishes so he can rest before starting his afternoon classes.

Now it is our turn to have lunch. By this time, there is not much left of the rooster; our share is mostly bones we can suck. Mother breaks the bones before putting them on our plates, adds chicken broth over the rice to give it a little more flavor, then calls each of us by name to receive our portion. The family licks the bones clean, sucking out the marrow, and relishing the food prepared in honor of the mullah's visit.

Although I love the meal and look forward to it, I do not like the mullah; I have to kill one of my beautiful roosters once every week for a person who beats up my brothers regularly. What would have happened, I wonder, if I had dared to criticize the religion teacher?

As the numbers of students grow for the Quranic classes, the local leaders of the village find an old, abandoned house and dedicate it as a classroom. This house stands at the corner of some rice fields behind our primary school near the river and is surrounded by trees. Girls, as well as boys, attend these classes together, because their parents believe such classes will benefit them as well. Some of the girls are a little older, already maturing, their feminine curves noticeable in their colorful peasant dresses. It isn't long before students begin observing the mullah touching these older girls in an inappropriate manner. I heard later that some of the older boys were also targeted. A few of them complain to their parents about how the mullah is taking advantage of the opportunity to touch the students familiarly when other students are absorbed in reading the Holy Book.

This news spreads through the village like a brush fire and makes the local leaders extremely angry. They devise a plan: one day, people are asked to gather in the market to watch the consequences of a religious leader or anyone else who abuses children. The mullah is walked around the marketplace, weighted down with a thick chain, an iron pig trap, and a large funny dunce hat, looking like a ridiculous clown among the crowd of villagers who laugh for hours. This cleric leaves the school forever, and the students have a vacation until a replacement teacher arrives[1].

––––––––––––––––––––––––––––––––

[1]After the 1979 revolution, the Islamic government decided that local courts were not in a position to try mullahs anymore. The mullahs were granted a sort of diplomatic immunity in the country since they were said to be the representatives of the prophet Mohammad, and more than that, the representatives of

God himself on earth. In support of them, for any kind of major crimes, they were tried in special courts established by the government exclusively for its clerics.

~ * ~

Childish Shenanigans

One summer at dusk, two of my brothers are under the kanduj, shirts saturated with sweat as they pull the newly harvested rice stalks into a bundle preparing to have it hauled up into the kanduj by a hook dangling from the end of a rope let down by my father. I take my horse, tired from carrying the crop from the rice lands to the house, to the open field nearby to rest and graze.

While I wait for him, cars slowly moving on the dirt bypass get my eye. Due to the construction of a new bridge over an irrigation channel, the main road is closed and an unpaved detour winds around past our house. On rainy days, like today, the bypass is nearly impassable, and cars often get stuck and need to be pushed. All of a sudden, a pickup truck full of Mashadi melons, famous for their sweet flesh, comes from the direction of the sea, slows and turns right onto the detour. I know the load is headed for the next town for tomorrow's weekly market.

Since this detour was built, it has been the entertainment of many of the neighborhood children to chase the trucks laboring through the mud, climb into them and grab some fruit. The thought comes to me suddenly, as a challenge, to see if I can do it. It is dark and nobody is around. The truck struggles forward into the mud and I run from behind, catch hold of the tailgate and haul myself up. I see the mound of melons and I want all of them. I reach my hand through the bars of the tailgate and take hold of a big one, but it is too big to pass through the grill. Dropping it, I choose another, which has the same problem: still too big.

While I am deciding which one will be small enough to be pulled out, the truck gets to the end of the detour and starts out on the main road, accelerating down then up a steep bank. I can feel the truck moving faster and I still have not chosen the perfect melon. I've almost decided to forget it when I see a long, thin melon, grab it quickly and it slips through the bars.

With the melon under my right arm, I am holding onto the tailgate when I notice how fast the vehicle is moving. 'What do I do now?' I think. 'If this truck takes me as far as the next town, it is too far to walk back'.

My other option is to jump, which I do, landing on my feet still holding onto the tailgate and running at top speed until I have my balance, then let go while the truck speeds off into the darkness.

As soon as I see the melon still in my arm, I forget all my fear, and run back home, shouting all the way, "I got it! I got it! I finally got it!" When I enter my yard at a rush, Mirza and Kaveh are still spearing the rice stalks with the hook. "I got it! I got it!" I say again in absolute elation.

"What did you get?" Mirza asks.

"I got this melon from a truck on the detour road."

"What has he done?" the firm and commanding voice of my father asks from inside the kanduj.

"He has taken a melon from a produce truck," Mirza explains to my father.

"Catch him and tie him to a tree!" my father shouts. "Don't let him get away until I am done here, then I'll kill him!"

Even as my brothers are saying "Freeze, freeze!" they are motioning me to get lost. With the same speed I used when entering the yard, I disappear out of it again, not willing to face my father's anger. I have no idea what happened to that melon, even though I do know I still had it with me when I ran off.

* * *

One spring day my cousins and I are playing under a fig tree on the tea farm while my father, aunts and a few local workers are picking tea nearby. The other children are taking turns grabbing a branch of the tree to swing over an irrigation canal. Back and forth they go, first to one side, then to the other.

These cousins are all girls and they are older than I am, besides. Because of their gender, I feel I need to prove myself and take my turn at the swing, even though I am a little afraid. I work up the courage to say, "Let me, let me!" and run towards the branch. Grabbing it, I push off and up in the air I go. But midway across the canal and in the air, crack! the branch breaks off and together we fall into the canal, me first, and the branch on top. I land directly on a log at the side of the canal, my arm caught between the log and my body. Pain and numbness take over – my arm is very painful and my body is numb. Suddenly I am sweating profusely. Without a word, I climb out with the help of my cousins and return to where I was sitting.

My arm is really painful, but I mask my discomfort. One of the girls runs for her mother and brings her to me. Seeing me frightens her and she immediately calls my father who arrives in thunderous anger, saying, "Spring is such a busy season for me that I don't have time to die, and here you are making trouble for me and keeping me away from my work."

The women insist he take me to a doctor.

"You see?" he roars at me. "Now I have to take you somewhere to look for somebody to set your arm." We march off to the tune of my father's mutterings for a town near the Caspian, to a teahouse. Parting the guests, we walk past the lunchtime crowd to where the owner is working. Hearing the story, he gets to work breaking two eggs into a bowl and mixing in some powders, and begins to massage my arm with the mixture, me shouting in pain all the while and the guests watching curiously as they eat. After the massage, he splints the arm with two boards. We go home.

A few weeks later, when my father takes me back to the restaurant for a follow up, the owner can see my arm is set improperly.

"What should we do, then?" asks my father.

"We have to break it again, and reset it."

"Oh, my dear Lord God!" my father intones. "I can't," he adds, sitting back in a chair.

While some of the guests hold onto me to keep me from moving, the restaurant owner massages the arm and with a sudden move, snap! The arm is broken again, this time deliberately. He massages it with the same mixture, replaces the slats of wood to immobilize it, and the arm heals as it was meant to.

* * *

The good thing about working for neighbors on their land in the summer is the variety of meals offered after a day of hard work. Our next-door neighbor was an excellent cook; whenever I worked for them, she offered delicious lunches, and often dinner as well. Add to this, the warm atmosphere of the house and I was happy to work for them.

One early morning, my father saddles the horse and makes him ready for work, asking me to go next door first and after finishing their job, to go on to the lands of a more distant neighbor. Jumping on the horse, I ride to the neighbor and they send me on to their fields. After a few trips, it is still early and they have no more work, and I am ready to go on to the second job, when the woman of the house invites me to return for lunch.

Happy with this invitation, I take off and work with the second neighbor until about noon, when his wife asks me to stop and join them for the midday meal. Since their grandfather has recently died, I am afraid to go into their house, besides I have my appetite whetted from the first offer, so I say 'no, I must go, I have to go'.

No matter how much they insist, I leave their yard at a gallop to return home. In my yard, under the pear tree, I put out newly cut grass for the horse to eat and go to the well to wash my hands and feet, prolonging the act so my neighbor can see and call me for the lunch I am eagerly awaiting. She doesn't show up and I walk around the yard keeping myself visible so she will come out.

Now, my mother, noticing I am back, leaves the living room, comes out to the veranda and asks if I have had lunch. Not knowing how to answer her, since I know, by custom I would have had lunch with the second neighbor, I say, yes, I have eaten. By now it is one o'clock, and I have missed not one lunch, but three. Hungry and tired, and not brave enough to ask my mother for food, I take the horse and return to work.

* * *

Coming home on horseback one dusky evening, my father unsaddles the horse for me, gives him water and sends me with the animal to the grazing field. Holding the bridle of my horse, I walk it to the grazing area near the spring. While there, the next-door neighbor coming to fetch water stops to talk to me on her way past.

"Why don't you take your horse to land farther away which has better grass?" she asks.

"This horse and I are tired; we just got home from work. It is already dark. If I take him farther away, by the time we get there it will be time to turn around and return."

Laughing, she says, "I deserve this lesson from a child; why didn't I think of that?" and continues on to the spring.

Because her special sense of humor gave me freedom to say whatever I wanted, I would try to live up to her expectations and say things that seemed more mature than my age.

* * *

One autumn day when the ground is thickly covered with leaves whose colors are slowly fading, I am playing with a cousin in the yard next door, located between my house and my cousin's.

With a broom made from evergreen branches, the neighbor shovels the leaves into huge piles here and there under the trees to be bagged. Not able to hold a bag open and fill it at the same time, she calls, "Hassan, come help me." I hold the bag open and she fills it. No sooner do I go back to playing with my cousin than she calls me again, then again, and a fourth and fifth time. The next time she calls me to help I walk over and, with a childish frankness, speak without thinking, "Why do you call me Hassan, then? Call me porter."

Dropping the broom, she grabs me and starts kissing me and laughs, "Oh, I love how this boy thinks! He is a boy after my own heart!"

Years later, she was still telling these stories at gatherings whenever my name came into a conversation.

* * *

Once on a weekend, several of my classmates and I are headed to see my aunt in a neighboring village near the Alborz. To get there quicker, we decide on a shortcut that means crossing a river, tea farms and some orange groves.

The river is at the bottom of a steep embankment with a sandbank on the other side. Adding the 2-3 meters of the height of the bank to the five meters width of the river gives an idea of the distance from one side to the other. Not wanting to take the challenge with me of jumping over the river, my friends decide the best way to cross is to take off their shoes and socks, roll up their pant legs and wade through the knee level water.

I walk back a few meters to get a running start and propel myself up and over the river, landing, out of balance, on my toes and forehead on the soft ground. Getting up before my friends join me, I pretend nothing untoward has happened and we continue on our journey.

Soon I feel one foot is too tight in my shoe. I take off that shoe, see how swollen the foot is and begin to feel the pain that accompanies it. My friends want to go home but I push them to continue, saying I am okay. Not long after that, I have to admit defeat and we return the way we came, with me limping all the way.

Entering our yard, I say goodbye to my friends and limp up the stairs to the veranda and into our living room. My mother, worried, immediately brings a pan of hot water and sticks my foot in it and begins a massage.

When my father gets home, not daring to tell him the truth, I say I have tripped and fallen. He takes me straight to a traditional bonesetter in the lower village, who, after examining my foot, sends my father to a nearby town for ointment. Limping badly, I get myself home while my father goes for the medicine.

On the second floor verandah, I lay down in the autumn sunshine and fall asleep. I am still sleeping when suddenly a sharp blow to my buttocks jars me awake and I jump up. There I see my father standing behind me at the top of the stairs, now furiously bombarding me with curses. "You little devil, how dare you lie to me! I just talked to your friends and they told me everything. You deserve that pain and had I known, I wouldn't have gone so far to get ointment for such a troublemaker. That's your ointment; take care of your foot yourself."

He leaves while I scrabble for the tube, now bent almost double from hitting me. Seeing it immediately reminds me of the pain in my back.

Two weeks or so later, I am still limping around when a very old woman, a classmate's grandmother, walks into our yard to visit my mother.

"What happened to your foot?"

"It's sprained."

"Is your mother home?"

"Yes, she is up."

The old woman goes into the house and before long, my mother calls me in. "Your friend's grandma is a bonesetter," she explains, "and she wants to see your injury."

After a short examination, she instructs my father to bring a cylindrical-shaped tree branch about the circumference of my ankle and the length of my foot. The grandmother asks him and my brothers to hold me tightly in a standing position. She grabs my leg by the ankle and lays it atop the branch. Unlike her hunchbacked posture and seeming weakness, her hands are so strong I can't move my leg in spite of the excruciating pain. She asks the family to ignore my screaming while she rolls my foot back and forth firmly against the branch for some time. Finally, I have no more breath to shout.

After she stops, I feel almost immediate relief and can walk again within a couple of days.

~ * ~

First breath of ideas; from dream to reality

Each year during the month of Ramadan, my father fasts along with the majority of Muslims. Before daybreak, he eats a snack, prays, takes care of the animals, and leaves for work. At noon, coming back from the fields, he quickly performs his vozu, washing his hands, face, arms, legs and feet and quickly changing his clothes in preparation for hurrying to the mosque to join other villagers for namaz or prayer. Then back to work, exhausted from not eating and the hard labor.

Sometimes at eftar, or sundown, when the fast can be broken, Mr. Behrang, a neighbor and relative, on his way past our house, calls out to us on the veranda, and we invite him in. "Cousin," he says to my mother, "a cup of tea, please. I want to partake of the evening snack with Islam, because I want the reward God has promised those who share 'eftar' with believers." He knows this will drive my father to a frenzy.

"Do you listen to God's words?" My father retorts.

"I have great respect for God."

"Why don't you sacrifice even one day for Him by fasting, then?"

At this, Mr. Behrang begins to laugh, and my father continues with his characteristic use of foully friendly language, "You don't give a shit about sacrifice."

"Fasting is for righteous people like you; we sinners just keep our eyes on the rewards."

"On the Day of Judgment, God won't give a shit about you, then. On that day, while you are trying to cross the bridge which is thinner than a hair and sharper than a blade, when you can't answer His questions, he will not let you cross and you will fall into the Hell burning beneath it."

"What questions would those be?" asks Mr. Behrang, feeling free with my father to make fun of his religion.

"Who is your first imam, who is your second imam, who is your third imam, what taboos counteract vozu..."

"What, for example?"

"Small wind and big wind," my father names a couple, referring to silent or not so silent farting.

The mention of such social taboos sends Mr. Behrang into paroxysms of laughter. "What about the imams, then?" he adds amidst his mirth.

Asking my mother and brothers to bring Mr. Behrang more tea, and dates and sweets as well, my father continues, "The first imam was Ali; he was the most pious man to ever live on this earth. He spent his whole life in prayer, helping orphans and widows and he fasted most of the year, surviving on only one date a day."

Mr. Behrang laughs again and says, "How do you suppose he could beget more than 30 children on such a slim diet?"

"How do I know? Being a man of God gave him the power."

"Listen very carefully, my dear Islam. I know you; your heart is pure. I don't care if you believe these stories or not, but please don't shove them down your children's throats."

In his own defense, my father says, "I have no doubt of your love for my children and I know you want what's best for them but I am not as talented as you are. If anything happens, you have the influence to save yourself and your family, but I have nobody to defend them if these boys follow such ideas."

* * *

By the time I am almost nine, I begin to join my brothers at work on our tea farms, listening closely as they talk about a wide variety of topics, sometimes using words I do not understand. But it doesn't matter, my enjoyment is just being with them. Darius, my oldest brother, tells us about some books he has read which are banned in Iran. He explains ideas like sharing lands, gardens and properties with others, saying, 'If I have two eggs and my neighbor has none, I should give one to my neighbor'. Although I find such ideas very interesting, I become fearful for my animals, which I love even more than my brothers' theories. I don't want my brothers giving away my beloved pets to someone who has fewer than I do.

After winding down their discussions at the end of a day, my brothers ask me to keep these conversations a secret from my father whom they know is opposed to such topics. My father, who only sees things in black or white, has resigned himself to the life he leads. He feels that being born poor is his lot, and he will stay poor because of it, the same way the rich stay rich. He always seems to be angry and when he is around, our lives are filled with 'dos' and 'don'ts'. He is constantly working, leaving the house early each day and coming home, either at noon for lunch, or in the evening, with no energy left for his family. We have to maintain complete silence; no fooling around, roughhousing, loud talking or music are tolerated when he is in the house. Worst of all, he expects us to mind our own business and stay away from ideas or philosophies such as the ones my brothers read and talk about, which to me are as sweet as watching my favorite cartoons, but to him are absolute nonsense. The more time my brothers spend talking, the less work gets done on the farm and this gives my father more fuel for his fury.

My brothers are much friendlier to me than my father. They tell me stories and let me listen in on the discussions they have almost daily.

"The first political novel I ever read," Darius tells us one day at the farm, "was in winter, 1976. It seems like yesterday a friend handed me the book; my eyes darting around the market, I held my breath as I took it and immediately hid it under my overcoat. Heading home, my imagination conjured up agents of the Shah's secret army grabbing me from behind. Once home, I walked directly to the second-floor room and, locking the door behind me, rushed to the window to make sure no suspicious person had followed me. Then, I sat down and started reading it."

I listen as Darius and the others talk about sugar in Cuba, war in Vietnam, tell stories about racial inequality, the revolution in France and Algeria, and persecution and resistance. One story that particularly moves me is of a teenage girl who was detained and questioned about her brother's views and his whereabouts. I can still remember the many times I secretly pinched my fingers with the pliers to see how strong I would be in case I were ever questioned by police officers whom I created out of my childish imagination. There is no reason to caution me about keeping these stories from my father; I might lose my source should my brothers find out I have tattled, and then what would I have to entertain my friends in the pasture?

Sometimes when my father is away, my brothers' friends visit us at the farm. They laugh and talk and fool around, but after a while their conversations get serious as they explore ideas about social injustices, lack of freedom in the country, and the role of younger generations in bringing a change to society.

One day when I have an abscess in my foot from a thorn and am supposed to be at home resting, a friend of Darius' from a neighboring town comes to our house asking for him. Both my mother and uncle try to give him directions to our tea farm where my brothers are working but he seems confused so asks my mother for permission to have me take him to Darius. Before she can make up her mind, I volunteer and quickly limp down to the yard; the young man and I head south.

Our tea farm is in the woods near the Alborz Mountains and we have a long way to go. My brothers' discussions have taught me not to give information to any strangers, so I remain deadly silent as I limp slowly alongside my companion. Occasionally he wants to know how much farther we have to go. Tersely, I tell him that we are almost there. An hour or so later, we arrive at the farm. I am so excited to see my brothers that I start babbling non-stop. The young man, surprised with my sudden talkative nature, begins to converse with my brothers. "I thought this boy had a speech disability," he says in a funny tone, smiling and telling them how I treated him on the way. Darius praises me warmly, saying, "It seems that our teachings are not wasted; this is the first fruit." My heart warms to his commendation; being my oldest brother, he has made a very deep impact on my personality and I want to grow up to be just like him. We all laugh and chat for a while before the young man brings out a section of newspaper he is carrying. He reads an article stating that in ten years Iran will suffer famine.

They are discussing this article when suddenly Darius suggests I go gather fruit from the trees in the orchard. I leave them alone to pick delicious figs, cherries, blackberries and strawberries growing wild around our large farm. When I return with a full basket of fresh fruit, my brothers are still engrossed in their conversation.

~ * ~

The royal police in the yard

One evening in autumn, I am home alone. The area is quiet and none of my playmates is around. The sky is partially covered with clouds and rain seems to be on the way.

I am playing out front near the pomegranate tree when a military jeep appears by the main gate. The vehicle drives into our yard slowly and stops close to me; a few soldiers step out. They are in military uniform and display the discipline associated with the Shah's armed forces: shined shoes, erect posture, the politeness of the commander who takes the initiative in speaking. He has a pistol on his belt and holds a short shiny black bat under his arm, obviously stronger than all the sticks I have made for myself in our pasture. His neatly shaved face with its well-shaped moustache over the upper lip crowns a uniform with several stars on the shoulders.

This is the first time police have ever come to our house, although I have seen them in the yards of neighbors who needed help resolving domestic disputes. My father jumps up from the veranda, puts his shoes on, walks to where they are standing and invites them in. The commander thanks him and refuses the offer. There is no sign of anger in his voice; on the contrary, he is serious, but very polite and gentle.

"We are looking for Davood," he says.

Holding the commander's hand tightly with both his hands, my father politely asks to know why they need to see Davood and what is happening.

"I just want to ask him a few questions if I may; it is not very serious and you do not need to worry."

As their discussion continues, my mother sends me for water and I reluctantly take a few jars and leave. Once near the spring flowing from among the trees on the riverbank, I see my 15-year-old brother Davood, looking frightened. He has been trying to hide among the bushes and it is clear that he already knows the soldiers are looking for him. I can feel that he is more afraid of my father than he is of the soldiers, since most of his questions are about dad. I mention dad and the soldiers are talking. He asks me to go back home and not say anything.

Minutes later, he appears in the yard and surrenders himself to the soldiers, apparently convinced there is no chance to hide. The soldiers walk him to their car and ask him to sit beside two of his friends, who have already been detained. Then the commander tells us the boys are being taken to the police station in a town nearby, and the car leaves.

A short time later, the news of Davood's arrest disperses throughout the village like black ink in water. Many of our neighbors congregate in our home and suddenly the silent evening is replaced by the noisy disorder of everybody talking at the same time. Sometimes it is hard to find who is talking to whom in the chaos.

"I know what happened," someone, whose child was also detained, says in a loud voice. Having just returned home from the police station, she is enjoying being the center of attention and speaks animatedly. The crowd turns in her direction to hear her version of the story. After making sure everybody is listening, she begins to talk. "My son was with Davood when he tore down a picture of the Shah from a wall," she continues. "The soldiers detained my son as well. However, as you know, my oldest child is a senior officer in the army. He has a picture of himself taken with the Shah. I took that picture to the police station and that convinced them my younger son was innocent and they released him."

We listen in shocked silence as she speaks. The news hits the villagers like an explosive; people can hardly believe their ears. No one ever imagined Davood would be foolhardy enough to tear down a picture of the revered and respected king. My old uncle always used to tell me there were two gods in the world. He described one god as God the Creator of the universe, and the other as the Shah who was God on earth.

My father, angry enough at first to be reluctant to give Davood moral support, is finally convinced by the neighbors to go to the police station and arrange for his release. A couple of hours later, he comes home empty-handed, madly restless and without a clue what to do next; the police have decided to detain Davood a little longer. It is the first time I clearly notice how deeply my father loves his children, since he doesn't know how to demonstrate his love for us either in words or actions.

Hours crawl by. Finally, my mother intervenes, "I will get him home," she states, and sends me to find somebody with a motorbike. I rush out to a friend's place; in minutes, my friend and I are in our yard on his bike. With the help of our neighbors, we are walking my mother to the bike when suddenly my father starts shouting at her, "You have no right to go after your son; such a son deserves prison and I do not want him back."

We all stop, not knowing what to do. My mother ignores dad's anger and insists we help her get on the bike. "Take me to Mr. Behrang's home, my child," she says to my friend as she tries to settle herself on the bike. "I want my Davood back."

My father stands mute as the bike disappears into the darkness but I get the feeling he is secretly pleased with my mother's decision.

Mr. Behrang is a famous teacher and a very influential figure in our area, his father having once been the ruler of the entire village. Well educated, with an outstanding personality and always being very handsomely dressed in suit and tie in a village where the majority of the farmers wear coveralls, he delivers lectures about agriculture, economy, or world politics, and on important national days, he is always invited to deliver speeches to the public. His house is usually full of important people and distinguished guests from all over the country. Also, he is my mother's cousin and has a great love and passion for my family. He treats my brothers and me the same way he treats his own children, and we in turn love and respect him greatly. We work on his rice land in summer. He lives on the far eastern edge of the upper village, where the dirt road reaches the tea farms. Every morning after my father milks our cows, my mother gives me fresh milk to take to his house. He pays me very well for the milk delivery and welcomes me like a son. Each year he gives me a sum of money for New Year's that is more than all the money combined from my other relatives. Mr. Behrang was my brothers' teacher and principal at different times, and later becomes my literature teacher in secondary school. His example inspires me to memorize thousands of poems and stories, just as he has done. My brothers and I are his top students so he has high expectations of us, but there are times when we are not prepared in class, and that makes him terribly sad. I remember the day he called me to the blackboard[1] to ask questions about our literature assignment. I had not studied this material and did not know the answers. During the break, he called me to the office. 'Look, Hassan,' he told me in a low voice so other teachers could not hear, 'I feel terrible when you and your brothers do not study well. Do you want to be an illiterate farmer like your father?' I listened to him in silence and when he finished speaking, I promised to do better. His kindness and the message he delivered were too impressive to resist. In the next class I volunteered to answer several of his questions before giving the other students a chance; he was so happy he gave me two 'A's for my hard work.

On the night of my brother's arrest, my mother has no doubt that only Mr. Behrang can solve this problem. He soon appears in our yard; my father comes out of the house and they leave together. Before bedtime that very same night, Davood is back.

----

[1]In old days, students went to the front of the class whenever they were to answer questions. Iranians say, 'biya pa ye takhteh', which translates, 'come to the foot of the blackboard'. Teachers believed this would help students overcome their shyness and act more maturely.

~ * ~

Bright expectations; unfulfilled dreams

Davood's arrest brings changes to our house; my father becomes stricter and pays closer attention to our activities. However, with the passage of time he gradually lets us watch movies at the neighbor's again.

Like many others, we do not have TV at home and almost every night, with a group of young people from different parts of the village, we gather at our neighbor's. Usually we enter their yard before they have finished their meal, and wait outside in the dark under the trees until they are done. While waiting, the older children climb the fruit trees in our host's garden without permission and stuff the fruit into pouches formed by tucking their pajama tops into the elastic of the bottoms[1], then climb down to pass the fruit to the rest of us. We eat a plum or a peach or two, and take the rest of the fruit into the house.

Every single night, the house is like a small movie theater with about twenty children in the room, chatting loudly during the shows. Tarzan, Laurel and Hardy, Detective Canon, John Wayne, and American Live Boxing Championships are a few of our favorite programs. Sometimes our hosts want to listen to the news, which comes on before the movies and we have to be quiet for a while. When I was younger, I decided that the news broadcasters liked me more than they did anyone else since I noticed they always looked directly into my eyes. To check to see if I was right, I would sit in a different place every night; they still spotted me very quickly. I wondered whom they would look at when I was not there. It was a long time before I figured out this phenomenon.

After the news is over, and the parents gone off to another room, we turn off the lights and settle down to our movies, our stash of sunflower and pumpkin seeds and the fruit we have brought. Sometimes the host's children accuse us of picking the fruit from their trees but we insist that we have brought it from home. Of course, they do not believe us, but when they see us slurping and munching the fleshy fruit, temptation overcomes them and they join us. By the end of the night, the room is filled with the aroma of seeds and fruit, and the heavy smell of our dirty socks. The host's older son and daughter act as their parents' representatives, keeping the door and window wide open to get fresh air and tidying the room of our clutter.

Some children have suspicious black areas on their faces or backs the next day. Like my father, their parents are also very punitive and want to keep their children under their control at any cost. Many of them do not even want their children to leave home to watch TV. Parents are afraid such gatherings may lead their kids to get involved in the political activities that are gradually taking shape around the country.

Darius and Davood, my two oldest brothers, are at the top of my father's watch list. Whenever they return home late, we all face violent arguments the next day. My brothers insist that they were watching movies while my father believes his children are involved with some of the villagers who are marked as political people. Little by little, my brothers become bolder and begin to talk back to my father, making him furious. He is strongly against any kind of political activities in the village while my brothers believe society needs changes; common people should not have to work so hard and have nothing to show for it while certain individuals are rich from exploiting poor villagers.

Ideas like these are what my father is against, and hoping to keep us from getting involved in anti-Shah activities, he says, "No one ever came to give my parents anything for free, and no one will ever come to give me things for free, either. Those who tell you such nonsense, which you find so sweet, want to deceive you. People can be like Satan. One day, Satan took me to a cliff; from that viewpoint, we could clearly see a river below us. I could hear the roar of the water and Satan told me that this was a great place to pee down into the river. Not trusting him, I asked him to go first. He pulled his pants down and started to urinate. I could see him releasing the water, see the arc of the stream leave his body, fall and hit the water below. He said, 'You see? It's that easy.' I followed suit, pulling down my pants and starting to urinate, but immediately I woke up and realized my bed was wet. Listen, children, people get you involved in something and even give you a demonstration, but when you do it, you put yourself in danger because you do not know how to avoid trouble and they do."

If he feels we aren't listening to him and insist on going our own way, he loses control and throws things at us or beats us all either with his belt or a branch from a tree, and kicks us out of the house. When this happens, we spend the entire night outside or at the home of friends or relatives.

When we continue to disobey him, he decides to leave home himself and disappears from our lives. To be frank, in the beginning, I feel free when he is not around. In his absence, my brothers and I pay more attention to our daily tasks and are more cooperative with each other. He has been gone for about two weeks when one of our relatives who lives in Ramsar, a nearby city, happens to see him working in an orange grove. They talk and my father explains his heartbreak and frustration. Finally, his cousin convinces him that we are young and he needs to have patience with us and suggests he will urge us as well to have more understanding of our father's concern for our future.

One evening while I am playing, my father walks into the yard. Seeing him, I realize just how much I have missed him, although I try not to let anyone know. Everyone gathers around dad in the living room, sitting close to him. You can tell by the way my brothers are silent, how sorry they are for making their father angry.

My father's absence is effective for a while; he holds his temper better and we are more obedient. Unfortunately, this peace is short lived and the nightly gatherings to watch TV begin again. Like many older youths in the village, my brothers leave home late in the evening with excuses that they are going to watch TV, not to return until the middle of the night. What they really do is leave to join their friends and resume the activities in which they are involved.

Before long, tension increases throughout the country and revolution sweeps over the nation like a deadly plague.

----

[1]Dressing in pajamas for visiting is an old and almost obsolete custom in my province. These days, only very close friends feel free to dress in pajamas when going out or receiving guests.

~ * ~

Talk the language of the village

The number of youths leaving home to watch 'television programs' grows nightly. Sometimes the following mornings, we see funny caricatures of the Shah and his family on walls and trees throughout the village. To talk against the government becomes more common among the younger generation.

Some say Farah, the Shah's wife, bathes in deer milk every day. They say Prime Minister Hoveida leaves to gamble in the casinos of Turkey every night. Then comes the comparisons between our life and the life of the royal family. At night, we have to fetch water from the well, boil it over the fire, then carry it to a tub under the trees to bathe, while Farah, whom I love and admire, bathes in deer milk. We cannot afford a taxi to visit our local bazaar in the nearby town once a week while the prime minister is flying to Turkey in his private plane. The worst is we believe the rumor that he always loses his bets and is wasting the money and assets of the nation. The conclusion we draw is that we are poor because Farah bathes in deer milk and the solution is to get rid of the Pahlavi[1].

Every night more and more military jeeps appear in the village, and every morning additional revolutionary slogans can be seen on walls. 'Death to the Shah' and 'long live freedom' are sprayed on almost every wall. The village youths become acquainted with the names of political leaders who have been arrested and are either still in prison or have been executed by the Shah. Suddenly to be part of a political group is in fashion and the younger generation is less reluctant to talk about their political heroes.

Simultaneously, we are being introduced to a new mullah, said to be the Prophet Mohammad's appointed man. His first name is Ruhollah, which means 'God's Spirit' in Arabic. We start admiring everything about Ruhollah Khomeini, since to see such an appointed person is a dream fulfilled for a nation that has lived with a religious creed for centuries. Before we know it, Khomeini replaces the Shah in our daily life; for us he is God's representative on earth and we fall in love with his speeches. A religiously oriented political fervor overtakes the country.

From the early stages of the revolution, Khomeini focuses on two major factors; this makes him more popular than other organizations. He emphasizes religion as the first priority, and he uses language common people understand. While other political organizations and parties use difficult words and concepts such as feudalism, bourgeoisie, proletarianism, lompanism[2], character assassination and rumormongering, Khomeini talks the language of the village; as a result, he establishes stronger relationships between him and the people who are thirsty for what they believe he is offering.

Although several communist-based organizations launch serious movements throughout smaller villages, especially the ones in the north, including ours, which are closer to Russia, for the majority of people, who, even if they are secular, have religious roots, it is very hard to accept there is no God or that everything was created by accident.

With the communist parties discounted, two other major movements have a better chance to gather more followers. These are the Mojahedin organization[3] and Khomeini himself who is showing up as an extraordinary figure, a religious leader unattached to any political party.

In addition to these, other, smaller groups and movements spring up here and there, as the revolution spreads its roots throughout the nation. However, since all the political organizations have one common goal in the very beginning, unity exists among them. They believe they can meet their goal of overthrowing the Shah and settle their ideological differences later.

* * *

One night a group of military forces is chasing some villagers just behind our home. My father and I watch through the window as the men jump over our wooden fences and disappear into the dark, leaving the soldiers behind on the road.

"Those fellows broke down our fence," my father says, his voice forlorn.

"How else could they have run away from the soldiers?" replies my mother from where she is sitting in her bed.

"Why do you think the government doesn't chase me?" asks my father angrily. "Because I am sitting here in my home minding my own business. If those men hadn't been doing wrong, nobody would be chasing them. I don't go to Atku - an imaginary mountain - and the bears on Atku don't eat me."

I have a very special concept about the word 'government'. In my mind, government is an enormous metal machine in the shape of a fat man. The metal man is sitting in the middle of a huge palatial room, and there is a big slot over his stomach from which money flows. Listening to my father, I wonder how such a machine can get angry with people.

"These crazy young people," my father adds through clenched teeth, "are destroying our home. They have no idea what they are doing."

Nobody answers him, and we continue to watch the soldiers who are talking to each other in low voices.

"I have seen the time of Mosaddegh[1] when he took the power from the Shah; we all yelled 'Long live Mosaddegh' on the streets one day. But the next day, we, the very same people, rushed into streets again and shouted 'Death to Mosaddegh'."

Exhaling a deep breath, he turns to my mother, "They know how to deal with us; we are just like marionettes with ropes on our hands and legs, the other ends of which are in the hands of puppeteers who turn us in any direction they like and we start dancing."

Suddenly he looks at me as if he has remembered something, "where are your brothers?" he asks with a frown.

"They are watching TV."

"Why did you come back home then if they are still watching TV?"

"They said the movie tonight was a horror movie and not good for children so sent me back home," I mutter without daring to look him in the eye. I can feel my answer does not satisfy him but he remains restlessly silent. A few minutes pass and a couple of military jeeps stop for the soldiers and disappear from sight.

"I really hope everything will turn out all right," my father murmurs, as he and I look out onto the empty road in the stillness of the night.

----

[1]Mohammad Reza Shah Pahlavi, the second king of the Pahlavi Dynasty.

[2]The concept of lompanism refers to the parasites of society, those without employment or work skills who hire themselves out

as instigators of trouble, those who by using violence impose their unjust views on others.

[3]Founded in late 1960s by a few university students, the Mojahedin organization was known as a progressive movement combined with both Islamic and Marxist ideologies, which appealed to the majority of people. I do not know too much about its original politics, but from checking their web pages today, it appears they are now focused on dogma similar to Khomeini's when he was in power.

[4]Dr Mosaddegh was elected as the prime minister of Iran in 1951 and became a hero with his achievement of nationalization of the oil industry. In 1953, with the people's support, Mosaddegh revolted against the Shah, forcing him to flee Iran. He had the people's support for two days; on the third day, with the help of the American CIA, people flooded the streets again. This time, they were supporting the Shah against Mosaddegh. The prime minister lost his newly gained power in a coup led by General Zahedi and backed by the American government. The Shah returned to power. Mosaddegh was arrested, tried and sentenced to three years in prison.

~ * ~

We want teachers, teeee...!

I must be in grade three when Khomeini and other leaders of the revolution announce a nation-wide strike against the Shah. The strike starts from the oil industry and sweeps almost all major organizations and ministries throughout the country. Schools are closed and there are no classes. When our parents still wake us up early in the morning, and insist that we go to school every day, we all collect in the schoolyard and play until noon, then feeling hungry, we head home.

We are pleased with the holiday; it is great fun and we really get a kick out of it. Sometimes we take part in the daily demonstrations held against the Shah while our parents think we are at the schoolyard.

These days, to say *'Death to the Shah'* evokes a sense of pride. Even the first grade students have learned how to write 'Death to the Shah' on walls with a piece of chalk. Those families who remain neutral are called shameless traitors. Every single day, at the top of their lungs, the protestors repeat 'bi tarafaa bi sharafan', or 'neutrals are knavish', in an effort to push the undecided families into getting involved in the anti-Shah manifestations. To avoid being the targets of harsh chants, more and more households join the mass movements daily. Night and day, the military forces scatter people and break up assemblies, arresting a couple of their organizers in the province. A high school student is shot dead in a nearby town. Fear and hope are everywhere; the more the soldiers intervene, the more seriously we protest.

On one particular morning, we gather in the schoolyard as usual, playing and chasing each other in the absence of our teachers. Suddenly one of the students jumps on the cement platform of the flag post, which now stands bare and flagless. Calling us all together around him under the post, he demands we listen to him. He is a fifth grader who doesn't have the shyness of a village boy and is more outspoken than most. With a loud, aggressive tone, he begins talking until we quit our games to listen.

"What the heck do you think you are doing?" he yells, "I don't care about the younger kids but you older ones, who will have final exams[1] this year, better listen to me. You ought to realize that the longer your teachers are absent, the worse your situation will be during final exams. We must make our teachers break their strike and come back to school. Whether they come to work or not, your teachers are still getting paid. Who loses then? You do. So I ask you all to show the public that you are not happy with your teachers being on strike."

To my understanding, what he is saying seems logical. Some children who are about his age begin to talk back to him.

"We are too young to protest."

"Nobody would take us seriously."

"Take it easy. Let's enjoy the unexpected holiday."

"Who would listen to us, anyway?"

Such an exchange of opinions persists for some time. Then this same speaker shouts at us to be quiet so he can talk. "I'll tell you what we'll do. Today we'll start our own demonstration to let people know that we are mature enough to care for our future. We'll put our books on our heads and march along the road towards the market."

Since demonstrations are something we really love, before he can arrange us in rows, we rush out of the schoolyard and flock by the main road, just like my little group of chickens who hurry to me when I call. The instigator runs after us and joins the group there. He stands in front of us and says, "while walking, cry out this phrase: we want teachers, we want teachers, teeeeechers".

We follow him, our chants filling the still morning air. Since we do not have any slogans or placards, some of the older students deviate to the nearby bushes and trees where they break off several branches and pass them around. We each raise a branch up in one hand while holding our books in the other. Waving them high over our heads, we walk towards our market where crowds of people are preparing to stage their own anti-Shah demonstrations.

We children, believing we are supporting the revolution by demonstrating, chant cheerfully. The police patrols, knowing we are actually supporting the Shah, pull over near the mosque and watch us silently from the comfort of their car, while villagers, including some of our teachers and the principal, seeing our deception, look at us aghast and no one steps forward to interrupt. The police don't stop us and people can't stop us for fear of the police. When we realize the soldiers aren't trying to interfere, we become braver and holler even louder until hunger gets the better of us and we head for home.

Later the same day, the principal of the school, who is a close friend to my oldest brother, asks me to accompany him to a corner where he begins to talk to me in a serious but gentle manner.

"Look, Hassan," he says, "what you did today disappoints me. I am your brother's close friend, as you know. I would never have expected you to take part in this kind of subversive activity. You are too young to understand what you are doing. Let me tell you that what you did today was totally against the revolution. I am going to ask you to tell me who organized this demonstration, who provoked the children, and who gave them those tree branches. As you know, we are on a strike along with other teachers throughout the country. People will question my supervision here if my students try to break such an important strike."

Even though I love my principal because of his friendship with my brothers, I remain stonily silent to avoid betraying my schoolmates. The more he encourages me to cooperate, the more I repeat 'I don't know, I don't know'. Because the Shah is still in power, he is afraid to push me too hard so, in the end, he asks me to go home and tells me not say anything about our meeting.

* * *

Later it becomes evident that the family of the schoolmate who encouraged us to break the strike supported the Shah until he left the country. Soon after the revolution his family, particularly one of his older brothers, joins the Khomeini regime and becomes part of the local paramilitary forces called Basij[2] whose job it is to demolish any kind of anti-Khomeini movements. This brother is the one who, with the Basij leader, impudently walks into our house in his dirty boots on a day that turns out to be a very bad day.

---

[1]Based on regulations in Iran, all grade five students have to pass final exams before being eligible to enter secondary school.

[2]Basij was a very radical paramilitary force Khomeini established soon after the 1979 revolution, which still exists to this day. Its members were people of little education who would kill upon order without question.

~ * ~

The Imam in the moon

One night, we are having dinner while my old uncle sits on the steps of the veranda. The stairs that connect the first floor to the second are a suitable place to relax and watch the yard and surrounding areas. Whenever we have nothing else to do, from somewhere on the stairs we watch the animal activity around us as well as people, cars and motorbikes: local taxis with one or two passengers, sometimes behind the driver, sometimes perched atop a basket of tea, sometimes over the gas tank in front of the driver, moving along the country road.

By squatters' rights, the stairs belong to my uncle. His wife and the baby she was carrying died in childbirth before I was born and he now lives alone in his room, close to us, as part of our family. Feeling lonely, he often comes out and positions himself on the stairs while we talk, adding his opinions to our conversations. He is very straight-to-the-point, never minces words, and freely criticizes everybody and everything without self-censorship, disparaging our neighbors' activities and ceremonies; this makes my father's temper flare. Uncannily, just before his brother completely loses control, uncle leaves for his room and stays there until things calm down again. Although he is the older, he has acceded leadership to my father since childhood.

The walls in uncle's room are thickly smoke-darkened from the fire he makes in his open fireplace every day. In winter months, with snow swirling silently around the house, the fire in his room beckons us; we sit in front of its bright flames, roasting potatoes under the hot ashes and listening to his tales and songs. Potatoes ready, we peel off their skins, salt them and together savor the tastiness of their hot flesh.

When uncle begins to sing, he closes his eyes and forgets about us. Sometimes my prankster brother Mirza hides a cup of cold water in the room, waiting his opportunity. When my poor uncle is immersed in his songs and oblivious, Mirza pulls the waist out to dump the water inside the old man's pajamas with a quiet and sudden move. As soon as my uncle feels the water on his lap, he jumps up and down and at the top of his voice, rains curses on us and on our teachers in abusive and foul language, since it is his belief that our teachers are the ones responsible for not teaching us manners. We laugh and try to calm him down. Uncle is accustomed to our practical jokes and doesn't take offense for long.

This night while he is seated on the stairs, one of our friends arrives. He greets my uncle on the veranda and we invite him to have dinner with us.

"How can you sit and eat while the whole village is out?" he asks. His words make us curious; we beg him to explain himself.

"A miracle has happened," he exclaims. "Come out and see it with your own eyes. The imam is in the moon".

At first, we think he is joking, but his expression is very serious so we rush out to the veranda to see what he is talking about. My uncle, who deeply loves the Shah, begins to curse us, and the entire younger generation, in an attempt to keep us from leaving. We hastily grab our shoes and run off anyway. By the time we catch up with the crowd standing along the road, staring with transfixed gaze at the moon, we can no longer hear uncle's grumblings.

"Can you see that?" says a man who is involved in organizing demonstrations in our village. "Isn't it amazing?" he shouts with great excitement, adding, "The imam is in the moon."

Dozens of faces lift to the sky.

"Yes, I can see him."

"I see his face."

"He seems to be praying there." More descriptions follow and it seems everybody can picture the imam's image in the full moon.

"So what are you waiting for?" interjects the leader. "Come on everybody," he yells, "say it then."

'Death to the Shah,' we chant.

'Say it'

'Death to the Shah'

'Come on'

'Death to the Shah'

'Everybody'

'Death to the Shah'

'Say it'

'Death to the Shah'

'Say it'

'Death to the Shah'.[1]

Our loud chants bring my old uncle out to the road. "What's happening?" he asks.

"Look!" says one of the crowd as he points to the sky and details the features of the image on the moon's surface, "Imam Khomeini is in the moon."

My uncle stares at the moon for a while. Suddenly he turns to us and roars an invective. "F**k your teachers for teaching you such bull," he yells, "it's too bad you wasted time going to school. Those black spots have been on the moon at least since I was a child."

We all burst into laughter and shoo him back home, continuing our chants in the middle of the road until a car stops by and a couple of men dressed in nice suits roll down the window to ask us the reason for such a gathering. "What's up?" asks the driver.

One of us runs to the car and says to them breathlessly, "The imam is in the moon."

The men look at the sky through the window of the car, and then look at us without saying a word. As the car is leaving, the window rolls up.

A few minutes later, the older moon gazers are haranguing and chastising the culprit who spoke to those strangers, beginning to worry that talking to the people in the car will bring incriminations against the crowd. They wonder if those men belong to the Shah's secret army, or SAVAK, as it is called. Although the number of people who support the revolution has increased a hundred fold by now, the Shah is still in power and there is fear that his secret army patrols among people, attempting to identify key revolutionary figures. Discussions continue and since no clear decisions can be made on this, our crowd decides to join other villagers whose loud chants we hear coming from the marketplace. We all move towards the market where we are warmly welcomed by a larger group of villagers standing around our local mosque, chanting. Our chants and theirs mix and generate a more powerful voice.

'Say it, death to the Shah'
'Say it, death to the Shah'
'Say it, death to the Shah'.

The person holding a field speaker and leading the crowd is the son of a dominant local leader. When the revolution weakens the Shah's power, villagers who used to serve as local leaders, begin to shift their allegiance to Khomeini. One of these leaders lives among us and people have always had to carry out his orders. As revolution sweeps the country, his oldest son, with a bully's reputation, leaves Tehran for our village to become active in the anti-Shah demonstrations going on all around us. A second son has similar weaknesses; besides being a bully, he drinks and uses drugs, and many believe he has contributed to the ruin of several youths by introducing them to drugs and alcohol and supplying them with these substances. Huge and brave, once when two groups of youths converged on our village to fight, he stood up to some 15 carloads of people and caused them to disperse.

When we arrive at the marketplace on the night of the sighting of the imam in the moon, with the field speaker in his hand, this thug is leading the crowd in chants, his shouts inflaming and unassailable. At intervals between chants, he makes very short speeches to the public, during one of which he pronounces the word, 'Imam Khomeini'. The crowd begins to show its respect to Khomeini by saying in chorus, 'peace be upon Mohammad and his family'.

Praising the prophet Mohammad and his family whenever the prophet's name is mentioned is a religious tradition, people nearly always wing a word of praise heavenward on hearing his name. Beginning with the revolution, we were supposed to show the same respect to Khomeini. Whenever somebody said 'Imam Khomeini', we were coached to praise the leader in chorus. This is what we were doing every time we heard the imam's name, but this threatening son of our local leader shouts, "I don't understand. You praised the prophet Mohammad once and praised our very own imam only once as well?"

For a while, we don't say anything and then suddenly break out praising Khomeini continuously for three repetitions. I have no idea why we choose three rather than two or four or some other number. From this night on, we praise Khomeini three times whenever somebody calls him by his name during daily speeches. Then this same bully shouts into the speaker and calls out the names of some families who have children serving in the Shah's army. "Your child may be an officer," his voice reverberates through the speaker, "but come out and see. Our imam is in the moon." Long, loud chants express our joy at his words.

'So, say it,' he tells the crowd as he punches the air.

'Death to the Shah,' we shout.
'Say it, death to the Shah'
'Say it, death to the Shah'
'Say it, death to the Shah'.

Calling for men, he says, "Brothers, say: 'unless the Shah is dead'." Turning to women, he coaches, "Sisters, say: 'there is no future ahead'."

In the new, religious nation, women are referred to as 'sisters', while I and all other males, are known as 'brothers'. The brothers start first, 'Unless the Shah is dead'. Sisters echo, 'There is no future ahead'.

'Unless the Shah is dead'
'There is no future ahead'
'Unless the Shah is dead'
'There is no future ahead'.[2]

We chant one revolutionary song after another until long past midnight.

The next day we hear that nearly all Iranians throughout the country saw the phenomenon of the imam in the moon. Later on, as people start harboring doubts about what they have seen, the anti-Shah demonstration organizers broadcast that the Shah spread this rumor to destroy Imam Khomeini's reputation.

----

[1]The chant in Persian:
Begu marg bar Shah!
[2]The chant in Persian:
Ta Shah kafan nashavad,
In vatan vatan nashavad (This nation will not become a nation)

~ * ~

Each rise has a fall

In August 1978, when a big movie theater called Cinema Rex catches fire in Abadan City, more than three hundred people are burned alive. The Shah visits the scene immediately and expresses his condolences with the families of the victims.

This fire unites the people more than ever against the Shah; we believe he killed those people deliberately in an attempt to defeat the revolution. We feel his sympathy to the families of the victims is insincere and deceitful. His actions take on monstrous proportions in our minds, deepening our hate for him and his family. Looking back, I can't help but wonder how this catastrophe could possibly have benefited the Shah.

No more than one month has passed when another major tragedy hits the nation. On a Friday, demonstrators are attacked in Tehran by the Shah's soldiers. Five thousand people are said to have been slain in Jaleh Square in the capital city. Self-proclaimed eyewitnesses say the waterways around the square were filled with fresh blood, which, according to hearsay, reached their knees in several places. The day becomes known as Black Friday and we blame the king for his lack of mercy for his subjects. Rumors and more rumors reach our ears daily, rumors vilifying the Shah and glorifying Khomeini.

In an effort to calm the nation, the Shah begins replacing cabinet members, including the prime minister. With each new shuffle in the government, we chant new songs.

'Brothers' chant first and 'sisters' follow with the second line.

'We say we don't want the king'
'Prime ministers get changed'
'We say we don't want the donkey'
'Its saddle gets exchanged'[1]

As the revolution sinks its roots into our soil, the majority of the families who have been supporting the Shah turn to join Khomeini. Victory is so close that even my old uncle begins to think it is the end of his second God. The Shah's rule is all but over; most people have no more patience for his tactics and the few who still have hope that he will keep power, remain silent.

Parts of the Shah's final message, which he delivers via television in a last-ditch attempt to pacify the nation, say, "At such historical moments I want you all to be apprehensive about the condition of Iran. Let us not ruin the future of our country. I promise to give you the fundamental freedom and the social justice you are calling for as soon as current tensions abate. Let us all pull together for the sake of our homeland."

Personally, I do not like listening to this speech, nor do my brothers. Our theory is that this dynasty has had fifty years to think about the nation, and isn't now a little late to start? In our opinion, he has come up with a new way to deceive people. Later we find out almost no Iranians were in a listening mood when the Shah delivered his final words.

Then one morning in mid January of the following year, one of the country's most prestigious newspapers gives out the biggest news yet about the revolution. In its largest font, the headlines read: 'SHAH RAFT' (the Shah has left). The pretext for his travel is 'for the sake of his health'.

For us, his leaving is a victory and we begin to chant again. Brothers yell, 'The Shah has decided to take a trip'. Sisters echo, 'Shit in his mouth, spit in his face'.

'The Shah has decided to take a trip'
'Shit in his mouth, spit in his face'
'He has reshuffled the cabinet'
'Shit in his mouth, spit in his face'
'He has made a fool of Bakhtiar'[3]
'Shit in his mouth, spit in his face'.[4]

Daily we continue to chant such phrases all over the village, celebrating the occasion of the Shah's leaving with our shouts of victory filling the air. Now even the shy children cry out such phrases freely. My old uncle constantly complains about our foul language and curses our teachers, blaming this filthy talk on them; he believes school is a sacred place where children are only taught good behavior along with scholastic material. His efforts are in vain; we believe such language is permissible as long as it is used to denigrate the Shah. We are thoroughly convinced that the king of Iran is our country's biggest enemy.

Soon chanting a new song that says, 'When the devil leaves, an angel appears', we call for Khomeini to leave Neauphle-le Chateau in Paris, where he is believed to be heavily guarded by the Shah's agents, and return to Iran. He is our hero and we love hearing any news whatsoever about him.

* * *

The Shah was not a perfect man; our daily life had difficulties and a lack of freedoms was noticeable in a monarchical state where the king was the owner of the nation and everything was considered his property, but the country was becoming modernized at an acceptable rate. His rule had felt like a dictatorship to us so we fought to overthrow the throne. Now that I compare his policies with what came after him, I believe he would have been a better choice for the nation; modification of the system would have benefited the country a lot more than a fundamental revolution. Looking back, we certainly had a happier and more stable life under his leadership than what followed in his footsteps.

----

[1]Streets in Iran, particularly in major cities, have waterways on both sides, which we call jadval or joob.

[2]The chant in Persian:

Ma migim Shah nemikhaym, nakhost vazir avaz misheh, = We say 'we don't want the Shah', his prime minister is replaced.

Ma migim khar nemikhaym, paloonesh avaz misheh = We say, 'we don't want the donkey', its saddle is replaced.

[3]Bakhtiar was the Shah's last prime minister. He fled the country after the revolution and was stabbed in his residence near Paris in August 1991; the Khomeini regime was said to be responsible for his death.

[4]The chant in Persian:

Shah azm e safar kardeh

Goh khordeh ghalat kardeh

Kabineh avaz kardeh

Goh khordeh ghalat kardeh

Bakhtiar o khar kardeh

Goh khordeh ghalat kardeh

(You can foresee the future of a revolution grown in the soil of such charming words!)

Bakhtak

At the time though, we close our eyes to the Shah's good works and focus on every single negative we can think of, including some of which are rumors, like the deer's milk baths of his queen. All we yearn for is the representative of God on earth, whom we are convinced is Imam Khomeini. We are very thirsty for religion, and Khomeini knows it.

Words cannot describe the feeling I have the day the Prophet Mohammad's appointed man lands on Iranian soil and I see him with my own eyes; our lifelong dream for a religious leader is coming true a few days after the Shah abdicates.

"Wake up, Hassan!" my father calls to me. "Go bring the horse from the stable," he orders, "he needs shoeing today."

"Today?" I ask half-awake.

"Yes, today."

"But I cannot go with you today."

"Why not?"

"Because Imam Khomeini is coming back to Iran this morning; I want to see him on TV."

My father looks at me as if he were looking at a fool. "This horse cannot work properly without being shod, I need it done today."

It is useless trying to dissuade him; he wants the work done, and now that he knows Khomeini is coming today, he is more determined than ever to do it.

An hour or so later, we are near the blacksmith's store that is tucked into one corner of a market now looking as if it has been deserted for years; all you can see are the doors of shuttered shops plastered with paints and colored chalk. Khomeini's picture is on many of them and several others are decorated with funny caricatures of the Shah and his family. Revolutionary slogans are splashed everywhere. From among them, two phrases stand out: 'Death to the Shah' and 'Greetings to Khomeini'. Nobody is around; everybody is home waiting to see Khomeini arrive. I hold my horse's bridle and lead him as my father and I walk through the market. Reaching the fork that leads to the blacksmith's store, we have hardly begun to walk into the dirt alley when we hear voices from inside an old teahouse. Young people and old who want to be with friends during the televised presentation of Khomeini's arrival have crowded inside this teahouse, the only business open. A big black-and-white TV is hanging under the rafters above the cashier's head just behind the entrance, and the room is full of smoke from cigarettes as people drink tea and wait for the live broadcast to start.

"I told you nobody would be working today," I say to my father with a smirk.

"Go to the blacksmith's home and tell him that your father is waiting right here. He will come," my father commands in a voice that doesn't seem to belong to him. He is more stressed than usual and pretends not to pay attention to the people inside the teahouse. Like many other people of his generation, he is determinately obstinate about accepting that the revolution has overthrown the Shah.

To be sent away on this special day feels like a cruel punishment. The old blacksmith lives at the other side of the lower village and it will take me quite awhile to get there and back. Running towards the blacksmith's home, I notice that, like the marketplace, the lower village also resembles a ghost town. From the corner of my eyes, I can see that each and every single space on walls alongside the village road are covered with the words of revolutionary chants. I already know which chant is written on which wall because I am running along the road where we marched and shouted 'Death to the Shah' thousands of times. I have a flashback of the place where one of our teachers of whom we were fond, when he once told us to say, 'Death to the Shah', and we weren't responding loudly enough to satisfy him, said, 'saying Death to the Shah is a lot easier than memorizing a geography book'. We had laughed and started chanting louder.

Breathing hard, I finally walk into the smithy yard. My father's message delivered, the old man grumbles a bit as he begins looking for his clothes. I wait for him outside and we walk back to his store together. The blacksmith and my father greet each other warmly and soon begin to chat. Like my father, this old man is disgusted with the activities of the younger generation. He loves the Shah and has no use for Khomeini.

Lighting his smithy's furnace, he looks around for suitable shoes and gets to work. Nodding at the teahouse, he comments, "Do you see those people in there? The Shah was of help to all of them. Not so long ago they did not have anything to eat; this very same Shah gave them jobs and supported them, both financially and with encouragement. While the rest of us had no bread to eat, they received handouts from the government."

Once the fire is hot enough, with his large tongs, the blacksmith grabs hold of each shoe and puts it in the flame; the iron shoe soon turns a translucent red color. He takes it out and holds it against a short iron pillar affixed to the middle of his shop, and begins to form it with heavy, sharp blows of his large hammer. The more he talks about these sycophants, the angrier he becomes and the harder the blows of the hammer. "The Shah supplied their daily needs," he continues. "He gave them free rice, mutton, beef, cooking oil, tea and even sugar. Most of these people have such a good life that they no longer need to send their wives to work on the lands. Now they are waiting for Khomeini to come. Let's see what this mullah will put into the hands of such people."

After forming each shoe, he dips it in cold water; the shoe hisses and steam escapes from the container. He repeats these steps three more times.

When it is time to place the horseshoes, I hold onto the bridle, and my father lifts one leg of the animal. The blacksmith starts cutting the waste parts of the horse's hooves, while continuing his monologue. "These young people think the mother of the groom has wrapped a big chicken for them. They don't know this mullah has put garbage in the package', which only looks beautiful from a distance." Both my father and the blacksmith are laughing as they continue with the other legs. The final blows delivered to the shoes' nails, the blacksmith stands up and sorts the hammer and some leftover nails into separate boxes. My father straightens and dusts off his clothes; the horse is shod and ready.

While my father and his old friend are still talking, I take off and run back home so fast my lungs are burning. All the long way back, I desperately pray to get to the neighbor's house on time. When you are in a hurry the road never ends, but I finally reach home and head next door without wasting time. Houses have the festive air of a village wedding ceremony. As a sign of celebration, most villagers have turned on their veranda lights. Some have even washed and cleaned their yards and put flowers in every room. As I enter the house, I face a crowd of people, some of whom are distributing candies and flowers, others sitting still waiting to see the imam arrive. I join my brothers, squatting down beside them on the carpet. They ask me a few questions about the horse, which I answer in monosyllables, my mouth full of cookies and my eyes fixed on the TV.

Suddenly we see the imam's plane landing at the airport. Everybody cheers. We continue conversing in clipped words until Khomeini emerges at the door of the plane. It is one of the most exciting moments in my entire life. Watching the imam, who is as important as a prophet to us, I feel joy like warm honey bubbling up from my heart and spreading throughout my being.

One of our neighbors is lounging in a corner, his legs stretched out open on the floor. Seeing Khomeini appear on the TV screen, his son asks him to sit politely in front of the imam. The old man gets angry and mutters, "Stop such nonsense. Remember, he is also a mullah like the one who abused our children at school." Since we all have similar problems with our parents, we focus on the imam and pay no attention to his words.

The live program is abruptly interrupted and a picture of the Shah superimposed on the TV screen. The old, familiar national anthem plays once more and we begin to curse the Shah afresh. Right now, he and his national song are an unpleasantness we are reluctant to face. Having heard rumors that the Shah's forces might try to kill Khomeini at the airport, we are worried and pray that such a thing will not happen. Nothing happens and the imam finally steps on Iranian soil after nearly 15 years in asylum.

* * *

Khomeini fell on our lives like 'Bakhtak'[2] - a vampire - and judging by his example, I don't think the Iranian people will ever again be open to a religious government.

----

[1]Before the revolution, a wedding ceremony lasted several days, when youth had a lot of fun together. An old custom in our village was for the mother of the groom to wrap a succulently prepared chicken in bread and papers on the seventh and final day of the wedding. There was close competition for the chicken, considered the gold medal of wedding trophies. With the bride

surrounded by youths in the yard, her mother-in-law would climb to the upstairs veranda, and from that height would throw the package containing the chicken into the crowd. Everybody held their hands up in flushed anticipation, pushing and shoving in their fervor to grab it. The importance of this trophy was it brought you delicious chicken and foretold a life of fame. Now the old blacksmith was comparing Khomeini with the mother of a groom, who was standing at a higher place than the people of Iran while holding a package, its content hidden in his hands.

[2]Bakhtak is an imaginary creature with various forms – demon, Satan, nightmare, incubus and tick, depending on tribal lore – whose function is basically the same; it sits on the chest of a sleeping person and suffocates him or bites him and drinks his blood.

Man is born free, and everywhere he is in shackles
................Jean Jacques Rousseau

Three

When 'Nothing' is loved

"What are you feeling now that you are finally returning home as a victorious leader?" a reporter asks the imam during the plane ride to Iran.

"Nothing," he replies. We even love his 'nothing'.

The imam comes and the transitional period between the age of dynasties and the kingdom of religion moves faster than people could ever imagine.

"The malicious Shah has destroyed the nation," he states in an historical speech upon his arrival, "and has made the cemeteries luxurious."

We are amazed by his words.

'Yes, he is right'.

'Do you recall the high school student whom the Shah killed in the nearby town?'

'I can still see his poor mother's face as she cried over the coffin'.

'His father could not even speak'.

'Poor parents'.

'What a huge crowd of mourners showed up that day!'

'Do you know how many more people mourned during the revolution?'

'The Shah killed five thousand innocent people in just one day[1]'.

'You see, the imam knows everything although he has been away from the country for such a long time'.

'That is why he is a leader'.

Conversations like this spread throughout the village as we are led blindfolded deeper into the next stages of our 1979 revolution.

Apart from his initial deceitful claims about giving freedom to the nation, Khomeini was very clever in the wording of his speeches; what we took for promises he was making us, really weren't promises at all. We heard: 'I'll make water and electricity free, I'll make oil free, I'll make buses free'. Recently I listened to his speeches again and heard: 'Do not be satisfied (if someone says) that we will make oil, electricity, and water free'.[2] But back then, in our thirst to hear what we wanted to hear, we interpreted his words to match our own longings.

* * *

American and Israeli products disappear from our local markets. People take off American clothes and throw them away: no more America; that is the new order.

Soon after the revolution, one of our neighbors gives me a twenty-toman bill and asks me to get him a pack of Winston's, the highest quality American cigarettes available in Iran. One dollar, or one hundred pennies equals seven tomans, or seventy Iranian rials, and twenty tomans is a lot of money[3]. I hold the bill tightly in my fist and run to the market. There are no American cigarettes available and I return home empty-handed. As I walk into the yard, my neighbor, who is still chatting with my father under the trees, fixes his eyes on my empty hands. "What happened?" he asks. "Is the market closed again?"

"No," I reply, "the market is open, but they don't have American cigarettes."

"You younger ones pissed off our country by your revolution," he says as I put the money in his hand. "I used to be able to buy five boxes of fine American cigarettes for this amount of money." Then he shows the twenty-toman note to my father and says, "This is just the beginning. I can foresee the day when this money is not enough for a kilo of lamb[4]."

"Don't say that," my father counsels his friend, "I hope such a thing will never happen. What would we eat then?"

Pointing to me with his hand, his friend smiles and says, "Ask these young people."

"We did not revolt on behalf of your cigarettes," I object.

"What did you revolt for then?"

"We revolted for God, not for stomachs," I answer in a serious tone.

He turns to my father and says, "Don't give him food for one day. Go ask your imam to give you dinner tonight," he tells me.

I leave for the house to do my homework. Schools have opened part-time and we have to attend classes again. Aftershocks of the revolution dominate the atmosphere of classrooms and no order is established; only a few teachers show up and books are missing, but we limp along with leftover supplies from before the strike. Our school's name goes from Khayyam to The Imam Musa Sadr Primary School, the name of a Lebanese religious leader.[5]

Gradually new schoolbooks arrive and when our teachers pass them out to us, we see that all the pictures of the Shah and his family have been replaced with a single picture of Khomeini at the beginning of each book.

As the days go by, we come to realize why Khomeini never laughs; based on our teachings, the God-fearing person whom Khomeini considers himself to be should always feel sad since man, who is born sinful, has no reason to feel happy in God's presence. In our religion classes, teachers begin to instruct us not to laugh loudly anymore, following the example of the imam. We learn that only for those whose objective is power will victory bring laughter. Khomeini is not fighting for power and there is no reason for him to be elated when he returns from exile as a victorious leader. We love how he discredits himself and praise him for making himself so humble before God.

The phrase 'a true believer always has a saddened heart' hits us from all sides. To support their ideas, our teachers tell us many stories about the Prophet Mohammad and his family, managing to ferret out direct and indirect quotes of the prophet, saying a truly pious person never laughs. Especially for girls, loud laughter equates to immoral behavior. If a girl laughs aloud in public, friends and relatives say she just needs a husband to tame her, while others call her a prostitute. Word pictures of this nature are created in our heads on a daily basis as we learn more about the examples of our religious leaders in history.

Stories and parables about the prophets and their families creep into our class work. One story I remember in particular is about the Prophet Mohammad who gives twelve darhams[6] to Imam Ali and sends him to buy a shirt. Later that day, the imam returns with a nice shirt in his hand.

"How much did you pay for it?" the prophet asks him.

"Twelve darhams," the imam replies.

"I don't like this shirt very much. I prefer a less expensive one. Will the shopkeeper agree to a refund?"

"I don't know."

"Go see what he says."

Returning to the same shop in the market, the imam talks to the shopkeeper and says, "The prophet of God prefers a less expensive shirt. Can we get a refund?"

Getting his money back, the imam returns to the prophet and together they go shopping again. On the way, they come upon a little girl sitting tearfully beside the road.

"Why are you crying?" the prophet asks the child.

"My master gave me four darhams to go shopping for him," the girl answers, sobbing, "but I lost the money. I don't dare go home because I am afraid my master will punish me."

The prophet gives the little girl four darhams and asks her to go buy the items her master has ordered.

While in the market, the prophet buys himself a shirt for four darhams. On the way back home, he sees a person who is so poor that he can't afford clothing. Taking off his new shirt, the prophet gives it to the man and returns to the market to buy another one, Imam Ali at his side. The two are walking home when they come face to face with the same little girl.

"Why didn't you go home, then?" the prophet asks.

"It's very late and I am afraid my master will beat me for the delay."

"Show me your home; I'll go with you and tell your master to be kind to you."

Saying this, the prophet walks the child to her home and calls out for the lord of the house. There is no answer. He calls for the second time. Still no answer. After the third time, the child's master opens the door, offering his greetings to the prophet.

"Why didn't you open the door the first time?"

"My lord," the man explains, "your voice is a blessing to this house and I loved hearing it again and again."

"Your housemaid is late and I have come here to ask you not to chastise her."

"In honor of God's prophet coming to my house today, I will set this slave free."

"Praise be to God," the prophet says. "What blessed money it was. It covered two people and set one slave free."

We drink in such stories and still feel thirsty for more. Honestly, the religion teachers are great masters in this field; they can find no end of stories about the prophets and their lives that haven't been dug up in thousands of years.

Soon these new stories replace all we have learned about old Persia. We begin to overlook our national heroes in history, now labeled 'stupid ancestors', and concentrate our learning on the early Moslems who have become the Islamic symbols of discipleship on the path to God. One day, one of our religion teachers tells us that based on the Prophet Mohammad's words, the future of Islam is destined to be in the hands of Iranians, and we convince ourselves that we are his true offspring.

For us, Khomeini, who is said to have private conversations with God and with Mahdi, Islam's promised messiah, is the right person at the right time, and nothing can replace him in our hearts. We feel ashamed when reminded of pre-Islamic Iran in which, for thousands of years, we lived under tyrants with 'meaningless traditions' but now are exonerated because Islam has come to save us.

Soon we forget there have been kings and dynasties in Iran for more than 2500 years. Kings, dynasties and kingdoms are suddenly regarded as unholy. Their historical and cultural relics are called unclean. Huge numbers of priceless books are destroyed to promulgate the religious Cultural Revolution. The new Islamic government begins to destroy historical monuments and buildings throughout the country. Sites like the tomb of Cyrus the Great are attacked as if they are our enemies.

* * *

Years later, the new government built a huge dam close to this tomb; experts believe water will one day destroy this monument to the Charter of Human Rights.

----

[1] This refers to Black Friday. Recently I saw a documentary movie about Iran, which estimated the real number to be about 250.

[2] This is Khomeini's original words, not meant to be colloquial English.

"We not only want your physical life to become tranquil and prosperous, your spiritual life we want to be enriched as well. You need moralities. Our moralities they have taken away. Do not be satisfied (if they say) that 'we will only build you houses', 'we will make water and electricity free', 'we will make buses free'; do not be happy with just this much. Your moralities, your spiritualities we will glorify. We will guide you to the place of humanity. They have deceived you. They have exalted the world in your eyes so much that you think everything is this."

[3] One American dollar equals some ten thousand rials today.

[4] One kilo of lamb sells for about 10 thousand tomans or 100,000 rials these days.

[5] Originally from Lebanon, the family of Musa Sadr moved to Iran, where Musa was born in Qom City in 1928. By 1960, Musa was back in Lebanon and held a position of Islamic Shiite leadership.

[6] An Arabian coin.

~ * ~

Islamic Republic of Iran

To decide on the political system and change the name of the country to reflect that it has somehow been 'born again' in Islam, Khomeini asks for a national election. He denounces suggestions coming from any political parties such as 'People's Republic', 'Democratic Islamic Republic', 'Democratic Republic', 'Social Democracy', and any titles with the word 'democratic' in them. Since the first part of the word 'democracy', 'demo', is close to the Farsi word 'dom' meaning tail, Khomeini says, according to our teachers, no tails are needed in the title of our political system. He believes Islam is a perfect religion and does not need any democratic titles. The suggestion he finally submits as the political system, the Islamic Republic, is put to the vote. At the polls, the majority of Iranians, whose only choice is 'yes' or 'no', vote in favor of his option. Based on the outcome of the election, a natural sequel is to call our country the Islamic Republic of Iran.

* * *

We have no more flag-raising ceremonies in our school nor do we sing the national anthem in the mornings. Our teachers instruct us that Islam is our first priority and soon the concept of religion replaces the concept of self, family or nation. We are guided to think globally since the new leaders believe world powers are suppressing the nations and only Islam can stop them.

Mornings before classes, children with good voices are asked to read aloud from the Quran and then a chorus of students sings revolutionary songs; these activities replace the flag-raising ceremonies. The choir is formed from students of all grades; I am picked from my class as one of its members. To this day, I still remember the main part of one song we sang almost every morning from the top of cement stairs leading to the school's entrance hall. It said,

'Khomeini o Imam!
Khomeini o Imam!
You the Mojahed[1], the symbol of dignity,
You have laid down your life for your goal,
Your name shakes the foundation of tyrants,
Tyrants have knelt down before you,
You are the Lord in protecting God's sovereignty,

71

You are the protector of people, religion, and the Book,
Your chant is to fight for the truth,
We greet you. We salute you.
Khomeini o Imam!
Khomeini o Imam!'

When we are done, one of the students commands 'Takbir'[2]
in a strident voice and the rest of us punch the air with our fists
and all together chant a phrase,

'God is greater,
God is greater,
God is greater[3].
Khomeini is the leader.
Death to anti velayat e faghih[4],
Greetings to the militants of Islam,
Greetings to the martyrs,
Death to the USA,
Death to the Soviet Union,
Death to Israel'.[5]

Before the revolution, we brought our hands together in
clapping whenever we wanted to show our agreement with the
speeches. We also whistled through our fingers enthusiastically to
show the speaker that we supported his words. Now our teachers
ask us to forget clapping and teach us how to support a speaker
with the help of Takbir. So, when we finish our morning songs,
somebody says 'Takbir', and others repeat the above phrases.

The topics of our composition-writing classes undergo a
change. We used to write about nature, the advantages of cows
and other animals, our holidays, and the heroes in our traditional
literature books. We would also compare wealth with knowledge
and decide which one we preferred and why. These days we are
expected to write about the revolution. We are asked to share our
memories of the revolution with others in the class and
encouraged to write about arrogance, tyrants and the suppressed
people of the world and in particular the Zionist regime, the USA
or the Great Satan as Khomeini calls it, the former Soviet Union,
and England. Our recommended reading is books on how
obediently the followers of the Prophet Mohammad fought for
their faith to the very last breath. We begin to learn about Arab
heroes like Ammar, Yasser, Abouzar, and even Salman Farsi, who
escaped from Iran to serve the Prophet in Saudi Arabia. One after
another, symbols of sacrifice like these are substituted for the

national heroes in our books. We have to actively take part in mourning ceremonies held in commemoration of these people. In contrast, our own traditional festivals such as Norooz, Mehregan and Char Shanbeh Suri are said to be unholy legacies left to us by our 'stupid' ancestors.

Refreshments at school come to an abrupt halt. During the Shah's reign, we had free snacks every morning and afternoon: bananas, apples, biscuits, and even bread and cheese of the highest quality. Once the revolution was in motion, we began to criticize the snacks provided by the Shah, saying, for example, that the cheese was made of camel or mare's milk, and even that he was giving us unclean food. But we needn't have bothered; once the revolution takes hold, we are given no more snacks, either clean or unclean.

The increasing unavailability of our basic needs such as sugar, cooking oil, petrol, chicken, mutton, beef, and even bread drives the prices of the meager supply of them higher by the day.

I remember there was once an old man who had a small store behind our home. He was our longtime immigrant neighbor who had moved into the village years before I was born. One day on the way back home from the market, I step into his store to ask him if he has matches for sale. He nods his head yes, as he leans his elbows on the table separating him from his customers, and bends over to the other side. I get two packages of ten small boxes each for two tomans apiece. Since I have no money with me, I tell him I will pay later; he knows me, so there is no problem. I hold the matches in my hands and ask him if he has heard the news.

"What news?"

"A few minutes ago when I was in the market," I explain, "each package was selling for five tomans. But, I am telling you tomorrow when I come back, I will pay two tomans for each one because that's our agreement. I just gave you the news so you can start selling them at this new price immediately after I leave your store." He agrees and I walk home.

The next day when I return to pay for the matches, he asks for five tomans each. I begin to argue, "We agreed yesterday on two tomans each. I bought them yesterday, and I will pay you the amount you asked for them then."

The old man answers, "Actually, I did not believe you yesterday. Otherwise, I would not have sold them to you for only two tomans. Yesterday after you left, I closed the store

73

immediately and went to the market to check. You were right. It was five tomans. So you must give me yesterday's price."

I have no choice but to give him what he asks and, parting with the ten tomans, leave the store. In the evening, while I am playing in the field nearby, he calls me back to the shop and returns six tomans to me.

The unpleasantness of this transaction colored how I felt about that shopkeeper who had been like my uncle.

----

[1]Mojahed means the one who lays down his life for his goal. In the world's new order, however, such an action may be called a terrorist activity.

[2]To this day, frankly I do not know the meaning of the word 'Takbir'. All I know is that it is an Arabic word and we knew to say these phrases in response to the word.

[3]The common translation of this phrase is 'God is greatest'.

[4]Velayat e faghih refers to the Shi'a governmental system in which the supreme leader represents God on earth until the Messiah comes.

[5]By the 1980s, 'Death to hypocrites, and Saddam' was also added to the phrases we chanted. Hypocrites was the title the government gave to either political dissidents or anybody else who stood against 'the representatives of God on earth'.

~ * ~

'Ask yourself what you have done for this revolution'

My brother Davood has left for the mountains, where he is spending a few months bringing first aid to the villagers, victims of a huge forest fire. The rest of my brothers are getting more seriously involved with friends in political groups and organizations taking shape here and there in the area. With them scattered, I am the one whom my father seeks when he needs help.

Shops start having lines for many commodities. There are quotas for this, there are quotas for that, there are quotas for everything. We have coupons and have to queue for whatever product is being offered on a particular day. When we hear that a certain commodity is available in the market, my father usually shoos me off with money to purchase our share. Soon I find myself in a different line every day, a chore I abhor. I hate it that I have to leave the friends I am playing with, I hate it that things are in such short supply, I hate it that lots of people first argue, then begin to fight over their place in line, each one claiming he was here first.

'This is my place'.

'No, I was here before you'.

'We didn't see you'.

'I got here last night'.

'There was nobody around when I arrived at 4.00 AM this morning'.

'Do you see that small rock in the line? It represents my place; I put it there last night as I was going home'.

'My shoe is missing; I left an old shoe just behind that rock'.

Such discussions often lead to fistfights. Former friends speak, argue, push, and finally hit each other; each one looking out only for himself. In addition to clashes about food lines, the villagers raise various social and political issues, which also give them fodder for disagreement. Tensions peak when, hours later, we hear that the chicken we are waiting to purchase is sold out.

The fuel lines are the longest and there is little crude, especially during winter when it is vital. Some young people, including a couple of my brothers, voluntarily work in the small gasoline station in our village to make sure everybody receives some. In order not to betray people's trust, they never save any for our family and very often, I return home in the evening, after long hours of trembling in the cold, my container empty. One day when I go home empty-handed, my father asks, "Where is the fuel?"

"There was not enough for everybody today and I couldn't get any."

"Your brothers are working there for free and you could not get any fuel?" My father is so angry that he denounces his entire generation for having good-for-nothing children like us, who offer 'khar hammali'[1] to others and deny their own family.

"We are not working there to get something for us," my brothers tell him later that night. "We are helping people."

"Who the blazes am I, then?" my father shouts. "Do I not belong to this 'people'? Your brother stood in line all day and you did not give him any Goddamn fuel. I don't believe it."

"What's the difference between my brother and all those other kids who also went home empty-handed?" my brothers reply. "If there is no fuel for them, there is no fuel for us."

My father and brothers rant at each other for a while. Then my father resorts to blows. In frustration, he smacks us all with his belt and kicks us out of the house.

With time, we become inured to the situation at home and our father's anger; we begin to talk back more often. My brothers ignore his advice and concern about their future and continue to meet their friends who are marked as political people in the village.

* * *

To take advantage of the freedom of speech and ideas Khomeini promises during the early days of the revolution, Darius, my oldest brother, starts selling books he brings back from Tehran, many of which are novels by political figures, such as 'The Little Black Fish' by Samad Behrangi. He spreads a cloth on the ground where he can display his library, since he doesn't have a stall in the market, and keeps additional books at home to replace the ones which are sold.

I am ecstatic to have access to so many books and begin to read new stories everyday. When I have finished reading all my brother's books, I borrow from the local library until Darius can bring me a fresh supply from Tehran. I remember once in summer I walked to the library five times in one day to hand them the book I had just read. After the fifth trip, the librarian suggested giving me a few books each time so that I did not have to walk that distance several times a day.

While I am enjoying the world opening up to me through books, our parents are grumbling about the scarcity of supplies and the subsequently high prices. In response to the complaining, the imam appears on TV and delivers another historical message. 'Do not keep asking what this revolution has done for you', he says, 'ask yourself what you have done for this revolution'.

----

[1]Khar hammali, a taboo word parents usually use against children in anger, means 'to offer free work or service to others without expecting rewards'. The word 'khar', donkey, may convey a concept of simple-mindedness or stupidity. Its meaning is similar to the English 'altruism'.

~ * ~

New faces of revolution: Either jewels or prostitutes!

Before coming to power, Khomeini accuses the Shah of suppressing freedom in Iran. In reference to a quote of the Shah that 'Iran has reached the gate of civilization', he says, 'A civilized nation is one where there is freedom of press, where its people are free to express their ideas and vote for their candidates. But in this country nobody enjoys freedom'.

Once he is holding the bridle of the country himself, Khomeini delivers a contradictory speech: 'Now that we have gained freedom, what are we going to spend it on? Does it mean that I am free to do whatever I like? To hurt anybody I wish? To write anything that comes to mind? Even if it is against Islam? Even if it is against the interests of the nation? Is this the freedom we wanted? Did we really want this kind of freedom, or did we want freedom under the shelter of Islam? We wanted Islam. Islam offers a freedom distinct from that of infidels'. He goes beyond this and calls freedom of speech supporters 'stupid', saying, 'a handful of stupid people' support the idea that 'certain groups who do not even believe in Islam, should be free to say and do what they like, even if what they do is contrary to the teachings of Islam and the Quran'.

* * *

Suddenly, women aren't allowed to let any of their hair or the curves of their bodies show, decree the new revolutionary rules. The government says women are very precious to God and should be protected from use as advertising slogans on TV or in movies. In the same way that diamonds are hidden from view, hiding women under cover is their safeguard from the eyes of men. They are encouraged to leave the work force and make the environment of the home pleasing to the family, to cook and bear children.

Morality becomes the precondition for any kind of social activity. Men are banned from shaving their beards or wearing colorful clothing, or jewelry. A person can lose his job if he doesn't go to Friday prayers, or doesn't know the names of the 12 imams in order, or doesn't fast during Ramadan. It is immoral for a woman to use makeup or nail polish, to wear tight or gauzy dresses, even at home, or to show her ankles.

People, the majority of whom are women, hold a public demonstration against hijab, or forced veil, saying they have taken part in the revolution to get more freedom, not have freedom taken away. The new paramilitary forces, founded soon after the revolution, intervene and treat the protestors with physical and verbal abuse, calling them prostitutes. They tell the demonstrators that the revolution never needed and does not now need their help, and that their protest supports an immorality contrary to the tenets of Islam. These same government forces say the Shah made the whole country a huge public brothel, and now Khomeini has come to wash away all traces of sexual immorality.

Every local religious leader and teacher describes a huge fire where on the Day of Judgment God burns immoral people. After hearing this, and hearing it again and again – and again, we can almost feel the heat of the flames licking away at our sinful nature.

No longer are there girls in our school. Like their mothers, who are learning new spiritual lessons, girls, with their hair covered, are sent to segregated schools. During our religious and Quranic classes, our teachers tutor us about how they want us to deal with women. 'Do not shake hands with women or touch them,' they teach, 'do not look at their faces or other parts of their body, cast your eyes to the ground when you talk to them; if you happen to look at a woman by accident, do not deliberately look a second time'. Based on their behavior toward boys who used to be their playmates, we know girls have similar classes.

We pray and fast as is befitting very committed believers. Words such as Islam, veil, temptation, freedom, martyrdom, sacrifice, blood, victory, dignity, independence, arrogance, politics, Heaven, Hell, and even enemy, become part of our daily vocabulary. Such ideas are so deeply carved into my brain that one of our neighboring girls once doubted my manhood.

More and more Arabic words and phrases filter into our daily usage until there are literally hundreds of them watering down our native Farsi[1]. We start using them with pride, but soon begin to feel inundated, without knowing that our sweet Persian language is being submerged in the flood.

* * *

Some people join communist-based parties[2], while the majority of those of us who don't support Khomeini, turn to the Mojahedin organization, which we believe to be progressive without sacrificing the religion for which we yearn. In parallel with the government activities, these new political organizations and parties establish their small offices in the four corners of the village, and sell their newspapers, magazines, and tapes as revolutionary songs blare from speakers within the shops.

To join daily discussions taking place among the members of different organizations becomes our daily hobby. Seeing us selling newspapers and attending different political discussions in the market whenever he happens to go shopping weighs heavily on my father's heart; he doesn't think we should hang around that atmosphere and keeps begging us not to become involved with inflammatory political groups. Still angry with us for our part in the revolution, he begins to intercept the new activities of my brothers once again, pleading for our patience. "Let's see what this mullah does to us first," he says, his imploring tone somewhere between hopelessness and eagerness. "Then decide whether he is good or bad. The revolution is just over and this mullah is new in power. You fought for him. What the Hell is your problem now? Why is he not good enough all of a sudden?"

His fear is that our home will be torched in retaliation for our activities and we will all be killed. Thousands of times he repeats his pleas to us, 'I see it now, our house is on fire and I am looking for you everywhere but I cannot find you anymore'. But the poor old man is trying in vain; we have decided that Khomeini has shown his true colors and is not the one we want.

When he gets home, he tells my mother that he has seen his children all over the market, busy pushing political propaganda. He swears, 'As God is my witness, my children will one day be wiped off the face of this village. These political activities are like an ocean and these foolish kids are like small needles who if they fall into it, I know they will never be seen again – they don't know mullahs. These mullahs are people who, if they needed to, would sell their own mothers to stay in power. If necessary, they would pull their pants down in public and offer their fish-belly white cheeks to people in order to grab attention and support'.

My poor mother, who can do nothing about any of this, listens in silence while preparing tea and putting a steaming cup of it in front of him. Once my father's words run down, she tells him not to get so worked up about it, the boys will wake up to the truth sooner or later.

"Later is too late," my father always roars in his pain. "All of them will be killed; I am absolutely sure of it. But my children refuse to believe me."

Sometimes when he loses his temper, he begins to bawl out my mother and her antecedents for giving birth to such disobedient children. No matter how much his temper flares, my mother, always patient by nature, says, 'you are tired. Drink some tea and you will feel better'. She knows from experience that fresh hot tea will change his mood. After my father has calmed down, she tells him that being angry is not good for his health. Then in a friendly tone, she smiles and says, "What my ancestors have to do with your problems, anyway, I'll never know."

In spite of my father's beliefs and warnings, we continue participating in our usual political activities around the marketplace.

"At least join different groups," he asserts when he fails to stop us. "You are five brothers and it would be wiser and safer for each of you to be part of a different group. In this way, if something happened to one, we would always have others to help support the family."

"This is not about business," my brothers state, siding against him in unison, "this is about ideology and belief. How can we be part of a group whose ideology we do not accept?"

Often feeling helpless, my father talks, shouts, weeps, beats and begs us to obey him. He cries out in frustration that he is our very best friend and wants to see us lead a long, happy and peaceful life.

At times, my old uncle fans the flames between father and sons. Since he is retired and is often in the market, he cannot help but see us communing with political factions and selling propaganda. Even though we warn him, and he promises not to tell dad about our daily presence there, by nightfall he usually forgets. It is hard to fathom just how much harm his tattling on us does when he begins giving my father information, whether true or pieced together out of his imagination. What I do remember are the nights we were banned from the house due to his untimely comments.

----

¹Farsi = Persian language
²With our entire society steeped in religion, members of these parties reflected a kind of 'religious communism', flavored by Islam and hardly recognizable as the Russian dogma.

~ * ~

The other side of the war

In September 1980, Iraq invades Iran and a massive war is imposed on our country. When the fighting starts, Iran is still in transition to a new system and now people are being asked to lay down their lives for the nation by supporting our fragile army. Economic, social, and political stability already lost because of the revolution; now we have a war to deal with, a war which winds up lasting eight years.

* * *

Many of the senior officers of the army, who supported the Shah and are no longer in favor, have already been executed or fled their homeland. A new military system with which the soldiers are not familiar has been imposed on the army, causing chaos. Officers who are still at their posts but do not want to do their service under Khomeini, stage a coup against the Islamic government two months before the outbreak of war. The coup fails, resulting in the execution of an unknown number of military personnel.

An interim government is in power and the new president, who ostensibly is in charge of the military in the beginning of the war against Iraq, is impeached and given a vote of 'no confidence' by parliament and when the opportunity arises, flees the country. With the advent of a new president, the paramilitary forces feel the need to 'purify' the Shah's army, and many of the old soldiers are pushed to the sideline of national affairs. This happens before the new forces have gained experience in military strategy, or knowledge of how to combat a warring nation.

To establish a secure wall around him, Khomeini strengthens his new military and paramilitary forces so they eventually will be able to take over the power from the army. The Islamic Revolutionary Guards Corps, the Komiteh (Committee) which dedicates its energy to what is called immoralities, a cluster of mercenaries, and the Basij forces are actively supporting Khomeini, trying to gather as many members as possible. According to the country's new religious leader, 'a nation with twenty million youths should have twenty million Basij members'.

All these forces that are playing vital roles in breaking down the anti-Khomeini demonstrations, also selflessly fight in the war against Iraq. To their credit, I do not think Iran could have survived this war without such an army. However, as becomes clear along the way, Khomeini is not only trying to unite Iranians against Iraq, he is also trying to get the Iraqi people to rise against Saddam Hussein, with the hope of overthrowing their existing government. While the Iranian soldiers believe they are fighting to defend their homeland, their spiritual commander's agenda is to use Iraq as a step towards spreading his version of Islam to the rest of the world. A popular chant during the Iran-Iraq war is 'to free Jerusalem we need to walk through Karbala'¹.

Several political leaders try to persuade Khomeini to call for a cease-fire as soon as Iran has the upper hand but because he won't listen, war continues and a generation of Iranian youth goes to battle and dies. This Ayatollah uses the war to his own advantage by putting emphasis on a government with himself as the representative of God on earth and the military as God's army against what he calls world arrogance. He believes only Islam, in the concept he has introduced, can bring peace to the world and repeatedly says that his 'Islam must be exported to all nations'.

Political organizations and parties, most of which are not allowed representation in parliament, accuse Khomeini of monopolizing power and are not willing to support the government against Iraq; there are debates that the Supreme Leader might use this war to unite people under his own flag.

The more Iraq, supported by the West, pushes at our country from outside, the better Khomeini manages to gather the backing of the nation; it is a matter of standing united against a foreign invader.

----

¹The song in Persian:
Bahr e azadi ye Ghods az karbala bayad gozasht
Az kenar e marghad e an 'sar joda' bayad gozasht
Khiz ey razmandeh sheer
'Khaneh' az doshman begeer.

Translation:
To free Jerusalem, we must walk through Karbala
We must pass by the shrine of Imam Hussein

Get up o you the brave soldiers
And get your 'house' back from the enemy.
Cleansing tears begin to fall over the land

Very quickly the entire nation is in mourning and the word 'martyr' generously peppers our vocabulary. Burial ceremonies abound and often are also broadcast on national television.

Then one day our village's first martyr arrives in a box. He was a neighbor and our friend, a supporter of the Mojahedin organization, and was doing his compulsory military service when he was killed. He is the second casualty from our village. Before him, a young police officer under the Shah was executed by the new Islamic Revolutionary forces, but this death is different; we are going to have a glorious service for a war hero. There is disagreement about his burial. The Mojahedin are of the idea that they have the right to be hosts because the martyr was a supporter of their organization, while the government forces believe the young man laid down his life for his country and they should bury him. In the end there is no decision; the government does the honors.

Right on top of the first, our village has its second, third, and fourth martyr. As the numbers increase, the government forms a new committee that deals with all sorts of burial affairs for the martyrs. This committee, named Martyr Foundation, whose primary mission is to hold ceremonies to console the families who have lost sons to the war, is actually used as Khomeini's machine for propaganda; through holding weekly prayer meetings, readings of the Quran, and sermons by mullahs, the government pushes for building stronger relations between themselves and the peasant population. This mechanism is so successful that the younger brother of the officer executed by Khomeini becomes an active member in the Basij forces and voluntarily goes to war and loses his life.

We are kept busy attending the burials of our friends, relatives and classmates, some of which last as long as forty days. On the first day, the burial rite is held. The body is waiting at a morgue some distance away, where a convoy goes to pick it up and bring it back to the village to be buried. The funeral usually doesn't end until evening when people visit the family, read the Quran, pray and weep. Visiting and mourning continue throughout the second day. On the third day, a mosque service is held with either a guest panegyrist or a tape reciting the Quran while mourners weep and wail. Then a mullah, sitting on a menbar, or raised pulpit with stairs, relates a story in which infidels kill Imam Hussein[1] and his family and followers, and the wailing becomes more intense. Afterwards the eulogist returns to sing and chant from the Quran or another religious book, allowing such intense mourning that finally, the family and friends of the deceased feel some release. The procession to the cemetery follows. Once at the gravesite, relatives bemoan the demise of the martyr before having had a chance to go to university, marry, have children, see his children grow up, and fulfill his potential. Crescendos of wailing and weeping fill the air, and once in awhile, someone faints. By early evening people return to their homes, then later visit the parents of the victim, where they spend their time reminiscing about the life of the martyr. This ritual is repeated on the 7th day, the 40th day, the anniversary of death, and every anniversary after that. These are the formal observances; in informal services, friends and family get together to remember the fallen soldier, play tapes of the Quran, and share memories.

During the 8-year period, when besides the thousands and thousands who die, scores more become disabled, suffer battle fatigue or disappear in action, it is a daily event that speakers at local mosques air revolutionary chants and recite Quranic verses. The whole village turns into a big auditorium where you can hear loud religious music, Khomeini's speeches, encouragement not to forget the war - as if we could! - and the radio teaching moralities and telling stories of, for example, how immoral people have been handled by the 124,000 prophets since Adam and Eve. Programs about martyrdom, sacrifice, prayers[2], and world arrogance intersperse the other portions booming from the loudspeakers.

Our classes are often cancelled to make time for us to attend the burials and remembrances held by the government to praise the martyrs. These gatherings become increasingly more crowded as more and more families lose a loved one to the war.

* * *

A couple of the parents of such victims, who have been cooperating with the Basij, now become representatives of the government. They can hardly read and write but it is their position to judge applicants on morality and decide who will get a job, or enter a university. They decide the fate of the village and we have to respect and bow to the wishes of those who hold our future in their hands, if we want to get ahead in life. These scarcely literate villagers replace the old leaders and create new standards of conduct for us. From their offices in the mosque, the new leaders take everything under their control. Unlike the old days, when we were praised for knowing ancient Persian literature and being talented scholars, now priority is given to those who attend Friday prayers and who can read the Quran in Arabic. In parallel with the religious and cultural aspects of our lives, our social lives are affected as well; these new leaders further organize the quota system with which we have already been living since the beginning of the revolution so that they are the ones to decide which person or persons deserve the few commodities available.

The Basij forces, who have already confiscated the properties of the former leaders in the village[3], support these new leaders with their military clout. If they want something someone has, they find an excuse to take possession of it, appropriating house, lands, or other properties, and leaving the owner with no recourse nor complaint, unless he wants to be taken to prison. They commandeer the best houses in the village, including our local library, to use as their military bases. Some of the old leaders, who have lost their property, flee the country and die in exile. Those who remain face humiliating and sometimes terrible conditions. After living like kings, the loss of their possessions and social standing is intolerable; often they too die soon after being dispossessed. Government forces justify their actions by quoting either Quranic verses or the words of other Islamic leaders as precedents.

Our mullahs preach that true Moslems are those who love one another and hate their enemies; new songs espouse the idea that killing our enemies is our goal[4], since according to the new teachings enemies are always wrong and must be killed. We are taught to hate those who shave their beards or don't cover their hair, wear short pants, slacks or short-sleeved shirts or blouses, shake hands with a person of the opposite sex, forget daily prayers, listen to music, dance, laugh loudly in public or insult a religious leader. Anyone having any kind of link outside the country is automatically put under suspicion. Death or severe punishment could await you if the government decides you are an enemy of God or 'disloyal' to your nation.

* * *

One day while playing soccer in our old field at the side of the local cemetery, our ball rolls into the graveyard. Seeing it, a few relatives of martyrs, who are mourning at their sons' graves, walk into our field. We watch them in silence, feeling guilty for enjoying ourselves so close to the cemetery.

"Your classmates are sleeping in their graves over there and you are laughing over here," one of them scolds us. "You have no respect for our martyrs."

"My child was your age when he was martyred in the war," adds a woman wearing a long black veil.

They give us our ball and walk away. We play half-heartedly for a while but soon cancel the game and go home. Not long after that, the authorities announce publicly that our field will be used as a burial ground once all the cemetery spaces are full.

With the passage of time, rows of cold flat stones begin to invade the green land around the cemetery, and a heavy silence replaces our cheerful afternoon laughter in the playground.

----

[1]Imam Hussein - third imam in Shiite Islam who, along with his family and about 70 of his followers, was slaughtered in 680 AD by a large army whose caliph was Yazid, considered a renegade Moslem leader by some Islamic nations. Hussein has become a symbol of courage, resistance, and martyrdom for Shiite Moslems.

[2]According to the statistics presented by IRNA, the Islamic Republic News Agency, during the years 2004 through 2007, over 6,000 hours of radio and TV a year were devoted to teaching namaz, or daily prayers, to children.

[3]Soon after the revolution, the Basij took control of the properties of the former leaders in the village. These lovely gardens, orange groves and pine forests were flooded with locals who took out the trees to transplant in their own gardens. The

homes on these properties were used as the Basij offices and local prisons.

"The killing of enemies is my culture/custom/path/goal' (keh doshman koshi rasm o rah e man ast).

~ * ~

Lack of tolerance; old friends, new enemies

Political discussions are a daily occurrence among the youths. The members of different groups who were once friends become less tolerant with each other, resorting to bickering and arguments. The gap is especially deepening between those who support Khomeini and the combination of opposition organizations actively gathering members in our village.

'Why don't you agree with my reasoning?'

'Because it does not satisfy me'.

'Do you have something more logical?'

'No, but I do not like your way'.

'Very interesting. How can you say I am wrong when you do not have a better suggestion?'

'I don't know. I just don't like the fallacy of your reasoning'.

'You are accusing me of sophistry? We are at least trying. What about people like? All you have learned to do is disagree without coming up with solutions.'

Onlookers to these squabbles, who nearly always support one of the organized groups, laugh at the one who, although he has no better ideas, refuses to be persuaded by the politics of the party.

In every family nearly all of the children are actively involved in one group or another, and will not listen to their parents' fears for their safety; the entire village is drowning in emotions emanating from the political activities of the youth who make themselves 'available on demand' to the leaders of their particular activists.

During harvest season, work groups spring up to help the farmers with their crops. Political parties gather their followers in large numbers on a farm and raise outsized rectangular pieces of fabric printed with a message visible from the road several hundred meters away. As volunteers work on the crops, they play their newly-composed revolutionary songs through tape players with loudspeakers, which passersby can hear from afar. No matter how much their parents try to stop them, the next day these work groups are back again.

Our opponent, the Basij, has in turn appropriated many young people for military training. Every evening, we see young boys and girls line up in front of the Basij base in the market and, holding their military guns across their chests, march southward to the riverbank, singing Arabic psalms and Farsi chants such as 'party only Hezbollah, leader only Ruhollah'.

In our village, generally we don't study at home, but walk back and forth beside our property or along the river, studying and learning our lessons. Although there is no communication between boys and girls, a sort of buzz or electricity polarizes them during these study periods, which makes studying outdoor attractive.

Once these young Hezbollah forces - as the Basij members call themselves - start drilling their troops in the area alongside the river, we no longer study there, and our 'study hall' is converted to their exercise field. They conduct a couple of hours training a day during which we hear loud explosions and gunfire. The same boys and girls who used to be our study mates are now either dressed in military uniforms or covered in a long black cloak called 'chador', to serve in 'the army of God'.

* * *

One evening when it is about time for the military drill to pass by our house, I watch while my brothers and their friends, as a prank, tie the end of a long wire to a tree beside the road, then wait. Once they hear the forces chanting in the early dusk, they tie the other end of the wire to an opposing tree across the road, pulling it taut.

The Basij has interrupted my brothers' activities a couple of times, and now they plan to take their revenge. With the wire stretched between the trees, each of them disappears in the dark while I head back home so I can watch the action from our living room window. No sooner am I back in our yard when suddenly I hear a motorbike approaching the area from afar. As I run across the yard towards our veranda, the rumble grows louder and louder. Suddenly there is a big crash and everything, including the bike, goes silent. My brothers hurry to the scene and so do I.

When we get there, we see a motorbike lying on its side in the bushes just behind our house, one wheel still spinning in the air. A voice emits moans of pain from the darkness. We rush to it, and find a neighbor sitting among the bushes near the bike. Seeing he has fortunately only suffered minor scratches on his hands and face, we try to get him up on his feet, but he refuses to budge, muttering gruffly, "I want to clear my account with those responsible for my crash."

"Who is responsible?" others ask.

"The first ones on the scene."

"Are you crazy?" my brothers tell him. "We heard the crash and came to help you."

"Do you think I am stupid?" objects the driver, "I know what happened; I know why you blocked the way with that wire. But you are so thick-headed you didn't consider that someone like me, a poor driver, would arrive ahead of your target."

Our neighbor knows everybody in the area. Although he has not had previous problems with the activities of the village youths, he insists that he will explain everything to the Basij forces whose drumming footsteps and the growing volume of their religious songs can be heard just around the bend. There is no time to convince him otherwise. Holding his legs and arms tightly, my brothers and their friends lift the man and duck into a nearby alley, while a couple of us wheel the bike and the rest collect the long wire to run after them. Seconds later, the forces pass by and see nothing suspicious to make them stop, and nothing comes of the episode.

* * *

As old friends gradually became new enemies, the physical barricades like our wire turned into spiritual blockades, and no one, except for our uneducated neighbor who inadvertently broke our first tripwire, thus preventing a major confrontation, ever tried to break these bonds with the intention of bringing peaceful solutions to the village.

~ * ~

Tensions grow like mushrooms

Activities, such as daily discussions, taking sides against each other, distributing pamphlets and hand-written messages, not only affect the relations of neighbors, but also change the atmosphere in schools. We younger kids, who have been bouncing our older brothers and sisters' ideas off us, soon form our own youth groups to support their organizations.

Dividing the school's walls among the groups, we use them as our advertising billboards, putting up pictures of our favorite political leaders, sticking several sections of our newspapers here and there around the pictures, then drawing flowers and birds everywhere on our board to make it attractive to others. Most of what we need we get from home and decorate our section of wall with disorderly freedom. Other children do the same. There are photos of political people all over the place. My uncle calls the school a barbershop, because according to him, as far back as he can remember, only barbershops are plastered in pictures, never schools.

During break times, followers of different organizations flock together and challenge each other to debates. Discussions progress along the lines of what we have learned from our siblings. When we run out of answers, we start accusing each other, we insult one another, and sometimes fistfights break out in the middle of the schoolyard.

One day a huge argument occurs among those of us who support the Mojahedin, and those who back Khomeini. Their board and ours face one other at the main entrance. Our problems with each other that day are major; somebody has torn down the papers of both groups. We believe they did it; they think the same about us. There is nobody to calm us down and neither group wants to withdraw. Shouts ensue until one of our teachers leaves the principal's office, and walks to where we are standing in the hall. He quiets us down and asks for an explanation.

"They have torn down our papers," we say.

"They are lying," our opposing group protests. "Look at our board."

Both parties surround the teacher trying to get him to look at their board first. The teacher, who is a native of our village, approaches our panel and glances at the few writings and pictures still left hanging in shreds. Raising his hand, he points to one of three pictures at the top of our board and asks me calmly, "Who is that man?"

I hang my head in shame. He points to the other two pictures in turn and asks the same question. I do not know who any of them are. Smiling, our teacher puts his hand on my head and leaves for the opposing group. Except for Khomeini and a couple of other famous people whom they can identify, that group is suffering from the same ignorance. Our teacher asks us to stop fighting and to pay more attention to our studies.

Later that day, my brother Kaveh listens as I tell him about the incident at school. He waits until I have finished, then says, "Maybe your teacher is right. It is time for you to learn more about this organization."

He consults Darius and Davood, who later raise this matter with their friends. It seems all of them have the same idea: we are entitled to learn more.

On the first scheduled day of our instruction, I go to one of my classmates' house in the lower village to attend class. My friend's family supports the Mojahedin, and isn't worried about letting us have gatherings in their home. When I walk into the room, I see my brother Kaveh sitting among several of my friends. After greeting everybody, we joke and laugh a bit while I find a spot to sit. Kaveh settles us down; he is to be our teacher.

"You are growing up," he prefaces, "and soon you will need to know many things about our organization." Taking a photo out of his pocket and spreading it on the floor, he says, "For example, you should know who these people are and what they stand for."

In it are pictured five people, three of whom are those at the top of our school board whose names I wasn't able to supply to my teacher.

"This one in the middle," Kaveh continues, "is the founder and backbone of our organization. Those two at his sides are just as important as he is in its formation. And finally, these other two are the first ever recruits. Through close cooperation and hard work, these five people have managed to found a very progressive organization, which you have now joined."

He proceeds to tell us about each person's life and background. The lives of these men are so interesting that I wish I had known about them a few years earlier. With them as my heroes, I would not have had to kill Bruce Lee in the stories I told in the pasture. After Kaveh is done with the founders, he picks up the photo and puts it back in his pocket, extracting another paper from a different pocket and spreading it on the floor. "This is the Mojahedin's logo," he goes on, "which you would do well to recognize. As junior Mojaheds, you also need to know what each symbol represents. First of all, the word mojahed means a person who lays down his life for his faith. The olive branch is the symbol of peace, which is our goal. The gun shows we fight for right if necessary. The star representing the five continents means our mission is global. The strong hand refers to ..." We listen to him attentively and eagerly absorb each single sentence and concept he teaches us.

One day he decides to split us up into two groups, one for the north, or lower village, and the other for the upper southern region, depending on where we live. When he is picking a leader for each group, I am almost sure my brother will choose me to represent the south. To my surprise and dismay, he chooses two of my friends for these jobs. I feel offended but say nothing. Later at home, I talk to him about how hurt I felt when he did not choose me. He laughs and says, "Don't judge like this; I know what I am doing. From my point of view, they were better choices." Refusing to give up, I insist on knowing what makes them different from me. "Why? I am a better student than almost all of them."

"I cannot explain the reason now," is his smiling response, "I hope that one day you will understand. Let me teach you a lesson, Hassan," he adds, patting me on the shoulder, "in the hierarchy of any organization, each person should know only what he needs to know. If you knew more than you should to carry out your orders, you might hurt both yourself and your organization. Do you want this to happen?"

Even though still not happy with his decision, eventually I accept the general idea that I am not the best choice. Seeing that group leaders are supposed to be available whenever they are called for duty and help others sell newspapers and stick up revolutionary posters in the market, I finally come to realize why my brother overlooked me; he did not want me in the marketplace every day, knowing this would feed my father's fury.

Systematically and methodically, our home group leaders give us more tasks to do during our spare time. There are no computers or typewriters and we younger kids are asked to hand-write several copies of certain of the messages, which are then put on walls or distributed around the village at night, and are known as 'night letters'.

* * *

I am in the first year of secondary school when the political tension reaches its climax. The Basij forces intervene in most public activities in the village, and the political groups have to try harder and harder to withstand them. The government has become more intolerant about demonstrations and gatherings, with oftentimes even the Islamic Revolutionary Guards showing up to break the groups apart and scatter people.

In general, there are now two hot political waves rolling towards one another in the village; one supporting Khomeini and the other, the combination of all those political organizations which have mushroomed, with new ones sprouting all the time, wanting to get rid of him. Although the members of the latter wave feel closer to each other because of their common enemy, they never do manage to unite in the same way as we witnessed during the revolution. Khomeini already has the experience of a united people against the Shah, and I think he now uses his influence to assure these groups will not unite against him in the future[1].

* * *

Steadily, old friends stand up against each other as real enemies; neighbors against neighbors, friends against friends, cousins against cousins, brothers against brothers, sisters against sisters, and parents against children.

----

[1]Even today, with many of these political organizations outside of the country, there is no unity among them, which I doubt can be by accident. Who else, if not Khomeini or his successors, would fear such oneness?

~ * ~

Instantly swallowed up

With everything happening so fast, and the whole village suddenly being swept up by opposing extremist religious and political ferment, we do not take time to think. Looking back, I find it very hard to believe a nation could have been so easily brought to its knees by narrow-minded religious ideas or be so instantly swallowed up by political obsession.

Iran is at war with Iraq and Khomeini is using religious beliefs to encourage men to fight and women to support them. If a soldier dies, he is immediately transported into the presence of the prophet in Heaven and if he kills, his killing of enemies pleases God.

Media programs air the claims of many people to have seen Islam's promised Messiah traveling on a white horse through the battlefields; on occasion, saving soldiers from death, indicating when they should take action against the enemy, or guiding them through the maze of battle. A popular story tells of a cloud opportunely covering the full moon, allowing soldiers to launch an operation safely. Some military personnel assert the Messiah has personally fired heavy canons on the Iraqi soldiers and has demolished their positions. We do not even stop to consider why the Savior of Islam would fire on Iraqi Moslems, who also claim the same Savior.

With each martyr, more people dress in black until black is the dominant color of clothing. In a green village where throughout history multi-colored gowns compliment nature, women and girls are no longer allowed to wear colorful dresses in public; dark shades dominate. The Hezbollah, or the Party of God, is everywhere demonstrating glimpses of the fires of Hell. Severe punishments await those who break the law.

* * *

Ideological interviews are a prerequisite to landing any kind of job. People applying for work have to be able to answer obscure questions about Islam and moralities. For example, whether you are a doctor applying for a position in a hospital, or an architect at a job interview, you might need to know things like the size and color of a mullah's turban, which foot to set down first in a toilet stall[1], the standard size of a shroud, how to enter a mosque and why, or the order of the ritual of ablution.

The religious leaders have created such a wide variety of scenarios that no sound person can anticipate what he needs to know. For example, what would you do if you were standing in a bus and a woman sitting in front of you gets off, leaving her seat empty? You would lose the job if you said, 'I would sit'. Why? Because the seat is still warm from her body. If you take her seat immediately and feel her body's warmth, it may plant a seed of temptation. Therefore, you must wait for about five minutes before sitting.

Another example is what should a woman do if she is home alone, and there is a knock on the door? You are not moral enough if you say she might ask, 'who is there?' She should follow the example of the Prophet Mohammad's daughter, who first put her index finger in her mouth to make her voice ugly. Why? If the person who is knocking is a man, he may be tempted to sin if he hears a lovely voice.

Further instances of morality lessons: In which position should you sleep? Tell them 'it is none of your business how I sleep' if you dare! Wrong! You should know that your warm bed may make you sin if you sleep on your stomach. I remember when I was doing my obligatory military service an officer would come through our barracks at night and wake up anybody who was sleeping on his stomach, commanding him to sleep either on his back or on one side or the other.

What is the difference between a white and a black turban? Please keep looking for another job! Why? Because you don't know that only the direct descendants of the prophet Mohammad and his family members who are called Sayyed are allowed to wear black; other mullahs must wear white. Did you ask how does anyone know who is a descendent of the prophet? You would not pose such a question if you knew the consequences of shedding doubts on your leader's words!

* * *

Our religious leaders use various media on every possible occasion to preach about Heaven and Hell, describing Paradise as a lovely garden where pomegranate, quince, grapes and other heavenly fruit grow beside a poetic river flowing with wine, milk or honey. The righteous can lie down on grass under leafy trees close to hills carpeted in green, while radiant and virgin angels glide nearby, attending to their wants with glowing smiles. The deserving can have anything they wish for, most of which are banned in this world, like wine, singing, dancing and beautiful girls[2]. To enter this garden, we have to obey our Supreme Leader whom we are taught to believe has the key to the main gate.

Hell, on the other hand, is portrayed as a land of fire and melting lead. The dry hills are burnt due to the eternal flames and there is smoke everywhere. God throws the disobedient into the boiling liquid to be incinerated. Then He causes the sinful to rise, renews their bodies and burns them again, repeating this over and over for eternity. Such a land is the place of unbelievers or those who stand against the self-proclaimed representative of God on earth: Khomeini.

Listening to these depictions of the afterlife, there are times when we can almost feel ourselves sitting under shady trees tasting 'heavenly wine'; more often the hot flames of Hell practically scorch us, as these sermons are predominately rebukes.

Such teachings are everywhere and the entire nation is dogmatically religionized. The 'Spirit of God' speaks, his soldiers take action to ensure obedience and his supporters flood the streets to demonstrate their approval of the new regime, while in counteraction, the opposition forces gather their own followers to express their disagreement with the current situation. Each targets the other in a show of force; the ultimate goal for both sides is to ruin the opposite number's meetings in the village.

* * *

During a parliamentary election, one of the candidates for office, a man from a neighboring town, comes to our village to deliver his campaign speech. We believe the reason he is 'eligible' to run is his governmental backing. This makes the opposition groups livid since all their own candidates have been deemed 'ineligible' and banned from running. They band together and circle the man, trying to confuse him with many questions, which, if he answers yes, he creates enemies on one hand, and if he answers no, he creates enemies on the other. Since he cannot provide clear answers without taking sides, the younger generation pushes forward and, through aggressive speech and actions, asks him to leave the village. Suddenly in the escalating tension, a friend of ours, who is only sixteen years old, breaks through the crowd and, jumping on shoulders, makes his way to the politician and slaps him hard across the face. The candidate is quickly taken away for his own protection. We give a cheer in favor of our friend's action, and mark the day as a day of victory.

When this candidate later serves three successive terms in parliament, to then automatically become a parliamentarian emeritus, our village degenerates, marked as the 'black sheep' of the country. Our land sells for pennies compared to the land of villages around us. Our young people are denied admission to universities, and their job opportunities are limited.

* * *

This man walked into parliament, and our village started turning into a ghost town and became more deserted year by year. Hundreds of families, moving down from the mountainous areas, have now replaced the original population of my home village.

Recently I watched some video clips and felt brokenhearted to see the decrepit, overgrown market; I could hardly believe this was the same market where once restless youths gathered to pass their days and nights together. Back then, we chanted, we wrote on walls, we marched, we argued, we shouted, we laughed, we cried and ... we sadly disappeared from the face of our traditional market in just the way my father had predicted a few years earlier.

––––––––––––––––––––––––––––––––

[1]According to the morality lessons taught either through the media or in religion classes, in case you die at the door of a mosque, you would fall inside if you entered on your right foot; to die in a sacred place like a mosque is regarded as a blessing. It was also said you will fall out of the toilet if you enter on your left foot; to die in an unclean place like a toilet is regarded as a curse.

[2]I am wondering what will happen to 'deserving women' in this paradise; will the same number of radiant and virgin angels, the male ones of course, be around to tend them?!

In the end, we will remember not the words of our enemies, but the silence of our friends.
........................Martin Luther King

Four

Things happen too fast

In response to the increasing activities of political oppositions that have dominated the atmosphere in the village, more and more government checkpoints spring up on roads between towns and villages. If we happen to be seen out in the middle of the night, we are stopped and questioned.

The situation in bigger towns is even worse. It is impossible to go from one town to another without passing several checkpoints; cars are targeted randomly for interrogation. The older youths who go to school in a nearby town have to explain the reasons for their trip and indulge their destination: Where are you going? Where is your school? Why do you have school today? What exam do you have? What grade are you in? Sometimes the government forces examine your books to see if you are telling the truth. Many political activists prefer not to travel to neighboring regions anymore.

To hold public demonstrations becomes harder than ever, since the Islamic regime censors them severely, even by force when necessary. We have to be very careful whenever we see military Toyotas patrolling the village in the middle of the night. The most prudent thing we can do is hide somewhere safe until they are gone.

It is spring 1981. The rice lands are covered with young green rice plants. The tea farms are all freshly green. The air is filled with the aroma of flowers, the fresh smell of green tea, and the sweet piquancy of young buds on orange trees. On moonlit nights, a glow spreads peacefully and comfortingly over the village; however, the local people are too busy to enjoy such beauty. Most adults go to bed early at night so that they can start their work on lands at dawn the next morning, but we younger ones, preserving an age-old custom, almost never miss our nightly chats under the trees, in spite of working long, hard hours in the fields all day. Sometimes, when we are too tired to get together, each of us sits alone in his own yard until he feels sleepy enough for bed.

On the twenty-seventh night of the third month of this spring, called Khordad on the Persian calendar, I am sitting under our old walnut tree on the road, which connects the Caspian to the Alborz. The village is silent, very unusual for that time of evening when normally the animated voices of villagers having supper on their verandas, surround us. I suddenly hear whispers coming from several meters away near the fork in the main road. From my position under the tree, I listen to the whispers but cannot make out the words, nor can I see anything through the row of tall bushes and short fruit trees bordering our garden and separating our property from the road. I figure some of my friends are coming for a nightly chat. The whispers continue off and on for some time, but no one materializes out of the darkness.

All my brothers are out and about except Davood, who, in his final year of high school, is studying for his exams. Soon, he too leaves home for the village where his friends usually can be found. I see him walk away on the narrow shortcut that links our house, like a triangle, to the middle of the dirt road running through the upper village. The tiny pathway passes through our neighbors' yards until it reaches the unpaved road on the east leg of the triangle. Since this way is shorter, we nearly always skip the fork when heading east.

Minutes later, I am following him. By the time I arrive at the end of the narrow path and enter the road, I can see Davood and his friends standing in the dark, talking guardedly to each other in voices I can barely hear. This impresses me, as they are generally loud and boisterous in their conversation. When I join them, some are commenting on the unusual number of checkpoints they have seen throughout the village that night, as well as in all the surrounding towns and are fearful the paramilitary forces are planning a big operation in the area.

"There are a whole bunch of Basij forces just on the main road's fork near your house," one of them says to Davood.

Davood is curious enough that he decides to go and take a look. He always did have a mind of his own, and in spite of our cautioning him not to, he lays his index finger on his lips and asks us to remain where we are. He walks towards a bend in the road; from there the fork meeting the main road below can be seen in the distance. At that point, he is only about twenty meters away from a lamppost shining light on the men standing under it. He sits in the dark and watches them for a bit, while we remain in our places some fifty meters behind him.

Everything is motionlessly quiet when suddenly we hear a loud voice ordering a command to fire. A volley of shots spewing from shotguns shatters the silence of the night. Some bullets pound on the metal rooftops of village houses and create the continuous puttering sound of hailstones in spring. Once the sound of the shooting dies out, the lights of the vehicles go on and the armed forces leave the fork and head for the dirt road, where we are ensconced. It is as if the soldiers have planned an ambush.

All of a sudden, in the light of those oncoming vehicles, we see Davood running back. The moving lights project on the trees and bushes in front of them, and we see huge exaggerated shadows preceding the headlights, coming uphill in our direction. We watch Davood running all out, with the forces rounding the bend of the road, closing in on him. A few soldiers shoot their primitive guns into the air over his head, causing scores of tiny quince branches and blossoms from the trees belonging to our TV host to fall, victims of the shooting.

My friends and I are spooked and decide to run; there is no time to wait for Davood; everything is happening too fast. A few huge people brandishing sticks, lethal-looking machetes or shotguns follow after my brother, with a line of military Jeeps and private cars just meters behind them. We all scatter, running into the neighboring yards and gardens. I jump back into the yard of our neighbor and hide behind their wooden fences, hoping it is a safe place. Some of our friends climb over the fences of a garden across the road and try to hide among the trees on the riverbank. Several others reverse direction and run back towards the main part of the village.

At his highest speed, Davood passes me, a Jeep almost touching him from behind. He has already way outrun the ones of us who are headed in the same direction. I can see he will no longer be able to lose those forces by continuing along the same road. He will have to jump over fences or the walls alongside the road and hope to escape by running in a direction the Jeeps can't follow. It seems he knows this himself as reaching a wall, he tries to swing himself over it but once again luck deserts him because the highest row of the block wall is loose and part of it falls on his head and legs, knocking him to the ground. He has quickly scrambled to his feet again when the Jeep rams him from behind and throws him alongside the wall. Davood remains down and the driver bides his time. On the face of it, it seems to me that the people in the car want to know what has happened to my brother. While the men are keeping watch on him from inside their car, Davood struggles up again, attempting to run, with the lights of the Jeep shining in his face. His pale features mirror panic and helplessness. Before he can make a move to escape, some of the group begin to kick, punch and hit him with clubs and chains. Limping back to the wall, he tries to defend himself against them. As soon as these strong forces quit beating on him and step aside to make way for their vehicle, Davood makes an attempt to flee but the Jeep then moves up to push at him forcefully and ruthlessly until he is flat against the wall, where his inert body is dragged for a distance. Finally, the Jeep is prevented from forward motion by a log and Davood falls lifelessly to the ground.

At this time, other voices some ways away begin to shout; the forces have spotted a young teenager in the middle of a tea field on his way to the riverbank. In thunderous tones, they order him to stop. There is no way for him to escape; he can easily be shot at such close range before reaching the far end of the garden. He stops midway and laces his hands over his head, headlights focusing on him.

Our friend had joined us just seconds before the tension exploded, so we had not found time to explain to him what is going on. The paramilitary forces grab him and begin to beat him savagely. The unfortunate boy, who is not sure what is happening, cries out for help. His shouts attract the attention of the rest of the mercenaries searching the area, who gather like ants around a piece of bread.

Although our friend is in a very precarious predicament, we do not dare leave our hiding places to help him. Everybody else has already disappeared. Those, who like me had not dared take the risk of running, have found a place to hide somewhere in the area, watching, in helpless grief, the miserable state of a 16-year-old boy crying out for help while being viciously kicked and pummeled by paramilitary thugs.

At the expense of my poor friend, Davood has a little time to renew his energy. With what must be all the strength he can muster, he puts one hand on the ground and the other against the wall and forces himself up again. By the lights of the Jeep, I can see blood covering his whole face and body. His legs are wobbly and he has trouble controlling his balance. He is panting very hard as he stands up between the wall on one side and the vehicle on the other. Before the forces have a chance to take their eyes off the captured boy, Davood manages to run as best he can towards the center of the village. In seconds, he has disappeared into the darkness[1].

---

[1]Davood recently told me he almost died that night when the car hit him for the second time. He said, "After I fell down for the second time, I felt myself passing from this life. The feeling was so real it was like something I was living. I saw myself in my childhood and remembered all the episodes of my past. I felt I was flying through the sky on a spring day with flowers and trees in leaf below me. I flew higher and higher until finally I reached a point in the sky where I could see the sun, and there was a picture revealed to me within it. The picture turned into a bright face and seemed very alive. The face talked to me and asked me to go back to the earth, telling me that my time had not yet arrived. I opened my eyes and was painfully reminded of my condition. I got up and pulled myself together because I knew I had to remain alive."

~ * ~

The dawn of a long day

Early the next morning, friends tell us that neighboring villages and towns had also been the target of ambushes the night before. All the followers and supporters of different political parties now gather in the main market in a show of disapproval at the illegality of these attacks.

Like many others, I join the demonstration. The Basij forces have evacuated their base by early morning and those villagers backing Khomeini also prefer to stay indoors. The crowd grows larger and larger as more people arrive. Before noon, the whole market area is full of local people chanting loudly. The organizers of the gathering have prepared speeches and pamphlets, which are delivered to the public through a small hand speaker, demanding the unconditional release of our friend who was arrested the night before, demanding as well the right to express ideas freely, and criticizing the local Basij for using Special Forces to invade the village. The demonstrators emphasize that based on existing laws freedom of speech is the basic right of civilians.

As we sit in the middle of the road inside the market, listening to the speeches of several local leaders who are taking turns shouting their messages into the old speaker, loud noises reach us from behind. We turn our heads back around to see what is going on. Slowly, a few at a time, people sitting at the back of the crowd stand up and run to where a splinter group of demonstrators has gathered near the Basij base. At the sounds of the loud voices, I also leave the speech area and join the new group in front of our ex-library being used by the Basij as their base. When I get closer, I see that several young people are booing the Basij, shattering windows, breaking down the door and daring each other to storm the building. Others, who are already inside, come out carrying articles of Basij property - military boots, uniforms, packages of new notebooks, pens and pencils - anything portable. Just then, one of the boys who is still searching inside, calls out that he has a surprise for us. Appearing at the doorway, he holds up women's intimate clothing - bras and panties - items very peculiar to be found in the headquarters of the supposedly religious paramilitary forces. The crowd bursts out into loud and raucous laughter.

Stores are closed, not a vehicle moving. New revolutionary chants from the crowds flooding the market fill the air, pictures of

Khomeini are torn from walls to be replaced by new chants sprayed all over the place. News hits us that a teenager has found a military gun inside the library/Basij base and has taken it away with him. One lone pro-Khomeini person is spotted in the crowd and becomes the target of accusations of being one of those responsible for the attacks of the night before.

The market has been taken so easily it makes our heads spin. The organizers of the demonstration are no longer able to control the younger people. Fear of the consequences begins to sweep through the whole market like fog settling in for the night, bringing confusion. Awakening as if from a dream, the leaders know that the destruction and havoc around them is far from their original objective of simply condemning the Basij, but regardless of their collective conscience, the younger ones, heady with the feel of victory, are dancing, singing, shouting and living in the moment.

Finally around noon, I leave behind a crowd milling everywhere throughout the market. Once home, I find my father sitting up on the stairs talking aloud to himself, my mother, silent, on the veranda below. It doesn't take long to see how desperately frightened and helpless he is. His face is pale, and in a kind of monologue, he is calling on God for help, saying, "I raised these children from birth through childhood, I gave my life for them and this is how they repay my sacrifice. Look at so and so, a rich person, his children are sitting at home keeping their noses clean, even though they also know what is going on around here. When you go hunting for bear or boar, some of the dogs run ahead and are the ones who get hurt; why do my children have to make themselves the lead dogs? Why are they the ones to get hurt?" Calling to my mother, he continues, "Hanna, I am telling you, your son is dead. I don't believe he can survive the injury he suffered last night. I have worked all my life for nothing; it has all come to naught. No king has ever come to give my father something for free, and no one will ever come to give my children something for free; they are laying down their lives for nothing. The world is too complicated to be changed by their actions, but my children listen to their friends; they don't listen to me. In destroying their lives, they have destroyed mine as well."

My mother is shroud white with shock and does not say anything back. I pass them with a clipped greeting and enter the living room. Just inside, I stop short, facing something shocking. On a pallet[1] under the window opposite the door, lays a body

106

covered in white bandages from head to toe. Only his mouth and eyes peek out from the gauze. I step in and walk to the body. It is Davood. His lips are swollen and bruised, and only with effort does his voice come out in a hoarse, garbled whisper I cannot understand. I sit beside him quietly for some time, holding his bandaged hand, a lump in my throat and my heart beating wildly.

After a bit, my mother calls from the veranda for me to fetch a rooster so she can prepare a meal for him. I leave and grab and kill a young rooster without second thought. While she is beginning to cook the chicken, I walk over to where my father and his friends are standing together in the shade of the trees.

Not much time has passed before we see several big trucks heading toward us from the south. Each of the trucks contains brawny powerfully built thugs, chanting, "God is greater, Khomeini is the leader".

They are the Special Forces from the night before, not military people, but villagers from the mountainous regions who work for the government during emergencies. When needed, the local Basij hire them to keep the area under control or spread fear among the villagers. These mercenaries who have little, or no education, show no mercy on dissident families and are pleased to kill for money and because they believe us to be infidels.

Wrath on their beard-covered faces, they approach us rhythmically brandishing big knives, thick strong clubs or machetes over their heads or waving chains or hunting guns in the air, their shouted chants of 'death to anti Khomeinis' making the earth tremble. We watch silently as the trucks pass by our house in convoy. With religious sayings scrawled across the front of their fabric headbands, the mercenaries stare at us belligerently and impudently, raising their voices even louder as if they want us to know they know we belong to the dissidents. We stand stock still and quiet until the last truck of the long caravan has disappeared down the road.

My father, wavering badly, begins to call on God again. "O God, please help! They are headed toward the market." Then looking at me, he asks frenziedly, mad with worry, "Where are your brothers?"

"I don't know. I didn't see them in the market this morning."

Seconds later one of our neighbors returns from the market with the report on the events of the demonstration and the ensuing damage to the Basij base. He describes the forced entry into the library and relates the story of the stolen gun. All strength has left my father's legs, and he crumbles, sitting heavily on the ground. "O God please! O God please! O God please!" escapes from his murmuring lips.

The neighbor has hardly finished his story when we hear gunshots from the market. I run to the road and head out quickly. My father shouts and calls me back. I tell him that I will not get close to the scene; I just want to get news. He offers no further protest and I sprint towards the market, passing our school and few other houses on the way. Then, there is nothing on either side of the road except the newly planted rice fields and a few closed stores. The more gunshots I hear from the marketplace, the more people leave for the rice lands and other neighboring areas. Each person is trying to find shelter for himself. From that distance, the whole market along both the east and west sides of the road looks like a huge battlefield under heavy smoke. Not daring to get any closer, I squat down at a safe distance, and become absorbed in the events going on. Huge numbers of people, men and women, are running everywhere as if wild animals have attacked them. Nobody is trying to resist the mercenaries; too strong to be challenged, they are slashing at people with large knives, clubbing them with huge sticks, flogging them with heavy chains and shooting the fugitives with their primitive hunting guns, accounting for all the smoke in the air. The majority of the villagers has managed to escape; those who are still trapped inside the market are desperately seeking a place of refuge.

Suddenly, here comes one of my friends running out of the market and rushing toward where I am sitting at the side of the road. Before he gets to where I am hiding, he veers into the rice lands at the very southern edge of the market, with several of the mercenaries close behind. Trying to lose them, he leaves the main road and heads west in an effort to get home by cutting across the vast rice lands which border the river. He has scarcely gone halfway when chasers shout from the road. "Freeze! Freeze! Don't move! Don't move or I'll shoot."

My poor friend, whose name, like mine, is Hassan and is only a couple years older, is too frightened to hear the warnings. He is not part of any political group in the village. Like many others, he was attracted to the market today by the shouting and loud voices coming from the small hand speaker set up by the demonstrators, curious to know what was happening. The armed forces yell at him to stop but Hassan keeps pulling his legs out of the mud, first one sucking step, then another, and continues inching forward, hampered by the conditions in the rice field, without even bothering to turn back to look at the gigantic bullies at the edge of the road.

Hassan is still running when one of the forces aims a gun at him and fires. This innocent boy falls onto the young rice plants growing out of the water, blood pouring from his wound. He gets up hastily but has hardly taken a few steps when, energy failing him, he falls again and the forces rush at him from behind. These mercenaries, experienced boar hunters who rarely miss their target, reach the boy by now struggling against death in water and mud. Grabbing his legs, they drag him away like slaughtered prey.

By this time, more and more people have left the market and run in my direction. Like my friend, most of them have the idea of crossing the rice lands to reach a safer place. As I see them coming, I also turn and run back southward, with the troops some two hundred meters or more behind me. I draw farther away until when I am near the school, I look back and see that I have outdistanced them. Villagers are scattered throughout the rice lands on both sides of the road, struggling to reach the trees beyond.

The more people leave the market for a safer place, the more dangerous the safer places become. The forces have already reclaimed the market and are now trying to catch as many of the demonstrators as possible, chasing people all over the area, their guns blazing all the while.

I see they have spotted a fat young man in the middle of the fields closest to the road. Although he is from a neighboring town, I know him pretty well since he is my oldest brother's friend and I have heard him deliver speeches in public from time to time. A very knowledgeable person, humble, and with a great sense of humor, he is well known by everyone and adored by many village youths, however, compared with his lightning fast brain, his fat legs are very slow. The forces soon catch up with him and begin hacking at him with large knives. He struggles for a short time, but his body soon falls and crushes the young rice plants. I watch as his blood begins mixing with the water to turn it red. Then the Hezbollah forces lift him and drag him away, his body plastered with blood and mud.

* * *

Unlike my friend Hassan who was released later, Zia, the chubby young man of twenty, spends a couple of years behind bars before the Army of God decides that he deserves death. As has been the case with so many thousands of other innocent Iranians, the government of the revolution executes him without the world knowing about it, and his name still leaves a burden on my heart.

* * *

For about three decades, the people of my country have continued to be suppressed, tortured and killed by the present government and no foreign nation has paid adequate attention to this issue. On the contrary, the commercial world has been trying to further relations with the Iranian government to quench their oil thirst, ignoring the plea for help from its citizens until recently, when the Iranian nuclear energy crisis has caused concern. I wonder if the basic human rights and lives of my people have any importance in the world's new order.

----

¹It is the Iranian custom to use bedrolls on the floor for sleeping. They are rolled up and stored during the day, so that the bedroom at night becomes the living room of daytime hours.

~ * ~

Silenced by force; soldiers of the revolution in the yard

A couple of hours pass. The shootings have stopped and the village is hushed, as if holding its breath. Papers and debris are strewn throughout the streets among the branches of trees shot down during the skirmish. Strips of cloth used for loading guns add to the litter. Nearly all the villagers have abandoned the area, some to hide in safe places around their houses, and others scattered in the woods or in the gardens of neighboring homes. A lot of the young plants in the rice fields are flat, smashed by the fleeing crowds. The mercenaries swarm everywhere like angry hornets whose hive has been disrupted.

My father, who has asked us say, if asked, that my brother was involved in an automobile accident, has just left for a neighboring town with the hope of filling the prescriptions he has from the hospital. We hope by this ruse to keep Davood from being taken away in his present condition. I am home with my mother, Davood, in his white bandages, who is not in any condition to tell me what I should do and there is no sign of my other three brothers. Aimless and not knowing if I should hide like everyone else, I leave the living room and walk out of our yard towards the road. Through a couple of villagers who rush by fearfully and silently, I hear that the forces have started systematic home searches and we can expect them to arrive at our house soon. I wander around the yard for a while, the events in the market and the blood I saw inside the rice lands playing over and over in my mind like a mad movie. There is nobody out and about, even the kids my age have evaporated. I amble towards the barn where the sticks, which I have collected over the years and whittled into different shapes to pass the time while in the pasture, are stored. I grab one of them and leave for the riverbank across the road and down a ways from our house. Deciding to hide like the others, I find a safe place by the river and lay down in the tall grass beside a felled tree.

An hour or so passes uneventfully. Nothing can be heard from that far away. I am tired and bored and the fear that the forces may break into our house to take Davood away in my father's absence gives me the urge to go back home. Guardedly, passing through first the rice field beside the river then the small garden, I am crossing the road when I see a gigantic person right behind our house standing exactly in the middle of the road some twenty meters away from me, a long hunting gun resting in his arms. As his gaze moves around, our eyes lock. We stare at each other, both of us startled to see the other and neither of us wanting to be the first to look away. Then just behind him, I see several others returning to the main road from where they were searching.

From what I learned just hours ago, I know that I should not run in spite of a feeling that pushes at me from inside telling me to. I walk across the road very gingerly, keeping myself busy with the stick in my hand, using it like a walking stick such as farmers normally carry with them on the way to and from farms. The man watches without speaking as, containing the dread which is consuming me, I walk into our yard past the pear tree to where he can no longer see me.

As I rush onto our veranda, I rationalize that I am very young for the forces to be looking for me. I step into the living room and go directly to the window to look out at the road behind the house; there the forces are, still in the middle of the road. My mother sits speechless beside Davood; I warn her that the forces are behind the house and to expect them within minutes, then add my silence to hers. Painful dread and uncertainty squeeze their way into a room already filled with fear.

A few minutes have hardly passed when, hearing voices from our front yard, I leave for the veranda. There are several armed people scattered around the yard, others inside the garden and barn and climbing the ladder to check the rooftop. More soldiers walk onto the veranda and enter the house to search each room. A few climb the stairs and rummage around the second floor. Finding no one either in the house or outside, they gather again on the veranda, push back the curtain covering the door to the living room and spy Davood on the bed wrapped in his bandages.

"Who is he?" one of them asks my mother from the doorway.

"He is my son," she replies from where she is sitting beside Davood. "He was involved in an accident and we just brought him home from the hospital."

They look at Davood more closely. The size of the wounds around his lips is enough to tell them the accident story is real. Convinced, they walk back to the veranda.

Just as they are about to leave, a few local Basij members arrive. Unlike the mercenaries, most of the Basij forces are from our village and know everybody. They disappeared that day to make themselves scarce during our morning's fulminating demonstration. However, after the massive mountain people have reclaimed the village, they come out of hiding and, murderously furious and seriously wanting revenge, begin to help these Special Forces.

The leader[1] of the Basij base and his friend[2] jump up onto our veranda and begin to talk with the mercenaries.

"Did you find anybody?"

"No, the only person in this room was injured in an accident."

The leader and his friend walk into our living room with their military boots on, knowing full well that it is part of our culture not to enter the house wearing shoes. Eyes lighting on Davood on his bed, the friend who is also our neighbor, calls to his companions, "One of the hypocrites[3] is here."

As the vigilantes step in, this Basij member aggressively and spitefully spits out, "You, the peasant population, do not deserve freedom. There must be force to control you at all times. We just gave you some time today to see how you act and you proved by your activities that you deserve punishment. This crackdown is just an example of the way the Basij can take control of an area whenever it wishes."

"He had an accident," the Special Forces repeat.

"This accident is different," our neighbor replies, asking them to bring the car around for Davood.

My mother, who can't show her love in words and rarely expresses anger or talks back to my father, or asks to be favored due to her health problems, begins to beg the young man to give us some time so that we can treat Davood's wounds first.

"You are like my child," she tells him, "and I could be your mother. My son cannot move; there is no way for him to escape. Please give him a few days. I promise we will take him to you as soon as he is feeling better. His father, who has gone for medicines, will soon be back. How will I explain my son's absence to him? Please, I beg of you. Please!"

"Don't worry," our neighbor boy says. "We have great doctors. They can cure him faster than you." He leaves the room and orders the others to take Davood to the vehicle. With him leaning heavily on them, they walk Davood out slowly to where a small pick-up truck, belonging to one of our neighbors, is waiting in the yard.

Seeing my brother being taken away, I lose control and begin to murmur to the thugs angrily. "When did Islam say to treat people like this? He is injured and can't walk. If you were a true Hezbollah you would be able to forgive people...."

"If you don't shut your trap," says one of them to me, "then I will have to get my whip from the car."

I shut up and they put Davood on the back of the vehicle. The truck leaves the yard, and so do the others.

We are picking up Davood's bed when my father returns[1] from the drugstore. Like our friend who was detained earlier that night, Davood does not come back home for some four years.

----

[1] The leader of our local Basij, who was from another town, married one of his fellow compatriots from our village. One night, the couple fell asleep in their new home in a neighboring village and never woke up again. Police announced 'unintentional death by gas' as the cause of the incident.

[2] This young man was the older brother of my schoolmate who encouraged us to break the strike during the early stages of the revolution, by taking us out on a march to call for teachers to return to their classes. He married one of his fellow Hezbollah, or Basij force members, soon after the domestic tensions swept the village. His wife, while cleaning a weapon, 'accidentally' shot and killed him. Since she was one of Khomeini's loyal soldiers who had permission to carry military weapons, she was absolved of guilt in his death. His permanent absence made many villagers, who believed he, like the Basij leader, had been involved in several executions during the eighties, happy. When he died, I heard one of his relatives say, "he is not a bad guy, but he certainly deserves death."

[3] Hypocrites referred exclusively to the Mojahedin in the early 1980s because of the similarity of these two words in Farsi: Mojaheddin and monafeghin. Gradually the government generalized this term to cover all dissidents and enemies. It served in a similar way as the word 'terrorist' does in the world today.

People were very easily labeled hypocrite if they opposed the government in any way.

'Years later, Davood told me when the local forces took him away in the truck, suddenly he saw his father, a bag of medicines in his hand, making his way toward the taxi stand. He was heading south towards home while his child was being taken away in the opposite direction.

~ * ~

Atku does have bears!

The long day finally turns into evening. By now, there is absolutely no sign of life in the sorrow-stricken village. Even the mercenaries have left the area, and the villagers are staying out of sight. Except for an occasional elderly passerby on the road, there is nobody around to be seen.

Feeling the need to meet some of my friends, compare notes on what has happened, and maybe find my brothers, I wander out to the road and walk to where the narrow dirt path branches off. Heading on, I pass by the block wall where Davood was hit the night before; his blood and scratches made by the vehicle are still visible on it. I get to the eastern edge of the upper village, without seeing anyone, as if the village has long ago been evacuated. In frustration, I head back home.

About halfway back, I hear a girl's voice calling me from behind the tall bushes and trees bordering the fence surrounding her house. I recognize the voice as belonging to the sister of one of my friends. She calls me to come through the gate and close it. When I get to where she is waiting, I can see how nervous, tremulous and sad she is.

Their house, very old and very large, sits at the edge of fields and is fairly isolated, and since her parents have passed on, she and her brother are its only occupants. Now her brother is gone, and I can feel she dreads spending the night alone in all that emptiness. She asks me for news of her brother or any of the other fugitives, as well as for news of the marketplace. Fearful of being arrested if she leaves home, she asks if I will go cautiously, without being seen, and find her brother who she thinks might be near the tea farms adjacent to the riverbanks.

Taking the narrow path south into the groves of trees, I depart on this mission and come across a group of about fifteen men, all but a couple of whom are very young, sitting in seclusion, chatting in low voices, apprehensive and waiting for nightfall. Both her brother and my brother Darius are among them; I walk directly to where my brother is sitting. He gives me a big hug and a kiss, then immediately drills me to make sure I have not been followed. Soon, everybody is taking turns asking questions about the presence of the Basij and the whereabouts of some of their friends, or how their families are doing. I tell them everything I know. After talking amongst themselves for a while, they ask me to go back to the village to collect warmer clothes and bread for them.

I go around to each of their houses, one after another, to report to their families and collect what they have requested. Some families want to know if a husband or children will be home by nightfall. Not knowing the answer to their questions, I keep telling them the same thing, 'don't worry; everybody is fine'.

After making the collection, I put everything into a few black plastic bags and head back south. No sooner do I reach the riverbank when a loud whistle catches my attention. I stop and look around, but see nobody. I start walking again but soon another whistle brings me up short. When I turn back, I see Mansoor, one of my friends, running to me from his garden; I wait for him. He has been as lonely as I have and seems very happy to meet up with me. His older brother is missing, so he decides to go along, hoping these fugitives may have news of him.

I hand Mansoor a couple of the bags, and we run one behind the other along the same narrow path beside the river. By the time we reach the group, everybody is getting ready to leave, thinking since I have taken so long to collect their supplies that I was unable to get what they asked for. They are afraid to hang around any longer where raiding militia forces may be searching. My friend and I quickly distribute the bags.

The fugitives dress in the warmer clothes, meanwhile passing bags of bread around. These fellows, who are often either related

116

to each other or have been friends all their lives, represent a variety of political organizations. Now, they are united in one common goal - to escape the enemy forces of the new Revolutionary Guards.

Their concerted cooperation makes quite an impression on me; I watch in silence, remembering. Some of them have previously had arguments over land and other property, especially if their rice fields or tea lands are adjacent. Squabbles in daily interactions are inevitable, and come to a peak particularly during spring and summer when the water table is low and crops need irrigation. However, at this moment, there is no sign of the petty grievances of the past, and in fact, talk among them is friendly and open, sharing with each other extends even to shoes and clothing.

A hand on my shoulder brings me out of my reverie; my brother Darius wants to give me a final hug. I look up to see that all the refugees are dressed and ready for what seems will be a long trip. My brother admonishes me to be of extra help to mom and dad in his absence, and to study hard and behave myself. He goes so far as to ask me to tolerate dad's anger with more patience and offer help with washing dishes and laundry. Mournful to see him leave, I agree to his wishes.

A few seconds later, Mansoor and I, two little boys, are watching as the group lines up for an arduous journey into the Alborz range and begins to disappear from our sight, on an extension of the same constricted path we just arrived on.

* * *

That night at home, I feel very alone and empty. The house is blindly quiet in the absence of my four brothers. I perch on the top step of the stairs at the point where they reach to second floor; my old uncle has parked himself on the same staircase down near the first floor, my father crouches in the yard under a tree, while my mother sits alone in the living room. Nobody has anything to say; there does not seem to be words to express our misery.

In spring and summer, the whole family used to sleep on the second floor veranda. We would spread our beds on the wooden floor under the metal rooftop of the house. During mosquito season, we also set up netting to protect ourselves from the thousands of mosquitoes buzzing around our heads. Once our beds were ready, my brothers and I would talk; we had long chats under the mosquito netting before falling asleep. Sometimes, we talked so long that our father would shout at us to go to sleep so we would be fit to get up early the next day and be ready for work in the fields.

Usually, we lay down with our heads stuck outside the net and watched the calm, lovely night, its silence broken only by the sound of crickets and the occasional bark of a dog or a bovine mooaaaa. The moon against the clear, dark sky appeared huge and incandescent, and those millions of stars, invisible by day, looked like brightly lit chandeliers hanging over forests of trees heavy with leaves, huddled in the darkness below them.

When it rained, we listened to rhythms drumming noisily onto the rooftop, and watched water cascade onto trees, our neighbors' roofs and onto the ground. We have a local saying about the fierceness of our rainfall: 'the rain is so dense you can catch the tail of it to climb into the sky'.

It pains me to admit this, but one of our regular entertainments was the great time we used to have playing pranks on my old uncle. He preferred not to use the bathroom to relieve himself during the night. Instead, he loved watering our trees and flowers at the far eastern side of the house. There was a quiet place there, on the very border of our neighbor's orchard, which he used as his field toilet.

Sometimes when my uncle assumed we were sleeping, he left his room and headed for those trees. He stood up in the dark and urinated, hitting the pieces of tin my father had used in building our fence, and making a loud noise. He usually passed gas when he passed water. After he was done, he cleared his throat loudly. When this happened, with my brother Mirza as the ring leader, to amuse ourselves we picked fruit from the branches of our neighbor's trees which hung over the second story veranda and threw them at the old man below us on the ground, hitting the fruit against metal objects in the dark and creating an earsplitting racket. Once we had managed to startle the old man, we would hide inside the mosquito net trying to control our sniggers. Although we tried to hit only objects near him, we sometimes missed our targets and hit poor uncle by accident. The hard fruit stung him and made him shout at us in the middle of the night. As always, he cursed our teachers for not teaching us good manners, while we were upstairs making fun of him.

118

Now everything has suddenly changed. Even my old uncle does not feel up to going outside to pee at night, and my father no longer wants to sleep under the mosquito net. The beds are ready and the mosquito net is set up behind where I am sitting as always, but the usual chatting, laughing and whispering of my brothers have been silenced. The house, part of which was built centuries ago, is more like a deserted historical monument than my home.

Finally, I begin to feel tired and without making any noise, crawl back to creep inside the net and into my bed. I lay there looking at the mosquito netting from the inside, miserably conscious that no forms are sleeping on my brothers' beds; no heads make dents in their pillows. In this silence, I conjure up each of them, one by one. I stick my head out of the net so I can look around at the surrounding area and watch my father until he leaves for the living room to sleep.

It is almost midnight when I fall asleep to the sound of my dog barking on and off. When he is still barking this way the next morning, we figure that strangers spent the night around our house. Since my brothers are in hiding, we believe our house was watched in the hope of catching them.

~ * ~

Political haste, Khomeini in control

Two more days and we still have no news of my brothers. Then, the thirtieth day of Khordad arrives, a day which changes the path of life for most Iranians when the leaders of the Mojahedin organization order a national protest against the Khomeini regime. A huge domestic war sweeps the entire country, deeply involving even those political organizations who have no orders of participation. The Islamic Revolutionary Guards, the local Basij forces and all those strong mercenaries show their faces afresh in our village to repeat extensive home searches. Now there are two main groups in the area: the chasers and the escapees consisting of all the members and supporters of different organizations and parties.

By nightfall of that day, the local Basij are peacefully resting at their base playing, through the loud speakers of the village mosque, a wide variety of revolutionary songs, archived speeches of the Supreme Leader and other clerics, and sermons. Interspersed between these broadcasts, they urge followers of all political groups to surrender voluntarily in to order to get leniency.

A military Toyota patrols through the village, a field speaker on its top airing religious chants. Every now and then, the Basij use the speaker to coax people to help them find the fugitives and even try to cajole the fugitive families to surrender their own children. Promising to be forgiving and to treat everyone justly, they ask the fugitives to turn themselves in at the mosque and sign pledges of repentance and willingness to avoid collaboration with anti-Islamic government groups.

In a matter of a few weeks, risking the danger that the Basij may renege on their promise, several younger ones including my brother Mirza, who is around fourteen, surrender; each one signs a paper that affirms he will never again support any political organizations. After vowing to keep out of the public eye, my brother and his friends are permitted to return home. However, all those fugitives either in the mountains or held up here and there in unidentified houses are our friends or relatives first and members or supporters of different groups second, who desperately need food, clothes, shoes and money; we cannot abandon them.

* * *

Mirza and I are the only ones at home. Kaveh, who has just turned sixteen, is still missing. Davood, at eighteen, is already in prison and Darius, by now twenty, is hiding in the mountainous areas to the south. All these factors are convincing enough to encourage everybody, including those who have signed the papers in the mosque, to remain involved.

My brother Mirza and I work on the lands and tea gardens even harder, as if we can somehow make up for our missing brothers. The tea farms are located among the woods some distance away from the village, giving the younger children who

120

are still at home, the opportunity they need to keep in touch with the fugitives. Like us, youngsters of other families are working hard to fill the empty places left by their brothers and sisters. Farm work creates ideal occasions for us to get together and exchange information about those in hiding. When there are fugitives staying nearby, we bring extra supplies to send along to our family members in the mountains. This is a very risky activity and we have to hide our doings from our parents, who fear for us and repeatedly ask us not to do anything 'stupid'.

In the mornings, with a few snacks and a flask of tea in a basket, we leave for work. At noon, we go home, take care of the animals, have lunch and rest for a while before starting for the fields again. By evening we hurriedly return to the house; it is important to be home before dusk to avoid interrogation by the Basij.

~ * ~

Cloaked in darkness

Weeks continue like this until one dark night rocks the village. The government forces announce an all-night curfew; it is public knowledge that the Basij are going to bury Behdad.

Behdad is the first case of a Mojahedin member from our village being executed. He is my oldest brother's age and comes from the lower village near the blacksmith's home. Simple, honest, friendly and an excellent soccer player, Behdad was an inspiration for many younger boys, including me; I used to wish he were my brother.

During the curfew, my parents spend a lot of time talking about Behdad and his family. His father is an illiterate farmer and his mother has worked all her life on other people's lands to raise several children with a near-empty pocketbook. I imagine other families are bringing up the same issues; discussing Behdad reminds people of their concern for their own children and other relatives who are either in prison or in hiding.

Late at night, the Basij forces take Behdad's body to our local cemetery, asking his parents to be available at the gravesite.

Nobody else has the privilege of attending the funeral and the family is warned not to make any noise or do any mourning or crying. In the middle of the night, Behdad is buried at the corner of the cemetery where it meets our traditional soccer field. He was executed in the Islamic holy month of Ramadan while the majority of Moslems are fasting.

There is no longer the sound of loud chatting voices on people's verandas. We take our nightmares to bed with us, only to be awakened at dawn by the sound of gunshots and explosions. The electricity has been disconnected and the village is cloaked in darkness. Since we do not have even one telephone in the village, it is not easy to find out what's going on, so we wait.

Later in the morning comes significant news by grapevine: After the Basij forces left the cemetery for their base, they held their nightly prayers for Ramadan and prepared themselves for fasting. While they were busy with a light meal and ablutions, a group of people broke into the base, captured all the forces and controlled the base for an hour or so. Then after killing one of the Basij members, they left, taking all the weapons with them.

Through covert publications, we learn that this action was in retaliation for Behdad's execution. What I find astounding, when I discover it later, is that the Basij who was killed was the one who asked me to shut up when Davood was taken away.

After this attack, the government forces are furiously out of control. They impose new, tougher regulations, detain and even abduct people for questioning, convinced that such an ambush on their base could not have been done without the cooperation of local residents.

Most of the young people who signed papers in the mosque are called in again. One wrong answer to the questions put to them means years of prison. The Basij members, now wildly hostile, are just looking for excuses to mete out punishment; some of the local youths who leave for work in the morning never return home.

My father is doing his best to keep Mirza and me safe, very carefully scrutinizing our daily activity. His main concern is Mirza, who is not allowed to go to the marketplace, even to shop. My brother is only permitted to travel between home and our lands, further than that, makes my father livid. I, on the other hand, young enough to fall below the radar of the Basij, am instructed to go directly to the market, buy the supplies and return without stopping to visit with friends or loiter along the way.

* * *

The Hezbollah forces begin tearing down from the walls all the former banners bearing chants and slogans left over from the ex-political groups, and start replacing them with new Islamic chants. For the very first time, we see the pictures and words of one single person on every wall. There is Khomeini, Khomeini, Khomeini, nothing but Khomeini everywhere.

One morning, we see a couple of Khomeini's pictures on the wall of our house. Someone has jumped over the fences onto our property and put the pictures up right near a window facing the road. It was very clearly done on purpose to see our reactions. And, if they are watching, they must be satisfied, as this makes Mirza very angry.

"They don't have the right to put their pictures inside our property," Mirza tells me.

No matter how much I ask him to take it easy, he has torn those pictures off by evening and stuffed them into the fireplace to be burned, not considering somebody may have seen him.

Later that night, when my father comes home, he is irate. He already knows about the pictures; one of our neighbors caught Mirza in the act and stopped my father on his way from the market to report it. My father knows our neighbor is not malicious, but tends to gossip and disclose peoples' secrets indiscriminately.

Night has hardly fallen when the local Basij forces arrive at our house and take Mirza away. Unlike many detainees who never return home, Mirza is lucky enough to come back to us after spending about four years in prison.

* * *

Some months later, government forces arrest a large group of Mojahedin in the neighboring province to ours and take them to a national TV station. This use of mosque, radio, or a TV station as the venue for confessions is a common practice, and sentences are supposed to be lighter for those who confess publicly. In this case, the group is expected to admit their wrongdoing in belonging to the Mojahedin and to seek for forgiveness with an apology. The interviews continue for several nights on national television. The leader of the faction is an engineer who says he has several diplomas from the most reliable universities in the world, which he mentions by name, one after another. He talks about the activities of the group members, how they survived in hiding and whom they have killed.

He admits that they are responsible for the attack on our local Basij base after Behdad was executed, saying they captured it very easily with simple weapons. Since they did not know how to use the military guns and grenades they found in the base, they ordered the Basij members to teach them. He says everything was going well until one of the Basij tried to attack one of the invaders; a gun went off and the Basij was killed.

Mr. Moqaddam, the group leader, and his deputy, Mr. Hallajian, direct their message to all Iranians and express regret for any possible trouble they have made for people. After the interviews, the government declares the entire group guilty and executes them.

Public displays like this are used to convince people that anyone who opposes the regime is 'corrupt on earth, an enemy of God and the Prophet' and deserves death. With television airings like this, coupled with sermons, brainwashing and lessons on morality, the new regime manages to engrave on the minds of the populace that it is the true representative of the Prophet and God. Their propaganda is so strong that several families even disclose the whereabouts of their relatives and neighbors to the Basij forces, convinced it is the right decision. The majority of such population, including dissident families, although feeling guilty when their loved ones are executed in prison, is of the opinion that Khomeini is not aware of the executions going on around the country; they think the young Basij members and the Revolutionary Guards are acting on their own.

* * *

Soon after Behdad is executed, the local Basij forces arrest Bahram, a friend of Behdad and another supporter of the Mojahedin.

His father died when the children were very young and his mother raised them alone. Bahram was barely more than a boy when he started his own business to help support the family. He opened a store inside the village market and sold chicken, a job lucrative enough to allow other members of his family to continue their studies.

Now, as he is crossing a rice field to visit his mother, a neighbor who works for the Basij sees him. This old man[1], who believes in the Basij forces as God's soldiers on earth, runs to the base to let them know.

Bahram hardly reaches home when the paramilitary troops surround his house. He tries to escape through the rice lands but the forces shoot him in the leg and capture him, beating him so badly that he almost dies on the way to the base. A night or two later, they bury Bahram next to Behdad, and cover his grave with a black cloth[2].

Within a few months, the number of those black coverings has grown to seven. Whenever nobody is around, close friends and relatives take advantage and secretly mourn on the graves. Eventually, the local Basij forces find out about these silent mourning services and become worried that such gravesites will turn into a source of problems. To prevent more gatherings in future, the executioners start burying people in either unknown or remote places. In many cases, even the families of the victims do not know the whereabouts of these graves without which many are still hoping that one day their loved ones will return home.

----

[1] The old man was a Basij member and a baker in the village. He had a reputation of being hard-nosed and always angry. People, including his family, were afraid of him, referring to him as a type of religious 'Hitler'. He was killed in an automobile accident a year or two later. His own family forgave the driver on the scene, following up with a police report that they were dropping the case. According to the Iranian judicial system, the family of someone who is murdered decides the fate of the murderer.

[2] To this day, there is no marker on his grave or on the graves of many others; sometimes not even the close family and friends know their location.

Far from familiar voices

Gradually, I get used to my lonely life. Mirza, Davood, and Kaveh, who has recently been arrested, are in prison. My oldest brother Darius is in hiding, leaving me home alone with huge farming jobs on my hands and the very harsh temper of my father who is now more agitated than ever. Even during the revolution, I never saw him in such a state; a single move or noise can make him rabid, my getting home after dark terrifies him and any kind of mishandling of daily tasks sets him off like a landmine.

Sometimes when my patience runs thin, I talk back to him, parroting his anger. My mother keeps out of the discussions, except to cool us down. At the tender age of twelve, I have to do all the daily chores by myself; care for the animals, milk the cows, work the lands and the gardens, and sometimes help my mother wash the dishes and laundry. I am not allowed to spend any time with friends; gatherings by day or night are history and it is even hard to convince dad to sit alone in the dark under the trees in our yard.

My father, who in spite of his tough disciplinary regulations for his children, had such a great sense of humor that he was a popular guest at shab neshinis, or nightly get-togethers and often the host would set back the hour on the clock to fool him into staying longer. For the entertainment he provided, neighbors were willing to pay him to join them at work during the harvest. Now he gradually withdraws inside himself and becomes a loner, no longer even wanting to work on his tea lands where memories of his children there are too painful. All day long, he sits either on the stairs of the veranda or under the trees in our yard staring at the road, a road now empty of the old familiar voices.

The one thing he does cling to is his outdated transistor radio, which he carries with him everywhere, eagerly listening to a serial program aired daily about the soldiers in the Iran-Iraq war. The part he doesn't want to miss is the end of every episode when a few soldiers send messages to their relatives and the names of several martyrs are released.

Dad in front of his deserted monument, alone and lonely

* * *

One day a week, my mother, sometimes accompanied by my aunts or other relatives, cooks an abundance of food. When the food is ready, they store the dishes in containers, wrap them in a clean cloth and stack them equally in separate handbags. Once packed, I take the bags out to where my father is sitting under a tree and lay them by his side. He reluctantly lets his eyes roam from bag to bag, traveling in his thoughts for some time until my mother breaks his silence by giving him instructions for their disbursement. "The green bag is for Davood," she says, "the black is for Kaveh, and those two others are for Mirza; he is thin and needs more nourishment. I am worried about his health."

Dad murmurs a few words as his anger begins to mount until by the end of my mother's instructions, he bursts out yelling, "If your children wanted good food, they would listen to me and stay out of trouble, but they have preferred prison to eating healthy food at home." Still muttering, he gets up, grabs those bags, and trots off for the neighboring town to visit his children, my brothers, in prison.

It is a frequent occurrence that the prison authorities do not allow parents to visit their children. On many occasions, I see my father, who left early in the morning, return home late in the afternoon with those still full bags in his hands. When this happens, he does not have the courage to go to the prison the following week so my mother has to call her sisters for help. As her personal pony express, I secretly take her messages to my aunts or other relatives and tell them mom needs their help on such and such a day. When the day arrives, they gather at our house early in the morning and work hard to prepare the food before my father notices what they are doing. Although not happy with the tactics my mom employs, he usually remains silent with chagrin after he sees mom dressed up for the prison visit, but sometimes, he loses control and shouts angrily. "Your children don't deserve this food. They don't love you as much as you love them, because if they did, they would stay at home to help you instead of you having to deliver food to them such a long way away."

My aunts, seeing my mother defenseless, take her side against my father and say, "Instead of sitting here complaining and blaming this woman, go back to work."

"I don't care what happens to the lands anymore," he replies. "I have lost my children after all these years of working for them. I gladly paid for their notebooks and pens and would have sold my eyes for their education. I put all my ambition in their future but they stepped on Khomeini's cock and made him angry. Now they have disappeared like four tiny needles in a huge sea. Whom should I work for, then? Why should I work? I cannot convince myself to continue working on the lands. Those places remind me of the sight and sound of my children. I feel agony when I see their empty places around the farms. I hear their voices everywhere. Although I punished them occasionally for wasting time, I was always delighted and never felt fatigue when we worked together side by side. Now they are gone, all four of them. Every single day, I sit around this house and stare at the road with the hope of getting news. My nourishment has become tea and cigarettes. I have been listening to all the messages the soldiers send to their families from Iraq. I even wish one of those martyrs' names were for me; at least then, I would know the fate of my children. Now, I am confused; I don't even know whether they are dead or alive. Why should I work? My children are gone. All of them, except this little one."

With this last remark, my relatives remind him of how he had his heart set on a girl at the time of my birth, saying, "This is the boy you didn't want. Do you remember? Now this boy is your comforter. God had a purpose after all, when he gave you this child."

"What kind of purpose is this, to take away all my children? I don't like this purpose. Let me take away one of God's children, see how He likes it."

To placate him, the relatives commiserate, "You are angry and blaspheming God, but He will forgive you because it is your sorrow speaking."

"I don't want him to forgive me," my father replies in anger. "I just want my children back."

My aunts walk my mother through the yard to the road and wait there with her while I call a taxi. Then the women help mom get in the car first. From inside the car, she gives me final instructions about where to find food and other kitchen things my father and I will need in her absence. She asks me to give dad his meals on time and not to leave the house until they are back. While she is busy talking to me, the relatives climb in beside her on the back seat and I put all the bags of food in the car on their laps. My father keeps watch on us in silence from under his tree in the yard; he knows better than to intervene when he sees how set my mom is on visiting her children.

~ * ~

Nothing can replace the sound of your footsteps in the house

Several months pass and still we have no news about my brother Darius. Then one day, a friend who is still around because he signed the Basij papers earlier, brings me a letter from Darius, saying he is fine and, as was his habit, asking me to behave myself and mind our parents. Knowing from his letter that my brother is still alive gives us new hope and we are almost delirious with happiness.

Gradually, those of us who remained in the village find the time to reverse the earlier disorder and confusion that has dominated it. Everything happened so quickly we still thought, looking back, that we had dreamed it all. Now that the earlier unrest is gone, we begin to pull ourselves together a bit and manage to set up more organized meetings during which some, who are in touch with the fugitives, give us news about our brothers and sisters and instruct us in how to deal with the government forces in emergencies. The most common advice is to avoid the forces in the village and change shirts to another color as often as possible, making it harder for them to keep track of us. The ruse of pretending to remain sleeping whenever the forces break into our homes, a regular occurrence, is also recommended. This sleeping tactic works well; during several home searches, I pretend to be asleep and thus avoid answering any of the several questions they may have about my daily activities.

Months later, I receive a surprising message from my brother saying he wants to visit mom and dad at home. Although we know it is extremely risky, my parents can hardly control their joy when I give them the news. We impatiently count down the days in anticipation.

On the promised night, I turn off all the lights in the house and we pretend to be sleeping. In the silence, I wait for Darius at one corner of our front garden, at about midnight I hear footsteps crackling the tiny dried branches of trees that have been raked to one corner of the garden floor. I look carefully in the direction of the noise and see Darius walking towards me from deeper within the garden. I stand up so he can see me and, holding my breath, wait for him to come closer. Then with a sob, I throw myself into his arms. He kisses me and asks me to get hold of myself, saying his friends are waiting at a distance and are anxious to return to a safe hiding place, so he has very little time. We head for the darkened veranda and step through the door of our living room. My father hugs Darius tightly in his arms for a long time before sending him to sit close to my mother on the floor. She holds both his hands firmly in one of hers, while with the other she begins to stroke his head and shoulders. I scurry out to my old uncle's room to get him to come see his nephew. He jumps out of his bed and, darting ahead of me for the veranda, runs to the living room, grabs Darius and starts kissing him on the hands, face and neck, bursting into tears.

After spending only a few short minutes with them, my brother asks me to go stand watch in the yard and to be on the alert for any suspicious movement around the house. I walk back outside and position myself in a safe place behind one of the pillars that holds up the kanduj. Seconds later, Darius leaves the living room without making a sound, followed by my father, uncle, and finally my mother trailing him to the veranda. They kiss him goodbye not knowing that it is to be their last meeting.

Darius disappears in the dark like a dream on awakening, leaving us with an unsettled feeling which we don't have time to analyze before we hear footsteps on the veranda; a sudden sharp hammering on the door brings us upright in our beds. I lie back down in bed immediately and whisper to my father to turn on the light and take a look. When he opens the door, through squinted eyes I see a man in uniform and with a military gun in his hand, whose frame fills the entire threshold. From where he is standing at the door, the soldier stretches his neck in and, eyes roving around the room, asks if anyone visited earlier that night. While my father is denying having visitors, more uniforms appear on the veranda, climbing the stairs and checking around on the second floor, including under the metal rooftop of the house; there is no sign of my brother.

Before leaving, we are instructed to report to the Basij base immediately if we receive any news about Darius. My father agrees and they turn and go. Closing the door behind them, we are just settling down to sleep when we hear more voices on the road. I kneel up and look through the window to see armed forces, both men and women, still behind the house. Among them is a neighbor girl. Her brother, also named Darius, and mine have been very close friends and pals since childhood, and have spent days and nights at each other's house. Now she and her brother, part of the local Basij forces, are on a mission to search out and arrest their old buddies. Our house is searched five times before morning.

* * *

One day, this Darius comes to me, saying, "I sent a message to your brother asking him to surrender and repent so I personally could defend him in court. Do you know what he told me?"

"What?" I ask.

In a voice laden with disappointment, he continues, "he told me 'winter will pass but the coal will remain black-faced[1]'. I am sad to think that Darius considers me his enemy."

*   *   *

'Soon after the first wave of tensions abates, the local Basij forces, who have been training boys and girls together in the village since the 1979 revolution, begin forming more intimate relationships. Thrust into close proximity during their training, these young people develop romantic feelings for each other, marry their ideological partners from the base and share their conjugal life along with their military duties.

For many of these proponents of morality and family values, rumors abound about sexual promiscuity and abortions, relationships end in divorce and for the women, often the next step is prostitution. Such was the case of the neighbor girl who helped in the hunt for my brother. A few years after marrying one of her fellow Revolutionary Guards, her husband took their children and abandoned her to her fate.

----

[1] A proverb meaning time will reveal who is telling the truth.

~ * ~

132

Green trees are felled in my village

Softly falling snowflakes soon cover the entire village with a thick, downy silk fabric, making the trees bow down as if in prayer; white silence is sovereign. With people indoors, the village is free of bustle and commotion. All you can see are a few light tracks made by chickens, dogs and cats leading from one spot to another, crisscrossing each other and forming curious patterns on the snow's surface. Nights are especially lovely with the large silver disc of the moon shining down on trees laden with their weighty winter wraps.

The cold brings a wide variety of migrating birds. We habitually set traps to catch them, or hunt them with our air rifles. I can painfully remember how groups of us would go hunting at night, breaking through the drifting snow, guns in hand, traveling among the orange groves and using flashlights to pinpoint birds sleeping peacefully on the branches of trees. One of us would fasten the light on a bird, while another focused the sights of the gun on it, and bam! The bird fell and a smear of red would form a hollow in the bluish-white snow.

I remember after one memorable night, when we returned with a bag full of game, happy with our results, my mother asked, "How would you feel if your brother were sleeping and someone pointed a gun at him and shot him? These birds have taken refuge in our orchards and it is very cruel to kill them while they are sleeping."

We didn't take this very seriously then, but with time and the circumstances surrounding us during the tensions of the domestic unrest, we quit hunting at night, and finally, a few of us quit hunting altogether.

* * *

With the onslaught of winter, Darius and others who are still in hiding desperately need our help. My friends and I continue collecting money, food, and clothes and scheme to find a safe network for delivering them. Each time a messenger is caught, another person steps up to take his place. Our families, although afraid for us and wishing we weren't involved, can't abandon their children in hiding either, so turn a blind eye to our courier services. In deference to their fears, we take great pains to keep the details from them.

Farid, the one who first gave me a letter from Darius, is detained one day, taken to the village mosque now being used as the Basij logistics room, and whipped. Within the mosque, a religious building dedicated to peace and love of God, they give him seventy lashes, while his poor disconsolate father cries for him outside. Then they release him. A short time later, Farid is arrested again and executed almost immediately[1].

* * *

The following spring, the villagers receive an edict from the government saying that within a few months all the trees around the villages are to be cut down.

Prior to this time, we were not allowed to cut any trees at all; during the 1979 revolution, when there was no established order in the country, my father and other villagers cleared parts of their own lands for tea farms and were taken to court over it once the government was well organized. The farmers had the choice of a fine or time in prison. Some chose prison. My father, who was fined a few thousand tomans, told the judge, "I kissed my own wife, why should I pay you, then?" The judge answered, "It is true that you kissed your own wife, but you did it in public, and you know that this is illegal."

But now, the ear-piercing roar of chainsaw motors shakes the forest from morning till night, as grove by grove, orchard by orchard, forest by forest, all our stately, majestic trees are felled. In a few months, thousands of hectares of green woods turn into flatlands across the province. In what had once been carefully-preserved lush rainforest, we can hardly find one ancient, towering tree anymore. A deadline follows for the removal of all underbrush in which someone could take refuge; defiance of this order means having lands confiscated.

With the green woods gone, my brother and his friends have to withdraw several kilometers deeper into the Alborz Mountains to the south. Our messenger Farid is dead and we go without news about those in hiding until some time later, seventeen-year-old Farbod, who also signed the Basij papers after being accused of supporting a communist-based group, volunteers to take his place. Because all of the fugitives are either close friends or relatives, he feels compelled to help. No sooner does he become our messenger when he connects me to my brother, but even with this contact, we find that, with the trees gone, it is becoming increasingly more dangerous to be in communication with Darius. It doesn't take long until the local Basij forces arrest Farbod and take him to prison where he languishes for six or seven years before he is executed.

Gradually, to survive in such a situation becomes more difficult for those in hiding; more and more local people, the majority of whom signed the Basij papers, have been arrested. The Basij is in full control of the village, and an overwhelming number of the fugitives who have begun leaving for other provinces, are caught in the act.

* * *

Mr. Behrang, my literature teacher, is busy finding channels to save his sons who are already in prison. He calls in every advantage within his power until he finally manages to save his children from the death penalty, and have their sentences reduced to a few years in prison.

My father, desperately looking for a miracle to save his own children, and perhaps remembering my mother's success in the past, pleads with him for help, believing Mr. Behrang capable of using his power to change the situation of my brothers.

Many times Mr. Behrang, sitting with a cup of steaming tea my mother has prepared, swears to God that, even though he loves us exactly as he does his very own children, he does not have any clout anymore. "Do you think I don't love your children?" he asks my father. "But you must understand the times have changed, they belong to the young Basij forces. I would do anything in my power, but I no longer have any power; I have run out of favors. You know, Islam, it cost me plenty to save my boys." "How is it possible?" my father wonders in the face of his protests, "that such a respected person as you are in the community, can do nothing?"

* * *

Coincidentally, not long later, one of Mr. Behrang's daughters marries a boy from a Basij family. The groom, it turns out, is the older brother of the person who spotted Davood in his heavy bandages on that unfortunate spring day. Mr. Behrang has just become a grandfather when he dies of a stroke while walking along the road on the way to the market. His untimely death shocks the village and my father begins to blame himself for passing judgment on someone who was 'a friend in need'[2]. Such is my father's pain at losing his friend and such is the warmth with which he remembers him, that it isn't long before he, as his disenchantment with the revolution mounts, begins to question his life-long beliefs and reflect Mr. Behrang's words and ideas himself.

* * *

In an effort to stabilize its power, the government continues systematically decimating our village youth by vigilante execution. In parallel with the dissidents, the majority of the war martyrs are under twenty years of age. Some of them used to be my classmates, who have, since it is fashionable, voluntarily joined the Basij forces and gone to war. A popular supposition is that some young men have run away from home to join the fighting in order to escape the limitations placed on them by religious parents. Increasingly family members die of heartbreak, psychological pressure or apoplexy; the more people die, the more we cry, and the more we cry, the more Quran and other religious creed is thrust on us as an antidote[3].

People use burial and related ceremonies to exchange anecdotes and stories about the martyrs, each person trying to outdo others with claims that he or she was closest to the person who lives no more. The government hosts and supports these services with a more sinister motive; they glorify these meetings to further involve the grieving relatives in their propaganda and to distract public attention from the executions.

Thousands of stories and dreams, created during these sessions, change the course of many people's lives. For example, in a neighboring town there was a girl whose brother had been killed during his military service in Kurdistan, west of Iran. At the same time, a friend of mine was also killed while serving in Kurdistan. The burial ceremonies for the two martyrs were held at the same time, and that is how these two families became connected. Although my friend was a supporter of the Mojahedin

136

organization, he was titled 'martyr' like all the other war casualties. When these two fell, victims of the fighting, ceremonies commemorating their life and passage lasted for more than forty days. My friend's parents never stopped wearing mourning; they started attending weekly prayer sessions that the government forces held at different locations and soon their children joined them. One day, someone, I don't know who, dreamed that she had a commission from one of the martyred boys to talk to the parents about arranging a marriage between this girl and the younger brother of my friend. An agreement was reached and the couple married. Hardly more than a few years had passed when this young couple decided they were not suitable for each other after all and they divorced. The father of the groom, an athletic and still quite young man, soon passed away.

----

[1] With his death, and later losing an older son to illness, the sorrow of both parents was so deep that they never got over it, dying before their time.

[2] After these many years, from time to time, I still see our old friend in my dreams. When I first arrived in China, under the suffocating pressure of not knowing what to do and about to run out of money, I had a dream that Mr. Behrang said to me, "Why don't you go to them for help?"

"Whom?" I asked.

"The same ones who have been helping those people."

"Which people?"

He didn't speak anymore but the faces of some of my students in India came to my mind. I woke up and tried to figure out what his message to me was, but was unable to understand. Soon daily pressures took precedence and I forgot the dream. Weeks later, as I was heading into an office, no sooner had I stepped through the door when I clearly remembered my dream and knew this was the place he had meant. Tears came to my eyes when I realized just how much he had cared for my family, and that his spirit was still demonstrating the same care to me in my dilemma.

[3] From among the people I knew, either in person or through family relations, and according to the names I can still remember,

in less than ten years, more than 21 members or supporters of various political groups were killed by the government, and around the same number died in the Iran-Iraq war. These figures do not include the parents or relatives of the victims, who died of grief or illness. The many more people who spent years in prisons because of their political ideas, the number of soldiers who were taken into captivity in Iraq during the eight-year war, and the dissidents who fled the country and hence were wiped off the map of the village, are also excluded from this list.

To go beyond is as wrong as to fall short
...............................Confucius

Five

Morality leaves you without a helping hand!

By the time I have started the second grade of middle school, no longer is there any political campaigning among the students; there are only the pictures and words of Khomeini and other government members plastered on the walls. What matters most in our lesson plans these days are moralities and Quranic verses. Incorporating Arabic words into our vocabulary becomes obligatory and commonplace.

In our new Islamized textbooks, stories abound about different prophets as well as the Islamic symbols of innocence, purity, resistance and sacrifice. Figures like Joseph in the Quran, who strongly resisted temptation, become very popular. During our classes, teachers continue to place emphasis on where the righteous will spend eternity, as well as where evildoers will go to spend their life after death. Many of the religious rules and stories we learn are based on parables and commandments from the Old Testament.

Rules such as 'do not steal', 'do not lie', 'do not commit adultery', 'do not kill', 'respect your parents', 'do your daily prayers on time', 'read Quran in Arabic to get greater rewards', 'do not pee while standing', 'wash yourself carefully before prayer', 'wake yourself up in the middle of the night and cry to God to forgive your sins', 'keep in mind that a true God-fearer is always sad', 'resist temptation', 'do not eat pork', 'do not be happy with your good deeds but strive to do better', 'cast your eyes to the ground when talking to a woman' and 'protect your namoos[1]' are only a small part of the commandments drummed into our heads every day.

In most cases, each topic has its own stories and parables to help bring the message home. One of our teachers, who parrots the words of the town's mullah in every one of his classes, seriously encourages us to eat rooster and not pork. His logic is that roosters defend the hens in their coop against neighboring roosters bothering the females, while pigs are totally indifferent when another pig invades their sty. 'That's why', he concludes, 'we chicken-eating Moslems have gheirat[2] but Westerners, because they eat pork, aren't concerned if their women interrelate with other men'. This teacher tells his stories with such self-appointed authority that, whether they are true or not, we are not encouraged to doubt him.

In class, we are not supposed to head our compositions with the Persian word God any more. Teachers say it is immoral to write the exact word on paper since God's name is holy. What if such a paper were accidentally dropped either under someone's feet or in a toilet stall? Wouldn't God be offended? The solution is to use an Arabic phrase, 'besmehi taala', in the name of He Who is on High, at the top of our papers to show respect to the Almighty.

We are strongly admonished to perform ritual ablutions called vozu before Quran classes. Even with clean hands, since God's word is holy and we are mere mortals, to touch the Arabic verses of the Quran is considered a sin; whenever we read this Book, we very carefully touch only the edges to turn the pages. To avoid uncertain repercussions and/or cruel punishments, we have to obey our teachers in this and all other regulations.

As we grow up inside these religious teachings, we get accustomed to accepting without understanding and begin to apply the rules we are learning to our daily life.

* * *

There is a young girl about my age in our neighborhood, who begins to work with me in our tea gardens one spring. Every morning, taking our baskets filled with snacks to keep us from getting hungry during the day, we walk together on a riverbank and cross through the bushes and the greenness of nature around us, heading south to reach our tea farm in the middle of hundreds of new young volunteer trees. Charming and lovely in her youthfulness, this girl still wears her colorful dresses in spite of all the black clothes being worn in the village. She laughs and jokes around a lot, saying whatever comes into her head without thought for tact or diplomacy and doesn't seem to have been impacted much by any of her classes of religion and morality. In my opinion, she knows more than her age indicates when it comes to relations between the sexes; I can clearly feel the sexual vibes she sends out when we are together. However, since she is also kind of village shy and does not have the temerity to disclose her feelings freely, she expresses her emotions through joking, and even by telling taboo stories about boys kissing girls. When I do not react to her efforts, sometimes she carelessly leaves a few buttons undone on her shirt so when she bends over the tea bushes to pick the green tea, her young firm breasts are partially uncovered. Although very tempted to look, I force my eyes away from her when she exposes herself that way.

Every night, a huge war wages inside my brain. At first, I convince myself that the next time she comes on to me I will respond, arranging a scenario or two in my head to direct our conversation towards my goal. 'Tomorrow, I will kiss her', I whisper to myself. By the time I am sure about my plan and ready to go to bed, I am beginning to feel uncomfortable. Suddenly all the words of my teachers circulate through my mind and my resolve sizzles out like a fire drowned in water. After struggling with this dilemma for an hour or so, I have an idea. In the middle of the night, I creep out of the mosquito net and crawl into the spare room on the second floor. Once there I get my big nail cutters out of my pants pocket, the ones purchased for me by my relatives years before. With its sharp blades, I grip parts of the skin of my manhood tightly, pressing hard enough that two sharp lines are painfully engraved on the skin. The temptation vanishes and I go to bed with new determination, which lasts until the next afternoon. Towards evening on the next day, with the self-inflicted pain dulled, the sexual desire surges again. Soon I am back to the same battle of the night before.

This conflict goes on nightly until by the end of spring the girl ridicules me, saying, "Hassan, you have nothing in your pants!" With that, she turns and walks away and I am left to harvest the tea without help.

----

[1]Namoos means the female members of one's family including but not limited to wife, daughters, sisters, and mother.

[2]Gheirat includes but is not limited to the zealous defense of one's family.

~ * ~

'Hassan doesn't like this!'

Afraid the government will call them sympathizers and use this against them in the future, the majority of the villagers won't take the chance of working for fugitive families. In most cases, we either do our chores alone or barter work with a group, laboring together to finish the jobs on one farm, then continuing on to the next.

During spring and summer, my days start before dawn when I leave for the local bakery, and it is still dark when I return with several pieces of freshly baked bread in my hands. After wrapping the bread in a piece of cloth, I lay it in the corner of our living room near the samovar, and leave for the barn to milk the cows, mix mash for the chickens and feed the other animals[1].

The farm chores done, I have breakfast, then put snacks in a bag and leave for the fields. Our two main crops, tea and rice, overlap, so I have one foot in the tea farm and one in the rice lands, as we say in Persian.

When it is tea-picking season, every evening after we have cut and gathered it into a gunnysack, I hoist the sack onto my back and walk out to wait at the side of the road for our contracted motorcycle carrier[2] to get to our fields. When he arrives, with the driver's help, I load the sack on the bike first then jump on top of it to head to the local factory[3] where the crop is inspected for quality, weighed and emptied into huge containers for drying and processing. The factory does not have enough space for the huge amount of tea from the village farms and while I wait my turn in line, like everybody else, to put mine on the scales, sometimes it starts to decay and turns brown in its sacks. If that happens, I wind up with a container full of about fifty kilos of rotting leaves, which I have to throw away.

By the time I finish my business at the factory and return home, the cows, the sheep and my horse are noisily awaiting their dinner, and I repeat the feeding chores of the morning.

* * *

One day while at the tea farm, I notice Mansoor, whom I haven't seen for quite some time, at work in an adjoining field. Mansoor has been working with his father on their land since his brother, who was detained and released, has left to begin his own life in a nearby town. At break time Mansoor crosses into our field, we have our snacks together and make plans to join up later at his house.

Unlike the gregarious Mansoor, his father has always been unsociable and kept to himself, often not responding even to people's greetings. Knowing he doesn't like any of his children's friends coming around the house, I plan to wait until Mansoor's father has gone to work before my head appears in their yard, as we say in Persian. I don't want to, as I have in the past, get to his house while his father is still there and have him say to me, 'Mansoor doesn't want to see anybody', when I stammer lamely, 'I wanna see Mansoor'.

Little by little, my friends and I grow used to his father's personality and begin to incorporate many of his phrases in our daily jokes. All we need to do is to replace a couple words of his original sentences and then apply the new phrases. For example, when a friend wants us to do something for him, and it happens that we have neither the time nor the inclination to do it, we simply say, 'Hassan doesn't want to help anybody'.

Mansoor, contrary to his father, is always available, no matter who whistles for him. As he and I start spending more time together, his father softens his behavior toward me, returns my greetings and asks after my family, something almost unheard of for him. However, our spare-time activities often make him angry. Being very particular about his motorbike, and not liking it to be touched, he locks it up every day before leaving for work to make sure we don't fool with it.

Mansoor usually is still sleeping when I get to his house, climb the stairs and go into his room. It takes him less than ten minutes to wake up, use the bathroom, wash his face, and have his breakfast. Swallowing several pieces of bread and gulping a cup of tea to chase the food down‘, he is still chewing as he dons a shirt and pants while searching for the bike key, which his father hides in a different place in the house everyday. He finds it within a matter of seconds and unlocks the large chain hanging around the tire. We have a good time biking around our village and neighboring areas until we figure it is time to get the bike home to beat his father's arrival from work. Sometimes Mansoor miscalculates the time and we arrive home after his father, who is angrily waiting for his bike. If this is the case, I avoid going to their house for several days, leaving Mansoor to deal with the situation, who handles it by laying low until his father calms down. A day or two later, he appears again and we go back to our habit of joyriding his father's motorbike.

* * *

With a lessening of tensions, the village youths form a soccer team. Bereft of a field, we play in the rice lands after harvest season, gathering in the early evening and playing until it is too dark to see the ball. My father is not happy with me going to our makeshift soccer field, so I have to hide this from him. Consequently, I always plan to leave early, but there are times when I get so absorbed with the game and the fun I am having, it is totally dark before I notice. I am supposed to be rounding up the animals and bringing them home, but with the light gone, I have to search for several kilometers around the village to find them. I leave my fun behind and, running through the darkness, stumbling and falling in the mud, I keep in mind that if I go home empty-handed, I will be in big trouble. First, I pray to God to help me find the animals, then, surrounded by animals from the neighbors' farms while mine are nowhere to be found, I start cursing my bad fortune. It's my lucky night if my horse responds to my whistles quickly so I can ride him to look for the other animals, but it often happens that I go home without them. When I enter our yard late in the evening, there is my father sitting under a tree in the dark. Seeing me walk home in my clothes all wet and muddy from my hasty searches, he cannot contain his anger; my arrival in the yard in such a sorry condition, alone and without the animals, sets him on a rampage. He is beside himself with fury, and shouts and shouts and shouts until he falls asleep. Nights like these are the worst of my entire life; Hassan doesn't like this!

The good point about playing soccer is that it gives me a chance to meet with my buddies every day; getting together for these games becomes our only entertainment after more than a year of isolation and allows us to renew our friendships. Without voicing our thoughts, we feel close to each other because most of us have in common brothers or sisters in prison. We decide to create afresh the cooperatives of our past, helping out on each other's lands and gardens, since with our older siblings gone we are all short of laborers. Through such cooperation, we find that handling our own farming jobs is a lot easier and considerably faster, leaving us with enough time left over to earn a little cash from the few other people who would hire us.

—————————————————————————

[1]During these years, I learned a little animal husbandry when I was left to deliver several calves by myself.

[2]Before the revolution, a government truck would travel around to the tea farms to pick up and deliver the harvested tea to the local factory and wait around to return us to our homes. This service was free to the farmers. Now, we were obliged to contract with a carrier and, once he dropped us at the factory, he was off to deliver a load for someone else, leaving us to walk home.

[3]The local tea factory was built under the Pahlavi long before the revolution, and was always subsidized by the government. My father, who was a small boy at that time, still remembers the opening ceremony with its live band and the crush of women dancing in traditional dress. The building accommodated the amount of tea that was being grown, but by the time I was helping out with the tea harvest, there were many more tea growers, and the factory had not changed or been modernized; hence the long waiting lines. Today this factory, officially abandoned by the government, is about to close its doors, going the way of our bank and post office; they are all history.

[4]Since he never bothers to brush his teeth, and he is very fond of chocolates, his teeth, badly decayed on top of being crowded and mal-positioned, become the brunt of our jokes; whenever we see things in disorder and messy, we say they look like Mansoor's teeth.

~ * ~

Where is his son?

One day when we are working in our tea garden, I suddenly see somebody hiding in the bushes not too far away. I stare and then am shocked to recognize who it is - my brother Darius, making a gesture of ssssh with a finger to his lips. With the excuse of taking a leak, I leave my friends and, walking to the outer edge of the garden where there are trees, I wind my way deep into the bushes. I cannot believe my eyes. It is not a dream. It really is my brother. While Darius walks towards me with a big smile on his face, I run to him and jump into his arms, holding onto him tightly. He hugs me back, pressing me hard against his chest. Nothing about him has changed; his manner of speech, his big smile, and the smell of his body are still part of the old, familiar Darius I remember. He has the same short moustache, the same black hair and the very same big, dark eyes.

Darius has come a long way to meet me in this garden where thousands of bittersweet memories lay buried. In the couple of minutes we have to talk, I give him news about mom and dad as well as our three brothers who are in prison. He encourages me to behave like a real man at home, and asks me to say hello to mom and dad. As he talks, I feel an overwhelming sense of joy bursting from my heart like fireworks, leaving me unfocused, without the use of my hands and legs, as we say in Persian. Abruptly, he embraces me once again, saying he has to get going and leaving as suddenly as he arrived.

* * *

A little later Kaveh and one of his friends escape from prison, and in their fury, the prison authorities launch extensive searches for them throughout the area. Within a week or two, the Revolutionary Guards arrest Kaveh's friend and execute him immediately.

* * *

My father regularly goes to the Islamic Revolutionary Guards' base in a neighboring town at the Caspian beach to visit my other brothers who are still incarcerated. This base used to be the house of a local ruler under the Shah until revolutionary forces confiscated it for use as a prison.

One day, he comes back home late in the afternoon, feeling so depressed that my mother and I think the government has executed either Davood or Mirza or both. After a few minutes rest and sipping a cup of tea my mother prepares for him, he starts talking, "Today while I was waiting outside the main prison gate to visit Davood and Mirza, the gate opened and I saw scores of men scurrying from different parts of the Revolutionary Guard's base into the yard. Armed with various types of guns and ammunition belts, they rushed like ants towards machine gun-mounted Toyotas. Along with other parents there to visit their children, I stood watching as the forces, laughing and smiling, swarmed the back of their vehicles, leaving in convoy and disappearing with a roaring of motors and clanging of gears. After they left, officials informed us there would be no visiting today and sent us off." Letting out a sigh, he continues, "I hope they are not going after my Kaveh or Darius. I hope my children are safe."

My mother begins to comfort him, soothing his anxieties by coaxing his thoughts from the troubling events of the day. She assures him that, God willing, soon everything will be fine and the kids will come back home. However, no matter how much my mother invokes God's name, my father is so seriously convinced that the soldiers were planning a diabolical mission that he is unable to be quieted even by her.

A couple of days later, early in the morning as I am heading for the bakery, I find a handful of papers lying on the stairs in front of the living room. I pick them up and, skimming through them, I notice that they are night letters from the Mojahedin, which is strange because we have not received any for a long time. After hastily checking several pages, one stops me cold in my tracks; I read that Darius and several of his friends have been slaughtered in a surprise ambush inside their shelter on the high Alborz Mountain range in a neighboring province. Also on the list of names is Bijan, a very intelligent and talented student of mechanics, who at one time was my role model. The date of the assassinations on the paper matches the day when my father saw the Revolutionary Guards leaving their base in a hurry.

* * *

Like many countless others in the post-revolutionary years, Darius and Bijan are buried in unmarked graves hidden away in unknown places. The government does not even bother to report anything about my brother's death to my parents. It is as if to them he never existed.

My poor father embarks on a grand search in the hope of finding a grave to give substance to his child's death. With a picture in his pocket, he goes to the neighboring town where Darius was killed and begins to interrogate people about the ambush in their area. He shows the picture to everybody he sees and asks if anybody has ever seen the person in the photograph. Depending on whom he talks to, details diverge, yet there is one common thread to all their tales; they all mention that nine youths were killed on that day.

~ * ~

Keep out of the way of the bull's horns

Kaveh disappears completely for several months after his escape; we don't know where he is and he doesn't try to contact us. But one evening I see a car drop somebody by our gate and leave. To my amazement, Kaveh walks into the yard, smiling. I run to him but, without taking the time to embrace me, he grabs my hand and says, "Let's go into the house quickly before neighbors or passersby see me."

Seeing us enter the living room, my father, who is sitting near a new, freestanding fireplace, one whose smoke dissipates through a stovepipe instead of filling the room and blackening the walls, jumps up with arms open wide, and rushes to Kaveh, embraces him and bursts into tears. After his initial reaction, my father calms down a little and steps back so Kaveh can kneel down on the floor near the samovar where my mother is always sitting, and give her a big hug. Then both mom and dad start questioning their son.

As Kaveh is briefly telling us how he and his friend escaped from prison and what has happened since, a smile turns up the corners of his mouth but doesn't reach his eyes. His face is pale and he squirms around restlessly, wincing; my mother wants to know what is wrong.

"I am having pain passing water and my urine is mixed with blood," he tells us. "I think I need medical attention and I know the only way to gain admittance to a hospital is to surrender myself to the government forces; that's why I came out of hiding."

At this confession, my father trembles, "They will kill you exactly like they did your friend!" he blurts out.

However, my brother's kidney problem is so serious that he wants us to talk to some of our ex-friends who are now members of the local Basij to see if they will intercede for him. After we discuss the suitability of a few persons, my father suggests our neighbor Darius, my brother Darius' old friend, as the best choice. Believing his family is more trustworthy than other Basij families, my father hopes they will help Kaveh for old time's sake.

We talk to Darius, now a senior ranking member of the Basij, who promises to do whatever he can. He consults important religious leaders about my brother; his efforts seem to bear fruit as the mullah, representative of the Supreme Leader in our area, writes a letter to the court asking for leniency in Kaveh's case.

After bringing this letter to us, Darius, our neighbor's son, asks my father to surrender Kaveh. Moments later, my brother leaves the house at the side of his ex-friend-turned-guard who is now taking him to the same prison from which he escaped months before. We each in turn embrace Kaveh and give him a goodbye kiss[1]. At my mother's direction, I pour water on the ground in Kaveh's tracks, symbolizing that with the footsteps gone, the person who made them has also been gone for a long time, so will soon return.

Although the letter secured for Kaveh seems very hopeful, our neighbor does not follow through with his support after handing my brother over to the authorities. Kaveh is sentenced to twenty years in prison; in our disappointment, we content ourselves with just knowing he is not going to be executed.

* * *

To confound the parents, the government begins relocating prisoners to confinement in different cities and provinces; my brothers are parceled out to cities such as Rudsar, Amlash, Rasht, Karaj and Tehran. With Kaveh back in prison, my relatives, but chiefly my father, visit all three of my brothers' whenever they can, but with them so far away and scattered, even my father cannot visit very often any more. In whichever city he happens to find one of my brothers, after a few visits, visiting privileges are cancelled without notice. Then for weeks, he keeps returning to that prison and pushes to see the child who is supposed to be there until finally they tell him, 'Your child is not here any longer. Look for him in...', and a prison in another city will be mentioned.

Once a month or sometimes less, my father travels to see one of his children. When he comes back home from a trip, it always takes him several days to regain his sense of equilibrium and throw off depression before he can relate his story. "I take a taxi from here to the bus station at the Caspian," he starts, "then catch the eight o'clock bus which drops me at the Karaj junction on the highway around 3 a.m. The weather is icy cold and while waiting for sunrise, I climb down to join the homeless under the bridge where they invite me to sit near their fires to keep warm, and offer me tea and a cigarette. These down-and-outers want to know if I am traveling for business purposes but I say, no, I am trying to find my children who are imprisoned. Feeling sad for my plight, they want to know what crimes my children have been accused of - did they murder someone? Or steal something? I answer that I wish that were the case, but no, my kids got in the way of Khomeini's horns and were gored by him. I warned my children, I tell them, but they didn't listen to me. Their problem is they think that if nothing else, at least by their death they can bring a change to their country and their memory will live on, but I say, once I die, no matter if the country is free or not, or if I am remembered or not, I am gone.

"At daybreak, I leave my new friends and take a minibus to downtown Karaj where I stand on the street corner and yell, 'prison, prison!' and sometimes even private cars stop to take me there. At the prison, there are hundreds of people lined up behind high walls with barbed wire at the top. Like me, these parents have brought all sorts of food - tea, fruit, chocolate, bread, milk, and cigarettes – which they share with their neighbors while waiting their turn to enter. In the queue of parents can be found doctors, engineers and lawyers; I am a little man among them and when I tell them I have lost one child and have three others in prison, they call me their champion and jokingly want to know how a peasant farmer such as me can have raised four children against Khomeini."

----

¹It is the custom in Iran for men to shake hands and kiss, first on one cheek then on the other, when they meet after a long time or they want to take their leave. Women greet each other in a similar fashion.

²I only saw my brothers once or twice during the long years they were in prison. I don't know why, but I didn't ask to go along with my father and I wasn't invited either; I think my parents were too occupied to consider taking me. The couple of times I did visit the prison, it was with an aunt or uncle, who took me as an afterthought.

~ * ~

Mirza fulfills his destiny

During high school, one day I am washing my clothes and shoes by the well when a group of sparrows swoops down from a tree, noisily fighting and circling around my feet. I pick up one of my shoes and throw it towards them, to startle them into flight. To my astonishment, the shoe hits one of the sparrows and drops it down, dead. I jump up and hurry to the bird; when I pick it up, it is lifeless.

While I am still thinking about what to do with it, I see my father walking into the yard from the main road, my brother Mirza at his side. My heart starts pounding and I am confused, not knowing if I should run and hug him or wait for him to approach me first. I stand transfixed, eyes glazed and glued to the spot, shoe in one hand and bird in the other. To this day, I have no memory of what I did with that bird. Mirza has just been released from prison after four long years and having learned to adjust to the independence afforded by my brotherless life, I have almost forgotten how to interact with him.

* * *

Little by little, Mirza and I renew our friendship and begin to take care of the farming chores together. He is closed mouthed about his time in prison, and if we ask him questions, he changes the subject[1]. He often moans in his sleep; that wakes him and he sits bolt upright and rigid for a long time, unable or unwilling to go back to sleep. Other times, in his nightmares, he pulls his legs towards his stomach with sudden violent, jerky movements as if the soles of his feet were the targets of a vengeful master, groaning until we shake him awake.

During the first months after his release, Mirza has to check in at the prison once a week, then every two weeks, and the intervals become farther and farther apart until he is told he no longer has to report in, but he needs permission from the Islamic Revolutionary Guards base to be able to leave the province.

With his life gradually returning to normal, Mirza finishes high school with honors only a few years after his classmates. Since with his background he cannot enroll in a government university, he enters the Islamic Azad University, which charges tuition but has fewer restrictions, and graduates four years later with a BA degree in Economics.

* * *

On the day before I am to leave Iran, knowing my father is coming to Tehran to say goodbye to me, Mirza, who now has the chance to see all his relatives together in one place, wants to take advantage of this occasion to prepare the way for his marriage. Being too shy to broach the subject, he insists I be the go-between and talk to my father and to his girlfriend's father, my neighbor in Tehran, on his behalf. I agree and he immediately calls his girlfriend to let her know, so she can ready the house for a formal marriage proposal.

Mirza's fiancé and her mother have already prepared a sumptuous meal prior to when my father, brother and I arrive. Except for bride's father, everybody in the family seems already to know that we are coming on a marriage proposal mission. After lunch, as I am about to take my leave, my father says, "Hassan agha, wasn't there something you wanted to tell your neighbor?"

At this, everybody stops conversing and focuses on me.

"What is it, Hassan? What do you want to say?"

"Well," I stammer. "As you know, I am leaving the country tomorrow but before I go, I have a mission to fulfill. My brother has a favor to ask of you and wants me to represent him."

"Ok?" queries the girl's father.

"I am talking about a camel that sits in front of everybody's house," I laugh. "And that is children falling in love and forming new partnerships. Today, I have the honor to present my brother's proposal of marriage to your daughter and ask you to receive him in your family as your son. He doesn't have a job yet since he just finished university but he has our father's support and is ambitious; I am optimistic that he will create a bright future for his wife, inshallah."

Mirza's future father-in-law agrees to the proposal and the two families decide to hold the ceremony soon, but unfortunately not before my departure.

Everybody is still visiting and chatting when I put the party behind me and hurry home to my wife who has been packing my luggage for the next morning's trip.

"You know?" she begins as I join her to help with the rest of the packing. "We just had this very last day to be together but you spent it away from home."

"Oh, come on. I had to go. This was Mirza's only chance."

"No, I am not complaining," she interrupts, her spirits low. "I just want you to remember that you left me alone on this memorable day."

"I know how you feel," I begin in a gentler tone to comfort her, smoothing her hair and putting my arm around her shoulders. "But let me tell you something. In this real world, you simply need to be realistic. I know you are strong, but you will have to be even stronger."

Leaning her head against my chest, she bursts into tears, saying, "I am missing you already."

In an effort to change her mood, I begin to laugh. "Well, well." I exclaim, raising my voice to tease her. "At least there is someone in this world who will miss me! Do you really love me?"

"What a question! You know I do. I have always loved you."

"You have? Let me hear it, then!"

"Hear what?"

"That you love me."

She smiles but doesn't say anything.

"You see? You don't."

"I do."

"Say it, then!"

"I love you!"

"That's my girl! Now get up and let's finish the packing. Not much time left."

As we resume packing, I notice the movie Robinson Crusoe playing in the background.

"Look at this movie," I tell my wife. "This man never gives up hope of surviving. Do you know why he fights so bravely for his life on this remote island? Because he knows how precious his life is, and if he doesn't fight for it, he will lose it. This movie teaches us not to despair in the face of new challenges. So I am asking you to be brave when conditions are against us."

"Just like the mullahs, you always have an answer for everything," she says, smiling. "God has been very kind to mankind by not choosing you as one of them! You could easily sway people to your belief system!"

----

[1]For the rest of his life, Mirza remains in constant fear of the Islamic Revolutionary Guards.

~ * ~

First personal failures; replacing bad with worse

But I'm getting ahead of myself.

It takes me several weeks to get used to my new environment in high school. The school is in a neighboring town near the beach on the Caspian Sea, and students come from many different towns and villages; it is a considerably different experience from the world of my country village school.

At first, I am so overconfident that I volunteer to answer my teachers' questions in the class without preparation. This includes problems in algebra, which isn't my best subject; I base my answers on what I remember from the lectures of a week before. After a few weeks, it becomes more difficult to solve the equations without preparation, so I gradually stop volunteering, walk away from the blackboard and remain silent in class.

Based on the Iranian school system, students are required to take final exams at the end of each of three months of schooling; during the nine-month educational year, we have three such exams. Although the scores on the last one carry the most weight, teachers often average the scores from all three.

For the first time in my life, I fail in three topics during the initial round of exams and do not know how I am going to explain this to my father. In spite of all the troubles we have made for him the past few years, he has always been proud of our performance in school and now I am going to have to confess my failure.

"I want to talk to you," I tell my father.

"Go ahead."

"It's very private."

"You mean your mother is a stranger?"

"No, I don't mean that. But I can't talk in her presence."

"What's wrong?" he asks, puzzled, with worry beginning to show on his face. "Did they kill Davood or Kaveh?"

Assuring him that it is no such thing and waiting for my mother to leave the living room, I blurt out, "I want to quit school."

"What?" he barks with temper. "Why?"

"I don't know," I answer prevaricating, "I just know I no longer wish to study."

"Die or finish your schooling," he shouts. "All these years I have been proud that my children were the best in the school.

Now you are telling me that you cannot finish. This hurts me even more than losing a child."

Trying to justify myself, I add, "Each person is talented in a particular way. Maybe studying is not my thing; maybe I should try something else."

"What for example?" he interrupts me angrily before I can say any more.

"I want to find a job and start working."

"Your job is your books," he roars again. "Do you understand me? I do not need your money. I'll work and if you know what's good for you, you'll finish school."

My father's yelling grabs Mirza's attention; he walks in to see what's happening. "What's going on?"

"Ask your brother," my father answers in anger and despair. "He wants to leave school and become a porter."

When he hears what I said to dad, Mirza, who can't believe his ears, says to me, "Go! Get out of here; let me handle this."

While he placates dad by immediately agreeing with him, I leave for the second floor. Soon Mirza joins me there. On hearing about my failed exams, he tells me I am trying to make a bad situation worse, but he promises to convince dad to forgive me this once, warning me not to ever again bring up the topic of quitting school. Although not happy about it, I have no choice but to concede to my father's wishes and go back to classes.

* * *

For three successive years, the secondary school authorities in my village almost exclusively planted in my brain the seeds of religion and ideas of a political Iran based on Islam. In the beginning of high school, I once ask my chemistry teacher if objects like water and soil are alive or dead. He is one of those somber teachers who never smiles; even though I am being serious, he looks at me as if he thinks I am joking. Then, he tells me in a very cold voice, "Sit down and behave yourself. You need to learn that this class is for serious study, not for fooling around."

Topics such as algebra, chemistry, physics, and math churn my stomach and keep me from feeling my best. I grow to dislike the teachers of these classes; most of whom have no sense of humor and don't seem to enjoy teaching. Even after all these years, I remember them as cold fish and I have never missed them or their teaching methods, which made learning a chore instead of an exciting experience.

Even worse than the teachers are our principal and vice-principal, who supported the Shah until he left the country, then, soon after the revolution, switched their loyalty to the Khomeini forces, thus assuring themselves improved work positions. Now, in accordance with the new politically correct religious mores, they are overly strict about our 'moralities'. We have to watch ourselves carefully not to break rules in case either they are close enough to catch us at it or another student rats on us. If we are caught accidentally offending them - and by extension, Islam - we can expect to be badly punished both physically and in terms of grades.

One of our courses is called Discipline; there is no studying for this course. The principal has a diary in which each student's name heads a separate page; it serves as the Book of Life for us. At the end of the year, he reviews all those pages and gives us grades based on the log of our daily behavior, grades which will influence the course of our future life. If we happen to fail in Discipline, the doors of other schools and of institutions of higher learning will be closed to us. Most of my marks in this course are just inches away from failing since I don't seem to be able to please either the principal or the vice principal. Points are given for getting involved in religious activities within the school, joining the school's young Basij group, and even attending Friday prayer in town, but none of these activities is attractive to me.

One day, after we have gotten to know the principal better and are used to his character, several of my close friends and I decide to play a practical joke on him. About a dozen of us go to his office and volunteer to join the school Basij club. He becomes angry and roars, "No! I will not allow you to make the office of obedient children a place for loafers." Then he chases us out of his office and tells us to stop clowning around. We no sooner walk out when we burst into loud laughter.

The same way I hate mathematical equations and rules, which require certain disciplines, I equally love literature and getting involved in religious discussions. During breaks, when there is enough time, a few of us gather in a corner of the schoolyard and write satirical lyrics, to which a crowd of our classmates contribute by laughingly proffering words and phrases. In our poems, we mock our friends, the principal, his assistant, and even a few of our teachers. We also write tributes to those few teachers whom we like. When our poems are finished, we entertain ourselves by reading them aloud to the sound of the hilarity of the other students who always eagerly ask for more.

My friend Masood and I once write a saga about our class, describing our classmates one by one. Our literature teacher, who is one of those named in the poem, invites us to read it before the class. I walk to the front of the room and read the long poem while both students and teacher laugh throughout the entire recitation.

In addition to reading and writing poetry, as a student, I spent my free time practicing Persian calligraphy in the room on the second floor. This became my room when I was the last child at home.

~ * ~

Immediately stricken by cupid's arrow; a duplicitous love

I manage to finish the first two years of high school and begin year three.

One day, holding a shock of my horse's mane in my hand, I head with him to our rice lands down along the riverbank. Crossing the road, I see three young girls walking southward; the one in the middle catches my eye and I am immediately stricken.

She is taller and thinner than her friends while her honey-colored eyes, so different from the dark brown common to my country, flash golden sparks from a face bronzed by the sun.

The three of them, in their identical uniforms, are returning home from school. I know, since students pass along this road all the time, they are headed for a neighboring village at the foot of the Alborz Mountain range. Without a secondary or high school in their area, these students have to walk more than forty minutes every day to attend classes in our village school, walking by our house in the morning and again in the afternoon; I know many of them but have never seen this particular girl before. I fix my eyes on her until I reach the far side of the road, turning my head to keep her in sight as they continue on their way behind me, talking. Watching her chat with her friends even though I can't hear what she is saying, I let this girl's lively smile steal my heart on the spot; oblivious, she and her two companions keep up their conversation without paying any attention to a love-struck boy and his horse.

"This is a girl for me," I say to myself and my heart begins to ache in my chest, making me feel uncomfortable, beside myself, and restless. As they get farther away and their figures disappear around the bend in the road, I feel as if a part of me is being carried away with her. I take the horse to the rice field in a flash and run back to the walnut tree beside the road, looking for somebody who might know the girl and can tell me something about her.

I am still under the tree when I see my cousin run into our yard from the direction of the market. Two years older than I, he works part-time in his father's bakery in the market near the school these girls attend. As a result, he knows almost everybody in the area, so he is the right person to help me. Nasser rushes up to me and seems to be as happy to see me as I am to see him. We position ourselves on the west side of the walnut tree facing the road so we can clearly see anyone who passes.

Before I can start talking, he asks me to watch out for two girls who will be coming our way in seconds. As we stare at the road in the direction they will approach, he describes one of the girls, quickly filling me in about her brothers and sisters, what year she is in school and so on. He says he has been trying to figure out a way to get her attention for quite a while with no success since she has mentioned to a go-between that she wants to finish her studies and go to university and so has no desire to get involved with a boyfriend. Nasser is still jabbering when, moments later, two girls appear from beyond our house. They are from the same village as the three young students who left earlier. My cousin asks me to take a look at the one he has been talking about and let him know if I think she is beautiful.

Unlike the other three, these girls, already covered in the Islamic veil, called chador, when they see us sitting there, make a point to bend their heads down and hide their faces deeper inside it. Unable to see their faces, I cannot tell my cousin what he wants to know. My non-committal comments upset him and he begins to berate me but soon drops his criticism and launches into his long and arduous struggles to conquer this girl.

Finishing his tragicomic story, he calms down a little and that gives me time to tell him about the beautiful girl I saw earlier. With the hope of convincing him to come along with me, I tell him that she and her two companions should still be on their way home so we can easily catch up to them, and he can tell me who she is. No matter how much I try, I can't get my cousin to agree since the girl he has his eye on is from the same village and he doesn't want her to think he is stalking her and thus blow his chances with her for good. We do the next best thing: we agree to meet the following day under the same tree and keep watch.

Our patience pays off after awhile. A few days later Nasser and I are sitting under our tree chatting when my 'tall young lady' passes by. I jab my cousin with my elbow to draw his attention to the girl, telling him in a low voice that she is the one who has stolen my heart. He looks at the girl but does not say anything until after she is out of earshot. When he is sure the girl is gone, he turns to me and says, "Hassan, you dog! She is the sister to the one I was describing!" We look at each other for a while and suddenly burst out into guffaws.

With time, my friendship with Nasser grows stronger. We have found a common ground that draws us closer together: we each like a girl from the same family. He longs, at any cost, to trap Parvaneh, the Persian word for butterfly, in his net, and I am frantic for a young beauty called Mona. The two are sisters who have been traveling and will continue to travel on the same road past my house everyday for nine successive months.

* * *

Hundreds of days pass over the next two years and neither of us has yet had the chance to talk to these girls. Nor do either of them give us any encouragement, making us more determined than ever to pursue them. As time goes by, crowds of students from all ages and from different schools see us sitting there under the same tree every afternoon - sun, rain or snow - and give us first puzzled looks, then stares, and then finally begin to jeer and laugh at us.

To break this deadlock, I ask a friend to pass a letter to Mona through his sweetheart whom we assume knows which girl we mean. When the girl with my letter waits for Mona to pass by on her way to school the next day, my friend and I are watching from a distance. As a long caravan of students is passing, Mona and her friends show up among them, but this girl makes no move to give her the letter. Then we see her about to pass the letter to a different girl. I holler to my friend, "Boro! Bodo! Go! Run! She is about to give the letter to the wrong girl!" My friend takes off running and stops her just in time.

After all my trouble, Mona later refuses to accept the letter.

* * *

On days when the weather is good for biking, Nasser and I go to his dad's bakeshop where his father and some of his younger brothers are working at the hot oven. Nasser asks his father for the key to the motorbike so we can go to Mona and Parvaneh's village. His father has no objections to us using the bike unless the bakery is unusually crowded and he needs either his son or me, or both, to help out.

Sometimes when Nasser is busy, I get hold of Mansoor or another friend to give me a lift to Mona's village, nestled among orange groves at the foot of the mountains. Although I know I cannot talk to her, I feel comforted when I am close to where she lives. To me this whole area, already beautiful in its own right, has a special quality simply because of its proximity to Mona. The miles between us seem short to me and I visit her village several times a week.

A pond beside the dirt road and behind Mona's house is filled with water during irrigation season, but during the dry season, it is used as a sports ring by professional wrestlers and kick boxers. People from neighboring villages get together at night to see these matches, giving me a legitimate reason for being around.

Figuring it will be in our interest, Nasser and I get to know Mona's brothers very well and we become friends. Sometimes they even invite us to come for a meal at their house; the invitation makes me wild with the hope of seeing Mona. On such days, which I feel are the best of my life, songs burst from my heart and out through my lips along the way to pick Nasser up from where he is impatiently waiting for me in his yard and together we travel to Parvaneh and Mona's house for lunch or dinner.

I am crazy in love with Mona and every glimpse of her twists cupid's arrow in my heart with sweet pain. I want to kiss the feet of the chickens which walk on the same soil she has walked on, as my father always says, referring to the passion a young lover has for his beloved.

* * *

In post-revolutionary days, we have to hide our interest in girls from everybody, from our parents, relatives, friends, and more importantly, from the Basij forces, who can arrest us if they find out. Times have changed since the revolution and the Revolutionary Guards no longer allow boys and girls to have any type of relationship with each other publicly, and the local people no longer approve of casual friendships. All the religious teachings for the past several years have sown a seed of guardianship in people; they think it is their duty to prevent their sons, daughters, sisters, and even their neighbors from having anything to do with the opposite sex. It sometimes happens that friends and relatives fight and even come to blows over a son of one trying to get close to the daughter of another. If, for example, I want to propose marriage to a friend's sister, he will usually be offended and accuse me of making friends with him only for the purpose of marrying his sister, thus abusing his friendship. These limitations, although they may sound strange to you, make any relationships we form very precious to us.

Girls have to be especially careful to keep their interest in their boyfriends strictly secret from their brothers and parents. Those who are marked as having had a previous relationship with a boy jeopardize their future. Almost nobody wants to marry a girl who has once been interested in another boy even if she and the boy have never touched, let alone kissed or had intimate relations.

Usually only best friends or confidants know about your relationships and since they may need you to keep their own confidences, they refrain from gossiping. In some cases, although neighbors and other friends know or partially know your intentions, they prefer to keep it a social secret so even though everybody knows, he or she pretends not to know.

There are cases when people will tell a girl's family her secrets; this is a problem which forces the aspiring suitor to either withdraw or fight for his love. Those few who fight and conquer make the battle sweet. I once had a friend who fell in love with a girl and decided to go to her family on his own to propose. He introduced himself to the parents, saying, 'My name is Noor, I have no money, nor business nor academic learning, but I have studied a lot of books, am politically minded and have the gift of gab. I have fallen in love with your daughter, that's why I am here'. The girl's brothers asked him to leave and return with his parents, which he refused to do, insisting he was mature enough to take care of his own future and didn't need his parents' help to run interference with this proposal. The brothers grabbed him by the arms and legs and threw him out into the darkness and rain. He was soon back, however, refusing to give up until finally the girl's parents realized he wasn't going to go away and they decided to let their daughter marry him. He turned out to be a successful and wealthy businessman.

But our situation is that Nasser and I are trying hard to keep Parvaneh and Mona's brothers from finding out about our interest in their sisters. Parvaneh, of course, knows how Nasser feels about her, but even she doesn't know about my feelings for Mona, and Mona is oblivious to Nasser's interest in her sister. At the same time, each sister is hiding her secrets from her parents.

* * *

In our own village, if the other boys and I find a strange boy around, we figure he is after one of the neighborhood girls. His presence might be completely innocent and legitimate, and the girl might have no idea she is the object of our attention, but it is our duty to protect her, so we stop the stranger and tell him to get lost. If he refuses to leave, it could get ugly; the 'rooster culture' might emerge and the cock we were encouraged to eat would bare its talons. The same thing happens in reverse if we find ourselves in a strange village. That is why Nasser and I work so hard to make friends not only with Mona and Parvaneh's brothers but also with other boys in their village, so we can visit the area unmolested. In such a suspicious environment, Nasser and I have a long way to go to reach our goals.

~ * ~

Migrating birds

Mirza is attending high school in our village and Davood, after being released from prison, has finished his high school studies in Tehran and received his diploma several years behind his generation.

For three successive years, I have failed in several topics including English, but now in my last year of high school, I renew my determination to finish with good grades. After such a long time of being rebellious and not putting my heart into studying, I suddenly feel the same desire to apply myself to my books as I used to during primary and secondary school. Although far from being a good student and not knowing the rules of physics, mathematics or chemistry that everyone else already knows, I work as hard as I can to raise my academic standing.

The first few months go well and I am making great progress, when another accident shocks the village. One evening a friend and his sister, who are also our relatives, take their younger brother by motorbike to a doctor in a neighboring town. Later that night, as the three of them are returning home on the bike, a minibus approaches them from the opposite direction and hits the bike head-on at high speed. My friend and his brother die immediately; their sister suffers major damage to her skull and goes into a coma.

This dissident family from our village has been plagued by calamity. The oldest son, a military pilot under the Shah, was executed by Khomeini soon after the domestic tensions swept the country early in the 1980s. His mother spent time in prison due to her earlier cooperation with the Mojahedin organization. Another son went to prison for a few years at the same time as my brothers, for fomenting Marxist ideas. One of the daughters wound up executed after years of incarceration and the other one finally escaped to Iraq. All these tragic events happened within a period of about seven years.

The villagers, who are forbidden to cry on the graves of any local dissidents, use the occasion of this accident, with its victims outside the stricture on mourning, to not only mourn them but mourn the dissident victims of the government as well. Thousands of people from the surrounding villages and towns gather, a crowd that is so large that the Basij, keeping a watchful eye on them, doesn't dare to interfere. For the traditional forty days, people feel free to release their long-pent-up emotions and no government forces try to stop them.

My cousins' death has a profound effect on my life and this affects my school study habits. I miss a few days of classes, and even when I return to school, I cannot get the sight of crushed faces and bodies out of my mind. Severely depressed, I find myself unable to focus on anything.

Around the same time, Davood returns from Tehran to say his goodbyes to the family. He says, since he can no longer live a normal life in Iran because of his background, he wants to leave the country. Although the news takes us by surprise at first, we gradually become used to the idea, and even see Davood's logic and are content with it. My father has praise for his son's decision and says he will offer his support as much as his resources allow. That same night, he brings the local butcher to our house, showing and offering to sell him two of our cows; the money from the sale goes to my brother. Other relatives contribute as well and soon Davood abandons the country forever.

* * *

Before I am able to overcome the trauma to my psyche caused by my friend's accident, and return to my books and begin afresh, several months have passed. Then one day after I am totally recovered and studying hard again, a couple of my close friends come to visit me.

Omid, the younger of the two, has won several gold and silver medals in the province in the 100-meter dash and distance running. He is the same boy whom my brother Kaveh appointed as group leader during one of our home meetings years ago. His brother Navid has just been released from prison.

We go to my room on the second floor and the brothers begin to talk. They are planning to escape to Iraq to join up with the Mojahedin organization and want to know if I am interested in going with them. The brothers say a messenger from the Mojahedin has come to the village to facilitate the moving of youths to Iraq. Even not knowing this messenger, both Omid and Navid are convinced he is reliable. They say they gave him a short phrase to be broadcast by Radio Mojahed, which was aired a few hours later; a common way used to test the reliability of the organization's representatives.

With the hope of changing their minds, I begin to argue that all the dissidents have already been crushed and, conditions being what they are, it is useless to continue resisting. The more I talk, the less the two brothers listen. They sincerely believe that even a government as strong as the Khomeini regime can be overthrown. My young friends counter-argue that in case they are not able to defeat Khomeini, their acts of defiance at least will be remembered by the next generation as symbols of resistance against such a forceful dictator; neither will they be put to shame in the annals of history for having laid down their lives for freedom. I agree that Khomeini is a dictator but I disagree that so few people can bring any changes. They retort that many of the people who are kept alive in history are part of this 'few' I have mentioned.

These friends of mine, whose brother has already been executed in prison, are so determined that I am obviously wasting my time trying to persuade them. I reach for my bag and come up with a handful of money I have saved from working in the fields, my contribution to helping them escape. Omid wants to know if he can borrow my sports handbag. I give it to him and with well wishes, hug them both goodbye, expecting it to be the last time I ever see them.

Navid joins several others and leaves the village, headed for Iraq. A couple of days later, Omid follows suit, leaving with the second and last group. Unfortunately, on the way to the neighboring town, he is spotted at a check post by Islamic Revolutionary Guards who transport him to their base. It appears the guards were fully aware of plans for the journey and were waiting to intercept the group. Under pressure, Omid agrees to cooperate with the revolutionary forces.

The next day when my friends and I get together to play chess under the walnut tree, we see Omid, whom we believed had left the province successfully, walking along the main road, accompanied by a different young man, not the messenger we previously saw. We can see that Omid is not his usual jolly self; his face is red and he is walking with his head hanging down, staring at the ground. When we call out to him, he passes us by with only a short, clipped smile. The two of them take the east fork of the road in the direction of Omid's house.

Several hours later, the first messenger from the Mojahedin organization appears again on the road near the walnut tree; he says he has come back to pick up Omid. It then becomes crystal clear to us that the young man whom we saw earlier with Omid was from the Islamic Revolutionary Guards. The messenger waits around hoping Omid will find a chance to lose his guard for a few seconds. This opportunity comes when the guard needs to take a leak. Before he can finish and zip up his pants, Omid has sprinted at his top speed and lost himself in the village, leaving the guard behind. He and the genuine messenger disappear like water in soil.

* * *

With them gone, the local youths soon forget about the past and the final traces of the Mojahedin organization are washed away from the face of our village. Navid and Omid leave Iran as if they have never been born. Not a trace of them remains. Their father has since died of a heart attack, one of their sisters is suffering from depression and a brother, once chosen as one of the top students in our province, begins to struggle with anxiety and eventually abandons his studies. Their sister, Hasti, the only one who survived without major emotional damage, grew up to become a social worker and her children have given new hope to an elderly mother who is now lonelier than God, as our local saying goes.

~ * ~

A journey of a thousand miles starts with the first step

Nasser, Parvaneh and I have finally graduated from high school but Mona still passes our house twice a day on her way to and from her classes and I am still waiting for the chance to talk to her at least once. This young village girl, whom I know likes me, continues to ignore me. All the years of waiting under the walnut tree, all the years of borrowing motorbikes to ride to her village, all the years of writing letters she will not accept, is wearing me down. She is only three years my junior, but growing up in a highly protected environment has made her years younger than her actual age. Unlike the girl on our tea farm, Mona seems to have spent her whole life absorbing and applying the lessons of religious teachers. She is afraid to let her brothers, her father, her neighbors, or even her very close friend, who passes our house with her twice a day, know her attraction for a boy.

The walnut tree becomes a sacred place for many of us; some days, there are more than a dozen boys milling around, chatting and 'girl watching'. To keep ourselves occupied, we take a couple of chessboards with us and play chess until late in the evening; certain games such as chess, which were forbidden after the 1979 revolution, are allowed again. Like me, many of these boys have graduated from high school and are in a holding pattern, waiting for our two-year mandatory military service to start. We have a void of several months to fill before we are conscripted.

With the supporters and members of political organizations gone from the village, life is more stable and we can spend pleasant hours together without the Basij forces intervening. Besides, with no one to chase, the priority of these forces has changed. They have begun to spend most of their time focusing on ways to control what they consider immoralities; we have to be extra careful and playing chess gives us a legitimate reason to gather in one corner of our yard close to the main road where school girls pass.

Nasser is the first one of us to be called up for military service and is sent to Tehran. Mansoor and my other close friends soon follow; next, it will be my turn. While I am waiting for my military service to start, I am also anxiously awaiting the Islamic Azad University's national entrance exam results, which will be published in major newspapers.

Taking advantage of this free time, I decide to visit an aunt and her family in Tehran. One day, I am squeezed inside a crowded Tehrani minibus, carrying commuters from Inqelab square to Azadi square, when I notice a passenger sitting in the middle of the bus, reading a newspaper. From where I am standing, I can see long columns of names and as he turns the pages, I read the large-print title and see the lists are the names of those who passed Azad's entrance exam successfully. I ask the young man to loan me the paper; he hands it over and I begin to look for my own from among the thousands of names. The minibus is moving fast and I am having trouble keeping my balance; with the newspaper in my hand, I lurch forward, fall back again and sway side to side when the driver brakes, swerves or accelerates to overtake other vehicles. Seeing me speed-search the pages as best I can, passengers become curious.

"Are you looking for your name or someone else's?" one of them asks.

"Mine."

"God willing, you passed," comments another.

"I sure hope so," I answer, my eyes fixed on the paper.

"Give the paper back to its owner," suggests a third person. "He has a seat and can find it faster than you."

Returning the paper to the young man, I give him my name, the name of the city where I took the exam, and the topic of the course, English. He searches the paper while I hold my breath, then looks at me and says, loud enough for everyone around us to hear, "Congratulations! You have passed the exam!"

Passengers clap for me and congratulate me, saying, 'tabrik, tabrik, mobarak'! The news shocks and pleases me, but I feel a little shy and embarrassed by the well wishes and other inquisitive questions of my fellow passengers. Not sure how to respond, I mumble 'merci, tashakor, mamnun', causing people to start laughing and telling one another that the poor fellow is too overwhelmed by the news to think – 'hol kardeh bandeh Khoda'!

A couple of days later, going back home to my village, I walk into our yard to see my mother, sitting on the stairs of the veranda, burst into tears of joy; one of my friends has already given my parents a copy of the newspaper so they have anticipated my news. As she struggles to stand up, I run to the veranda and, grabbing her, we give each other a big hug. She takes my hand in hers, and pulls me with her into the living room, offering me tea and snacks.

We are busy chatting when we hear my father's voice coming from the yard, calling 'Hanna!' 'Hanna!' as is his habit. Hearing him, my mother calls out loudly and tells him that I am home. He rushes up to the veranda saying, over and over, 'well-done Hassan jan, well-done!' After embracing and kissing me, he holds my hand and tries to circle around me[1]. I take hold of him and stop him; we kiss each other on both cheeks again and again. He is so much shorter that, when we embrace again, his head lays against my chest as if he is a baby resting in my arms. He is beside himself with joy and tries to kiss my hands, but once again, I stop him. Finally, following the many years of tension and the losses he endured because of the revolution, my father is looking at a success; I am the first one in all the generations of his family who will be experiencing the life of a university student. My parents are so happy that they cannot speak for minutes; I have given them renewed hope and they believe at last this couple is going to experience an honor it has deserved.

In congratulation, many people in the village invite me to lunch or dinner and extend their best wishes. During the silence of the post-revolutionary years in which our neighbors did not even dare to work for us, now it is remarkable to see how happy the villagers are at my success. Nevertheless, they encourage and urge me to work extra hard with the goal of filling all the empty places in our home left by my brothers.

* * *

In autumn, I move to the city and begin my first year of college. After years of hating desks, chairs, benches, and blackboards, I begin to like the atmosphere of the classroom again. At the university, there are not so many restrictions as before and teachers do not call our parents if we happen to play hooky from time to time.

Boys and girls sit beside each other in class and I begin to understand what my father meant when he would say, 'the opposite sex makes the environment more beautiful'. However, most of the young students seem to mirror my own background; we all feel the burden of morality on our shoulders. Although we, as young girls and boys, are eager to talk to our classmates of the opposite sex, we struggle to shed the ingrained wariness put on us by the mullahs, and we fear the university Basij students among us who, if they see us breaking morality codes, call us to their office with warnings or expel us from school.

In the beginning, I am totally lost in my classes. Our teachers speak English exclusively and I have no idea what they are talking about; feeling it to be very embarrassing to admit to my limited English skills, I do not want to ask my friends, whom I have known for such a short time, for help. I take a look at those around me and notice all of them are listening very intently to the instructors; immersed in the lectures, they do not look around at me, even though I know they see me looking at them. Sometimes when a couple of students laugh at something a teacher says, the whole class follows suit and starts laughing. I have no idea what they are laughing about, but to save face, I join them.

At the end of every class, teachers give us assignments. One day when I feel more comfortable with the boy sitting beside me, I ask him about the homework. His face turns red and he begins to speak abruptly, saying he has been busy writing and did not catch what the teacher said. Then both of us turn to a third person beside us. He also pretends he was busy taking notes and does not have any idea what the homework is about.

During the break, I go hunting for a certain student who, being better able to converse in English with the teachers, is always one of the first to laugh at comments. Although his English is not very accomplished, he is levels ahead of most of the rest of the class. I find him in one corner of the yard surrounded by several of my classmates, explaining the joke that generated the laughter. Once he finishes the translation to Persian, all those students who laughed in class now burst out in true amusement, they just now get the point of the story.

Before I have a chance to ask about the homework, the students who are closer to him have already asked and are waiting for answers. It is then I realize I am not that far behind the others and decide to devote myself to my studies, spending more than sixteen hours a day with my nose buried in my books.

'To circle somebody represents love and respect for that person. It also shows a form of worship as we see in the Moslem pilgrims who circle a house in Mecca. To show equal respect to the people who want to encircle us, we politely request them to stop.

~ * ~

Sad but true; they are not here

Before autumn ends, feeling homesick, I decide to visit my parents since there is still no telephone in our home and it is hard for us to keep in touch with each other. Catching a bus going as far as a neighboring town by the Caspian Sea, I head to my province.

Stiff from sitting so long, I alight and walk towards the taxi stand where I come face to face with a neighbor who was also my teacher years ago in high school and who wants to know the reason for my trip at a time when schools are open.

"I am using several free days to visit my parents," I explain.

"So, you haven't heard the news?"

"What news?"

"Oh, never mind. How is school?"

"Not bad."

Then, he begins to congratulate me on my enrollment at the university, wishing me well for the future and reminding me that I am the new hope of my family. He says, "Your father has suffered through a lot of terrible conditions in his life in order to raise his children. Now it is your turn to support him. He may need your help now more than ever. He is growing older and you should act more responsibly towards him and your mother."

We continue to talk until the taxi drops us beside our house where we separate and I walk into our familiar yard. The old house seems handsome to me after not seeing it for months; I realize separation has caused me to love every board, every window, every door, and the way the veranda steps lead to the upstairs. I look around the yard holding my bag in my hand; there's the pear tree I picked fruit from when we had visitors, there are the fig trees with their luscious fruit, and over there the small orange grove my father planted in our front garden last spring.

After soaking in the sight of all aspects of the yard and buildings, I turn and step up onto the veranda, leave my shoes in the corner and enter the living room, calling, 'mom, mom'! My mother, who is sitting in her usual place on the floor beside the samovar and behind the door, turns when she hears my voice and reaches out for my hands. I sit alongside her on our worn carpet and she kisses my face, my forehead, the top of my head and my hands. Then I get up and go to my father who is waiting anxiously to embrace me; we hug each other tightly. Overjoyed, and like my mother, he kisses me on and on and even tries to kneel down to kiss my feet, which I prevent by holding onto his arms.

While he is calming down a bit, I walk over to a neighbor who happens to be visiting my parents. We shake hands and he congratulates me on being the man of the family and praises me for the hope I am bringing to my parents after their many years of hardship.

Finally, I turn to my uncle who is impatiently waiting his turn. With all his strength, the old man, considerably older today than the last time I saw him, pulls himself up straight to stand before me. He is too short and too arthritic to reach me, so I bend down to his face and we kiss each other. His embrace stretches out; then suddenly, his face on my chest, he bursts into sobs. "They killed all of them. They killed Kaveh," my uncle murmurs, choking on his tears, repeating this again and again. His words shock me to the core.

My father interrupts and tries to calm his oldest brother, "Hassan has just arrived and is very tired; let him rest first. I will talk to him later."

It is already too late for that; I urgently press them for the whole story.

"Take a deep breath, my dear Hassan," my father begins, going on to explain, "It was not only Kaveh; Ali, Farbod, Shirin and Reza, along with many others were executed in prison. This is life, my child. I want you to be strong. Don't let such happenings get you down, Hassan. Look to your future and build on it. We are counting on you. Keep your head down, lead your own life and don't go looking for trouble. I can't take more losses. Do you hear me? What is broken is broken; what is spilt is spilt; we must move forward with what we have left. We still have you and Mirza. We also have our dear Davood. I expect you all to fill your brothers' empty places in our home."

My poor dad talks so patiently that I can hardly believe he is the very same furious father I have always known. Through the pain in his voice, I feel him trying his best to fill me with hope for the future.

Not wanting my parents to see the impact this account has made on me, I leave the room to give myself some quiet time to assimilate the news. Kaveh had already spent six or seven years in prison, and the government had pardoned the last twelve years, leaving him less than two years left to serve. Now, this unforeseen execution has robbed me of the hope of seeing my brother again. I go to see a friend whom I think probably is aware of what happened. He adds several other names to my father's list; these men and women, like Kaveh, had also been prisoners during those same six-plus years. My friend says, "As you have heard from the media, the Mojahedin, now based in Iraq, launched a massive attack against the Khomeini regime. In retaliation, the Khomeini forces have executed thousands and thousands of political prisoners across our country."

Now I know why the Mojahedin organization was gathering their forces and moving them to Iraq. The leaders of the organization initiated their attack soon after the government of Iran accepted a ceasefire after eight years of bloody war with its neighbor. If Saddam Hussein, a mighty power at that time, had not been able to invade Iran even with the help of the chemical and mechanical weapons he had received from western countries, how did the leaders of the Mojahedin figure they could capture our country with the help of a mere few thousand paramilitary forces, as they had announced publicly? Unknown numbers of the Mojahedin were killed in this ill-fated attack with only about three thousand militants escaping the massacre and drawing back to their bases in Iraq.

It is the second time that the Mojahedin organization has failed in their handling of mass movements. The first time was during the domestic war in the early eighties and had been a resounding defeat. To this day, its leaders vainly declare both of them victories. I have a hard time believing an organization, which once had millions of followers, could so carelessly throw away the trust of their loyal supporters and the entire nation.

* * *

A few days after Kaveh is executed, the Islamic Revolutionary Guards send a message to my father asking him to report to their headquarters where he is blindfolded at the main gate and led to a small room. When the blindfold is removed, he sees two people awaiting him beside an old iron bed in one corner, which he feels is not an ordinary bed since it is not something one could sleep on, and the thought passes through his mind that it has been the site of torture sessions. He is asked to sit and answer their questions.

"How do your neighbors know what is happening in your house?" they ask.

He stands up in protest and wants to know why they are asking such a question. "Do you think my son was reporting events from inside this prison?"

"Sit down," they order. "You are here to answer questions, not to ask them. How do your neighbors know what is happening in your house?"

"Maybe, they keep a watch on it."

"What if they cannot see inside your house and still know about your daily affairs?"

"What should I say? I don't know."

"How do America and Israel know about what happens inside our country?"

"You mean my child, who has been in your prison for more than six years, made reports to the American government?"

"No, he did not. But your child was glad to see our enemies invade our country. What should we do with such children?"

175

"If you have killed my child, just tell me that you have done this and show me his grave, because I don't want to take more of your time."

Handing him a few of Kaveh's possessions, they say, "Go home and take care of the rest of your children. Keep in mind that you are not permitted to hold any kind of mourning ceremonies in your house; in fact, allowing people to gather in your home for any reason is strictly forbidden. If you meet our demands, at a later date we will show you where your son is buried."

My father assures them that he is too busy making a living to worry about attending any mourning get-togethers for his son. "But," he adds, "My wife is disabled and neighbors come to see her routinely; I can't stop them from visiting."

* * *

Months pass and my father is called in once again. This time, the Islamic Revolutionary Guards give him a piece of paper on which a number is scribbled. "Go to the Garden of Heaven in Rudsar," they say, "and look for this number. Your son is buried in that cemetery."

With the paper in his hand, my father locates the cemetery and looks for his son's gravesite. He travels among headstones but does not find number 22. Then he asks a young passerby for help. The man, after hearing the story from my father, tells him that such bodies are not buried inside the main cemetery court. He then takes my father to a remote part of the garden where rows of black cloths have darkened the ground; each with a stick planted at one end, bearing a number. Pointing out one of them, the young man says, "Your son is here." Then, he is gone.

My father kneels down near the black cover and begins to dust it with the palms of his hands. "Kaveh jan, salam," he mutters, "it's me; your father. I am here to say sorry because I am responsible for your death. I have killed you, my son. I personally surrendered you to the guards. But ... but I just wanted to help you. I am sorry. I wish you had been killed in the mountains along with your brother Darius; at least I wouldn't be blaming myself now. My very dear Kaveh, you are not a father and do not know how I feel. Last time when I visited you in prison, you assured me you would be released soon. What happened, then?"

In this miserable condition, my father is still crying when he hears voices coming to him from the shores of the Caspian; looking up towards the sounds and seeing a crowd of moaning people, he moves closer and learns that a young fisherman has drowned. Consoling himself with the thought that there is a season for dying for each person, whether in prison or in the sea, and that his child has fulfilled his destiny, lessens the burden he carries. He turns and walks home.

Each time my father visits Kaveh's grave, he tells us how the families of other victims have swept all the gravesites clean, sprinkled them with rosewater and put flowers on every single black cloth.

Then one day, he walks into the cemetery yard through the big iron gate to see several bulldozers and loaders working around the number which my father visits regularly. He searches all around carefully for his child's grave but does not find anything; there are no traces of graves anymore. He sits in the place where he believes his child was buried, and tears flow from his eyes. As he cries, some of the local workers come up to him to see what's wrong.

"I had a child who was younger than you are," my father tells them with a catch in his throat. "He was as strong as you are and worked on the lands with me for years. A good student, I was never worried about his grades. I would have sold my eyes to make sure he had an education. I went hungry to give him a better life than I had. I know I was not able to give him as much as he deserved but I did my very best to provide for him. Like his brothers, he stood against the Khomeini regime, and Khomeini killed him. I'm not saying the government shouldn't have killed my child; he was punished for what he did. But I have the right to cry on my child's grave. My child was here the last time I visited this place. Right here. Now I can't find him."

He starts sobbing again. The workers give him a drink of water and tell him that they have been digging in that part of the cemetery to prepare for construction and found no bodies under the soil.

My father walks away knowing his child is buried in an unidentified place like thousands of others, although to this day, he still hangs on to a tiny thread of hope that Kaveh, as well as Darius, are still alive somewhere.

~ * ~

Rats are everywhere, so are nets!

My cousin Nasser, who is done with his two-year military service, confesses to his family his feelings for Parvaneh and asks them to present her parents with a formal marriage proposal. Nasser and Parvaneh marry soon afterwards and on the strength of his success, I feel closer to my goal of a legal union with Mona.

I finally work up the nerve and write another letter to Mona, asking Nasser's sister to hand it to her. A couple days later, Nasser comes over and says he has something to discuss with me; he begins to talk about life's responsibilities as we walk southward along the main road. After only a few days of marriage, suddenly he is talking to me like a father to a son. Taking my letter out of his pocket, he holds it in one hand and uses it to slap the palm of the other to emphasize his logic. "Now that I am part of Mona's family," he says, "I feel as if she is my own sister and I am responsible for her, so it's no longer proper for you to court her through my contacts." He then proffers me the folded paper. Exceedingly offended, I turn abruptly and leave him alone on the road.

I find Nasser's action so selfish that the next day I leave the village for the university and, for months, do not come back to see Mona. One day after I talk about this to Abdullah, who has been my roommate for the past two years, he says, "You are angry with the person you love merely because of what your cousin has done? This is neither logical, nor fair to Mona. I suggest you go back to the village and talk to her in person before making your final decision."

Feeling happy to find a reasonable excuse to go after 'my love' again, I write a letter, put it in my pocket and travel back home, determined to give it to Mona in person.

* * *

I have been sitting under the walnut tree for a couple of days, the letter in my pocket, when two men show up in our yard; I ask how I can help them.

"We are teachers in the adult education program recently reopened by the government. Your father, one of our students, has suddenly disappeared, causing many others to withdraw as well."

"Why?"

"Many of them are your father's friends, and only come to class because they like his wit and sense of humor. We are glad to find you here today so you can help us convince your father to return, since we have been unsuccessful in our attempts."

I call my father to the yard to talk to his teachers. From the veranda, he runs with a smile to greet them and invite them in for tea and snacks. Holding their hands in his, he shows his appreciation for their persistence, saying, "I am so grateful to you for coming. You are like my children and I am proud of you for truly serving people."

"So, you will come back, then?"

"I'd really love to but please understand that I cannot, although I cannot explain why, I am really unable to continue."

"Why, Dad? What's happened? You told me you liked your class."

"I still do. And I have a lot of respect for my teachers who have come all the way to our village to teach me and others who missed out on school as youngsters. I am fully aware that being illiterate as I am is a type of blindness and these teachers have the ability to open my eyes." Turning to them, he adds, "I have no doubt about your goodwill but please accept it from me that I really can't go on." Heads down, the two instructors walk away.

I ask my father, "If you like your class and your teachers so much, why have you changed your mind, then?"

"I couldn't tell them," he starts, 'but let me tell you why I suddenly hated the class. It was going very well and I liked the stories in the books so much I often volunteered to talk about them before the class. Even though I was terrible about writing, I was good at speaking about the stories we learned. But suddenly we reached the story of this mullah coming to Iran and we had to read the poem, 'Khomeini, O Imam, Khomeini, O Imam,' and I couldn't force myself to let this man's name slip off my tongue. And because I couldn't tell my teachers about my reaction, I came home."

Saying this, my father returns to the living room and I resume my place under the walnut tree, when suddenly I see Mona walking home from school with her old classmate. I wait until they take the fork to their village, and then run to a friend's house to borrow his motorbike.

Mona and her friend are walking on the dirt road surrounded by freshly greened trees and vast tea farms when I spot them from a distance behind. The closer I get to her, the more frightened I feel; we have never exchanged even one word in the several years we have known one another and now I am planning to give her a letter stating my intentions. 'Here's a letter for you,' I think, 'no, this is not good. What if she doesn't accept it? A better way is to pass her and her friend, drop the letter in front of them and speed away; then she will have to pick it up'. My hands begin to tremble and every now and then I lose control of the bike so it wobbles and I have to concentrate on what I am doing to keep from falling.

I make up my mind, take the letter out of my pocket and keep it in my hand, ready to drop. By this time, the two girls are near a bend in the road, which would be an ideal place; I can drop the letter and quickly disappear. Driving very slowly, I approach them from behind and while passing them, I look at Mona. Our eyes lock for a second; immediately she looks at the ground and I, in fear and uncertainty, direct my eyes away from her and move forward about ten meters. 'Idiot! Drop the letter now,' I whisper to myself. But I just can't do that, 'what if she doesn't pick it up?' Not knowing what else to do, I stop the bike and turn back, thinking aloud, 'I must give this letter to her today'. I ride towards them, stop the bike in front of Mona and, without saying a word, I stretch out my hand to give her the paper, now folded and damp from the sweat of my palm. The two girls hide their faces inside their chador and pass me while my hand, with the letter in it, hangs in the air. 'What happened?' I think, 'she rejected my letter; did I do something wrong'? I look back at them, still hoping she will return; they disappear behind the bend without even looking back. I scrunch the paper into a ball, put it back in my pocket and drive home in anger and frustration.

Convinced that Mona does not plan to budge, I tire of the situation, leave for school and put her out of my mind.

* * *

The day, during my third year at the university, when one of my friends from a neighboring village, who was also a classmate of mine in high school, enrolls in the same institution, I ask my roommates if he can join us in the house where we live. Some six of us are living in a fairly spacious house surrounded by a yard with grapevines, cherry and fig trees scattered about. The landlord, an employee of the university, resides in a house he owns on the other side of the city and we feel totally free in his rental to do as we please. Being very talkative by nature, my roommates usually defer to me by unspoken agreement, and I wind up managing most of the affairs of our living quarters. They have no objections to my suggestion and my friend soon moves in with us.

Our newest roommate, Parviz, is not very cooperative in the house, often not paying his share of the expenses and not willing to help out with chores, but because he is an old friend of mine, we all tolerate him. With his outgoing personality, he soon makes friends with lots of students, especially girls; he is wild about girls. He laughs and jokes in an attempt to get their attention, which offends not only the authorities but also some of the guys whose girlfriends are targets of his clowning around. Several times, the Basij of the university have had to warn him to behave himself.

* * *

One day, Parviz tells me he has planned something that will be great fun for everybody, a night at the movies and wine. He has invited several of his local friends, saying they have homemade wine and porn movies but have no place to get together safely. Although drinking is strictly forbidden in Iran, we sometimes risk a party with alcohol. I talk to everybody in the house for a consensus, except Abdullah whose father was the butcher who purchased our cows when my father was gathering money for Davood to leave the country. Abdullah has become our roommate simply because our fathers know each other, although at the time he entered the university we did not know that he used to work for the Basij forces in his hometown and by the time we find out, he is already our roommate. Being sociable and warm, his staying doesn't bother us; besides, we think having him with us is a sort of security against being hassled by the Basij.

I ask my roommates what they think. They are of the opinion that we should not mention anything about the wine to Abdullah. However, they say he may like the movies since he has a reputation as a playboy. Going to Abdullah, I tell him about the movies; he feels affronted and states that watching such movies is a rebellion against God. I tell him coldly to move to another room if he does not want to watch the movies. Although angry, he finally leaves, sequestering himself in another room; we settle down to our porn movies, a first experience for many of us. Greedily downing quantities of a wine exemplary by the standards of what is available anywhere on the black market, with our eyes glued to the screen of our small black-and-white television, we are primed for the occasion.

We are still enjoying ourselves into the early evening when Abdullah, our Basij friend, leaves his room and goes outside to get some fresh air. An hour or so later, he returns and goes directly back to his room without speaking. Hardly any time has passed when somebody knocks on the door. I open to face one of Abdullah's friends, Heydar, who works for the university Basij office, while the others, as soon as they hear the visitor's voice, are busy turning off the TV and hiding all signs of the party. Heydar thrusts his head inside the door and looks around the entranceway, spying all the shoes piled upon each other in the doorway. He declines our invitation to come in and says he needs to speak with Abdullah. Seconds later, Abdullah greets his friend and invites him in; again, he refuses, saying he doesn't want to disturb the guests and the two of them can talk better outside. They disappear.

Once Abdullah is gone, some of us go to the rooftop to look for any suspicious movements around the house, thinking he and his friend may have gone to the Komiteh, a military body that deals with immoralities. From there we spot a young man, whom the local boys know as a Basij member, standing around closely watching our front gate. We run back and start getting rid of all the party things, packing the VCRs in bags, pouring the wine down the sink, washing the glasses, opening the windows for fresh air and generally cleaning up. Then we wait for darkness so Parviz's friends can take the VCRs and depart.

The next morning, the dean who, because he used to be a colonel during the Shah and now applies military-like strict rules and regulations to the university, calls for us and asks if we were watching pornography the night before. We deny watching forbidden movies, saying they were merely educational and were good for improving our English language skills. Although he knows we are not telling the truth, he decides to let us go this one time and warns us not to let it happen again.

A report like this could get us expelled from the university. Being thoroughly miffed at Abdullah, before the day is over, we catch up with him on campus and give him a couple of days to find somewhere else to live. Who would believe my roommate with whom I had shared my longing for a girl could sell us out so cheaply!

Heydar, Abdullah's friend, comes to us later in the day and tries to convince us that Abdullah is innocent of ratting on us, saying he is the one who reported everything to the dean of the university, not Abdullah. He says, "I was determined to send you to jail and to get you kicked out of the university, but you were lucky; it was a holiday and I was not able to get a home search permit from a responsible body in the Komiteh in time. Now that everything is over, I request you not to turn Abdullah out of his room."

"What we do in the privacy of our home is our own business," I tell him, "and we don't want rats living in our house. Without Abdullah, how would you have known what we were doing?"

In spite of his continued insistence, my roommates and I hold our ground and push Abdullah to leave. No sooner has he left than our landlord asks us to evacuate his house.

* * *

With this one exception, university life hums along uneventfully. One day when I decide to visit my parents again, my friend Parviz asks me to deliver a package to his family and say hello to them while I am there. During my stay, taking a trip to his village to see his family, I walk into a yard surrounded by a wide variety of fruit trees and colorful flowers, calling out to see if anybody is home.

After a few moments pass, a young woman appears on the veranda, smiling gently at me in greeting. Being at home, she is not in hijab but wearing a yellow T-shirt and a long black skirt and her uncovered hair falls in waves over her back and shoulders. Her eyes are a bright golden nectar shining out of a charming, dark-complexioned face. She is tall, solid and the female curves of her chest are so attractive that I almost fall over in a faint.

"Hello. You must be Hassan."

Smiling, I say, "And you must be a magician."

"Why?"

"You know my name even before I introduce myself."

"Ah, I see," she exclaims, delighted. "Actually, my brother called to tell me to expect you."

"And here I am, bearing gifts."

"How is Parviz doing?"

"Great! Bam's eggplant doesn't decay!"

We both burst into laughter at this familiar Persian saying[1]. She looks down on me from the veranda while I stand a short distance away in the yard, giving her a slightly censored version of news about her brother and our university life. Every once in awhile as I talk, I take my eyes off the ground and look directly into hers. Every time I do, she is looking at me so prettily it takes my breath away. Her beauty lures me, like a bird, into her net. I want to know her name. With her attractive smile 'trembling the foundation of my being' as we Iranians say, she tells me her name is Donya. We chat for a while about school and her ambitions for her life while I say nothing of consequence since her presence has me tongue-tied.

In spite of wanting to stay longer, I finally say goodbye and, my mind captivated with the picture of her face, I turn to leave when her laughter brings me back.

"What?" I ask in surprise.

"Are you taking the package you brought from my brother back with you?"

"Ah, I am so sorry."

"You sure are!" she chides me humorously.

Giving her the package, I walk out of their spacious yard, my feet not touching earth. I am leaving but my heart is already pulling me back.

----

[1] In Persian, 'bademjun e Bam afat nadareh. Humorously, you are saying nothing has happened/is happening /will happen to the person in question.

~ * ~

Shall I compare thee to a summer's day?

By the time I am only a few steps away from my bachelor's degree in English translation, the results of my hard work are gradually becoming evident. Although still a long way from reaching my personal goal, I have managed to draw the attention of the majority of my professors. To see if I can, I try my hand at translating Shakespeare's sonnet 18, 'Shall I compare thee to a summer's day?' I read the translation to my friends and they encourage me to show it to my instructor one day during a translation class; he is quite pleased with my work. Buoyed, I find the courage to share it with another professor whom I highly respect. Having received his PHD in English from the US, this instructor is on the board of those who decide what English material will be included in the country's schoolbooks. In the two years he has been my English teacher, besides teaching me a lot about translation skills, he has always been a source of inspiration, praising my work and urging me on to greater and greater success. I take my Shakespeare to him. Very impressed, he asks me if I will allow my translation to be published in one of the Iranian literary magazines; this possibility thrills me.

Once published, my translation is distributed all across the country. My friends bring copies to the university and tack one on the notice board in the hall as a message of inspiration for other students. That work becomes my final project at the university and I walk away elated after the long years of study to wait out the due time to start my military service[1].

* * *

While I am at home waiting, with nothing much to do, Donya and I keep in touch with each other by phone or I travel to her village on some pretext or other. We become more than friends; both of us clearly know this although we don't dare speak about it. Having a telephone at home now, our communication is a lot easier; I call her late at night and, with my talkative nature and her great sense of humor, we chat for hours, never tiring of such meetings. The more we talk, the deeper I fall for her; yet still, I am not brave enough to declare my love nor have I had the courage to touch her.

One day, determined to openly give her a marriage proposal, I set a time to meet her. When I walk into their yard, she is listening to a Persian song whose lyrics go: 'from among two lovers, my heart and I don't know which one to choose; this way to go, that way to go?' Hearing my voice coming from the yard, she turns off the tape player, leaves the room and walks out to the veranda.

During our usual chat in a quiet corner of their orchard, I suddenly brave unknown waters and say, "I want to put into words the message our hearts and eyes have been sending each other."

Breathing a bit fast and looking somewhat startled and uncomfortable, she asks, "What message?"

"You are clever enough to know what I am talking about. Don't pretend to be a fool."

"I am one," she interrupts me, smiling. "Otherwise, I wouldn't be talking to a na mahram[2] boy like you in this garden."

We both grin while I search my mind to find a suitable way to go on. "I will begin my military service soon and may not be able to meet you as often."

"May God's hands be with you!" she exclaims in amusement. "So you have come here to ask for forgiveness? But, you know? You are too late; the war with Iraq is already over. It's a pity though; we could have called an alley 'Martyr Hassan's Alley'! And what a glorious funeral ceremony we missed!"

"I am here to make sure that you will also cry on my coffin!"

"I will; don't you ever doubt it! I will also buy a new black dress to wear just for your sake! For forty days! And even longer until you send me a message from Heaven telling me it's enough! But please ask your angels to deliver your message quickly; it's not fair to keep people crying!"

"Enough kidding. I am serious; I want you to marry me."

Her face turns red and suddenly she is almost panting. Saying nothing, she busies herself with a piece of fruit to keep from looking at me. When she does begin to speak, she slowly says, "Hassan, we are friends. More than this, you are my brother's pal. You must not take advantage of his friendship. I don't want to give you any kind of false hope, nor do I want to promise something that I cannot fulfill."

I see she is insulted but not angry and hurry to assure her my intentions are honest and I do not want to take advantage of her, saying, "In all the time we have known each other I have never tried to abuse our friendship. There is nothing wrong with wanting to marry you."

"But I don't want to marry; not now, not ever."

"Why? Do you want to become a 'virgin sister' in a holy place?"

"Something like that!"

Asking her to think about my proposal, I say goodbye. Yet as the days go by she grows colder and more distant, leaving my head full of bewilderment and chaos. I cannot believe she does not love me back. We have spoken and behaved like real sweethearts, but now she is telling me that she doesn't want to marry. We draw a bit apart, during which time I use all my persuasive ability to change her mind.

Gradually, she gets over her pique and we start our long chats afresh. I am allowed to talk to her about anything I want except marriage; whenever I bring it up, she changes the subject. Soon after that, I leave for the capital to fulfill my military obligation.

* * *

A year or more of my military service has passed when I receive a phone call from my father telling me his brother, my uncle who has been a part of our lives as long as I can remember, is gone.

"Hassan, please don't reproach me, but I have to tell you not to grieve about your uncle, who has been released from the pains of this life."

"No, don't tell me that. How?" I ask, memories marching through my mind of how he would side with my brothers and try to protect them from my father's anger, how we used to roast potatoes on his fire while he sang to us and told us stories, and even how forgiving he was when we played tricks on him.

"What is this silence?" My father's voice brings me back. "His was a long and full life. I will go too, when my time comes. You know what I did for his memorial ceremonies?"

Trying to focus on my father's words, I say, "Tell me."

"I didn't invite any Mullah to come and deliver a eulogy. And listen carefully, I want you to do the same for me when I die. Don't waste your money on any Mullah, spend it on musicians to play and sing on my grave."

"What's the point?"

"Mullahs take your money and make you cry, but for the same money, a musician makes you happy."

"Dad, thank you for trying to lighten my mood; don't worry, I just need time to absorb the news."

* * *

I still call Donya and we talk on the phone for long periods. We also meet whenever I go home. I haven't changed my mind about her; she remains my one hope and desire. I finally tell her that I have decided to talk to her brother and tell him I want my parents to visit his and ask for the hand of their daughter in marriage.

A few days later, I track down Parviz in Tehran in spite of Donya's opposition. His answer shocks me. "I never expected you to betray me," he tells me in a sad tone. "We have been closer than brothers. You could go to my house any time you liked, whether I was home or not. Now you are telling me that you were in touch with my sister during all these years. You have no sisters and do not have any idea about the responsibility of being a brother. But let me tell you that from now on, you have destroyed my ability to trust anybody when it comes to my sister."

Trying to calm him down, I say, "We have been friends all these years without me even thinking of betraying you. I have had no intimate relations with your sister. We happened to fall in love with each other, which is not something predictable. Before today was not the time to talk about it. Now I am asking for your permission to be allowed to send my parents for a formal proposal."

Parviz says he will not agree to it. He feels very offended, believing I have strengthened my friendship with him merely because of his sister.

"We were friends before I knew your sister," I explain, "and it is not true that I have used you to get closer to her. I cannot see any problems with a friend marrying his friend's sister, anyway."

Parviz and I had become very tight back in high school; by the time we were in university together I was helping him out of scrapes, tutoring him for classes and lending a hand with his chores. Now, he dares accuse me of making overtures of friendship because of Donya, not for his sake. After an hour of debate, I finally convince him to talk to Donya and he promises to give me an answer later.

* * *

Before Parviz can get back to me, I hit up another friend for advice about the situation. I tell him everything while he smokes and listens to me in an odd silence all the way to the end of my story. At the conclusion, he says he can give me no particular advice on my problem.

Shortly thereafter, I hear through the grapevine that he is also in love with Donya. What surprises me is that the same scenario Donya and I have going, she had going with my old friend as well, while both he and I managed to be oblivious to the intrigues of this young lady.

Later I am shaken to hear that two other young men had a serious falling-out with each other over the very same Donya, both claiming to be her suitors and both of them able to back up their claims. Everybody being desperate for this Donya makes her brothers more determined than ever to prevent their sister from having anything to do with anybody.

In spite of what I know, my desire to marry Donya doesn't waver; I wait for Parviz's answer. When he finally says 'no' to me, we break up our long-term relationship forever. To help me overcome my rejection, I rationalize that Donya was too complex for me. I go see her for the last time and wish her well, and then return to the military base.

* * *

Only a few months remain before I finish my service when one day a phone call comes to the base for me. When I pick up the receiver, a girl's voice is on the other end of the line, saying, "I want to talk to Hassan."

"This is Hassan speaking."

"Salam," she says in our local dialect, then pauses before asking, "Do you who this is?"

I search my memory for a face to go with this voice but come up with nothing. During my university years, a few girls were interested in me but because my heart had first belonged to Mona and later was totally absorbed by Donya, I never made an effort to get involved with them.

While I am absorbed in going through my memory bank, I hear a breathless voice say, "This is Mona speaking. Do you remember me?"

I feel a shock pass through me and say nothing for a minute. Is this the same Mona who ignored the boy eagerly awaiting her under the old walnut tree all those years ago? The anger I had harbored then comes to life in a flash. Why is she calling me now? What can I say to her that doesn't sound reproachful?

"Hey. How strange that you are thinking about me after all these years!"

"Well, anything is possible, stranger things have happened in life. I just got to Tehran and thought I would say 'hello'. I asked your cousin for your phone number on the pretext that I want to learn English."

"You aren't calling from Tehran?"

"I have just enrolled in the University of Tehran's School of Social Studies program."

"Oh, have you! My congratulations. So, you finally managed to break through the crowded gates of academia and earn a slot in the university lottery?"

"Thank you, you are too kind," she answers with a little laugh. "Actually, it wasn't easy, but I am too stubborn to give up and here I am; in fact, I just moved into the university hostel, so it's official."

She gives me the address of a place, only minutes away from my house, and goes on to talk about her classes and the struggle of a village girl to adjust to a big city environment. The more we talk, the more I recall her flashing eyes and infectious smile. The sound of this uncomplicated village voice warms me and my severity and resistance melt like last winter's snowman; I want to see her face to face. After all, she was the object of my first longing; maybe I should see if the spark is still there.

"Listen," I suddenly jump into her tale, "I can't talk long on this phone. Can we meet somewhere later?"

"Ok," she answers with delight and we set a time.

----

[1]Mandatory conscription in Iran is postponed as long as you are enrolled as a full-time student working on a degree.

[2]Na mahram is a combined Farsi-Arabic word that denotes anyone not of one's family, or if a family member, far enough removed to be marriageable.

It was the best of times, it was the worst of times, it was the age of wisdom, it was the age of foolishness ... it was the spring of hope, it was the winter of despair ...

....Charles Dickens

Six

Break with custom if you want warm kisses!

It is lunchtime and Mr. Lee calls for a one-hour break. We agree to meet again at one and head back to the main hallway, weaving through people still standing in lines. Saying goodbye and leaving the building, I stroll to a nearby restaurant for lunch.

An hour later I enter the building again and ask for Mr. Lee at the same table as before. While waiting, I keep myself busy by pacing back and forth and finally strike up a conversation with a few people standing in line. Some individuals, with a smile of relief, now have their passports in hand, others have applied and their faces show hope that their paperwork will be approved, and still others are nervously and hesitantly taking care of legal procedures before they can leave China for different parts of the world.

Ten minutes or so pass before my interviewers approach me in the hall and together we descend to the first floor. Once seated in our room, we spend a few minutes making polite conversation, smoking and having a glass of water.

"Eating food finished?" Mr. Lee asks me.

"Yes."

"How fast! Where?"

"Close to the second ring road there is a restaurant near the overpass bridge."

Smiling, he says, "Is there a restaurant there? How come I don't know that?" Turning to his colleagues, he continues, "Foreigners are faster than us, are-aren't they?"

We laugh and he asks, "Have you become used to Chinese food?"

"Yes, I like it."

"What about your children?"

"Oh, they love Chinese food."

"In your home you cook Chinese dishes?"

"Yes, my wife does."

"How she knows?"

"Through neighbors and friends. She also watches TV programs about food and writes down the instructions."

"Very clever! Can she read Chinese?"

"No."

"You?"

"No."

"Such a long time in China; how come still can't read?"

"How can we?"

"Your office, they don't help you?"

"In 2003, they gave us a volunteer teacher for a couple months. But during the SARS, when all businesses were closed in Beijing, our classes were cancelled. After the SARS, we asked the office to resume the class. They said, 'not possible' anymore."

"Why?"

"They said there was no budget."

"So, no help with learning, no entertainment, nothing?"

"No. Let them have their entertainment; we are more worried about the basics. Please, if you can, don't let them cut back our payments."

Smiling, Mr. Lee changes the topic, "Ok, begin again?"

Taking a deep breath, I begin.

'Having no place of my own and with her living in the hostel, Mona and I start meeting several times a week in different streets and parks around the city. Our friendship grows deeper until it transforms into love.

One evening, we are sitting side by side on a bench under a tree in Park e Laleh. It is almost dark enough that people cannot make us out. While Mona talks, my concentration wavers. I so want to kiss her but am not sure how she will react. Working up my courage and before I can change my mind, I abruptly bend to fold her in my arms. She tries to draw away to the other side of the bench but cannot because my arms are tightly wrapped around her while my lips, without giving her a chance to talk, are hungrily chasing hers. After a bit of struggle within my strong embrace, she tires and relaxes, and I steal a very sweet kiss. I don't know how long we stay like this before I release her, but when I let her go, she pulls away and begins to cry, not having anticipated such an unexpected move.

People are passing by and I worry they will notice a young girl crying in the dark. There is also the real fear that Basij forces patrolling in different parks and streets to discover young girls and boys together, may arrive at any moment in response to agents who roam the park. If we happen to be detained for being alone together, the whole bunch of our relatives will disown us for such a disgraceful act. I remind her of the possible dangers we face and tell her that I will run away and leave her alone if Basij forces arrive. Although we both know I am kidding, she begins to calm down and finally falls silent; I feel joy surge through my heart.

Mona does not speak much on the way back to her hostel where we say our goodbyes. I watch the door close behind her before turning to sing and almost dance my way home under the streetlights. After looking at life through the dark lenses of moralities, I finally see face to face the euphoria I have been cheated of, and am relishing my first taste of it.

That night when the tingly feeling of Mona's lips fades from mine, I begin to agonize that I have messed up my chances with her, and this girl will not want to see me anymore. I spend the night kicking myself for my rash behavior so the next day when she calls even earlier than before, I can hardly contain myself.

* * *

With financial help from my brother Davood, who is now a Canadian citizen, I shop for and buy a house in Tehran. Now Mona and I do not have to be afraid of the Basij forces in parks, streets, or even inside movie theaters where we used to go in the case of rainy or cold weather; now she can come to my house and we can spend as long as we want together.

One night after having dinner, I bring my photo album to show her. As we go through the pictures, I relate relevant stories.

"Do you remember this boy on the horse? He is the same boy who spent months and years chasing you!"

"How can I forget that boy?"

"But you never turned to answer him!"

"I really couldn't. I was afraid of my family, especially my brothers."

"They didn't know anything."

"That's what you think. You are like an ostrich hiding its head in the sand, thinking nobody can see it. My brothers knew about your intentions but didn't tell you anything; because of your family's background they felt embarrassed. But on the other hand, they put a lot of pressure on me to make sure I stayed away from getting involved with you and kept my nose in my books. Believe me or not, I always wanted to talk to you."

"You talked a lot! You never once said one word to me and did not even acknowledge my letters. You could have accepted the last one and written back to let me know how things were, and I would have been more cautious."

"You mean the letter you tried to pass me from the bike?"

"Yes, it was a perfect occasion. What would have happened if you had just stretched out your hands to get it?"

"You see? You know nothing! My grandmother always says 'lovers are blind', and I now know she is right! On that day when you believed no one was around to see you, the whole bunch of my aunt's family was picking tea in their garden just meters away. They were all watching us."

"But I didn't see anybody."

"That's why I say you think nobody sees you. Let me tell you something. Last year, I passed the test for the medical course. Had I started I would now be in my second year at medical college, on my way on becoming a doctor. Everybody in the family, including my father, encouraged me to take the course, but I refused simply because the university was not in Tehran where I could find you. They didn't push me too hard because the course at the Azad University would have been very expensive. So I waited one more year at home with the hope of getting into a government university in this city, regardless of what I studied. Is this convincing enough to prove that I have always loved you?"

* * *

Having permission due to the automatic rank accorded to me with my university degree, I leave the military base everyday at around two when my job is finished and find a few freelance teaching jobs to save money for a wedding shopping spree.

Prior to the Iranian New Year in 1995, we join old friends and go from store to store until late into the night. After trying on and rejecting many suits and shoes and rings and such, we finally manage to purchase all we need.

The New Year is only a couple days away when Mona and I pack everything we bought and leave for the central bus station in Azadi square. We are just two of thousands of people who are desperately seeking to buy tickets in the many crowded lines across the huge bus station, but by checking out the different ticket sellers, after several hours we manage to get the ones we want. By nightfall, Mona and I are on a bus that is leaving for our province, Gilan.

"What if our parents do not agree to our plans?" Mona asks on the way.

"They will. My father would never say no to me on this matter and yours is, as far as I know him, very open-minded the spouses his daughters choose."

The bus arrives at the neighboring town around midnight and I take Mona to her village in a taxi and return home wondering where to hide the wedding paraphernalia we have just bought until after we talk to parents still blissfully ignorant of our intentions to marry during the New Year holiday.

How can I possibly talk about having a girl in my life and wanting to marry her to parents, particularly to my father, who have suppressed our sexual energy and amorous emotions since we were born? Stuttering and stammering my way through a rationale for needing to get married, I begin, "Er, as you know, I am 25 years old, have graduated from university and will soon finish my military duty. With your help, I have a house in Tehran that lacks a woman's touch and I lack a bride; wouldn't you like to have a daughter-in-law?"

Smiling, my father jumps in, "Of course we would, but who would that girl be? You know, my son, we are talking about a lifelong issue, not a matter of buying a shirt today and throwing it away tomorrow when you get tired of it. You need to be aware that you are choosing a partner who will live with you for the rest of your life. Do you have anyone reliable in mind?"

"I believe I have."

"Who is she?"

"You know her family although you may not know her."

"My dear Hassan, I have raised you and I know that you have chosen the right girl but as your father, I need to meet her."

Although it is a monumental task, I agree to his demands and later ask Mona to come over to our house to visit with my parents. It is a totally unreasonable request because nobody in the village considers such behavior proper; it goes against village customs if a girl visits a boy at his house for the purpose of arranging a formal marriage proposal. All Mona's relatives will ostracize her should they know about such a visit; a girl can be branded as immoral if people know she has visited a boy's house.

It is proof of her love for me that Mona accepts taking such a risk. We set a time and wait until the day arrives. When it does, many of my friends are sitting in our spare room on the second floor, busy playing chess[1]. None of them can know anything about our secret plans. I ask my brother Mirza to keep everybody busy upstairs until the visit is over. I also ask for the help of Mansoor who has been my close friend during all the years since we met, even after the two of us moved to Tehran.

Mansoor sets up his lookout on the main road west of the yard and keeps watch on the whole area until the road is free of passersby. When everything is clear, I signal to Mona, who has been waiting on the road behind our house, to hurry into the yard. She joins my parents on the veranda, who then escort her into the living room, with Mansoor, Mirza and me walking in behind them.

For half an hour or so, we chat about everything and nothing, getting to know each other and becoming comfortable together until, deciding not to push our luck at keeping the meeting a secret, we take Mona out the way we brought her in.

My mother, who already knows Mona, is very happy with my choice for her future daughter-in-law. However, Mona has one fault from my father's point of view: she is quite thin. Most Iranians, especially the older generation, believe girls with a little more weight can bear children easier and have healthier babies. No matter what kind of girl my father prefers, he can see his point doesn't carry much weight in this argument. Mona is my choice and I insist that nobody but Mona will do.

* * *

A few days later, Mona and I marry on a cloudlessly bright day when the sky is blue and the weather is unusually warm for such early springtime.

Unlike many other provinces in Iran, men and women in my province still dance together during wedding ceremonies, in spite of all the Basij forces' intervention. This has been our custom since way back in history, some believing that because of the greenness of the landscape, people are happier by nature, regardless of the earlier conflicts.

Now, after all those tensions in the eighties people are reverting to the happy weddings of earlier days even though the Basij often break into the parties and detain and may even fine the groom, holding him responsible for the dancing and other illegal activities in the new Islamic Republic of Iran. However, when scores of men and women dance around us under orange trees within Mona's yard, we do it without the benefit of an official permit. This is the very first marriage in my family and many people, who had wanted to sympathize with us during all those bad years but didn't out of fear, now try to make up for lost time by taking part in our happy moments.

Crowds of guests, enlivened by a few women dressed in folk costume, dance or form a circle around the periphery of Mona's yard, clapping to the live music. I can clearly see that everybody has wished for my family to have a blissful day such as this.

Even my father, who to my knowledge has never danced in his life, cannot stop dancing. My mother, in spite of having a hard time sitting in a chair for very long because of her infirmities, still wants to stay longer when we try to take her home that evening. The ceremony continues until nightfall without incident; no Basij forces show up.

By evening, when the exhausted wedding guests leave for their homes, a couple friends and I take my new bride to the seashore to shoot videos and snap photos.

The waves of the Caspian Sea reach us on the
evening of our wedding day

----

¹Because my parents had no daughters, our house, both
when my brothers were around and later when I was the only
child left, was always a place for friends to get together without
worrying about someone misunderstanding their intentions.

~ * ~

Count on 'personal pronouns' to help you find a job

A few days after the wedding, Mona and I leave the village
again; she needs to get back to classes and I have a few more
months to serve as a soldier.

Normally before a bride officially moves into her husband's house, a second ritual takes place at the home of the groom's parents, but we decide to make life simpler; Mansoor and the others who live with me move out and Mona moves in. To this day, she kiddingly tells me I still owe her a wedding ceremony.

Happy together, everything is going well until the ugly face of reality shows up; we cannot spend the rest of our life on a honeymoon. I have depleted all my previous savings, and my freelance teachings are no longer bringing in enough income to support two people; the time has come to look for a real job – quite a task in a city the size of Tehran with its high rate of unemployment. While keeping my part-time teaching and translating jobs, through networking I find employment at a travel and tourism agency which I hope will be long lasting, but after working for a few months I am asked to fill out forms about my background; shortly after that I am called in, told the company is over-employed and sent home. As I am leaving, the company representative says he will get in touch with me if vacancies come up later, but I am never once contacted.

An uncle of mine, who has a son taking English classes from me, says, "I have a distant relative who works in a well-known high school in this city." After talking to his relative, he hands me a name and address on a piece of paper, saying, "On _ date go to this school and look for Habib."

On the day of the appointment, accompanied by Mansoor, I enter the courtyard of the school; impressed, he whistles, "Wow! Are you going to teach here? This is a beautiful huge old campus." Intimidation drains my confidence as we walk through the students into the building and ask the custodian for Habib.

"What's your relationship with him?"

"He is my cousin."

With that, we are taken to an office, offered tea and cookies and courteously asked to wait while he calls Habib. Minutes later Habib walks in with a heart-felt welcome, asks after my family and offering us seats, then walks behind the desk and sits in his own swivel chair.

"What can I do for you?" he asks with a tentative smile on his face.

"Actually, as my uncle mentioned when he called you, I am looking for a position."

"So, you have finished your college studies?"

"Several years ago; since then I have also completed military service."

"Wow! How time flies! It seems like yesterday when your parents told me you were enrolled in university."

"That's true. Now the carefree days of youth are over; I have a wife to support and want to start my career as a teacher. I am hopeful that you have connections you can use to give me a hand."

"Well, Hassan, this institution has a very creditable reputation with strict guidelines for choosing employees; I am only a small part of it. I doubt it is possible for me to help you find a job here but I have friends who work in other language institutes, and maybe I can connect you to them. Do you have a contact number for me to call you later?"

"Unfortunately, I do not have a telephone but you can get hold of me through my uncle."

Thanking him, we stand to take our leave.

"Not yet," he says, "I haven't seen you for so long that I insist that you stay to lunch." Then, without giving us time to react, he leaves to take care of some business affairs before returning to escort us to the canteen.

As soon as he exits the room, I turn to Mansoor and say, "Let's enjoy the free meal now; he won't be calling me."

* * *

With its frequent repetition, I learn to despise the phrase, 'we will call you later'. My being unemployed creates financial difficulties Mona and I struggle to overcome; to reduce our daily costs, we reluctantly decide she should go back to her hostel.

At one interview, I am required to take the TOEFFL test for English proficiency. This test contains a vocabulary of multi-syllable and seldom-used words I have never in my life heard and cannot imagine ever needing to know; I fail.

Unhappy with my result, I give the interviewer my opinion about the obsolete nature of the English test and ask him to let me teach a topic of his choice before judging my competency. He declines, saying they have their rules and passing TOEFFL is the first requirement. I walk out of the business and into another nearby, where at reception a young girl listens as I tell her I am there to apply for a teaching job. Looking at me, she asks, "How old are you?"

"I am not here to propose marriage that you need to know my age; I am applying for a job."

Offended, she says, "I am asking your age to determine your experience; experience is very important. Now do you want to tell me your age?"

"Soon to be twenty-six."

"Sorry, we only hire teachers who are forty or older."

* * *

I begin asking my long-time friends if they know of a suitable job for me. Unfortunately, none of them is in a decision-making position and so can be of no help.

Carrying a copy of my Shakespearean work in my bag, I begin checking the many translation agents in Tehran, showing it to them as proof that I am a good translator. Almost no one wants to read my published work. In one of those offices, I face an old man sitting in a room among several young people. Giving a brief description of my background, I say I am interested in working for them if there is an opening. The old man takes a long look at the cover of magazine then turns to me and, in a quivering old man's voice, says, "What are the subjective pronouns in English?"

I take this as a joke. Smiling, I tell him that I am serious about needing a job. He smiles back and says he is also serious.

"I have given you a translation of one of Shakespeare's poems, and you are asking me about personal pronouns?"

"You would know how important pronouns are if you were a good translator," he comments with a gesture that shows he has no doubt about being right and is raising a very important point.

I feel insulted and even regret that I have talked to such an old goat who has spent his entire life using grammar by rote like a machine. His spoken English is about as good as mine was when I was in my second year of university. However, everyone in the room seems to side with him, sitting there nodding their heads in agreement to everything he says.

"You must be very intuitive to know my translation abilities just by hearing my recitation of pronouns."

"That's my job, young man," he retorts, returning my magazine to me. "Excuse me," he switches from Farsi to talk in his poorly pronounced and incorrect English, "my saggeshen is you go other place. Possibell, they give job to you, God wishing."

I turn and leave the room. What was the use of studying English so hard when afterwards there are no jobs to be found? The old man has seriously damaged my ego. Try as I might, I cannot clear that experience out of my head; I decide that for the future I will not depend on my university qualification for getting a job[1].

Hope evaporates. I talk to a couple of my friends who are in the same situation, and ask them if we can put our minds together to come up with a solution, since it seems impossible for us to find any kind of professional job. One of them suggests marketing. We seek out the names of companies listed in the newspapers and note down their contact information and then check every address and ask if anybody needs salesmen for their products. Many of them are not interested, some say they will call us later, and a couple of them, including a sausage company and a plastic cups producer agree to contract out services to us. However, they want us to give them a promissory note as a guarantee that if we mishandle the job the guarantor will cover the loss. We are responsible for their products; if they are lost or destroyed, those notes will be used against us in court and we will have to pay for the loss. We do not have any guarantee except our national ID cards, which are unacceptable.

We keep looking. I think of a friend who knows some professional tailors who produce women's underwear wholesale in a big factory and export their products to other provinces. My friend can get me articles of clothing from them without me paying anything in advance. The tailors want 200 tomans for each item while the retail price in stores is about 500. Besides that, they will give me 15 percent of the sale. It is a good offer and I decide to try it.

Since all my neighbors know me as an English teacher, to save face, I take all my papers and books out of my bag and fill it with ladies' lingerie and every morning leave home with the bag in my hand, broadening my territory to cover stores on more distant streets and look for customers who don't know me.

All shops which sell intimate ladies wear are run by women and I find it hard to work up the courage to convince myself to step inside them. If there are crowds of women in a store, I wait outside until all the customers have left, before, briefcase in hand

I hesitantly step over the portal. When the employees inquire how they can help me, I turn red and begin to sweat. Then, with clipped, choppy sentences, I ask them if they need new inventory. In contrast to my embarrassment, the clerks are totally relaxed when they want a description of the clothing I have, but 'bras' and 'panties' are words which won't come out of my mouth; I just open the bag and expose the merchandise inside.

I have hardly begun to find a few repeat customers when my friend tells me the clothing factory has gone out of business; I rush to find out for myself. When I arrive at the main gate, everybody is busy packing machines and clothing to be loaded into a big truck waiting nearby. While I stand outside smoking a cigarette, the truck leaves and takes my job away.

–––––––––––––––––––––––––––––––

[1]Many years later, I chose the subjective pronouns as the basis of my English and Persian lesson plans. To be frank, this method is very productive for beginners. But still, even today, I have no idea what personal pronouns have to do with professional translations.

~ * ~

Ghol gholi, the strongest party in Iran!

Towards evening, I am once again out in the streets looking for a job. Night is falling and I don't want to go home to an empty house; I call an old friend.

"Hey Masood, how're ya doin'?"

"Hassan! Long time no see! Where are you?"

"At Inqelab Square; near your house."

"Come on over! My wife and children are on a trip to Gilan and I am home with only Hamid to keep me company."

"But since I am in a melancholy mood I might not be good company."

"You just get on over here and let us change your mood! I'll be waiting for you."

Saying this, Masood hangs up and I step out of the public phone booth to call a taxi. Masood, Hamid and I were really close friends in high school during which time we wrote hundreds of satirical poems together.

The taxi drops me near their alley and I climb the spiraling staircase to his fifth-floor house. Masood opens the door to my ring and as always, we embrace each other heartily. Walking into his flat behind him, I see Hamid, grinning, rushing from the kitchen to greet me with wide open arms.

Settling in, we chat and review many old school events, and laugh at our former high school principal, his assistant and other teachers until our reminiscing brings us up to the present.

In contrast to Masood who is making a reasonably good living in the black market, Hamid has been looking for a job for a good six years and has yet to find work he feels worthy of him. He is one of those individuals who is exceptionally intelligent and has lots of plans and ideas but so far has done nothing important with his life. Hamid's philosophy is contained in a line from Hafez, 'fortune is something that should come to you without your effort'. As far back as I can remember, he is always waiting for good luck to fall into his lap, but it never does.

Masood interrupts our friendly chatter to leave for the kitchen and comes back a few seconds later, holding in his hand a small glass jar partially filled with water. Placing the cylindrical jar on the carpeted floor beside Hamid and me, he makes another trip to the kitchen and brings back a plastic bag, a short metal wire and a rubber band. He sets these things on the floor near the jar and turns to the kitchen again. Hamid grabs the plastic bag and secures it tightly around the jar with the rubber band.

By this time, Masood has brought a small primus stove to add to the rest of the paraphernalia. Hamid lights it and starts heating the wire in the flame. When the section of metal is red hot, he removes it and pokes it into the lid at separate points, creating two tiny holes close to each other; the smell of hot plastic penetrates my nose. Then he sticks the wire back in the flame and picks up two straws, one of them the size of a drinking straw and the other a bit wider and thicker. He passes the thinner straw at a 45-degree angle a few centimeters into one of the holes he has made, leaving the majority of it outside the container. The second straw goes vertically through the remaining hole until the end is under water. He separates the sliding cover from a box of matches, rounds it slightly into a cylindrical shape and puts the shell over the vertical straw, checking all the fittings a couple of times to make sure the new instrument is in working order. Then, the needle in his right hand, he impales an amber-colored ball about the size of a pea on its tip and cooks it over the flame for a few seconds.

Although I have never tried it before, I already know the apparatus, having seen it in the home of a friend whose father uses it daily. We call the jar ghol gholi; a homemade hookah used for smoking opium.

"Well, Hassan khan," Masood begins, "we indulge in this from time to time; I hope you are not offended."

"No, it's ok. Go ahead."

We each grab a pillow and lie down on the floor around the flame of the stove. As my friends take turns inhaling, I watch how they operate their makeshift machine. Holding the needle with the opium ball at its top in one hand, with the other Hamid heats the wire. When the metal is almost red, he takes it from the flame and moves both his hands to the matchbox cover on the jar's lid, as Masood bends over the jar and puts his lips around the thinner straw. Hamid touches the hot metal wire to the ball inside the matchbox, smoke begins to rise; meanwhile Masood inhales the air in the jar through his straw, causing the water to bubble. The more he inhales, the harder the water quakes, as if it is boiling. Since the water sound it makes is called 'ghol ghol' in Iran, people have nick-named the instrument 'ghol gholi'.

Soon Masood changes places with Hamid, and the process is repeated. My eyes fixed on the machinations of my friends, I am caught by surprise when Masood asks, "Hassan, do you want to try it?" Nodding agreement, I move my pillow closer to the stove. A couple of inhalations make me high and I do not dare take another. I feel so light that I am sure if I try to fly, I will not fall and seem to have enough supernatural energy to work the whole night through without fatigue. Different parts of my body itch on and off; the more I scratch, the more my skin likes it.

* * *

A few months later, I notice most of my friends already have a long-term friendship with ghol gholi but have not dared to tell me, worrying I would pass judgment on them, since they knew about my strict rules for no smoking in the house back when I was a non-smoker. Although they know that, after the debacle with Donya, I had started to smoke myself, here they are a step ahead of me smoking opium, and not being sure of my reaction, they have kept it a secret from me.

We begin to make it a habit to gather around ghol gholi, and our get-togethers become more and more frequent. The best part of the ghol gholi parties is the warm conversation; the thoughts and ideas we exchange around this jar are as valuable to us as the opium itself. Passionately, we explore ideas about creating job opportunities for ourselves, debate about sports, social and political issues, travel, music, movies, books, poetry; one of the best activities of our ghol gholi sessions is writing poems - when the chemistry of the group is right, we compose verse after verse of poetry, bouncing ideas off one another.

Sometimes, if one of us is adamant on a subject and the others have different opinions, serious arguments develop; however, the ghol gholi is stronger than our disagreements, and, with a few puffs, reduces serious tensions and unites us under the flag of the golden ball. Those who seemed angry calm down when it is their turn to inhale the smoke of the jar.

No matter how busy we are and no matter how empty our pockets are, we always find time for these gatherings around the little golden balls.

* * *

The opium, with its initial feeling of euphoria, gradually makes me paranoid and fearful. During the smoking of the opium, I feel a joy that, after I leave the group and am alone again, turns to guilt and drains me of any motivation to improve my life.

Paranoia also prevents me from standing up for my rights; people often crowd in front of me in bus lines and I don't have the nerve to complain. If I get into an argument with someone, since I already feel guilt I think the worst may happen: I will get in a fight, be arrested and given a drug test.

As time passes, to make sure I keep a low profile, I start going out of my way to avoid the government forces that roam the streets.

~ * ~

From a journey on high to a journey too far

Looking for a job in a capital city with a population of more than ten million, I happen to run into Behnam, a friend from earlier Tehran days. With a degree in English translation, he now works as a translator in a large organization. Listening to my struggles with finding permanent employment, he suggests that I take the entrance exam for freelance translators in his office. He explains that the office has its own dictionaries and references, which serve for choosing the language they want in their work; this dictates their strict rules and regulations for choosing freelancers. About ninety-nine percent of the applicants, who have to know the philology of the company in order to pass the exam, are rejected; without having a contact inside the translation department, it is almost impossible to get hired. "But don't worry," he adds, "Come and visit me at my office and I will introduce you to my boss; I will ask him to give you an article to translate as a proof of your ability."

His enthusiasm is contagious; I apply to take the test, pass and become a freelance translator. Now, all I need to do is go to the office for articles, translate them at home, and deliver them to Behnam's boss. The jobs are few but I make enough to keep myself alive.

* * *

The day comes when, as we are enjoying our warm ghol gholi chat, Milad, an old friend, joins us. He is from a neighboring town in my province and spent a few years in prison as punishment for his involvement in the same political movements as my brothers. Although he doesn't smoke and isn't involved in drugs, he always comes to our ghol gholi chats when he travels to Tehran.

Milad already has a Bachelor of Science and tells us he wants to leave the country to further his studies abroad. The pros and cons of leaving Iran soon take precedence over earlier topics; while others are comparing life in our own country with the unknown quality of life in a foreign land, I suddenly blurt out, "I'll go with you."

Everybody lying on pillows around the primus stove looks at me and suddenly the chat focuses on my life.

"But you just got married."

"You have a house in Tehran; a major advantage."

"You have a Bachelor's degree in English and your wife will soon graduate as a social worker."

"Best of all, you love ghol gholi."

Laughing at me, my friends conclude, "this is the ghol gholi speaking, not you."

"Maybe you are right, but what I don't seem to have here is a future."

"This is your future," Hamid says with irony, holding out the golden ball to me, "You belong here."

* * *

Milad and I begin collecting information about various countries we might consider as our destination and finally choose India; we hear that living there is cheap and getting a visa seems easy.

While Milad goes back to the village to see if he can get funds from his parents for the trip, I contact Behnam, my freelance supplier, and ask him for additional translation work. When I tell him about my recent decision to leave the country, he encourages me and promises to see if he can throw more jobs my way.

The first big project he gives me is a book to be translated into Persian. I tackle this project of much bigger proportions; it will net me somewhere in the vicinity of 200 thousand in Iranian currency, enough to take me to India. Working on the translation day and night, I finish this six-month project in less than two months and take the final draft to Behnam at his house. Although he knows I have done it hastily and therefore not as well as I could have, my long-suffering friend does all the hard work of editing. He finally submits it to his boss, who accepts the translation, and I receive the payment I have earned with Behnam's help; money I plan to use to change the path of my life.

* * *

While translating this book, I hear a written exam for teaching jobs in the Tehran high schools is being offered; I sign up, take the exam and am waiting for the results to be published. A successful written exam is only the first step in a long line of obstacles I would need to surmount in order to get a job in the public schools. If I pass, I will then have to take an oral proficiency test to demonstrate my ability in spoken English. Other steps follow these two.

I keep watch in the state's newspaper until the results are published and I see my name on the lists. From among a couple thousand young applicants, I have managed to pass the written exam favorably. The positive outcome of this test is a giant step forward towards qualifying me for a permanent teaching job. The newspaper gives the successful applicants instructions for attending the spoken English exam; I follow up with the date and address on the paper and join a few dozen others who have arrived in compliance with the instructions.

A couple of weeks after the oral exam when I return to the building where I took the test, I am relieved and happy to see my name up there on the board among the remaining few who have passed the second hurdle.

The third proficiency will be an ideological examination. I can't imagine any problems with an exam of this type since I have extensive background training in moralities and religious rules and rituals. The first two tests have greatly improved my morale and bolstered my confidence about the third. Once the ideological portion is mastered, I will have renewed hope of being able to remain in the house I own and with my wife by my side. I will no longer feel the need to leave my country and establish a new life in India.

In the warmth of my self-assurance, I mention to my friends around the ghol gholi that I may not go to India with Milad after all, but stay and take advantage of the new opportunity. They all laugh and say, "We knew all along you were not going anywhere."

Before I know it, I am sitting for my ideological interview in a room at the human resources department of the Iranian Ministry of Education in Palestine Square. My interviewers are two friendly men in their fifties, both with long and well-shaped beards similar to those worn by religious leaders. Half an hour or so later when they say the test is over, I ask if I can add something. With gentle smiles, they let me talk.

"After my own long struggle with English during my first years in college, I feel I can help upcoming generations discover more successful study methods. My desire is to teach English to students new to learning the language. I know I am far from an experienced teacher but I believe I can be successful at this endeavor. As for my personal life, I am a newlywed, I own a house in this city and my wife will soon graduate as a social worker, giving me every reason to stay here to serve my own people. I am telling you this because I was planning to study for my master's degree in India, but to be frank, I would really rather not take such a step. If you allow me a chance at this job, I will be able to further my studies within my own country while serving my fellow citizens at the same time. My future lies in your hands; please don't deny me this opportunity."

"Your test has raised no red flags of alarm."

"You mean I passed the exam?"

"If God is willing, yes. On such and such a date, report to the Ministry of Education office in Khazaneh Square; by then, a list of successful applicants will be posted on the bulletin board."

One more hurdle remains for me to jump over. This final test requires no action on my part; it consists in checking my background. My life will be finitely scrutinized, going all the way back through university and high school to my childhood in the village. It is the Iranian version of what many countries these days call a security check.

That very same day, I call my father in the village and, giving him the news about the teaching job I all but have in my pocket, ask him to get in touch with our high school principal right away in case the security check includes talking to him. He is so happy he almost cries with joy, and agrees to comply with my request. The principal promises my father to give a positive report should he be asked.

Finally, on the day of the results, I leave home early for the Ministry of Education facility. When I walk in, a small group of young people, including a few of those who were in my university, have already gathered around the white board inside the building. Parting them to get closer to the board, I skim the list to the very end looking for the name Hassan. There is no sign of my name. I check the list again and again. My name isn't there.

My legs are quaking, I stumble into a nearby room hunting for someone who can tell me the reason my name is not included in the list. The people I find tell me they have no idea about the process of elimination. They have been told to put those papers on the board; that's all. I continue to insist on an answer until a gentleman with a sparse salt-and-pepper beard and thin wisps of white hair walks over and speaks in an effort to comfort me with his soothing words. Assuming I have failed the security check, which he says he is not in a position to control or change, with a hand on my shoulder, he encourages me not to lose faith at such a young age and to funnel my energy into a positive attitude instead of feeling frustrated. "Life is full of failures," he intones, "and each failure is a chance for a new door to open."

I leave the room in a surreal silence as if my senses have failed me. "How can I tell my father who has such faith in me?" I wonder. "How can I tell Mona? The prospect of this new job has given her such hope that I will not have to leave the country. I am about to destroy all the beautiful dreams she is contemplating about how our life will unfold. Although she has never tried to convince me to stay, I can clearly sense that she is upset and unhappy about my plans to go to India, but now I will have to tell her that I am really leaving after all."

These thoughts make a continuous and futile circle through my head as I keep walking aimlessly around the streets and parks until my stomach starts to complain. Grabbing a sandwich, I walk back to a park where I sit on the first bench I see and munch on it, my mind a blank. People come and go around me and I wonder bitterly why everyone has a normal life except me. I do not know why I cannot succeed like others; I have never been behind bars and have no personal problems with anybody. Still, I cannot qualify for a job or earn enough to bring my wife home to live with me. Life seems so unfair.

All afternoon I ponder these thoughts, then putting my misery aside, I call Mona and tell her the news. She feels devastated and asks to come over to our house and stay the night with me, but I am neither in the mood to comfort nor to be comforted. She accedes to my wishes and we hang up.

I call Mansoor; he is home with a few other friends and asks me to join them. When I walk in, they are sitting in his room around a primus stove and, looking at me, figure out at once that I am not in a good mood. After giving them my disappointing news, they don't say anything for awhile then start trying to console me. Someone asks me to take it in stride. Someone else lambasts the teaching profession while still another reminds me of the fresh bananas and coconuts to be found in India.

I know each one of them is trying in his own way to give me hope and encouragement, but at the moment, I am so angry that their words of comfort don't penetrate my brain. In my frustration, I begin cursing every single person in the government, all of whom, I believe, are the reason I have been rejected as a candidate. A discussion ensues about the government and its responsibility for the woes of the country. Some, who have been through similar situations, share their personal testimonies with the rest of us.

The discussions continue for a while, when out of the blue, Mansoor asks me, "Have you ever participated in any national elections?"

No one speaks for a bit. Then, suddenly, we all burst into laughter.

"What a stupid question!" I say. "What is the relationship between my qualifications and the country's elections?"

We continue ridiculing him but it turns out he is serious about getting an answer from me.

"Nooo," I reply at his insistence.

"You mean you have never gone to the ballot boxes since the revolution?"

"Well, no. I was too young to vote during the revolution. Then, after I grew older, I could see the candidates had all been selected by the government and my vote was merely to confirm their choices."

"You mean there are no seals or affidavits on your national ID card to prove you have voted?"

"No."

"Do you think the government is stupid?" he queries. "You have never voted for this government and now you are expecting them to let you teach children in their high schools? What could you possibly teach them which would be approved?"

"There are many people who have never voted in their lives," I argue.

"Do they have jobs in government offices?"

"I don't know. What I do know is that I have never acted against this government since high school. I have never participated in any kinds of sensitive demonstrations during all the years from the time I left my village till now."

"You ought to know that written proof works a lot better than claims; you never gave the government a chance to trust you: you shave your beard, you don't attend Friday prayers and you never take part in government-sponsored activities. Why should they believe you have changed and are now supportive of them?"

"But governments are not political organizations; they are the representatives of the nation and the guardians of the country."

"Ideally, yes, but not our government."

We toss this topic around until after midnight while the water in the jar bubbles away.

* * *

When I call Milad a few days later to ask him if he is ready for India, he says he has not been able to arrange the necessary funds, and has decided to cancel the trip.

More than ever determined to leave the country, I get in touch with another friend from university days, Fardin, who, while still a minor, was taken to prison where he spent several years for his involvement with a splinter political group during the eighties. Like my brother Kaveh, his was executed while serving a sentence in prison, and that brought us together on common ground and we became very good friends. When he hears about my plans to leave Iran for India, he decides to go with me. He has always been a good companion and I am sure we are going to have a great time on this journey.

In 1996, I say farewell to my parents, to my village, to Mona, to my closest friends, and to my cherished ghol gholi; Fardin and I are gone before many of our relatives know we are going.

The UN Declaration of Human Rights laid down what any person might reasonably expect, yet there are remarkably few people who enjoy these rights

....................Peter Gabriel

Seven

Behind closed gates

Tourist Camp, located near the railway station in Asaf Ali Road on the border between New and Old Delhi, is a large garden with more than a hundred single- and double-room dwellings nestled under trees, resembling a small village. Because the area has a large, quiet garden, is restricted to guests and is cheaper than many hotels, I, like many other foreign tourists, soon hear about it upon arrival.

* * *

Years before, Fardin, while in prison, developed bleeding ulcers and whenever he eats spicy Indian dishes, he gets terrible stomach pains. His digestion isn't helped by the trouble he has chewing with jaws previously broken during torture sessions and when he eats, I can hear the 'tick-tuck' sound of his jaws grinding in their sockets. Unable to tolerate life in India, he decides to go home. Once home, he faces interrogation by Iranian officials and flees to Europe.

With my companion gone, I talk to friends I have made since arriving, and find out where the United Nations' Indian headquarters is located; afraid of facing similar interrogations as Fardin, and knowing I have no money to flee again and go someplace else, like Europe, I decide the best choice left for me is to seek asylum. I buy a train ticket and head for Delhi.

A cycle rickshaw takes me to this camp called Tourist Camp. It is densely populated with Farsi speakers when I step into the yard. Embarrassed by my situation and leery of all Iranians¹, I try

216

to be in as little contact with my fellow citizens as possible, checking into a single-bed room, the size of a solitary confinement cell, in the far back corner of the garden.

Inevitably, however, I make a few contacts with other Iranians and through them learn that the majority are Armenians from Iran who have just arrived and like me, don't want to say what brought them to India. In addition to this group, who form the largest community in the camp, there is a big group of Iranian businessmen waiting for the Pakistani border to open. A few other Iranians, who, like me, are travelling either alone or with family, are nestled away in isolated corners. Here and there between their Iranian neighbours, tourists from other countries occupy many of the rooms.

It takes me a couple days to find the address for the United Nations High Commissioner for Refugees. Alone and lonely, uncertain about the future, and with a limited budget in a foreign country, I pass the bend in an alley and walk forward, address in hand. A huge crowd in the distance meets my startled gaze; there are literally hundreds of people standing several deep in a long line directly behind the high walls of a heavily guarded office, where flags are waving and mural-sized pictures of victims of human atrocities are plastered on the walls. Waiting their turn in line, people hold newspapers or cardboards over their heads to shield themselves from the hot Indian sun. Some children are playing silently in a small triangle-shaped field nearby. At one point in the line, I spot a whole bunch of the Iranians who live in my neighborhood in Tourist Camp. With their backs to me, these refugees or asylum seekers are facing a small, closed iron gate crisscrossed with bars and woven metal nets. Some have formed clusters and are chatting together, making the line resemble a dormant snake that has swallowed several fat frogs and is waiting for them to digest, something my old uncle always used to say about the way we formed lines at school. Every so often, a couple of Hindustani soldiers open the gate, letting a few applicants walk out with a handful of forms; a number of people equal to the number who have just left, are let in.

Even though in order to get my refugee application, I know there is no other way, I do not want to come face to face with the Iranians standing in the line; to avoid calling attention to myself and not knowing what else to do, I turn back and walk away from the crowd.

* * *

I am only at Tourist Camp for a few days when I meet a slight wiry man from Quebec whose name is Alain but who calls himself Ali Baba, a name he has chosen as appropriate for this part of the world, and who works for a Canadian travel and tourism agency, being a tour guide by trade. Trying to learn a couple of words in any language he comes into contact with and using them whenever there is somebody around who speaks that particular language, Ali Baba is very open and warm with everybody and always has a few words of greeting for the residents of the garden. He is very high energy; his friendliness and hyperactivity keep people around him in a good mood. We immediately hit it off; I am impressed by his extensive knowledge of so many topics; he likes that I can help him communicate with my fellow countrymen and picks my brain about Iranian tourism and culture as well as its political and social systems. He has time to spare while waiting for his tour to arrive from Quebec; we become fast friends within a couple of days and I, piecemeal, confide to him my situation. On hearing the story of my life, he in turn expresses fascination, astonishment and indignation and finally, at its conclusion, offers to help me in any way he can.

"I would like to get a refugee application form from the UNHCR office," I tell him, "but there are lots of Iranians standing in the long lines everyday. I don't care if they find out later that I am a refugee. However, I would rather not be marked as an asylum seeker while there is a possibility that the United Nations may reject my case and force me to repatriate; I don't want to cause more troubles for myself in Iran if the government one day finds out that I once applied for refugee status in India."

Even before I can tell him what I need, Ali Baba, who has a solution for everything, says, "I will do it for you; I like such challenges." No sooner having said that, he stands and, picking up his bag, pulls me by the hand from my sitting position and asks me to prepare for a new adventure.

In less than half an hour, a motor rickshaw drops us close to a double-storied building attached to the UN office and adjacent to the open area where asylum seekers are lined up. An Iranian flag sways at the top of a post inside its yard and the word Ambassador is written beside a huge plate-glass window on the wall of the house, telling us clearly that the building houses Iranian officials. We both begin to laugh with surprise to see such an incongruous building just meters away from the United Nations' refugee office.

The long viperous form seems to have been napping; it remains basically unchanged since I last saw it. Ali Baba, who has already planned how he wants to handle things, leaves me walking around at a distance out of sight of the Iranians but soon shows up again with a form in his hands. Since he does not look Asian or African, he has not had to wait in the line like other asylum seekers.

"Hey Hassan," Ali Baba calls out, laughing and walking towards me in a rush, "let me tell you something funny. I asked a lady in the office for a form and she inquired about my nationality. I said, 'Canadian'. She was shocked and said they could not accept a Canadian citizen as a refugee in India. I told her that I needed the form for somebody else and she smiled. I also told her about this Iranian ambassador's house here. I said they could take 'chick-chick' pictures," he makes a gesture of using a camera, "of the asylum seekers very easily from this distance. But she said the office could do nothing about it." We laugh together as Ali Baba hands me the form. Relieved with the ease of his success, I thank him and we double back, stopping on our return to spend some time sightseeing in an ancient garden before heading home.

A couple of days later, I submit the completed form to the UNHCR office. Now I have to wait until they call me for an interview. When Ali Baba's group arrives and he leaves on his tour, I begin to spend most of my time sitting on a chair in the garden of the Tourist Camp's outdoor café along with the other Iranians. There is no longer any way to hide the truth from each other since we can't help meeting one another in the camp every single day of the week. It is then we realize that we all have the same goal: to get refugee status.

The large group of Armenians left a lucrative life in Iran after hearing the gossip buzzing through Tehran at the time; rumor had it that the UNHCR office in India was accepting Christian Iranians and resettling them without delay in the USA. Most of them have sold their houses and businesses in anticipation of their relocation. Of course, upon arriving in India, the rumor turns out to be unfounded.

The second largest group in the camp belongs to the Iranian businessmen who have been trading between Iran and India for several decades. A few of them have fourteen- or fifteen-year-old children with a Hindustani wife plus another wife and several other children in Iran. It is rare that the families in Iran know about the second family in India and vice versa. These people are principally from a minority tribe in Iran close to the Pakistan and Afghanistan borders. Another handful comes from Mashad, a religious city in northeastern Iran. These traders deal in fabrics and precious and semi-precious stones purchased by the tens of thousands from India and transported to Iran via Pakistan in huge containers. The border was closed by the time they were ready to leave India and they were told it would be a wait of about forty days before the Pakistani government would allow their cargo to enter that country.

We are all waiting together; tourists for visas, businessmen for borders to open and we, the asylum seekers, counting the days until we can get into the human rights organization office for an interview.

'When I first left home, I felt compelled to avoid my fellow countrymen. I gradually came to realize that the Iranians I met outside Iran all had the same distrust of each other, a legacy from the new regime.

~ * ~

First tastes of freedom; cultures colliding

Every evening, crowds of Iranians, free from earlier restrictions on alcohol, gather inside Tourist Camp in front of their rooms under the trees, play loud Hindi and Persian music and drink until late. They generally strike up conversations with foreign tourists in the garden, hoping to convince them that, contrary to the bad image of Iran abroad, Iranians are very friendly, hospitable and open-minded. However, if they offer drinks to foreigners and are politely refused, the offer may be pressed on the guest with insistence, and in the end, this offends and sometimes angers the foreigners. Those not familiar with our cultural custom of ta'arof occasionally leave to look for a more peaceful place to pass their time. By the end of the night, a few of the Iranians are slurring their words, unsteady on their legs and quarrelsome, soon starting to shout at one another and then progressing to brawls.

The same story plays out several times a week while guests from other countries look on in surprise: how is it that the very same people who fought the night before, collect again the next night and share food and drinks like old friends?

* * *

I come to know a neighbor, an Iranian named Kasra, who is neither Armenian nor a businessman. He, along with his wife, a woman from my province, and his young son, has left his homeland to find resettlement somewhere else. Kasra, a humble man who always stands in respect when a newcomer arrives, is very sociable and wears a smile perpetually. In his late 30s, and as a result of having grown up in different bazaars, he has experienced a lot in his lifetime; he is a professional home and industrial electrician, an excellent mechanic, a talented chef and on top of that, a non-stop drinker.

Kasra and I start meeting often, enjoying each other's company. His wife usually asks me to have lunch or dinner with them, a huge comfort for me since I, like Fardin, cannot tolerate spicy Indian food. Food I am unaccustomed to and the broiling Indian weather have been upsetting my system since I first arrived and I have already lost more than ten kilos. With these intestinal problems, stomach pain sometimes forces me to lie down for hours.

I end up joining Kasra's group. He is part of a smaller group of mostly a few older men who drink every evening until past midnight. However, barring a few occasions when outsiders initiate a skirmish, this convivial group is not always fighting like

221

the younger ones around them. Most of them are in their fifties or sixties and all they want is to single out a quiet corner and share a bottle; I find myself joining them in toasts and singing into the night. These men like to share memories of their life experiences with each other, stories which I listen to avidly. Except Kasra and a couple of others, all are business people who are waiting for the border to open.

There is also a member of this group, who calls himself 'Khoda' or God. A tall, white haired, fair-complexioned and Aryan looking Iranian, he had felt compelled to leave Germany, his home for twenty years, due to bankruptcy, and had chosen to move to India where the cost of living is lower. Khoda speaks four languages: Persian, German, English and Urdu. When once I ask him his age, he looks at me seriously and says, "It seems that you still have doubts about me being God."

"No, I didn't mean that," I answer quickly. "I mean how many years have passed since you first entered this world?"

He smiles and says, "That is a better question. It has been about sixty years."

For him life is pure entertainment and he tries to enjoy every single moment of it. He seriously believes he is God and supports his claim by a Persian poem, 'when you become aware of yourself, you are God'. Such talk often upsets the more religious Iranians around him, who try to get him to admit to being at least a little lower than God; he insists, 'no, God; I am God'.

If not God Himself, Khoda is surely the god of backgammon; consequently, his main source of income is his game board. His talent is such that almost all of his competitors are soundly defeated, which is good because he needs to win since he is always broke and unable to pay off a debt if he loses. If he does happen to lose a game, he will push to play again for double the stakes, and keep at it until he wins. For months, I accompany him to various restaurants in Delhi where he has his backgammon corners and plays with his cronies. Cash and drinks are used as tender; I always have a wide variety of free drinks when God is with me in a restaurant.

* * *

When evening rolls around and our friends return to the camp from their daily activities, they walk directly to the area where Kasra and I live. Each person brings something: vodka, whiskey, mutton, beef, cold drinks and ice. Putting everything inside the small icebox in my room, we begin setting up our table under the trees and I go next door to get Kasra.

As soon as everyone has arrived, we start our nightly social routine. Many of the tipplers, especially Kasra, are excellent chefs. Never in my life have I had food as tasty as what Kasra makes. His dishes, mostly his kebabs, are so flavorful that a few of the camp's guards, who are Hindu and have never eaten meat, break their taboo and secretly join us, asking for kebabs.

One day when we are in the midst of our evening meal, a fellow I don't know walks into the front yard of Tourist Camp and, looking around him, sees the group of us in a far corner of the garden. My friends know him as Amu; they have all been meeting off and on for the past twenty years or so in the same camp whenever they happen to arrive in New Delhi at the same time.

Amu walks over to us and we all stand up and shake hands with him. He has a receding hairline and grey hair but moves his short and muscular frame energetically, belying his age. In contrast, his speech is a slow measured drawl, his features unruffled and his conversation positive and optimistic. He left Iran during the 1979 revolution and has never been back but he loves Iran so much that his Persian accent is unchanged and, unlike many newcomers, he never uses a single English word in his sentences although he can communicate in spoken English if he wants to.

In less than half an hour, Kasra and Amu who are meeting for the first time, act as if they have lived side by side for years. Kasra, with his talent for listening to a person with undivided attention, is a master at praising people, inflating egos; we never tire of listening to him and his outgoing personality complements a longing the introverted Amu seems to have for such a companion.

Amu is also waiting; however, he is waiting not for the border to open but for his baggage, since the custom border officials in the New Delhi airport have seized his luggage. He was bringing several cameras and camcorders from Singapore and Malaysia to India but did not have the necessary permit to present to customs. Since it is illegal to take expensive cameras into India without permission, he was asked to pay one hundred fifty thousand

Indian rupees[2] for the release of his property. Not wanting to pay such an amount, he allowed his belongings to be confiscated by customs.

He tells us he cannot convince himself to pay import taxes on his goods, so routinely takes a chance on crossing borders without being stopped. As a result, customs officials single him out and stop him at airports. When that happens, he looks around for a lawyer who can plea bargain his case and hopefully have his customs tax reduced and his property released. He is now waiting for his lawyer to fix his current problem.

From that day on, Amu's visits to Tourist Camp become more frequent. Soon he is addicted to our nightly meetings and, although he doesn't join us in drinking, Amu loves the interaction of the chats and also loves playing cards with us. When he wins a game, he says, "at last I won one." Usually when he loses, he looks at me and says, "You see? Even I can lose if the cards are not right!"

We laugh and play and look forward to our meetings among the green trees, bushes and flowers of the camp. The more time Amu and I spend together, the deeper our friendship becomes.

----

[1]Iranian culture dictates that a person offer to others whatever he has, whether it is drinks, food or possessions. Self-sacrifice is another aspect of ta'arof; putting the comfort of guests before one's own wishes and desires is a part of hospitality.

[2]One USD was around 42 Indian rupees.

~ * ~

Interviews: a chore I hate

"Hello, Davood; how are you?"

"Hi, I am ok. How are things going at home?"

"Well, I am not calling you from home."

"From where, then?"

"From India."

"What! Are you taking a tour?"

"Sort of; a long tour maybe."

"What do you mean?"

"Actually, I have no plans to go back to Iran."

"Why? What's happened?"

"It's a long story. I can't go through it in detail on the phone; it would take too much time."

"But you have to tell me."

"Ok, don't panic; I am going to apply for refugee status here."

"What! What are you talking about? Where is your wife?"

"She will remain at the hostel until she finishes school."

"Are you out of your mind? You left your wife, your home and your life behind to become a refugee in India? What the hell do you think you're doing?"

"Listen, I can't explain it now; it is very complicated."

"You always make things complicated! Why didn't you talk to me first before leaving the country?"

"I really wanted to, but I was afraid you would try to change my mind."

"Why afraid?"

"Because I feel you still consider me the school boy I was when you last saw me."

"I am your brother! You should have asked for my advice."

"Ok, Davood; it is too late for that. What I need from you is your help."

"What can I do?"

"I have an interview at the UN office but I don't have any documents and was wondering if you have any papers to support my claims."

"Why didn't you apply for a visa through the Canadian embassy if you wanted to leave the country?"

"The conditions in Iran are not right for getting visas; countries hardly issue visas for Iranians these days unless you have connections or a lot of money."

"This is what you think! I see a lot of Iranians arriving in Canada everyday."

"Different people have different conditions but for me it would have been impossible. Let's forget about Iran; I am now in India and need your help."

He lowers his voice and says, "Go to the United Nations and tell them your life story; the officers there will surely accept you."

* * *

Finally, I get a letter from the UNHCR office with an interview date scheduled for January of 1997.

The line in front of the building is as densely crowded as always when I get there. I am shuffled from one small room to another until finally a young Indian lady, who is to be my interviewer, comes and asks me to follow her. We climb iron stairs just behind the waiting area to a small room on the second floor, where we sit and she starts questioning me; nervously and hesitantly, I give her the details about my life in Iran.

After finishing my story, she asks for the death certificates of my two brothers who were executed. We do not so much as have the body of my brothers and she is asking for legal papers to prove that my brothers are dead! Of course I have no such papers, so am asked to go back to Tourist Camp to wait while my petition is considered.

A month or so later I get another letter from the refugee agency. Their officials have rejected my case due to my inability to provide proof of my claims but do give me one month to appeal.

When I show this letter to my friend, Shahrooz, one of the members of the eclectic group in the camp, after a moment's consideration, he looks me straight in the eye and asks, "How did you act during the interview?"

"What do you mean how did I act?"

"I mean did you talk brashly with your eyes fixed on the interviewer's?"

"No, what's your point?"

"You just answer my question. Where were your eyes fixed when she was interviewing you? Did you look her in the eye or not?"

"Well, not exactly."

"Why?"

"Because she was a young lady and I felt embarrassed."

"Khak tu saret¹; that's the reason for your rejection."

"Nonsense! How stupid!"

"No, this is not stupidity; when you cast your eyes to the ground while talking to people, especially in such circumstances, it indicates you are lying."

"But that's how I learned to behave."

"You have learned bullsh...! If you want to survive in the outside world, forget what you learned and look people in the eye."

I call my brother Davood again and ask him for help. He has a specific document I need and sections of newspapers, released from the Mojahedin organization after the fact, listing names and sometimes pictures that prove my brothers were killed by the Khomeini regime, all of which he sends me and I put them together and submit an appeal.

While I am waiting to hear back, Kasra's wife and son return to Iran. There is no possible way for them to get visas for any country and Kasra does not want to apply for refugee status in case at some future time he decides to return to his homeland. The more his wife insists, the more Kasra resists visiting the UNHCR office. So, he sends his family back to Iran while he himself remains in Delhi with the hope of solving his dilemma.

After his family leaves, I move in with Kasra whose room is larger than mine but still so small we do all our cooking, eating, and visiting outdoors. At night, Kasra provides light by connecting a long wire to an electric plug which he has uncovered in his room, and to which he has attached several wires; he uses them to connect to the hot plate we cook on, the fan, outside lighting and other electrical appliances as needed. Only he knows how to fine-tune this system depending on its use so as not to overload it. Several times, when I accidentally touch the wires, I get an unpleasant shock.

* * *

The Pakistani border is open again and most of the businessmen have headed out to Iran. For the six months I have been at Tourist Camp, some of the businessmen as well as some of my group have returned for their second or third time.

As for the Armenians, once their appeals were rejected, the majority return home. The ones who stay behind are too broke to leave and have to rely on relatives in other countries for financial help, but they, too, finally give up and decide to repatriate.

Things are considerably quieter with nearly everyone gone. Only those, like me, who have determined to stay no matter what or those who have no choice are left. That's how things are when I show up for my second interview at the UN office. This time my interviewer is a well-experienced and professional legal officer who seems very friendly and I feel more comfortable talking to him than the previous interviewer.

As we get into more details, he begins to interrupt me to ask questions, forcing me to be more explicit, adding the words 'why' and 'how' to the end of many of my sentences. I have to explain every single thing at length and convincingly. At one point, I am forced to surmise why the Revolutionary Guards in my village never arrested me. For many of these questions, I have no answer because there is no answer.

At the end of the interview, this officer looks at me from his side of the table and says, "There are no obstacles to you returning to Iran; you can go back home."

I am sitting directly in front of him in his comfortably cool, almost cold office, with its air conditioning going full blast. I stand up in anger and put both my hands on the table between us. "You are sitting in this chilled room," I start shouting angrily, "while I have been waiting outside in the hot summer sun for months waiting to talk to somebody who can help me. Now you are blithely telling me that I can go back to Iran if I want to, and live a normal life? It is now your turn to prove it. Give me a written guarantee that conditions in Iran are amenable."

With a patient smile, Mr. Rao, the Indian legal officer who is my interviewer, asks me to calm down and calls for a break. By then it is lunchtime anyway so I spend the hour wandering around a park near the office and smoke so many cigarettes that I am afraid I might vomit; feeling poorly, I lie down on the grass in the park under huge shade trees. At the end of an hour, I have returned to the place I left and am ushered in.

The agent is still determined to have me prove my words. For the first time in my life, I find myself speechless, no longer do I have any words to prove that the life I led in Iran is as I described earlier. He asks me to name two friends who lived through the tensions in Iran with me, to serve as witnesses. I search the far reaches of my mind to recall two of my village friends; it is no use. Not only have all the names of my childhood friends slipped my mind, I am so tense that my English knowledge completely deserts me.

Taking into account that I am too wrought up to think, Mr. Rao offers to call an interpreter, which I accept with relief. While waiting for the interpreter to arrive, he, being as gentle with me as he can, asks, "Do you know our interpreter?"

"No."

"He is from Iran."

"Oh, is he"

"Yes, he is a doctor."

"Does he work here?"

"Yes, but he is a refugee."

The doctor walks in and I blurt out in rapid Persian, "Pleasedoctortell themhowthesituationwasinIranintheeighties.Theyareaskingforthed eathcertificatesofmybrothers.How-can-I-come-up-with-legal-papers-which-don't-exist?"

Both the doctor and Mr. Rao do their best to smooth my frenzy. When I am calmer, the interview continues and finally Mr. Rao comes to the end of his questions and then advises me to report to the back gate for the committee's decision after about a month or so.

* * *

For six consecutive weeks, officials postpone that date by a week every time I report and still no decision has been made. After a month and a half, once again, I find myself in the crowded line snaking down the dirt road and I am going crazy with this treatment. When it is my turn at the tiny window, a woman sitting on the other side once again writes a future date and time on the paper I hand her.

I blow my stack. "Do you think I am an animal? There is no more space on this piece of paper for more dates!" I bellow, showing her the scribbled and worn scrap of paper which has made its home in my pocket for six weeks in a row. "If you insist on postponing the release of the conclusion," I add, "just tell me when to come back. Why do you continue to bring me here week after week? Do you enjoy seeing me stand outside in this line all the time?"

The refugees and the guards are mute with surprise. The agent, startled by my outburst, picks up the phone and begins to speak. After a few seconds, a man appears in the room. She tells him someone outside is shouting that their office treats people like animals. When she gives him my name and nationality, the man leaves the room and is soon back again. He sticks his head out the small window and says, "What was your name again?"

I give him the worn-out paper without saying anything. He takes a look at it and says, "I have good news for you. You have been granted refugee status."

Everybody cheers my success but I am still so angry that I can't force myself to smile. I stand there silently and the agent addresses me, doing her best to bring joy to my deadpan face, "Come on, laugh! You should be happy. You are now a refugee."

As the rumor makes its way down the long queue, many other asylum seekers side with her and tell me I should be bucked up with the news; my case has made them optimistic about their own proceedings. I perk up a bit when I'm told to expect only another week's delay in getting the refugee certificate.

From among the hundreds of Iranians applying, I become the first person whose case is accepted but the battle to get to that place has left me emotionless and drained.

Beginning in July of 1997, I join the thousands of people from many nations who have been granted refugee status and are waiting for resettlement, some as long as seventeen years.

---

¹Khak tu saret is a taboo phrase meaning 'dust to your head'; it indicates you have made a stupid, unnecessary or terrible mistake. The closest English equivalent is 'idiot!'

~ * ~

Puppy

Kasra, thrilled to see my refugee certificate, embraces me and says, "Now, I can go back to Iran happily. You got what you deserved."

A few days later, the last of the group is packing, ready to leave India. Kasra, who has been supporting me, by now has also run short of money and decides to return home.

It is a very painful day when I silently help him pack his luggage. In the afternoon, the Iranians in our group, who are heading out that day, stop in one by one until all of them have arrived. Departure time is eminent. I am not looking forward to saying goodbye to everyone with whom I have had such a great time for so long.

Helping with the luggage, I walk with them to the main gate where we hug and say farewell before I go to Kasra who is waiting in silence. We throw our arms around each other, a big knot in my throat preventing me from talking. When he notices my low spirits, he pulls himself back and socks me gently on my shoulder. "Come on man," he says, "If you are old enough to be a refugee, be a man and don't weep like a woman!"

Everybody adds words of comfort and, trying to lighten my spirit, promises to be back soon. I get control of myself and an empty smile touches my lips, while deep in my heart, I long to be going back to Iran with them.

Kasra puts his hand in his pocket and pulls out all the rest of his money, two hundred American dollars plus a few hundred Indian rupees. Counting the money and separating it into equal amounts in his hands, he turns to me and says, "You are like my child and I want to see you succeed. I am just sorry that I do not have much money left. Let us share it half-and-half. Don't worry about me; I am travelling with my great friends who will not let me down on the way."

Other friends agree with Kasra and I, red-faced, accept the money that I have to shamefully admit I need in the worst way. In seconds, my moral support has evaporated like steam in the sun, while I stand, unfocused, by the gate; had it all been a mirage?

When I return to my senses, I am still holding Kasra's hundred-plus in my hand. Putting it in my pocket, I turn to see Puppy just behind me, a little sweet dog Kasra and I have been raising. She is watching me attentively, her tail barely wagging. I take my eyes off the dog to look all around. There is no sign of life; the camp seems to have been totally evacuated. I can hardly believe nobody lives here anymore. Painful silence strikes me hard on that hot summer afternoon. How will I survive in such a funereal place?

Puppy, who is very sad as well, follows at my feet to our room. This little dog was only a few weeks old when Shahab[1], a young Iranian man who at that time was an asylum seeker, found her at the perimeter of the camp and brought her in with the hope of finding somebody to take care of her, introducing this cute cuddly dog to us as Puppy. Kasra and I decided to adopt her, and for the past six months, the dog has grown up at our side; you can't imagine Kasra's childish joy at running around the Tourist Camp with Puppy for hours on end!

Now she is lying silently beside my chair under a tree near the room. Clearly feeling her grief and loneliness mirroring mine, I pick her up and begin to stroke her coat. She curls up calmly on my lap while I continue to look uneasily around us: cook pans, the old kettle, wires, chairs, bottles, and the well-taped icebox are scattered everywhere; I have no desire to collect them since I am not going to use them anymore. What are they good for now? I want to kick all of them away. Each one of these gadgets brings to life a painfully hurtful memory.

* * *

After an hour or so, one of the managers of the camp shows up. He is a polite and friendly person who treats the campers as equals and, because his dark features, hair and eyes remind me of my brother Darius, I love him like a brother and sense he has grown to feel the same about me.

Sitting in the shade beside Puppy and me, he begins, "I am sorry, Mr. Hassan, I have some bad news for you: the management of this camp has decided that you cannot stay any longer; you have been here for months and it is becoming difficult for us to justify your presence with us to the police. Moreover, you no longer have a visa and we don't accept the UN refugee certificate; we follow regulations and I hope you understand that I have no power to change them, although for your sake I wish I could." Gently asking me to find a place as soon as possible, he walks away, his eyes cast on the ground.

I immediately lock the door and leave for Old Delhi to book a room in a run-down hotel where a friend stayed earlier. When I arrive, the manager isn't there and a worker shows me to my quarters.

Back at the camp, I sign out, grab my things and scoot to the hotel, but before I can change my clothes or unpack, there is a knock on the door; the manager is there asking for my visa. I show him my refugee certificate and he says it isn't a proper document for renting a room; only a visa will do.

Having no other option, I return to the camp where I come face to face with my camp manager friend who is still alone in the office and agrees to let me stay a couple of days while I look for another place. When he gives me some addresses of the areas where he hopes I can rent a cheap room with my UN paper as identification, I thank him and promise not to let him down. Smiling sadly, he says he has already been let go and is leaving the camp anyway.

Leaving my luggage in the room, I lock the door and run towards the camp's main gate to head out in the hope of finding Amu, who has recently returned to recoup his seized properties still being held in the capital's airport, which as far as I remember, were never released.

Puppy starts running after me. Usually she does not try to follow me, but this time won't let me out of her sight. Since she is not used to crowded streets, when I reach the gate, I tell her to go back, but she doesn't obey. She is so determined that she finally makes me angry enough to pick up some small stones and throw them to chase her back into the yard. All the way to my room, she keeps turning around and looking behind her, desperately hoping I will summon her. When I make sure she is safely home, I jump into a rickshaw waiting for passengers by the gate and ride away to look for Amu among the millions of people in this city.

––––––––––––––––––––––––––––––––

¹Tall enough to be a basketball player, athletic looking, quiet and polite by nature, Shahab had just come to India with a father who was determined to find him a safe place to live outside Iran. With his father's help, he had found and married an Australian girl in Mumbai and contacted the Australian embassy in New

Delhi for visas while his father returned to Iran. The process took them longer than expected as it became a challenge for the couple to convince the Australian government that their marriage was genuine. Shahab's wife, who had his child in her belly, turned out to be a drug user. A year or so later when I accidentally saw Shahab in Paharganj, he was miserably and painfully drowned in heroin just like his wife. He was among several Iranian addicts I knew who were living in India hoping for resettlement, some for more than a decade.

~ * ~

Amu

It is almost night and I am still checking out the different places where I hope to find Amu; he is nowhere to be found. Frustrated, I decide I might as well return to the camp.

When I walk in, most lights in Tourist Camp are off and not many people are around the yard, only a few asylum seekers are sitting in the garden of the restaurant. Out of the original assortment of residents, these Armenians are the only ones left. After greeting each other, we begin to talk. The UNHCR office has accepted some of their cases also and this makes them feel very hopeful. They welcome my presence and ask me to stick around and chat, so I pull up a chair and join in. Having seen these people go through lots of tough times recently, now I am glad to witness their new spirit of lightheartedness, even if I cannot share it.

"My interviewer was a young Indian girl," one of them is saying about his interview at the UN office. "After the session was over, I told my interpreter that I wanted to thank the young lady in English myself, since I know several English phrases. I just wanted to say 'thank you' to her. Trying to remember 'thank you', I don't know how another phrase came to mind; standing up, I said, 'I love you'. The girl appeared shocked and the interpreter began to smile. Suddenly it dawned on me that I had chosen the wrong phrase. Afraid that I might have made the lady angry, I worried that she would drop my case in retaliation, so could not believe it when I was finally granted refugee status."

Laughter ensues and the discussion continues. Everyone else is happy but I find I am having to force my mood. Apologizing, I leave.

The whole backyard of the camp is dark. Except for the companions I have left behind, there is nobody around. I make my way through darkness under the trees, open the door to my room, turn on the light and am depressed to see such a small quiet empty space. Kasra is not there but his presence is everywhere. This was the friend who had taught me how to be tolerant with different types of people, how to listen to others with an open mind to discover the truth behind their words and how to build relationships even with enemies. I learned a lot from him about these issues, although he considered me mentally clumsy when I had trouble borrowing an item he needed from another camper since, such was his way with words that he could persuade almost anybody to do almost anything. As we Iranians say, 'he could convince a snake to leave its hole'. He repeatedly told me, "You are my only failure in the art of persuasion." During the time we were friends, he played the role of a mentor to me in everything except marketing; marketing wasn't my forte.

Looking back, it seems as if I have known this man from childhood, but in reality, only half a year has passed since we met. Now he is gone and I find I cannot even sit in the room we shared, without seeing ghosts. I walk outside and try to find something to sit on but the Tourist Camp workers have taken away all the chairs and tables Kasra and I collected for friends to occupy during our evening visits. They belong to the camp and the workers probably figure I do not need that many chairs any longer. Finding an old stool and setting it down under the tree closest to my room, I sit on it for several minutes in the dark, smoking, when all of a sudden I remember that Puppy would be a great comfort to me at this moment. I begin calling for her but she does not show her familiar puppy face. I walk through the garden calling louder, but there is no sign of Puppy in the whole area; I am still searching when I run into one of the Iranians around the restaurant.

"Are you looking for your dog?"

"Yes, have you seen her?"

"Those mother-fucker workers kicked her out of the camp this evening," he says, showing me the point, a small cement-lined water channel, through which Puppy was chased, and I run out in search of her, looking in all the nearby areas, and only find her when I reach the one-way crowded street directly behind the walls of the camp. What a painful picture for me to face! Puppy, who was not street savvy, has been hit and crushed while trying to cross the road.

I begin to feel very guilty for keeping her inside the camp all her life. She would have grown older like other curs if we had not sheltered her so, but we had separated this lovely canine from her natural environment and it was her doom.

It is almost more than I can bear: in one day I have lost Kasra, I have lost my friends, I have lost my room, and now I have lost my sweet little dog as well.

* * *

Later that night when Amu walks into the yard towards where I am sitting, calling out my name from a distance, I answer warmly, forcing my thoughts away from my misfortune, and hurry to meet him.

"Hello, Amu, welcome!"

"Hello; what's new?"

"Nothing special; everything is fine."

"Why were you looking for me then if everything is fine?"

"How do you know I was looking for you?"

"A while ago when I went back to my hotel, people told me you had been there looking for me."

As we walk back to my room, he hands me a bag, saying, "I just had dinner and brought some meat and bones for Puppy. Where is she?"

"Actually the workers kicked her out of the camp today," I say, deciding not to tell him about the dog's unfortunate demise.

"What were you doing then?"

"I was out looking for a new place to live."

"So, they have also kicked you out?"

"Hey, hamchin begi nagi. Something like that."

"Kasra is gone?"

"Yes, Amu; he left this evening, but he said he will be back."

"What do you think?"

"What should I say, Amu?"

"I say he will never be back."

"Why, Amu?"

"Because he loves ghol gholi more than he loves India. Yes? Don't you remember how Kasra quoted an old Iranian, saying, 'I quit smoking opium for twelve years but the passion for it is still in my heart'?"

Finding a chair for him, we both sit, a miserable light coming to us through the doorway of my room and lessening the darkness of a small swath around us.

"Put that food in the room for Puppy; I am sure she will figure out how to get back inside."

I give him the news about the room I am being kicked out of, the managers' decisions regarding the camp, and mention that I do not know anywhere else I can go in that big, teeming city.

"I say," Amu begins, "instead of sitting in this camp all day long, everyday, drinking, if you had visited just one area in Delhi once a week since you've been here, you would know of at least twenty-four areas in this city where housing can be found."

"You are right, Amu."

"Whisky is better? Or a house?" He says in his short-hand manner of speaking, we both laugh; with that, he puts his hand in his pocket, pulls out a small bottle of brandy and places it on the old icebox, which will serve as our table.

"It was late and the whisky was sold out," he continues, "anyway, drink is drink. I knew Kasra was gone, so I got you something to warm your blood."

"But, Amu," I interrupt, "my problem is not that I need booze; what I need is to find a place to live."

With his usual high-handed gesture, he looks at me and says, "First put a glow in your stomach, then we'll see what can be done about your room. Now get up and bring a glass while I go get us sodas."

I make a move to stop him, but he is already heading for the restaurant, calling back to me to do what he tells me. I bring out two clean glasses and soon we are both sitting and enjoying ourselves, he with a virgin soft drink and I waiting for the buzz alcohol will give me.

"I wonder why Puppy doesn't come back," Amu muses.

This old man and Puppy have always got along famously together; he loves to spoil Puppy and usually brings her fresh mutton or beef from the butcher on his way to Tourist Camp.

"You really love this dog, don't you?"

"Yes," he confirms. "Ask me why?"

"Why, Amu?"

"This dog wags her tail for me whenever she sees me; no matter if I have something for her or not. If, instead of helping so many people, I had raised a few dogs, I would never be lonely. People are my friends only when my pocket is full but will not even give me the time of day if they know I have nothing for them."

After I have swallowed some of the brandy and smoked a cigarette, Amu says, "Is your motor running now?"

"Yes, Amu; this hit the spot!"

"Now get up; go find those wires Kasra had and turn on a light in the garden. I cannot see anything."

I get right up. When I have found what I am looking for, I hang the lamp on a small branch over our heads and take the other end of the wire back to the uncovered plug in the room, remove the bare fan wire with a piece of wood and put the unwrapped wire of the lamp in its place.

"Ok, it is on," Amu calls loudly from outside, "don't do anymore to it; it's working."

I have hardly left the room when he calls me again, "Bring that book with you as well."

I go back for the book of Hafez[1] I have lying on my bed. Although illiterate, Amu loves listening to the poems in this book; during most of his visits to the camp, he has asked me to read aloud from its pages.

Book in hand, I return to Amu knowing he will open it to a random page, put his right index finger on a poem, and, "read this one," he will say. His powerfully sharp mind absorbs almost everything it is exposed to; whenever I start to read a poem I have already read, he stops me and says, "We had this one before. Let me find another one." He can even pick out most of the pages he has viewed earlier.

As I begin to read aloud the poem he has selected, he listens with rapt attention, sometimes coughing when he takes a drag from his cigarette, and sipping his drink. After I finish reading, he looks at me for a moment and commands, "Ok, now tell me what Hafez says."

"Hafez says, 'it is amazing to see there are still flowers in our garden in spite of the long and bad winter. He says, 'keep trying patiently because God is not going to leave the garden to devils'."

"So, Hafez knew about the Tourist Camp garden?"

"No," I reply, "Hafez is describing Iran."

"He means the mullahs will eventually go away?"

"Eventually, yes."

With a sigh he comments, "I know these mullahs. I say they cannot run the country. They do not deserve to run it; their job is to see to religion. I say the only person who can make this country well again is the Shah's son. He knows what to do if only Tony Blair will let him do it."

"What does Tony Blair have to do with anything?"

"If two fish are living peacefully together at the bottom of the ocean and Great Britain finds out about it, Blair will do something to make sure these two fish start fighting."

We sit there until around one o'clock in the morning, my spirits becoming lighter by the hour, when Amu finally decides it is time to leave.

"Come to my hotel tomorrow morning and I'll find a solution for you," he says as we stand up to separate. "Also, don't forget to give the food to Puppy when she returns."

I agree and we say our goodbyes. Walking away, he begins to talk as if to himself, "I don't know what problems such a little dog could possibly make for this camp. Maybe, like Hassan, her visa has expired! Yes?"

We are both laughing as he disappears into the darkness of night.

'Hafez/Hafiz, 1325-1389 AD. Born in Shiraz, Iran, Hafez lived and died in his hometown. He had a wide religious education but little is known about the details of his life. Other than he served as a court poet to many rulers and perfected the Persian lyric poem or Ghazal, he lived at a time when freedom of speech was severely suppressed, so he had to convey his message through well-organized love songs, ambiguous, both in form and meaning, to escape the harsh reaction of the then rulers and religious leaders. Although the main part of his poems is believed to have been destroyed, the collection of his available works has 'sweet complexity' that can be interpreted to fit all times and any conditions. His book, the Divan of Hafez, is regarded as holy by an overwhelming majority of Iranians.

~ * ~

Forms are better, or money?

Within a few days, I say goodbye to Tourist Camp, which has given me the chance to become acquainted with diverse cultures and know dissimilar behaviors all congregated in one place. To me, the camp has been a miniature world where I have watched as hundreds of people checked in and checked out one by one, two by two, and in groups, lived in close proximity for a couple of hours, a few days, a week or two, or as in my case, for months. The travelers who checked in took showers, went shopping, cooked, swam in the small pool in the garden, made friendships, fought, reconciled, and finally, kept on traveling. Now it is my turn to step out of this beautiful garden just as others have done.

I transfer to a temporary place Amu has helped find and has even paid the deposit on, knowing how short I am of cash. One night, shortly after I have moved, I feel a stab of pain in my side that is so ferocious my muscles, hands and feet go numb. I kneel on the bed with my stomach pressing against my knees as hard as I can make it. Remembering a couple of my brothers who have had kidney stones and whose remedy was to jump up and down for awhile to cause the stone to pass, I figure I probably have the same thing, so start jumping up and down in my room until I run out of breath and fall flat on my bed. No stone passes but at least I am tired enough to fall asleep.

Pain wakes me up early the next morning. I dress and head out to ask Amu if he can lend me money. By the time I reach the street, I am doubled over in anguish and can barely walk. I hire a rickshaw and leave for the tourist camp where he has again rented a room. He is not in, and since I cannot wait any longer, I leave a message for him with Khoda and hurry out as best I can towards the hospital across the road.

I am faced with a group of people outside a half-open door, which a gateman occasionally opens to let a few people pass. Knowing I cannot wait my turn, I hobble to the front of the line and ask to be allowed in. The gateman says something to me in Urdu which, even though I partially understand, I pretend not to and reply in English, 'I need to see a doctor now'. People around me intervene and, by paraphrasing his words in Urdu, try to make me understand I need to go to the other end of the building. Although I know what they are saying, since I think they just want to get rid of me, I push on in English.

As our discussion continues, a good-looking young man, in a white lab coat with a sphygmomanometer and blood pressure cuff hanging around his neck and down his front, appears at the door beside the gateman, attracted by my loud voice. He walks out to where I am standing and starts speaking to me in English with very little accent, "They are trying to tell you that the outpatient ward is at the other side of this hospital."

"Please, Doctor," I start begging, "I am in bad pain. I cannot walk anymore. Please, I need your help."

Taking off his equipment and handing it to the gateman, the doctor asks me to follow him to the other side of the yard. Seeing me bent over like a crippled old man, he adjusts his pace and asks questions about my symptoms while I gasp out the excruciating details of my pain.

Then, "Where are you from?" he asks.

"Iran."

"Oh, I love Iran! I had a few Iranian roommates in Armenia, where I went to medical school. I am really looking forward to visiting my friends in Iran one day."

This young doctor goes on to tell me he is a brain surgeon or neurologist or something like that; I am in too much pain to take in exactly what he says. We talk all the way to a door at the back of the hospital. As soon as we walk into the building, we are facing a vast horde of patients crowded into a huge waiting room, some sitting on old sofas or chairs, while the majority lounges on the cool cement floor. My eye focuses on a dead body occupying a stretcher in the middle of the room, around which a couple of women and children are crying. Two nurses come and cover the corpse with a white bed sheet and push the gurney out while other patients look on mutely emotionless.

The doctor asks me to find a place to wait and walks away into a nearby room. Minutes later, returning to me, he says, "I told the doctors about your pain; they think they know what is wrong." Pointing out a nurse who is sitting at a table in a corner of the room, he adds, "All you need to do is wait until that sister calls for you. Now, I must go back to my own patients. Take care," he says, giving me his business card. With profuse thanks, I take it and squat on my heels against the wall.

It isn't long before the nurse comes to take me into a spacious room where I face a huge elliptical table which accommodates ten to fifteen doctors. Each patient goes to the doctor who is free when it is his or her turn. The doctor who sees me confirms the suspicion that a stone is trying to pass from my kidneys. He scribbles something on notepaper and sends me back to the nurse who takes the note and walks away.

Waiting again, a small group of patients who has lined up in one corner of the room draws my attention. Bottles, jars and other smaller containers in hand, when called, they walk to a nurse who is standing beside a barrel the size of an oil drum and give their prescriptions to her. She takes a look at the notes and asks for their containers. Then, with a fair-sized kitchen ladle, she dips up some syrup from inside the barrel and fills the containers one by one, telling each patient how much and how many times a day he needs to take the medicine.

Unconsciously I forget my pain by my habit of people watching until the nurse comes back with a small syringe in her hand and asks me to pull down my pants for the injection. I lean against an old sofa already accommodating as many people as possible, bare my cheeks to her and she injects me in a matter of seconds, right there in the middle of the crowd in front of God and everybody. She sends me home without giving me anything for pain and nobody asks for money. That is how I learn government hospital services are totally free in India.

Half an hour or so later, I am feeling much better. By evening, I have almost forgotten the pain and am falling asleep in my room, when suddenly I hear Amu's voice calling from the alley, "Hassan agha, Hassan agha[1]!"

I jump awake and run out to look over the terrace at him, "Hello, Amu, please come on up."

"Ok, but have the tea ready by the time I get there."

"Sure, Amu."

While I put a kettle of water on to boil, he walks into the house and I watch through a grill as he starts up the stairs to the third floor where I live. Amu's presence never ceases to be encouraging and I always feel relief from anxiety when he is around. By the time he arrives, I have hot water for tea.

He asks after my health, and I tell him the story of the pain in my side and my hospital visit. "When something bad happens, nothing but bad follows," I begin to complain. "Why is it that everything happens to you when you are already down?"

Noticing my low spirits, he starts relating some of his own hard-luck history in an attempt to make me feel better. "I was not yet five when my father put me to work in a bakery; at night I slept there so early mornings I could deliver fresh hot bread to hotels, restaurants and teahouses. I grew up working in restaurants, stores and various marketplaces in Tabriz before moving to Tehran. I never had the chance to go to school, but you have a university education. Why is it then you give up so easily?"

"You know, Amu, I think a person can only bear so much."

"So, you think as well! You'd do better not to think; you just do what I say."

"What do you say Amu?"

"I say, instead of giving up hope, give up thinking! Now, go find the playing cards; I haven't beat you for a long time."

As we start playing, he continues, "You need to learn to be patient."

"How, Amu?"

"You gain patience by detaching yourself from your losses."

We continue playing and drinking our tea while he goes on to tell me about the many times he has lost his wealth and possessions both inside and out of Iran. He doesn't take these things very seriously, saying, "Money is like the dirt on your hands. Here today, gone tomorrow."

In a couple hours, when he is ready to leave, he hands me a sum of money before walking out the door.

"Thank you, Amu," I say, knowing I am just one of many persons he helps support, "I hope God rewards your generosity."

"For the past twenty years or so, I have never given away one-tenth of my income to any religious leader, nor have I ever paid taxes to any government if I could help it. So, take it easy and don't worry about owing me. A couple of thousand rupees from time to time is not a big deal."

"I wish the people in charge of human rights organizations thought like you."

"Why?"

"You lend me money without asking me to fill any forms or to give you any written guarantee while the people in charge of the UNHCR are always having me fill out some form or other and are looking for any excuse to withhold my allotment."

"Forms are better, or money?"

"Money, of course, Amu."

"But why do they like paperwork?"

"I don't know, Amu."

"Who knows then? Blair knows?"

He turns and walks down the stairs.

* * *

Later that night, my insides are burning again. I have the urge to urinate but cannot. I jump up and down until I am able to void a little urine and with it, a small stone passes agonizingly. Immediately afterward, I feel like I have been born again, and, asking God to bless the entire extended family of the Indian doctor and that of all his colleagues for removing such a horrific pain from me with a single injection, fall asleep peacefully and don't wake up until morning.

---

[1]Agha in Persian means Mr. and is a polite form of address which may come either before or after someone's first name, depending on the pronunciation of the name; hence: agha Reza but Ali agha.

Great love and great achievements involve great risk
........................Anonymous

Eight

This zigzag path of life

One day early in January of 1998, I am washing my dirty laundry and the dishes which, for days, have been accumulating in one corner of the room. Early in the evening when everything is clean and dusted, I take a quick shower, dress in a hurry and, borrowing some cologne from my next-door friends, I fly out of the room and down the stairs, rubbing my hands over my face and neck. By the side of the road, I find a small three-wheeled motor rickshaw waiting.

"Going to airport," I tell the driver, jumping in without waiting for his answer.

As we take off, things around me become a blur and I let my thoughts wander to my main concern. "How do I start the conversation?" I think, "What issues do I raise first? What can I tell her about how my life has played out in this country? I have no money, no place to stay and no control over my status. Will she agree to stay with me the way things are now? Will she be strong enough to tolerate the current conditions? I have kept the realities of life in India from her and led her to believe the UNHCR is like Superman who is everywhere saving people, failing to mention how distinct the actual UN agency is from her picture of it. Now she is only a few hours away from learning the truth; how can I destroy her dreams?"

Worries, guilt and uncertainties weigh heavily on my shoulders. I am still pondering my options when the rickshaw arrives at the New Delhi airport. Making my way through a crowd near the exit gate, I stand behind iron fences and cast around for my wife. The eyes of passengers leaving the airport, bags in hand, rove through the crowd, waving in happy relief when they recognize friends and family. I watch as, one by one, every last person leaves the hall; there is no sign of Mona. Fear invades my gut as I hurry to a small information center to ask about her flight. The employee checks the computer system and tells me the Tehran plane will soon land in an airport a short ways away, leaving me little time to get there. Thanking her, I run out on the double, call a rickshaw and ask the driver to move as fast as possible.

At the second airport, I get caught up in a group similar to the one I just left, watching the passengers who are already emerging from the exit hall single file. I notice a few Iranians waiting in the crowd; their well-shaped beards, their demeanor of success and the way they are dressed clearly proving to me that they are Iranian embassy personnel. I hide myself among the crowd and peer around into the hall with the hope of finding Mona.

Suddenly my eyes light upon a young girl in a long white dress, her hair covered with a scarf like women use in Iran. Her face, although a bit more mature and self-assured, is unchanged. She is my very same Mona whose eyes are now roaming around everywhere in the crowd looking for me. I want to call out to her but not wanting to attract the attention of the Iranians, I hold off. When the embassy people have left with their arriving visitors, I raise my hands in the air and wave for Mona who, seeing me, picks up her pace; I start towards her with my arms wide open. We hug each other like long-lost friends, Mona resting her head on my shoulder. For a while, she snuggles in my arms but soon bursts into tears. "You are so mean," she sobs, "you left me alone for ages."

"Don't worry; you are here now and I am with you. I promise not to let anything come between us again. How was your trip?"

"Don't you ever leave me again," she adds through her tears without answering my question. "It was so painful and I was so lonely without you."

Getting her emotions under control, she pulls herself back out of my arms. "Let me tell you what happened to me in Mumbai, you won't believe it."

"What happened? Tell me."

"When I got to Mumbai, that friend of Kasra's, the doctor? who arrived from Iran on the same flight, offered to act as interpreter. Passing customs, we were in the exit hall when I asked the doctor how to find the domestic airport from Mumbai to Delhi. He walked over to talk to a couple of airport officials who then came to where I was standing and said something to me in English which I couldn't understand. The doctor and the officials exchanged a few phrases; they walked away and the doctor told me that my luggage was overweight and I wouldn't be able to leave until I paid a surtax. The charge was $50, which I gave him and he walked with it back to where the officers were standing. I could see him telling them something but I didn't see him give them the fifty dollars.

"Then the doctor escorted me to the departure gate for Delhi and, once again, through his interpretation, I found out that my ticket was not confirmed and I would have to wait until the following day for another flight. By then I was in tears because I knew if I missed this flight I would have no way to contact you. With the two or so words I knew in English, 'husband' and 'Delhi', and with an emergency phone contact I had brought from the Iranian travel agency, which the airline employee called to confirm, I was allowed to board."

I can see she has only brought one bag and not a very large one at that; it couldn't possibly have exceeded the baggage weight. Keeping these suspicions to myself, I say, "Welcome to life abroad! Let's forget about it and just be glad you are here."

Suddenly, she sniffs at my body and gives me a puzzled look. "You smell differently."

"Oh, maybe it's the cologne."

She inhales again and says, "No, it is not cologne. It has the scent of rain falling on dried soil or something similar to that."

"Now, I get it," I reply, laughing. "This is the odor of India. You will get used to it soon and then you won't notice anymore."

When I reach to take her bag, she pulls back and says, "No, I don't need help. In your absence, I have learned not to be dependent on anybody."

With a chuckle, I comment, "I must say you seem to have grown up a lot since I last saw you."

Laughing together, we walk to a rickshaw, the bag between us. Although we missed one another terribly while being apart, we now act like strangers, both of us exceedingly polite and feeling uncomfortable together. Time and circumstances have pretty much done away with the youthful yearning I nurtured for years under the walnut tree. I wonder if Mona has some of the same feelings but is afraid to say. Like me, she has matured; I hope her newfound confidence and self-reliance will be sufficient to get her through the hard times she has ahead.

* * *

During her first few days in New Delhi, I take Mona to all the places I have lived in or visited, or ones to which I have created a special attachment in my heart. I show her Tourist Camp's garden, now almost empty with no sign of Iranians; some have returned to Iran and those, like me, who have received their UN refugee certificates, are now living in alternative housing.

Mona and I sit in the outdoor café sipping sodas, and I narrate to her all those adventures I have experienced with Kasra and others while living here. She listens contentedly to me telling the story of how the residents cooked and lived in those small rooms resembling prison cells and the way I managed to survive without a job or money.

"Now you know what my life was like and how little control I had over it. Sometimes at parties when I was having a great time, I really wanted you to be here. You know, the same way you missed me, I missed you. But the point is, because hard times overshadowed the good times, I just couldn't call and make you worry. Still I read all your letters hundreds of times under these very same trees."

'My dearest Hassan,' I begin to read parts of a letter I pull out of my pocket. 'I do not know how your life is going in India. I guess it is very tough for you to survive in a foreign country alone. But, how tough could it possibly be? Is life so harsh that it does not even let you call your wife once in a while? For months I wait to hear your voice, no word from you. At least give me your phone number so that I can call you. My parents now have phone access in the village. New Delhi is a capital city. How come you have no phone number?

'By the way, recently I dreamed of you again. It was a wonderful dream and I want to share it with you. In it, you and I were traveling hand in hand on a quite narrow path when a huge wall appeared in front of us. I was afraid and began to feel sad but you comforted me and asked me to hang on. Looking for a way through, we came across a gate, you pushed it open to reveal an abandoned garden. We entered and walked along under overgrown, wild trees, some of which were dry and dead. At the far side of this garden, we came to a gigantic wall even thicker and stronger than the first one. Hopeless, I did not want to try to find a way ahead. Over and over, you gave me encouragement to be strong. After diligent search, we found a gate. Pushing and pushing, it finally gave way and we stepped through to the other side where a dazzling garden met our eyes and we both felt we had 'wings of joy'[1]. "You see?" you scolded, "I told you to be strong. This garden is your reward."

'Suddenly my eyes were drawn to a house on a steep bank and to you sitting on its second-floor terrace chatting with some of your former friends while I was down in the yard looking up at you, calling your name and waving but you didn't seem to hear or see me.

'The next thing I knew the scene had changed and you stood beside me in the garden. We started walking together alongside the carpet-like grass and among the delicate flowers stretching towards a series of high hills in the distance. The hills were lusciously green and there was a narrow zigzag path through them that disappeared into the far horizon. Showing me the track, you said, "That is the way we ought to take."'

Mona is in tears by the time I finish reading. "You still have this letter?"

"Not only do I have this one, but I still have all the other letters you sent me as well."

* * *

As we walk out of the camp, I look around for the Indian manager who reminded me of my brother Darius, but don't find him.

----

[1]In Persian, to have 'wings of joy' means to be extraordinarily delighted.

~ * ~

Use your powers of rationalization patiently

Mona has been with me for a week or so when I decide it's time to take her to meet the UNHCR legal officer in order to add her name to my case and change my status to family unification. It's going to be very difficult for me to start this discussion with her. I will be asking her say goodbye forever to her family, her profession, and her friends in Iran and making her a helpless refugee just like me; she is not used to such a life. Besides, she never experienced the political tensions I went through in Iran. All her brothers and sisters were among the few in the village who didn't get involved in politics and I fear exposing her to a situation like mine will be something beyond her tolerance level. Although she knows I live in India as a refugee, she doesn't have the vaguest idea of life in such terrible conditions. Will she be able to put her peaceful existence at home behind her? Does she love me enough to come live with me in cramped quarters and share my hectic lifestyle?

"No!" she cries out loudly, "you mean I'll never see Iran again? You mean we are going to live in this tiny room forever?"

"Not forever. Just long enough for the UNHCR office to resettle us in another country."

"But I have no problems at home. Why can't I at least visit my family?"

"Listen, Mona," I try to explain very patiently, "if you ever visit Iran while I am officially a refugee, you will be sending a clear message to the United Nations that I have lied to them. It means what I went through in my childhood was fabrication. Do you know how it makes me feel when my very own wife doesn't believe what I am saying?"

"No, it's not that I don't believe you. The point is that we have to replace our comfortable life with such a poor substitute. Even when you sold bras and vegetables around the markets, our lifestyle was a lot better than what we have here. You can go back to that type of work. I am sure you can do it. Besides, I will get a job. We already have a house in Tehran and we can make our life close to our families and friends."

"How long do you think I can keep selling panties and bras or vegetables? I did not study to be a vegetable seller in the market. I won't be allowed to live peacefully in the country of my birth and this will affect your life as well. The reason you don't understand, Mona, is you did not go through what I experienced. Please! Forget about your feelings and use your powers of rationalization. I am also suffering here. Do you know how much I miss my old friends? But, think about our future family, innocent children who are not even born yet. Why should they suffer the stigma of their uncles being executed? My family is marked as dissident and for that reason, you and I cannot go forward with our lives at home like others. Even if a better life in another country doesn't happen, at least by seeking asylum here we can send a message of protest, and this message is that we can't live in a land without basic human rights, and this is why we are tolerating such unbearable conditions away from home. I assure you we won't stay here forever. Who knows? Maybe this year the UN office will send us to Canada, close to my brother Davood, where our situation will be improved."

I guess at no other occasions in my life have I ever lobbied for a cause so hard and so long at one sitting. We look out at the surrounding areas from our sliver of terrace and talk until, late in the night, she finally comes to see my point of view and agrees to let her name be added to mine on the United Nations refugee certificate.

* * *

We start looking for some place cheaper to live, and find a very small room on the third floor of a house in a rather poor area called Bhogal. The three-story building belongs to an extended Indian family who together occupy the first and second floors. The owner is a venerated Hindu woman whose family consists of her sons, her daughters-in-law and her grandchildren.

Entering through the gate from a narrow alley is an open area that serves as the kitchen, dining room and living room and doubles as a workplace where mounds of clothing and linens are pressed several days a week. At the far end, directly opposite the main entrance, is a small windowless room about the size of a darkroom for developing pictures. This floor is occupied by the old woman, her oldest son and his wife and children.

In order to reach the second and third floors, as well as the rooftop, we pass through the dining room to climb the cement stairs against the left wall.

The second floor has two rooms, one facing the other; the right-hand one is smaller but has a pleasant view, being adjacent to the alley passing by the main entrance. It also has a very narrow terrace profusely covered with long branches of jasmine leaves and flowers. The room on the left, being windowless, even though larger, has no view at all. Two of the old woman's sons live with their families on this floor, one room for each.

The only difference between the third floor, where we live, and the second is it contains a toilet stall and a small shower between the two rooms. Sometimes, when the toilet outside the first floor is in use, whoever is in need uses the one scarcely a meter away from our room.

Squeezed between our room and the toilet, a square is cut out of the floor, and covered with an iron grill. This open hole serves as a natural air conditioner to cool down the scorching temperatures of the entire house during the long Indian summers. Through the bars, we can see the second and the ground floors. If we happen to be outside our room and someone from below is looking up, we are visible, so for privacy we keep the grill partially covered with a blanket. The second room on our floor is a rental like ours.

Ashok and his new human toy! Behind him are grills partially covered with strips of canvas from an old bag. A pipe comes out of the wall between the grill and the toilet.

We live in the smaller room on the right, the one with the narrow terrace. Like the terrace on the second floor, ours is covered with so many jasmine branches that when our neighbors across the alley come to their rooftops, they can just barely see me sitting on my plastic stool.

The main problem of this house as well as houses in many other areas in Delhi is water shortage, especially during the long summer. We get used to being awakened at two or three o'clock in the morning to a loud voice shouting 'get water! get water!' and taking all our empty jars into the shower and filling them under the taps.

The occupants of the second floor have to wait for the landlady to fill her containers first, and when it is finally our turn, we have to make do with any water that is left. It often happens that the water doesn't reach either the second or the third floor[1].

"We still have not got our water," we protest from upstairs.

"The water has not come on yet," comes the answer.

"We saw you filling your jars minutes ago."

"You were dreaming."

It's useless trying to convince them and we have to wait until the next night and try again. Often we cannot take a shower for a week or so at a stretch in the sweltering summer months.

* * *

When kids come up to use our toilet, if they find it occupied they squat outside the door in front of our room and poop on the floor. Since there is no water to clean the area, Mona and I have to close the door and stay in for hours until somebody comes and washes away the pile.

The sound of large containers of water being moved about finally brings us out with the hope of getting our share. Both Mona and I sit in our doorway in front of the grill, sweat dripping off our foreheads, and watch little children below splashing in big wash pans like a gaggle of ducklings while we go without water upstairs.

When I finally get fed up with the lack of water I start shouting, my anger drawing the attention of neighbors in surrounding buildings who are busy collecting water and who are kind enough to sometimes volunteer to share it. But the summer is long and their water supply is short as well.

Occasionally, I notice how the whole household seems to enjoy hearing me talk angrily to the owner of the house. This gets on my nerves; here I am shouting down to the landlady in anger and there she and her family are smiling up in reply. I suppose they are laughing because they find my Urdu usage funny, but no matter how much I shout, not only do my hosts not become agitated, they actually try to calm me down, amazing me with their tolerance of my bad manners. Even though all three of the owner's sons are stronger than I am and could kick my butt, their culture is such that they make a person angry, and then they refuse to fight.

* * *

As time passes, both Mona and I get used to our neighbors, and many of their children begin to visit us, first the kids from downstairs come, then they start bringing their friends, and finally, the friends also bring friends. I might come home to about twenty little boys and girls both in our small room and on the terrace, vociferously chatting with Mona and generally having a good time.

"Uncle Ji Namaste!²" They say when I step in.

Whenever we have enough potatoes, we make 'finger chips', which I nickname 'uncle chips'. These youngsters, already familiar with cooking, love the whole process and do not let anyone help them with their preparation. One of the children acts as chef and doles out tasks to the others; they cooperate in preparing the pan and peeling and chopping the potatoes. The older ones assign themselves the task of frying. The 'fingers' are all different shapes, some short, others fat and still others odd-shaped but we all relish the finished product. Then they wash the dishes and tidy everything. The 'uncle chips' days provide a good feast and attract even more children to Mona and me in our little aerie.

Through these children, we learn their language and local customs. It seems to us that most of them, because of the harshness of their lives, are more mature than Iranian children of the same age are.

If, after we have tired of their noise and activity, they want to stay long, I resort to anger and shoo them out; instead of going home, they head to the rooftop. Something which amazes and frightens us, even though it seems very natural to them and their parents, is how these children play on a roof which has barriers on only one side, and I see them leaning over the edges without a barrier, talking to people below.

----

¹This could happen for several reasons: if the landlady was not happy, if rents were a day or two late, or even if friends visited too often. Once when we first moved in and a friend was broke and needed to stay with us for a couple weeks, the landlady closed the tap on her floor, denying us water during the time our friend was staying with us.

²Hello dear uncle

~ * ~

Where is your flag?

Several months pass and we are still waiting for any news about our resettlement. During this time, we make good friends with an Afghan family; six children, their parents and an elderly grandmother all living together in one small room located in the middle of the roof of a three-story building. The front and backsides of the long open rooftop, enclosed by iron fencing, double as their front and back yard. Everybody in the family is a registered refugee except Balooch, the children's father.

Balooch, a good-mannered man in his early forties, has the kind of character that regales everybody with embellished stories in which he always plays the hero. In his accounts, he and Doctor Najib, the Afghan ex-president, had great times together in kung fu classes and various athletic clubs while their friendship deepened. One story in particular, which he relates over and over, is how he saved the president: once when he was flying with Doctor Najib, the pilot had a stroke and lost control of the plane. The president and his entourage were expecting the plane to crash and all of them to die. Everybody had lost hope when Balooch jumped into the cockpit and asked others to help him by taking the pilot from his seat and putting him on oxygen. Donning the headsets, he began to call for help and continued transmitting until he received an answer from a nearby airport tower. The main concern was for the president; ground control immediately made this plane top priority. By following instructions from the ground, Balooch managed to land the plane safely.

In spite of such tall, exaggerated stories, he is a warm, outgoing person with whom I love spending time. Seldom is he at a loss for words; poetry, politics, Iran, Afghanistan, refugees, and many less germane topics keep us engrossed for hours. Never able to sit still, even while we are talking, he is always working on fixing a child's bicycle, a fan or a radio. He loves his native country so much that he keeps himself busy writing patriotic stories and poetry, or lesson plans for Afghan children, paraphrased from old grammar books. When I ask him why he is writing lesson plans for kids who don't even have a school, he sighs and says, "That's OK. Maybe someday they will be of use."

Mona and I care deeply for this family and feel comfortable being with them. We wish Balooch could get refugee status like his family; however, he is too intractable to take any advice on his case. Several times I gently try suggesting to him that the UN agency might not believe his stories about the ex-president of Afghanistan. I ask him if he can prove his claim that he was a senior officer under Doctor Najib. As proof, he takes out of his pocket a very poorly done ID card with no specific information on it and shows it to me. A self-portrait is attached to the card with glue, and he has written his own name on it in ink. In the photo, he is in military dress, which, most probably, he borrowed from the photographer. No name or star decorates his uniform.

"What kind of card is this?"

"Look here, this is me in the picture. As you can see, I am in military uniform. So, that proves that I was an officer."

"But there are no officer's stars on your shoulders."

"That is not important. I knew lots of officers who did not put stars on their uniforms during their daily activities."

"This card has no official stamp or signature, either."

"There was war in Afghanistan for such a long time, and offices would remain closed for years. Besides, many government buildings were destroyed in the war. So, these things were not very important in my country."

The more I emphasize that such a card is proof of nothing, the less he listens. He goes to the UNHCR office and repeats similar stories during his interviews. In the end, the UN agents tell him that he is too important for the Indian office and they cannot guarantee his safety in India. He is asked to contact the UN Headquarters in Geneva directly to present them with his case, in the hope that the agency might decide to accept him as a refugee. That is how, even though he is the head of the family, Balooch plays no role in the family's case under the UN refugee Conventions.

* * *

I hear complaints from Balooch's children about having the same food day in and day out. Their meals consist of bread baked at home; to this, they add grains and beans, and only occasionally meat. To reduce daily expenditure, the family makes do with second-hand equipment, clothing, and home appliances.

In spite of their poverty, the whole family is kind, receptive, and hospitable. We are like family; in fact, I call Shadi, Balooch's wife, 'sister' while Mona calls her 'aunt' and both of us treat the grandmother, whose husband recently died and was buried in Delhi, like our own mother.

Balooch and Shadi have two sons and four daughters, the oldest of whom is about fifteen and the youngest five or six. The family lived in refugee camps in Pakistan for a couple of years before fleeing to India. They always describe life in the camps as 'a real Hell on earth' and are very happy with their new life here.

Relatives in the USA, Canada, England as well as other parts of the world send them a little money from time to time, some of which they have used to purchase a second-hand color TV. The TV keeps the children busy for hours with all sorts of Hindi movies while Balooch and I, sitting outside the room on the rooftop, exchange pleasantries. Sometimes a group of elderly Hindu ladies sitting in a circle in a small park below us chanting religious songs and playing tabla, an Indian drum, captures our attention.

"Look," Balooch exclaims, "what if women in our own countries had such freedom?"

"They would be called aging prostitutes!" I answer with a laugh.

"And they would be stoned to death!"

"What interesting countries we come from! Don't you think?"

"People in other parts of the world have traveled beyond the solar system and we are still stuck with such backward ideas. Why are we so proud of our thousands of years of civilization?"

Some of Balooch's children come out to where we are sitting to interrupt our conversation, wanting to explain the story lines of their movies to us. In order to be the center of attention, they compete to narrate the story, pushing and crowding in front of each other to get the chance to speak first, finally pleading, "Come on, uncle, come on, baba, let's go watch it together! Such a good movie!"

"No, my child," Balooch gently declines. "Uncle Hassan and I are talking."

"But you have already talked about these issues hundreds of times! We don't understand your conversations and they are not as exciting as our movies."

"The words of us, the writers, are different," Balooch explains. "How could you expect to understand such difficult topics? You would be better off to go in and watch TV."

When we decline their offer, they head for the kitchen where Mona and Shadi are busy preparing food.

* * *

Once when we are sitting outside their room in the fresh air, somebody knocks. Shazieh, the youngest girl, runs to the other side of the rooftop and opens the door to let a young woman enter. We stand and Balooch introduces her as Bibi, the wife of their neighbor from the third floor just below them. She is a very warm and friendly Sikh woman and all the children are very fond of her. Hearing Bibi's voice, the rest of the family comes to the rooftop to welcome her.

"The landlord was here today," she says to Balooch and Shadi, "and wanted to visit your place. You were not home and he said he would come back tonight. I was hoping to see you before then."

They thank her and Balooch immediately calls three of his children to him. "Did you hear Bibi, my child?" he asks his oldest daughter. "Be quick and take your sisters to your auntie's house until later tonight. I will bring you home when the landlord leaves."

Just like that, three of Balooch's offspring disappear. He has lied to the landlord about how many children he has since it is well known that nobody will rent a house to a nine-member family.

In addition to hiding children from the landlord, they also have to hide from the UNHCR representatives the small appliances they have managed to obtain. If the agents happen to find such luxuries as sofas, chairs or color TVs inside refugees' homes, they suspend the monthly allotments[1]. In order to get reimbursed for the missing allowances, refugees have to prove that they are in desperate need. Although the payment received from the UNHCR office every month is negligible compared with daily expenditures, it is still vital for survival.

The poor little Afghan girls have to take off all their fake bracelets, rings or necklaces whenever they are to meet people from the UN office. All bicycles go into hiding when there is a rumor of official visitors arriving. On many of these occasions, Bibi's timely warnings are of great help to this family.

In spite of Balooch and Shadi's friendship with Bibi, she almost never partakes of a meal with them. In her religion Moslems are considered unclean, so sharing food with them is forbidden and she wants to avoid upsetting other members of her family.

Her statements on clean and unclean things remind me of what I went through in Iran. I can clearly see that her religious lessons are more or less the same as the ones from our mullahs. Our teachers of religion teach us not to shake hands or eat food with non-Moslems since they say such people are unclean. Now, Bibi is telling me that she grew up in a parallel environment. This world village has many similar teachers!

I am amazed to actually see this happen in one of the most democratic countries of the world, India, where people are absolutely free to choose or even to invent the kind of faith they wish. As an example, there is a society towards the south of the country, where members smoke pipes filled with hashish, called chillums, shave their hair and dress only in long orange robes both in public and inside the temple.

One of their more interesting customs is how they deal with sexual temptation. Unfulfilled sexual desires distract one from relaxation and focus, but are easily solved by cohabiting with other members of the cult. I heard two Iranians, who had recently left their country, joined this community. As the result of restrictions in male-female relations in Iran, they had a strong desire for girls upon arriving in India. According to the 'orange robe' people, they were permitted sex with female members of the temple until their lust was satisfied. During their stay, their thirst for sex seemed unquenchable. In less than two weeks, the authorities kicked them out and told them that they had mistaken the temple for a public brothel (honestly, I wasn't one of them!).

Close to the Red Fort in Old Delhi, there is another temple where people gather and worship the male organ which is considered sacred because it increases humanity. A couple, on their wedding night, visits the temple where the bride offers her virginity to a stone phallus.

In a country as free as India, Bibi does not share meals with Moslems because of her religious beliefs. Don't you think the world of religions needs a new flag as much as we refugees do?

'Once, I changed my residence and did not report it right away. The refugee agency suspended my allowance and I had to push them for a few months to get the back payments. Deputies could withhold our imbursement arbitrarily, at a whim; they often visited our houses looking for a pretext to get out of having to support us. Personally, from my terrace I once saw Ms. Vinira, one of my UN caseworkers, at the nearby store talking to the shopkeeper. Later, when I was talking to him, the shopkeeper told me Ms. Vinira had asked him how much money I spent on an average every day and what I bought.

~ * ~

Mona's masterpiece!

It is 1998, the World Cup has just started and I am desperate to watch it.

Mona and I are home when Shazieh, Najieh, Yama, Hasib, Nabila and Tahmila - Balooch and Shadi's brood - arrive at our house raucously. Shazieh, the youngest child, is running up the stairs while her brothers and sisters chase her from a distance behind. She joins Mona and me on the third floor and greets us hurriedly.

"Uncle-Hassan," she blurts out, "my-father-said-you-like-soccer-very-much-so-he-has-sent-you-our-old-black-and-white-TV-to-watch-the-soccer-matches-we-have-our-color-television-and-do-not-use-this-one-anymore-my-father-said-you-can-have-it."

Shazieh utters all this in one breath to make sure she has finished her story before the others, who arrive behind her one by one, breathing hard, can stop her. Facing the angry frowns of her brothers and sisters who are yelling at her for not giving them time to tell the story first, she grabs my legs and hides behind me.

Seconds after the rest of the children, Hasib, the older son, appears at the door, wheezing, and carrying a portable TV in his arms.

"Uncle," he gasps, "My father said..."

"Shazieh already told uncle and auntie everything," the rest interrupt him.

"Shazieh, why did you tell?" Hasib asks his sister angrily. "Our father asked Tahmila to explain about the TV to uncle Hassan."

"Well, I said it first," Shazieh replies, feeling brave from her position of safety behind me. "So what?"

We quiet the children and help Hasib put the appliance on a small short-legged table they have brought along. With everybody helping, we connect one end of a wire to the TV and wrap the other end around an iron rail on the rooftop to take the place of the antenna we don't have.

* * *

The times Iran plays, Mona and I cheer the team on gustily in support of our country, even if it is in the middle of the night.

Our boisterous entertainment can be heard from several houses away but our neighbors never complain about our rudeness and lack of consideration for their sleep.

So hot! In India, I spent most of my life in 'maman dooz' shorts! Watching soccer on the donated TV, to the right is our tape recorder/player covered with cloth against dust.

This old TV comes to be good company; besides the World Cup, it keeps us occupied for hours with Hindi movies and sing-alongs to music. Mona and I sing at the top of our lungs, record our performance with a little tape recorder and laugh loudly at the sound of our own voices played back to us.

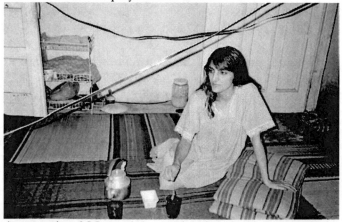

An emaciated Mona sitting under the wires connecting the TV to the roof. Our three-story kitchen fits behind the door on her right.

* * *

One day Mona and I are strolling in the Bhogal market when we decide to have some refreshments. Entering a nearby restaurant, we order two glasses of juice and start sipping them while chatting about this and that. With an abrupt movement, Mona puts her glass down on the table and says, "Is it ok if I don't finish my drink?"

She is feeling queasy and we decide to leave the restaurant. We have hardly stepped outside when she begins to heave. Her face is pale and no sooner does she stop vomiting when she starts in again. I take her directly to a clinic nearby. A doctor checks her and says, "Congratulations! You are pregnant."

The doctor expects me to be pleased but I am in shock and don't know how to react. Without enough to eat already, now we have to worry about feeding and caring for a baby?

"Is there anything wrong?" the doctor asks.

"No," I reply and to justify my reaction, add, "I am surprised, that's all."

She tells us that Mona is in her second month of pregnancy. All we need to do is to wait for some seven more months to pass, and then we will be parents.

We leave the hospital and walk back home in silence. After exhaustive debate, knowing it is a challenging situation, we decide the child has the right to life.

* * *

Our Afghan friends are elated with the news. The children, looking forward to playing with our expected baby, start a contest for choosing his name.

"Call him Hasib."

"Ok." I answer with smile.

"Call him Yama."

"Ok."

"Call him Najib."

"Ok."

"If it is a girl, call her Shazieh."

"Ok."

"No, uncle; call her Najieh."

"Ok."

"What are you doing?" Balooch calls to his children, "Uncle Hassan and Auntie Mona will have only one child while you have chosen several names."

But who is listening to him? Each child is busy lobbying for his own option and has no doubt that his choice will win.

Although happy about the news of the baby, Shadi and her mother are concerned that I cannot feed Mona adequately. With their experience as mothers, they begin giving me advice on what to cook and serve for proper nutrition during pregnancy.

This family has very little, but they often insist on having us to their home for meals, or coming to our house to prepare and serve a simple meal sometimes consisting of only eggs and homemade bread.

Here we are, two families living in close proximity in our neighborhood, both of us so poor we are unable to help each other out, but getting together for meals, sharing whatever we can afford to eat, laughing and having a good time in spite of our difficulties, in spite of being refugees and broke all the time.

Sometimes I wish people, once life situations improve, could still be as close to their friends as they are when they have nothing.

* * *

Thinking of how I might make more money, I contact the UNHCR office and talk to Ms. Vinira, the Indian officer, to ask if there are any opportunities for me to work within the UN office as an interpreter like I have heard many Afghan and a couple of Iranian refugees are doing. She makes no promises but says she will try to call me if anything comes up.

At the same time, I begin to look for students and find several Afghan and Iranian refugees who need an English teacher. Soon, I am spending hours in crowded buses everyday, traveling to different areas of Delhi to give lessons to my students in their homes. Although I'm not making big money, I make enough for the extra expenses occasioned by Mona's pregnancy.

With no money for drinking water and no refrigerator in our house, I wind up buying ice from the market everyday and filling a styrofoam icebox to keep our food safe from spoilage for several hours, and we boil water we collect from the taps. The boiled water goes into a clay jar we cover with a damp cloth and store in the shade of the jasmine branches on the terrace near where we leave food for the sparrows and chipmunks. At mealtime, when I, dressed only in above-the-knees shorts called 'maman dooz', stoop under the jungle of branches on the terrace to bring in water and all the birds scatter, Mona laughs and says, "You look like a primitive man and this place looks like a cave!"

Since we do not have an air conditioner and have to cook in this room, the heat from the small gas stove or the hotplate combined with the natural heat of an Indian summer makes the room as hot as the Hell my religion teachers described and I feared years ago. In order to get some sleep, we soak a large curtain in water and cover ourselves during the long summer days. The slowly turning blades of the large ceiling fan dry the curtain in minutes and, feeling the heat again, we get up, re-soak the curtain in water, and repeat the process over and over throughout the daytime hours.

* * *

One day, returning home from teaching, I come face to face with my landlady in the middle of their dining room floor. I say hello[1] to her and to her three daughters-in-law who are busy doing the ironing they take in. The old woman stops me with a sharp tone as I start up the stairs to my room. Her features are twisted with anger and she rages on and on at me while I stand there watching in silence.

Not being able to figure out what she is trying to tell me, I pretend by nodding my head and saying 'acha, acha', or 'ok, ok' in her language, and turn and leave for my room.

The old woman shouts after me furiously. "What acha, acha?" She bellows. All three of her daughters-in-law begin to laugh loudly and talk amongst themselves.

The door to my room is locked when I get there. Could the landlady in her anger have locked me out? But, no, it is locked from the inside, which means Mona is there but isn't answering my knock. In a wheedling tone, I ask her to open the door.

"No!" She cries out.

"Why not? Let me see what has happened."

To my continued insistence, she at last opens up. She is visibly shaking, her eyes are red and puffy, her face flushed, her voice fearful and angry at the same time. I hug and reassure her; when she becomes a little less agitated, I ask her to tell me what the problem is.

"I have told them over and over and over," Mona begins angrily, "that their children cannot leave human waste at our doorstep. But they think I am kidding. Today, I almost stepped in a pile of offal when I walked outside the room. I called downstairs for someone to come and clean up the mess. More than an hour passed and, although several people came to use the toilet, nobody cleaned up. Then, I saw red; I grabbed a broom and swept the whole heap down to the first floor through the grill."

When she has finished her story, I walk back out and look down through the bars near our doorway. I can see an identical set of bars on the second floor and below that, the women who are working down on the first floor. There are still scattered remains of Mona's 'masterpiece' smeared on the bars of the second floor.

Returning to her and with disbelief in my voice, I squawk, "You mean you shoved all the crap into their dining room?"

"No," comes her slow answer, "the old woman was working downstairs and it fell on her."

We look at each other for a few seconds. Then simultaneously both of us burst into loud laughter.

Hearing us laughing, the landlady screeches even louder from downstairs. What pushes her over the edge is she will have to wait until night before she can take a shower or wash her clothes.

"Why did you lock the door on yourself, then?" I ask Mona when our laughter dies down and she is calmer.

"I was alone at home and they were four; I feared they might beat me up."

"That is why Rashti are so brave in Persian daily jokes!" I chuckle[2]. She feigns anger and tries to punch me for making fun of her.

As a result of this incident, the landlady denies us water for a couple days but it isn't long until we reconcile with our proprietors again.

---

¹I always greeted the landlords with 'namaste', or 'hello', when I saw them, a Persian custom. However, this family was not accustomed to greeting each other every time they met. As a result of my frequently using 'namaste', one of the landlady's grandchildren, who was just learning to talk, called me 'Namaste'. That is how our friendship with these children started.

²Rasht is the capital city of my province, Gilan. We are known as Rashti.

~ * ~

Raise your voice if the occasion warrants

At the beginning of every month, Mona and I meet some of the Iranian refugees at the UN bank, where we receive our monthly payments. Most of these people used to belong to the larger group of Armenians who lived in Tourist Camp at the same time I did. From among some four hundred Iranian applicants, only about ten of us managed to get a refugee certificate.

Among them is a young man my age called Roberto, who was accepted several months after me and subsequent to persistent and numerous appeals. He is the first Iranian refugee I invite to visit us at our home.

Once, in the beginning of our acquaintanceship, when his payment is suspended by the UNHCR office and he is in desperate need, he comes to me for help. I loan him some money and he promises to repay me as soon as he can.

Months pass until one day when the office cancels my monthly allotment and Roberto does not offer to return the favor of helping me out, I realize he doesn't plan to pay me back and decide to confront him.

At the next scheduled payment day, when I am determined to talk to him, Roberto doesn't show up at the bank. Upset by his action and feeling that he is doing all this on purpose, I sit under a tree waiting until I spot him, papers in hand, sneaking into the bank at the last moment. When he emerges busily counting his money, I approach him from behind. With a look of alarm, he makes the excuse that he was late getting to the bank because he was visiting an embassy.

"Are you human?" I say in anger. "I loan you money, then you disappear. When you saw my payment was suspended last month, you just put your cash in your pocket and walked away. You have your beers whenever you want while I cannot afford to even feed my wife bread."

When he has apologized and paid me back, I let go of my anger towards him and that is the beginning of our friendship.

Roberto is quite a talker; he can talk from early morning until late in the evening without ever running out of words. He is also an encyclopaedia of information about resettlement regulations in different countries. Once he suggests that instead of sitting home and talking all day long, we talk on the way to present our applications to various embassies. That is how we start going together from one embassy to another along Shanti (Peace) Path in New Delhi, with Roberto as the instigator and me as the spokesman who translates what he tells me to say. Although nothing ever comes of our efforts, he won't hear of us quitting.

When we get to know him a little better, Roberto with his wife Mikkey, and Stella, one of their friends, become regular visitors. Stella lives alone in Delhi since her mother and sister have sought asylum in Canada. She has been waiting a couple years already for her mother to get Canadian citizenship and be able to sponsor her. I like her because she is a down-to-earth, unpretentious girl with contagious laughter, and her warm presence makes her popular in any gatherings.

Both Roberto and his wife are very excited when Mona tells Mikkey about her pregnancy. According to their information, in the history of the UNHCR in India, our child is the first ever made here and will be the first ever born here.

"Now you have set a record," they add, "this is something to brag about."

Although Roberto would have loved bringing a child into the world, Mikkey does not share this desire with him. She puts her foot down and says she cannot have a child until she has a homeland.

* * *

Each time I call my brother Davood in Canada, I have to endure lectures as if he were the teacher and I a schoolboy, so I limit my contact with him. He worries so much about me that I can't convince him I am an adult and able to make decisions on my own. Thinking I don't understand what he is telling me, he repeats the same message time and again.

"I get it."

"No, you don't. My words go in one ear and out the other. And this predicament of yours is because you never pay attention to what I say. You left your home, you left your country and you made your wife homeless as well, without consulting me to find out how to do it the right way. You could have applied for a visa through the Canadian Embassy in Iran. Now this is what has become of your life. It's all because you don't listen."

While he is lecturing, I keep my eyes worriedly fixed on the phone meter clicking off the seconds and minutes. Every time I call him, I spend several hundred rupees and end up with a whole bunch of impractical brotherly advice for my money.

"Put on nice clothes," Davood usually coaches, "and take your wife with you; do not go to any embassy alone. Officials may think that you are a single person; many countries do not accept singles. Both you and Mona should be well dressed. Go to the Canadian Embassy and ask for a meeting with the visa officer. Explain that you are a refugee in India and you have a job offer from Toronto through your brother who is a Canadian citizen living in that city. Very politely, tell them that you would be grateful if they could help you join your brother in Canada. Don't go to the meeting without a proper suit. Shine your shoes and put on a necktie. Watch what you say; don't elaborate, just answer their questions. Don't laugh, don't let yourself get angry, don't raise your voice. From the moment you step into the embassy until you leave, whatever you do will be noted, so be serious and do not try to joke around."

Davood talks non-stop until we say goodbye. He doesn't want to believe how many people stand in crowded lines outside most embassies in Delhi; I cannot make it clear to him that it is impossible to get past reception, let alone meet a visa officer. What he is asking me to do is not viable but I find it is useless to argue with him, so I begin calling him less and less until finally a year has gone by since we have spoken.

* * *

Mona is in her third month of pregnancy and I am teaching several days a week to add to the meager payment from the UN. One evening, I return home to her crying in a corner.

"Go call the doctor," she moans, "I have started bleeding. What if my baby dies in my womb?"

"What has happened?"

"Water came this afternoon and you were not home," she replies. "I filled all the containers with fresh water[1]. Trying to move those heavy jars to our room, a shooting pain almost knocked me over. Go call the doctor. I'm bleeding."

Without taking time to get more information, I pick up the phone number of the doctor who is closest to our house and run out to the street to find a public phone. Hastily and disconnectedly, I explain everything to the doctor who, confused, asks me to repeat myself and tells me to bring Mona to her house, behind ours, right away.

Once having seen Mona, checked her vital signs and asked about her symptoms, the doctor says, "I am not sure what's wrong with her. Take her to my clinic where I can do a proper check; I will be right behind you."

We walk back to the clinic, which is in front of our house, to wait for the doctor. After provisional tests are done, the doctor tells me that my wife needs to be admitted immediately and sends me to registration to fill out the paperwork.

"Ten thousand rupees please[2]," the receptionist says.

"How much?" I reply in uncertainty and confusion. As if coming out of a fog, it suddenly dawns on me that, contrary to my previous belief, not all hospitals in India are free.

"To have your wife hospitalized here, you need a ten-thousand rupee deposit first."

"But I don't have that much cash with me. I can give you a few hundreds down then go home to get you the rest of the money. I was not prepared for such an amount."

I argue with the nurse for several minutes. She cannot accept my proposition because she is responsible to someone else. As we continue to talk, I resort to shouting, a weapon which has served me in the past and at the moment the only one I have at my disposal.

"Maybe somebody does not have the money you want," I yell, "should that person's wife die because he can't pay the deposit? This is a hospital, not a business center."

At the sound of my voice, several people gather around me. Behind them, some of the doctors and hospital administrators appear. They rush straight to me and try to calm me down before I can upset others. Some employees try to explain to the crowd that everything is okay and request onlookers to disperse, leaving only a couple of the managers talking to me in a corner.

"Please quiet down," one of the men in white uniform says, "this is a hospital and there are many patients here who need silence."

"That is the reason I am shouting," I reply angrily. "I am shouting because this is a hospital. Your main job here is to save lives. But your employee tells me that my wife cannot stay here because I don't have ten thousand rupees cash in my pocket."

"Unfortunately this is the rule and she can do nothing," he answers calmly.

"Your rule is wrong and you should change it if you care for people's lives," I reply in a harsh tone.

They pacify me by agreeing to let Mona have a bed in the hospital and a nurse helps me take Mona to her room.

* * *

Knowing Amu is back in India, I leave the hospital and run to his hotel. He isn't in his room nor in a few other of his favorite places, but I finally find him in a restaurant nearby. He is his usual calm and peaceful self, but on noticing my agitation, he offers me a cigarette and asks the waiter to bring me a cup of milk tea which I drink while telling him the story.

"Maybe the managers of the UNHCR office are away on long vacations," Amu begins, "but our God does not go on such trips, does He?" I remain silent as he continues, "Hassan, patience is better, or anger? Baba, the sky hasn't fallen. People get sick and they get well again. This is life. I wasn't even half your age when I supported five families. Baba, I say pain is for man. Difficulty polishes a man's nature. Don't lose hope so easily."

He then shares with me a couple of stories from his childhood. About half an hour later, Amu leaves for his room and soon comes back with ten thousand rupees.

"Go," he commands, "your wife is waiting. I will visit her shortly."

* * *

Mona stays in the hospital until the very last penny of our deposit is spent; after it is depleted, the doctor discharges her. However, she has to return twice a day for a few injections. It is very difficult getting her there; she is advised against riding in rickshaws and she can barely walk. We investigate having a nurse come to the house but it is too expensive.

A few days of painful trips to the hospital later, Mona has an idea. "Wait a minute," she says, "with my training I know how to do injections. Maybe I can't do them on myself, but I can talk you through it. I'll prepare the syringes and tell you what to do."

We have been so busy worrying about how to get this done that we ignored the obvious: we could do it ourselves.

Never having touched syringes in a real-life situation and remembering how, back in my village, one of my classmates became disabled after an injection by an inexperienced person, I become nervous and try to persuade Mona to change her mind. However, she is so certain I can handle the job that I agree to try. After a couple of hesitant attempts, I do all her injections for about six months.

This is a major financial hardship for us as the injections, plus a powder protein the doctor prescribes, have to be purchased from a drugstore and are very expensive. The doctor requires Mona to come in for a checkup about every two weeks; each visit costs several hundred rupees. Mona is confined to complete bed rest for the first three months; after which I can take her to a free government hospital a little farther away for her monthly checkups, but we still buy and do the injections at home.

After three months rest, her health improves but she is very limited in what she can do. Still so weak she can hardly walk; she is prohibited from doing housework or cooking.

Our landlady and her family come to help us occasionally and loan us both their portable AC and their hand juicer, suggesting I make orange juice for Mona's strength.

With almost no money, we are always hungry during this time and Mona still remembers vividly how she never had enough to eat. I tremble now to remember those frightening days[3].

----

[1]Due to her ingrained habit of collecting water against the day there was none, years later, Mona was still saving water in jars.

[2]Ten thousand Indian rupees was about USD 250 at that time.

[3]It may seem strange if I tell you how much we still love and miss India; in this country, in spite of all our troubles, we tasted freedom for the first time.

~ * ~

Your mother-in-law loves you!

When Mona's hospital expenses are tallied, I take all the receipts to the UNHCR office for reimbursement. A couple days later when I meet with Ms. Vinira, she sends me 'after a black pea'[1] to a UN clinic across town for certification of the paperwork. I make five trips without being able to meet the doctor who, I am told, is either too busy to see me or away. On the sixth trip when I still am not allowed to see the doctor, my temper gets the better of me and I raise my voice, "Is this clinic closed? Every time I come, you tell me the doctor is not here. If you're running this clinic without a doctor, then close its doors and go home. And if a doctor works here, why is it he avoids seeing me? It seems your doctor is playing hide and seek with me. Today I am not going to leave this clinic until I meet with somebody who has the answers to my questions."

I keep up this tirade until the doctor appears. He takes a look at my folder and asks me to come back in a few days for his decision.

When I go to the clinic again several days later, there is no sign of the doctor. I am told he is away and will not be back that day. My papers are returned to me with a short note: "Since your wife weighs fifty kilos and her height is 165 centimeters, we believe she is in good condition. So, we regret to let you know that the UN is not able to reimburse your bills."

I would have killed that doctor had I found him in the area. He probably knew this himself and made sure he wasn't there when I came. I go back home empty-handed.

* * *

A few months later, I receive a letter from the UNHCR asking me to be available in one of their vocational training centers. It makes me happy to think that I am finally going to be given a job.

On the specified day, I arrive at the training center where several Afghan refugees, who welcome me in a warm and friendly manner, are working. I am asked to choose a vocation from a list of professions, among which are mechanic, refrigerator repair and air ticketing. Having once worked in a travel and tourism agent in Tehran for a few months, I choose air ticketing but add that I don't know enough about it to teach a class.

"No, you are not going to teach the class," comes the reply, "this is a free training course for refugees who are interested in learning a profession while waiting for their resettlement. Some time ago, you asked the UN to find you a job."

"Yes, I asked them to find me a job," I retort, "not to send me to a class as a student!"

"You need to learn first before you can work ..."

"I know," I interrupt, "but this is not what I asked for. I am short of money right now. I need a teaching or interpreting job to pay my bills. Do you know how long it will take me to learn a new profession? There are thousands of Afghan refugees and a lot of Iranians who need teachers or translators. I know many people who are currently working inside the UN office as interpreters whose qualifications are not as good as mine."

Just being in charge of the vocational training center, they have no idea where I am coming from and ask me to talk to the office about a job. I agree to the air ticketing class and leave the building.

Now, every afternoon instead of going to teach English, I have to attend air ticketing classes where I am the only Iranian among the group of Afghans. Although a couple of them speak good English, the majority have no English knowledge whatsoever. Some are my students in my own English classes. Most have problems understanding our young Hindustani teacher, whom I find to be a formal and boring instructor.

Ten weeks or so pass and I am learning to hate the class. Except for price calculations and flight terminology, there is nothing new or interesting for me. The only thing I remember from this class is arguing with the teacher who insists that the earth has seven continents and India is one of them.

Just a few more sessions are left and I will finally leave that class forever; I return home buoyed by that thought. When I get there, Mona is in the shower. I call out, "Hi, I'm home!"

"I just noticed that there was fresh water running through the taps," she answers back in a cheery voice. "So I decided to take the opportunity to bathe."

"Do you need a towel or anything?"

"No, thanks. I have everything I need. There is fresh tea in the pot. Go help yourself while I am washing."

I leave her alone out there and walk into our room and onto the terrace but have hardly finished smoking a cigarette when Mona steps out of the shower. We kiss hello and she asks me to go get Shadi immediately.

"Now what? Is anything wrong?"

"Everything is absolutely right!" she replies, "I think the baby is coming. We need Shadi's help."

"Wow. Really?" I cry out happily. "How do you know?"

"Don't you concern yourself with the details," she says, grinning. "We are going to be parents soon."

I kiss her again and, bending down, kiss her stomach as well. "Hello baby! Welcome!" I exclaim in joy. "Get dressed and be ready by the time I return," I tell Mona and take off.

* * *

The Afghan family is setting their dinner cloth on the floor when I arrive. The children are busy bringing dishes, bread, spoons and cups from the small backyard kitchen. They receive me with their customary warmth.

"Your mother-in-law loves you[2]," Shadi tells me.

We all laugh and I sit close to the grandma, shaking her hands. Everybody wants to know why Mona is not with me. Dinner is ready and I do not want to disrupt their meal with my news, so I tell them that Mona will be along later.

We all have dinner together, Shadi setting aside some food for Mona. After the meal, when the room is cleared and all the dirty dishes taken away, I begin to talk. "Actually, Mona sent me here. When I came home from my class this evening, she said the baby was coming. I am here to take Shadi with us to the hospital."

The whole family looks at me in wide-eyed disbelief, thinking I am joking.

"It's no joke; I am serious," I emphasize. "The child is anxious to greet you!"

"My God," Shadi exclaims loudly, "what kind of husband are you, Hassan? Your wife is in labor and here you sit calmly sharing dinner with us?"

She gets up quickly and, giving orders to her children on the way out, flies from the room with me at her heels.

In no time at all, Shadi, Mona and I are on our way to Safdar Jang Hospital in New Delhi.

----

[1]To send someone after a black pea (Kesi ra donbal e nokhod siah ferestadan) means to send someone on a wild goose chase.

[2]This is a kind of saying in Persian culture. Whenever you arrive at a house where a meal is being served, the hosts say 'your mother-in-law loves you'. It means you are just in time and they are happy to have you with them to share the meal.

Never be afraid to do something new. Remember, amateurs built the ark; professionals built the Titanic
....Anonymous

Nine

Hoya, Hoya!

Around eleven o'clock on that same night, Mona gives birth to a healthy, robust boy.

* * *

Once Mona is admitted to the hospital, she is immediately taken from her room to a delivery room; a doctor dismisses me and tells me to wait outside for a report. I walk around the grounds until Shadi finally comes out and says, "Hassan, congratulations, your child is born! Come on, let's go meet him."

We are met with a crowd of people leading up to the entrance gate, waiting to get in to visit their relatives. Pushing our way through, we reach the gate and the guard, seeing we are the only foreigners, beckons us forward.

"I want to get in to see my wife," I tell him.

He lets me in but when Shadi wants to follow me, he tells her to wait. He closes the door behind me and coaxes me to follow him into a small room off the entrance hall, where other guards are taking a break.

"Mobarak ho! Mobarak ho¹!" One of them says to me in Urdu.

"Thank you very, very much."

"Boy or girl?"

"I don't know yet," I reply, wanting to postpone telling them.

He rubs his index finger on his thumb, saying, "tips, tips."

"Let me see my wife first," I say, smiling. "Then I will certainly take care of you."

"No problem. You may go in and visit your wife. You can also take your friend with you."

With the help of his colleagues, the crowd gives way to allow Shadi to enter. Mona will be spending a few days in the hospital and the guards clearly know I will be back.

Upstairs, we go from room to room looking for Mona. One of the janitors offers to help us find her and leads us into a large room on the second or third floor. We walk in and there is Mona among several other women sitting or laying on their beds. So full of emotion I am practically speechless, I barely manage to say, "Hello, little mama! You did it!"

Shadi who has had this experience several times, says, "This 'little mama' must be very hungry!" and immediately starts feeding Mona the bread and a few spoonfuls of honey we have brought with us.

"How happy you must be, Mona!" she begins while she hands the small morsels of food to her. "Even though unfortunately your parents are not able to be here, at least you have your husband at your side. I delivered many of my children when Balooch was away and I was all alone, lonely and hungry and there was nobody to take care of me."

"That must have been very difficult for you," I comment, trying to comfort her. "But thank God, with six lovely children, you are not alone anymore. Balooch is here with you as well, so let's forget about the past."

Silently, Shadi continues to feed Mona while I look around the room. Since this free hospital is not large enough to accommodate all the patients who come to it, even though nearly all the beds are single, there are two women occupying each, two by two, feet to head, while some new mothers, on sheet-covered mattresses, are sharing the floor with a population of mice.

I watch the nurse who, each time she enters with a baby in her arms, walks to one of the mothers and gives it to her. Now it is Mona's turn. As soon as the nurse hands over my son to his mother, I take him from her very gently, staring in awe and wonder at this perfect little human who didn't exist until three hours ago.

"What do you want to name him?" Shadi asks.

"Sroosh," I reply, my eyes on him.

He is beautiful and the fact that he has not been affected by his mother's health problems and poor diet brings a song to my lips. Rocking Sroosh in my arms, I start singing him one of our traditional folk songs.

"Hoy, Hoy, Hoya,
Eesar osar telaareh,
Mashti Hassan savaareh,
Bisheh aroos biyaareh,
Ba donbak o diyaareh,
Dah shi poolam nadaareh,
Hoya, Hoya."

"For God's sake Hassan, what are you singing?" asks Shadi, smiling.

"Hoy, Hoy, Hoya,
A veranda here, a veranda there,
Mashti Hassan on a horse does ride,
On his way to bring home his bride,
To the sound of drum and tambourine,
Without a penny to his name,
Hoya, Hoya." The bubble of laughter escapes from my throat and everybody joins in.

Later, another nurse gives me a form and directs me where to go to register the baby's name and birth date. Shadi and I take the sheet and walk downstairs to leave for the yard where registration is located. We have hardly reached the main entrance when the guards who let me in see me again. They call me back to their room and one of them takes the registration paper out of my hand. Looking at the information on the form, he starts speaking.

"Wow, it is a boy," he comments with satisfaction.

All his colleagues side with him and say it is great to have a boy.

"Is he your first child?"

"Yes."

All his colleagues say it is great to have a boy as a first child.

"How is his health?"

"The doctors say he is in good health."

All his colleagues tell me how great it is to have a healthy child.

"Look, my brother," the man who has my document adds. "This is your first child. He is a boy. He is also healthy. So you have to pay more in tips."

I try in vain to postpone paying them until later but they are adamant. To visit my wife and child, I have no other choice but to acquiesce. I pay each of them in turn and head outside to where Shadi is waiting.

"Why did they call you in?" Shadi asks me.

"They wanted to congratulate me on having a baby."

After we have registered Sroosh's name, we return by the same route we have come. Shadi is sure the security personnel will not let us in a second time, but I ask her not to worry. From among the crowd, the tips patrol sees us and rushes to open the gate while some of the local people who think they are being discriminated against, protest.

"This poor man is a foreigner," the guard defends his decision, "he has nobody in this country."

The crowds quit complaining and we walk in, heading for Mona's room. We don't get far before the guard calls me back to his station.

"These two gentlemen are our bosses," he shares, pointing out a couple of fellow workers. "They are also delighted that your first child is a boy."

Like their friends have done, the bosses congratulate me and ask for tips, but will accept no less than one hundred rupees each since their rank is superior to the guards. I pay them the money to the gripes of those who have accepted less.

"Why did you give us fifty rupees and give them one hundred?" They want to know, asking for an additional fifty rupees for themselves.

"They are your overseers," I reply. "In all countries there is a difference between a soldier and an officer."

They laugh and let me go.

"What did you have to say to those guards?" Shadi asks me when I catch up with her.

"Nothing important," I answer, playing down the conversations. "Their bosses were also interested in expressing their pleasure that our first child is a healthy boy."

We climb the stairs and walk into the room where Mona and Sroosh are.

"Hello again, mama Mona!" I say, smiling. "What do you feel?"

"Nothing!" She answers satirically. "Well, to be serious, I am really happy that our child is healthy."

"Of course," Shadi confirms. "We need to give thanks to God for the gift of this marvellous baby. Hassan, you must give a sacrificial sum of money to the poor as a way of showing your gratitude."

"I already paid my sacrifice to the gatemen."

Shadi remains silent for a while, and suddenly starts laughing.

"I see," she chuckles. "Now I understand why the gatemen singled us out from among all those people."

* * *

In the early hours of the morning, we finally give Sroosh back to his mother, who puts him behind her in the crook of her knees. In the same manner, her bed partner puts her own child behind her knees in a line with Sroosh. The four of them will have to sleep like this on the same bed for the next few days.

~ * ~

God's voice is to relieve pain

Upset that we have not chosen any of their suggested names for Sroosh, the Afghan siblings find it difficult to call our baby by name for the first few days.

"What does Sroosh mean?" they finally ask.

"In Persian poems like those of Hafez, it means something like 'God's voice'," I explain.

"Uncle, why didn't you choose the names we gave you?" Shazieh wants to know.

"Because we didn't want to disappoint any of you," I answer, smiling.

They feel better and begin calling the baby the name we have given him. Soon Sroosh becomes a favorite toy in the hands of the Afghan and Hindustani children who all love to play with him. Sometimes they go so far as to fight over whose turn it is to hold him. However, Shazieh has a more authoritative voice than anybody else does, and when she commands, others obey. Protective of the baby, her main concern is what she refers to as 'those Hindustani kids'; she worries that they might harm him. We continually have to reassure her that nothing is going to happen to Sroosh.

However, Pooja, Diraj, Sohrab, our very dear Ashok, who, as a baby, thought my name was 'Namaste', Artie, Jortie, our Kashmiri Shazieh, Efrah, her lovely sister, Navid, their brother, and many other children in our neighborhood who are also our great friends, can't be denied their share of Sroosh. But for the most part, the Hindustani youngsters, many of whom are our landlady's grandchildren, wait somewhere on the second floor or the rooftop and leave the field to Shazieh until her parents take her home, before they dare come to play with their new little human toy.

With the help of Shadi and her family, Mona and I manage to learn childcare very quickly. Our landlords are also a great help whenever Sroosh wakes up in the middle of the night, crying. Knowing that Mona is still in pain and in need of rest to fully recover from the difficult pregnancy, the old woman and all her daughters-in-law often take turns coming to our room to help her comfort the baby.

When the news of us having a baby spreads among other refugees, they start visiting us. Except for Roberto, I have been ashamed to invite people to my living quarters. My friends and English students are aghast and incredulous that we live in such a miserable place; having visited their homes, I know our living conditions are worse than those of any I have seen.

The more visitors we receive, the more toys and baby clothes accrue for Sroosh. In spite of their financial problems, the refugees try to find a useful gift for our child. Their supportiveness is something that removes from my heart the pain of dealing with what seems to me an indifferent human rights organization. During the time my wife was on a strict six-month bed rest, the India Office of Human Rights never once came to visit or offer help.

From among the visitors, Stella, Roberto and his wife Mikkey are a great encouragement. They find a second-hand baby crib and mattress, musical toys, and whatever else they can get their hands on which they think will be useful, and bring them to us.

Although she and Roberto do not have babies, Mikkey has learned many things about caring for children from her mother. She has heard that a baby can choke on his tongue if laying on his back, so needs to be laid on his side. She is familiar with burping a baby; she knows of syrups for colic. If Sroosh is constipated, she advises massaging his stomach with oil.

Roberto falls in love with Sroosh and they play together by the hour.

"Look at this child," he says to his wife, hugging Sroosh and bouncing him on his knee. "Do you see how gorgeous he is? I do not understand why you would not like to have a baby just like this. Look, my wife, such a child would keep us occupied and turn our lives around."

"No," Mikkey always replies. "Let's find a country first. Then, I will give you a baby."

"Please!"

"No!"

"Only one!"

"No! Not even a half!"

Listening to Roberto's wistful urging to convince his wife, and Mikkey's defense of her decision, is a source of amusement to all of us.

* * *

The ceiling fan is the first object Sroosh recognizes. After a month or so of laying under it on an old military blanket which serves as our carpet, we notice that he is exploring the fan as it whirs and hums, and starts to complain when it is off. As long as the fan is working, he watches it until it lulls him to sleep.

At times, he moves his chubby little hands and legs in the air and makes cooing noises as if he were talking or playing with the fan in his imagination. When the electricity goes out, which happens a few times everyday, he begins to make louder noises like maybe he is angry that the fan has stopped or he is asking us to turn it back on. He keeps complaining until the fan begins to turn around over his head again. As soon as he sees the fan blades circling, he moves his round baby hands and legs in the air with glee as a child might do on finding his mother.

If the electricity has been off for hours and there is no sign of it returning, we fill a washbasin with cold water and, with Mona supporting him with her hands, we dip Sroosh in it. As much as he loves being in that pan, we love watching our duckling lay so peacefully in the water, cooling his little body in this scorching Indian climate. What a racket he makes when we take him out of his makeshift pond!

* * *

Having already missed my remaining air ticketing classes, I decide to put that career behind me and start teaching again to cover the additional expenditure created by the birth of the baby.

Mona can finally take care of most of the housework, leaving me with more free time. Several people, relatives of earlier students, had asked to be put on a waiting list if I decided to give classes; I contact them and make the necessary arrangements. My efforts are successful and soon my time is full.

In my absence, Mona still does heavy jobs like laundry and filling the jars with the fresh cold water whenever I am not there to help her; this makes me angry in my concern for her, and I insist that she not do it anymore. She still has some pain and I do not want her to struggle with health issues for the rest of her life. Remembering my mother's suffering, and how it affected my father, who always blamed himself for her being disabled, I don't want to repeat his mistakes and have to live with his regrets.

"Water came in the afternoon," she says, trying to convince me that she has done the right thing, "and you were not here. You know that whenever we have water during the day, we have no water at night, so I filled the jars. But don't worry. I was careful not move them. They are still in the shower waiting for you. Go bring them in if you are not too tired."

As usual, I move the jars to our narrow terrace, which we are in the habit of using for washing dishes and clothes, as well as bathing if the shower happens to be occupied. Water is so precious we save the used portions for flushing the toilet.

"By the way," Mona tells me while I busy myself with the heavy jars, "don't move that red wash pan. That water is for you."

Once the jars are moved, I wash myself in the cold water of the big pan inside the cramped shower stall. Winter and summer we both use cold water for everything; that's all there is. After we get used to cold showers they feel refreshing, even in the cooler winter temperatures.

In spite of the difficulties a child adds to our life, Sroosh gives us something to live for. Our normal routine of negative events is interrupted and replaced with a warm and happy environment which brings Mona and me closer together. Sroosh motivates and inspires us, Mona has a companion and our room becomes a home for the first time. I return after classes eager to spend time with my wife and my precious baby boy.

In addition to teaching English classes to refugees, I serve as interpreter for them or for their relatives when they have appointments at an embassy, a police station or church. The more I get to know these people, the more they share their life stories with me. Most of the Afghans have been suffering terrible living conditions for years in both their own country and abroad in places like Pakistan and now here in India. In some cases, they are caring for their friends' children who have lost fathers to war in Afghanistan and whose mothers have escaped to Europe to work until they can be sent for. Some of these children are still waiting for their mothers after years of separation.

* * *

With not enough to eat during the nearly three years we spend in India, our immune systems are unstable and we are prone to illness. I have hardly worked two months when I succumb to dysentery. In the sweltering weather, sweat pours from me, saturating my shirt in minutes. Dehydrated, I lose a lot of weight and look gaunt and undernourished. Nauseated on many occasions, I get off the bus and sit under a tree to keep from vomiting. This condition worsens and for several weeks, I have diarrhea and can't keep anything down. I cancel nearly all my classes, keeping only those few students whom I owe favors. Finally, I recuperate somewhat and resume my classes, only to repeat the same pattern of illness time and again.

During my recovery, what time I don't spend with Mona and Sroosh, I sit out on the terrace, 'our sacred temple' as Mona and I call it, reading the poetry books I still have with me. Once her chores are done, Mona usually joins me and we renew our acquaintance with Hafez and Rumi with fresh eyes. For hours, we read poems and discuss them, pondering their meaning, thoroughly relishing our new insights. Our literature teachers in schools never mentioned points which now seem obvious to us. I have been carrying these books with me for years and just now am discovering how astute their authors were.

In one of his most famous stories, Rumi, telling us each person can converse with God in his own words, presents a parable of Moses and a Shepherd[1].

'One day in the middle of a desert', he says, 'Moses came across a shepherd who was talking to God. The shepherd was saying, "O dear God, where are You so I can serve You, so I can mend Your sandals, so I can comb Your hair, so I can kiss Your hands, so I can massage Your legs, so I can set up Your bed for You when it is Your bedtime. May all my goats be sacrificed to you, may I sing praises to You day and night."

When Moses heard the shepherd talking to God in this familiar way, he approached the man and asked whom he was talking to.

"I'm talking to the One who created us, who created the universe."

"What nonsense is this you are attributing to Him, describing Him with the mind of a human?" Moses yelled in anger. "This is blasphemy. You do not show appropriate reverence of Him. You are offending Him with your feeble offerings of praise. Stuff a rag in your mouth and shut it up. You ought to know that sandals are suitable for you and me but God is bright light. He will burn your sandals. If you don't keep your mouth shut, a fire will come and burn people." The poor shepherd felt sinful in the face of Moses' words and repented immediately.

As Moses continued his travels in the desert, he heard 'Sroosh' or God's voice.

"Moses," God called to him, "I have sent you to help people come close to me. However, you separated me from my old friend; he is not talking to me anymore. We do not judge people based on how they look on the outside, or the way they talk; we look at what's in their heart and their spirituality. The religion of love is different from other religions. Those who walk in love, simply regard God as The Way."[2]

Feeling guilty, Moses ran back to find the poor peasant wandering the desert and called to him from afar.

"Don't worry about words and phrases," he hollered to the shepherd. "God told me there are no rules for worshiping him. What I called blasphemy God considers true devotion. Feel free to talk to him however you wish."'

Our Persian literature is full of such poems, fables and parables and as children we all studied them in our school books. However, in their final interpretations, our teachers never taught us that we should forget about different religions, languages, and regulations in order to unite with God. They all focused on Islam as the only way. I hope you did not have such teachers.

----

[1]In Persian classical literature, poets often attribute their stories, which in reality cannot be found in the Christian Bible, to a non-Muslim personality, such as Moses or Jesus, to avoid criticism by Islamic religious leaders. Iran sure has a long history of freedom of speech!

[2]This is a summarization of the original poem.

~ * ~

Strangers in luxury cars

From among a big group of crows which make their home in a huge cedar tree no more than one hundred meters away, there is one with a broken wing. During our stay in this place, the crippled crow is in the habit of flying over to sit on the electric wire scarcely a meter's distance from our terrace. Once settled, it caws several times and flies away again.

In our culture, a crow coming to our house croaking, heralds guests or a message. In the case of the lame crow, this superstition quite often proves to come true. Either a visitor or a messenger arrives on several occasions after the crow has cawed at us from his wire perch, even though looking back now it seems irrational to believe there was such a connection.

* * *

On one particular hot afternoon, while Mona and Sroosh are sleeping on the floor, covered with a large wet curtain, I am trying to keep cool on the terrace. The alley below me is lined on both sides by wooden benches on which elderly ladies sit and massage their grandchildren's hair with coconut oil to the sound of the arguing of a couple of our neighbors.

A woman from the second floor of a house nearby, when she sees a vegetable vendor calling out the names of different vegetables and hawking his products as he pushes his cart along the alley, stops him and asks about the prices, then sends down a basket on the end of a rope. The vendor puts a few vegetables in it and the basket is pulled up. Once she gets her basket, she examines the produce and sends some of it back for exchange; up goes the basket again. Satisfied, she sends down a sum of money in the same vehicle.

Taking his cash, the vendor continues along his way, calling out, 'buy cabbage, buy turnips, buy potatoes, buy onions, buy eggplants'! He disappears from sight, his voice blending into the loud sounds of a popular Indian song coming from the marketplace, 'Life, in each step, is a new war...'

I sit back on the stool, eyes focusing on the cedar tree. Under it, on the rooftop of a house, a couple of teenagers are throwing stuff into the air; having done this before myself, I know they are throwing waste meat high into the sky and the birds are flying up to catch it mid-air.

Mona on the balcony in front of the jasmine branches, electric wires and in the background the cedar tree which was home to the crows

I am still watching those teens when 'our crow' leaves the cedar and flies towards where I am sitting among the heavy jasmine branches. It sits on the electric wire right in front of me; I could have reached out to touch it by stretching my arms forward. The bird crows loudly several times as if something important is about to happen and keeps up the chattering until it wakes up Mona and she comes out to see what is going on. As soon as she appears on the terrace, the crow flies away. We peer down to the narrow alley to see if anything is happening around the main gate. Three people are talking to a couple of our neighbors whose small grocery store is attached to our house. After the conversation ends, the three step through the landlady's door and enter our house.

Suddenly, Mona and I remember our old black and white TV. We run back to the room to hide it before those people, whom we suspect of being UN agents, get to the third floor, but there already is not enough time to hide both the TV and the long wire which stretches through the room and out the upper part of our front door to the rooftop. At any moment, the officers will be close enough to see us through the grill, so we put the TV down and I reach for my shirt to get dressed.

Seconds later, the three people from the alley appear at our door and we invite them in. One of them is a young and quite beautiful Hindustani girl wearing a long blue sari. The second person is a middle-aged Hindustani man who introduces himself as the UNHCR doctor. His face seems familiar to me; I am almost sure he is the UN doctor who talked to me when I tried to get reimbursement for the expenses incurred when Mona was pregnant and needed treatment; the one who said since Mona was fine their office would not repay the bills. The third is a young Afghan refugee who works for the UN as an interpreter. The doctor introduces himself and his two companions and begins to talk.

"We have come from the UN clinic to visit your wife," he says.

"Why?" I ask in a stony voice.

"It seems that some time ago you contacted the UN office asking to see a doctor regarding your wife's condition," he replies calmly.

"When was it that I asked for a doctor?"

"Well, I do not know about the past. I was just told to visit your wife to see if she is feeling better."

"Do you always visit your patients in such a timely manner?" I query with a bit of sarcasm and anger. "I asked for a doctor when my wife was three months pregnant, in pain and afraid she would lose the baby. Now my child is three months old. You are nine months too late."

The Afghan interpreter intervenes politely, "Excuse me; you probably did not understand him. These people were sent here to visit your wife by the UN clinic not from the UNHCR office."

"Please don't interrupt," I retort. "It is not my intent to be offensive, but you are just an interpreter and would do better to stick to interpreting when you are needed. In any case, I don't know why the UN has sent an interpreter with the doctor."

Seeing me angry, the poor Afghan says no more and now the young girl jumps in.

"We are sorry," she says compassionately.

"But 'sorry' cannot solve my problem," I stop her with an angry tone. "Let me drop you down the terrace. Then I will say I'm sorry. What good would my 'sorry' be to you?"

She remains unruffled in the presence of my rudeness.

"Please," she pleads, "let us forget about the past. We are here to help."

"Ok," I agree as I pull my old bag, open it, and take all the hospital bills out. Giving the papers to them, I say, "All right. Now that you are here to help, maybe you can figure out a way to have this money reimbursed for me."

The doctor comes to the aid of the girl. "Listen, Mr. Hassan," he says without emotion, "we are not in charge of your financial situation; we are just doctors. After receiving some letters from you regarding her condition, the UN has asked us to see how your wife's health is. We cannot authorize the payment of your bills or anything else; our job is to report your wife's condition and let the UN make decisions."

"You have come nine months later to see if my wife feels well or not?" I almost yell. "Where were you when my wife was bleeding? Where were you the several times I contacted your clinic? Where were you when I needed you? I could not find even one doctor. Now you are asking after my wife's health? Please get up and leave my room this instant. I will only talk to somebody who has authority you do not have." I get up and immediately usher them out the door.

After they are gone, my landlords, who obviously have been standing on the stairs listening to my yelling, appear at the door. "What is the problem?" they want to know.

"Nothing. It is finished."

I begin to smile in an attempt to convince them that nothing is wrong, and invite them in. They start to amuse and pacify Sroosh who by now is crying.

Several weeks later, the office sends a letter asking me to attend a meeting. There are two women waiting in the interview room when I arrive; one of whom I already know: Ms. Vinira, an officer of the UNHCR for nearly two decades, is my caseworker, and the one I went to about finding a job as an interpreter. The second woman is a young French lady, who has just arrived in the New Delhi office on temporary assignment. Ms. Vinira is obviously edgy but trying to control herself. She wants to know the reason I treated the doctors in such an unfriendly manner.

I pour out my frustrations afresh: "Why do you send people in luxury cars to see me when they can change nothing? Now my landlords think I know rich people and I'm afraid they will raise the rent."

"Listen, Hassan," Ms. Vinira says, "the UNHCR office can only reimburse bills which are incurred in government hospitals. Your receipts come from a private clinic. We cannot honor them."

"There is no such hospital close to my home," I reply, "my wife was bleeding and what mattered most to me at that time was to save her life and the life of my child. Later when she was feeling better, I did take her to a government institution. What you must understand is that in the beginning I had no way to get her to a government facility or anywhere else any distance away; that private clinic was our only choice."

"I understand your feeling," she commiserates, "however we can pay bills from government hospitals only."

"But government hospitals are free of charge," I protest, "what are you paying for, then?"

"There are still a few procedures in certain refugee cases that need to be paid," she answers.

We debate back and forth for quite some time getting nowhere when abruptly Ms. Vinira changes the subject. "Listen,

Hassan; we have submitted your case to a country for resettlement. All you need to do is be patient."

"Which country?"

"Unfortunately I cannot tell you, but I assure you it is a very good country."

"How long will the process take?"

"It is hard to say. But I would guess about two years."

"How can we wait two years? We need money now. You have seen our room. You know the conditions in which we live."

Winding up the conversation, Ms. Vinira tells me, "Because your situation is a bit different, I will do my best to help you. What I can do is to authorize a one-time payment of three thousand rupees to support your family. But forget about those hospital papers. Frankly, we cannot reimburse them." She also offers to add seven hundred rupees extra to each monthly payment as a way of helping us out. I leave for home contented and give the news to Mona.

"You see, Hassan?" she tells me, "you were always worried about how we would survive once our child was born. Now you can see that a baby has blessed our house. We have survived miserable conditions; we found Balooch and Shadi, Amu and Roberto to substitute for our families not being near us; our child was born and we had nothing for him but people generously supplied our needs; we had bills we couldn't pay, but now the office will help with them. In spite of empty hands we have a healthy son and we will raise him because, as we Iranians say, 'the One who gives him teeth will also give him bread to chew.'"

A month or so later, the UN office gives me a paper to take to the bank. I am going to get three thousand rupees cash, an amount which will cover our room rent for two months.

For three weeks in a row I go to the UN bank; there is no money in my account. Ms. Vinira does not even authorize the extra monthly pay she promised. I feel I have been treated like a fool and begin to see everything through a filter of negativity which I generalize to all kinds of human rights organizations and movements, despising them for being, in my eyes, nothing but empty propaganda. I put all these pessimistic thoughts on paper and give it to the UNHCR office. The letter tells them clearly that I do not believe humanity matters to them or organizations like them.

~ * ~

Talk to Him in your language

"Hassan Agha! Hassan Agha!"

I know this warm familiar voice.

"Yes, Amu," I reply loudly from inside the room, run to the terrace, look down into the alley from where the voice originated and see a foreshortened Amu looking, from my angle, like a bulked-up weight lifter.

"Hello, Amu," I say as I lean over the fence railing to see him better, "please come on up."

"Do you have tea?"

"Yes, Amu."

"I just want to drink a cup of tea with Ahmad."

"Ahmad? Which Ahmad?"

"You don't know your child's name? His name is Ahmad." I laugh and he continues, "Yes, his name is Ahmad."

Amu walks into the building and I leave the terrace for the front door so I can welcome him at the top of the stairs. His voice comes to me all the time he is climbing to our floor, "I just arrived in Delhi yesterday. I knew about Mona's delivery but I didn't know if it was a boy or a girl. Today, some friends in a teahouse told me that you have a boy. I decided to call your boy Ahmad. Ask me why."

"Why, Amu?"

"All the Ahmads whom I have known in my life are smart people."

I laugh again. Mona joins me near the grill to welcome Amu.

"I am not here to see you," Amu says, ignoring my outstretched hand, "I came to see Ahmad; where is he?" He pushes past us into the room where the baby is.

"He is Ahmad," Amu says again. "You are Ahmad, ok?" He tells Sroosh. He plays with the baby for several minutes in the childish way he used to do with Puppy, saying, "he is Ahmad, he is Ahmad."

Both Mona and I are surprised to see how much Amu loves babies.

"You are very lucky people," he tells us, then turning to me asks, "How old are you?"

"Soon to be thirty."

"Your child will be thirty when you are sixty, right?"

"Yes, Amu, sounds about right."

"Do you know how old my children are?" He addresses both of us.

Mona and I look at each other. "Maybe thirty?" We answer in an uncertain tone.

"The oldest one is barely fifteen."

"We hope you will live with them for more than one hundred years," we tell him, quoting a traditional Persian blessing.

"No, that is not going to happen; I believe people should marry at an early age and have their children while they are still young."

Taking a photo from his pocket, he shows it to us. Pictured are three little girls playing together in a plastic pool filled with water. Amu married very late and his dream is to be able to support his children through university. We join him in hoping that he will live long enough to see that day arrive.

Mona and I listen with avid attention while Amu, with pride in his voice, tells us anecdotes about his daughters. "This little one," he says, pointing to the youngest child, "has a quick wit. Once she said, when I came home with a kilo of fruit, 'Dad, are you bankrupt?' When I wanted an explanation, she added, 'I thought since you brought home such a small amount of fruit, maybe you were bankrupt'."

After several minutes of conversation, I look Amu in the face and notice his eyes are completely yellow and his face is unnaturally pale. "What's going on, Amu?"

"Doctors say I have jaundice. They say my liver is hepatic." He pauses a little and continues, "I know these doctors. They are just saying that because they want my money."

"Yes, you are right, Amu," I side with him in an effort to appease and throw him off balance, "but just in case, we had better get you to a doctor."

It doesn't take much more than that to get him to agree with me.

"We will go to that nearby private hospital where you took Mona," he decides, "it is clean."

I acquiesce and allow him enough time to finish his tea.

"By the way, how is your financial situation?" he asks, changing the subject.

"Honestly, not that good. I have been thinking maybe it would be better for me to take my family back to Iran."

Then I tell him the entire story of what happened with the UNHCR office during his absence. He remains silent for a moment and then asks, "Do you like to go to Iran or Canada?"

I smile and say, "Canada, of course."

"If you had passports, can you take this Ahmad and his mother to Canada with you or not?"

"I don't know, Amu."

"Ok, no problem; while you are making up your mind, get up and walk me to the hospital."

We stand up.

"Take care of Ahmad," Amu tells Mona, putting a couple of hundred American dollars on Sroosh's pillow. "This is my gift to him; I didn't buy anything on the way because I didn't know yet that he was a boy."

Amu says goodbye to Sroosh, again calling him Ahmad. Raising his voice somewhat, he calls out, with a wave of his hand, "You are Ahmad, OK? Bye bye Ahmad."

Startled out of his imaginary world by the change in volume of Amu's speech, Sroosh unexpectedly jerks his arms and legs, making us laugh at him. Mona sees Amu and me off as far as the veranda at the head of the stairs.

The doctors order an extensive panel of tests for him and Amu is hospitalized that same day. For the next couple days, Amu constantly complains about the poor institutional fare. "Baba, how can I get well with this food? It is only water and vegetables! If I were spending this money in a hotel I would be getting gourmet meals and a lot of respect."

As a joke I say, "They give you this kind of food because they like you and want you to stay with them longer."

Starting the next morning, in spite of his objection that it is too much trouble for us, we regularly cook meals at home and take them to Amu at the hospital.

The tests have been completed but the results won't be released for a couple of days. Finally, one of Amu's doctors calls me out to his office one evening while I am visiting. "Listen," he begins, "unfortunately, I don't have good news for you. But remember that what I am telling you is based on our initial diagnosis only. We are still waiting for a specialist we have contacted to arrive; he will probably want more tests. To make an accurate diagnosis, we will have to wait for the results of these additional tests. However, since Amu insists on hearing what we know about his health, I am telling you what our initial findings indicate. We think Amu has cancer, so we have asked for an oncologist to give us his opinion."

The word cancer evokes a nightmarish vision; I remain as silent as death. The doctor tries to give me encouragement and repeatedly says it is not their definitive diagnosis. I ask him not to tell Amu what he has just confided to me.

When I return to Amu, I deliberately start talking about the weather and other distracting topics.

"What did the doctor tell you, Hassan?" Amu abruptly interrupts.

"They are waiting for another doctor to come visit you."

"What the Hell are these doctors doing then if they are waiting for someone else?" Amu replies a bit irate, "I am paying them good money and I insist that they tell me what the Hell is wrong with my liver."

"Don't worry, Amu. It can't be anything very serious."

"If not serious, why all the secrecy then?"

"You know how doctors are, Amu; they just want your money," I say, repeating his words in an attempt to amuse him.

"So they love money more than they love me!"

"Yes, Amu."

"What's the deal? Why does everybody worship money?"

"What shall I say, Amu? Money solves problems."

"Does it?"

"At least it does for Khoda. By the way, where is he? It has been a long time since I have seen him."

"When Khoda has money, you can't find him in Delhi anymore. He has gone to Manali¹ to escape Delhi's heat."

By the time we have finished talking about the attractions of this retreat and Amu has quieted down, it is late and I leave the hospital, a huge knot in my throat. On my way back home, I mutter to myself with a fury I don't attempt to contain, angry at my fate, my conditions and my UNHCR office. Heedless of being heard, I shake my fists at the sky and call out to God angrily. "Where are You?" I say aloud, walking along a small dark alley. "Why me? How long? You do not exist. You can change nothing. You just enjoy watching people in pain."

I am still talking when I come to a tiny Hindu temple where a couple of people are praying in front of a stone Buddha. Candles burn in the dark around the statue and a small red lamp brightens the short veranda a bit. I slow down and start watching the worshipers. They light more candles and incense sticks and place them near the Buddha with an attitude of humbleness. After ringing a bell, they leave.

Approaching the temple, I look inside. It is a rather small veranda consisting of three walls and a roof, like a large, upturned box, and there are short iron fence posts in front, which prevent people from getting too close to God. The Buddha is sitting in silence in the middle of the temple on a carpet of flowers, his face and body smeared with sacred paints and wreaths of religious blossoms hanging from his neck. Wisps of smoke mingle with the aromas of the flowers around him. The road is dark, and except for occasional passersby, there is nobody around. I put my hands on the fence in front of the Buddha and look at him in silence for a while.

"Hello, Bhagwan," I greet the statue, "I see you are enjoying yourself here. You have opened businesses everywhere. It must be very agreeable sitting here and watching poor people pay You such great respect. Am I right or am I wrong? I want to talk to You. I called to You in the Arabic language for about eighteen years, but You not only did not answer me, You allowed my life to be destroyed. These Hindustani people called to You in their own language. I was watching them. I was there in the dark when they put these candles and incense here. When are You going to answer them? I cannot talk to You in Your language. The only words I have learned here are about my case and buying vegetables in the market. We are taught to believe that such words are not worthy of You. You love religious words, which I do not know in Your language. But I know my mother tongue. I am talking to You in my language. I have heard You know everything. You know about my life. You know that from among millions of people in this country, I found an old man who has treated me like his own child. He planned to help me. He wanted to save the life of a family. But You gave him cancer. Why?"

I burst into tears and give way to my sorrow and frustration. From time to time, some local people pass by and look at me.

"Bichara koy mosibat hogiya[2]," a couple of them say to each other.

After my tears are spent, I feel better. "Sorry Bhagwan, to disturb You," I begin again, "I was angry. Really, I am sorry. At least You are patient enough to listen. Please Bhagwan, I need Your help. I know You are not this stone, and You know that I am human. Each person has his limits. I have had too much; I have surpassed my capacity. You are my witness. Please Bhagwan, please."

Head down, I walk away.

* * *

Sroosh is asleep when I get home and I walk across the room to sit out on the terrace in the dark. Teas in hand, Mona joins me. I light a cigarette and begin to sip the hot brew. When I can finally force myself to speak, I repeat what the doctor has told me about Amu's health. By the time I finish, tears are running down Mona's cheeks.

----

[1]Manali is a mountainous resort in India foreign tourists favor because of its wild greenery.

[2]This Urdu phrase means something like, 'poor fellow; misfortune must have overtaken him'.

~ * ~

Which way to go? This way to go? That way to go?

Eventually this endless night turns into dawn and I get ready to leave for the hospital again. Towards noon, the doctor from the day before arrives and calls me to his office.

"Mr. Hassan," he begins, a smile turning up the corners of his mouth, "I have encouraging news for you today."

His words make my heart beat faster as I await his report.

"Amu is suffering from a minor hepatitis, which is much more manageable than cancer," he explains. "It is in its initial stages and we hope to be able to stop the disease with special treatments over a period of several months."

"You mean he will have to stay in the hospital all that time?"

"No. His liver isn't functioning properly, which must be corrected immediately. This process may take some weeks. Then, he can go home if he likes. However he must continue medication at home following our doctors' instructions."

"Is he in mortal danger, doctor?" I ask, wanting to hear his reassurance.

"It could be if not treated properly; we will do our best with him."

I thank the doctor and hurry to tell Amu that the illness making his eyes and skin yellow is a simple inflammation of the liver and the doctors want him to remain as a patient where they can keep an eye on him until his body responds to the treatment. I assure him that the doctors are confident he is not in serious danger. His relief is palpable; he brightens and decides to take a walk with me in the hospital's garden to get some fresh air.

* * *

Although the doctors advise against us bringing our child to the hospital, we find it hard to deny Amu when he pleads passionately to see his 'Ahmad'.

"I have not seen Ahmad since last night," Amu often complains. "Bring him to me with my lunch. I want to play with my Ahmad."

When, after two weeks of treatments, Amu is able to leave the hospital as an outpatient, Mona and I take him home with us and he becomes part of our family. His being there changes our mood; even though we don't dwell on it, we miss being near our parents and find Amu to be a good substitute. He plays with Ahmad all day long as if he were our son's natural grandpa. Having Amu at our house helping out with Sroosh also gives Mona more free time to take care of housework and she is more cheerful. Once again, I am able to start teaching the students who have been waiting for my recovery.

Returning home from English classes, I always feel I am going back to my own place in my village as long as Amu is with us, a radio at his side much as my father used to keep his. His presence fills a void we didn't know was there.

"Still no change in the government, Amu?" I ask.

"Do you expect a change?"

"No, not really, but I thought you might be able to give me some news of Iran."

"Nah, ghorban[1], not yet. Sir Tony Blair is still happy with the mullahs."

A month from the time he first started treatment for the hepatitis, Amu is feeling much better and decides to join his old friend, Khoda, in Manali, believing fresh mountain air will help him overcome his poor health. He has a lot of faith in a Dr. Sardar Ji in that area who, in his opinion, is a miraculous traditional doctor.

Amu leaves and we return to our life without him, our spirits dragging. Sroosh has grown accustomed to Amu's confident voice and learned the names of many objects around him after hearing them repeated over and over[2], and he misses all the extra attention he has come to expect.

* * *

Poverty often overshadows our lives. A few months after Amu leaves us, I become ill again and a financial nightmare shows its face once more. Not knowing what else to do, I talk to Ms. Vinira in the UNHCR office about my condition and go so far as telling her that I am seriously considering selling our passports as a last resort.

"That is your personal affair," she replies, smiling tightly.

In order to survive, I am reduced to following through with my threat. Passports secure in my pocket, I visit a black market with a reputation for being a trafficker in such documents. In less than an hour, I have sold them to Afghan refugees in a teahouse for a sum of money that will only get us through a couple of months. What we will do after that, I can't force myself to think about.

The money is soon gone and I have nothing else to sell. In desperation, I write a letter to the UNHCR office and ask to be sent back to Iran. Ms. Vinira calls me in for another meeting but it changes nothing at all. I am encouraged to hang on until the office can resettle us in another country. Our main issue, putting food on the table and feeding our baby, is one for which nobody has an answer. Mona cannot produce milk to breastfeed Sroosh and we have no money to buy powdered milk or any other baby food. Despondent about the future, when I get home from the office, I bring up the idea of returning to Iran. Knowing the bleakness of our situation, Mona agrees with me; we decide it is time to contact the Iranian Embassy.

I pull out my bag and start searching it for a paper which Shahrooz, a friend from Tourist Camp, gave me several months before. Once in the 80s, while he was in India with his pregnant wife, they were granted refugee status but were still waiting to see what their final destination would be. Their child, Achilles, entered the world by way of New Delhi. With no news about their resettlement, he finally decided to send his wife and child to Europe with an Iranian smuggler. Once there, his wife married the smuggler and did not want to have anything more to do with Shahrooz. He tried for a while to get sent to the same place and when he had exhausted all his options with no result, he returned to Iran by himself.

In 1996, when I arrived in Tourist Camp, Shahrooz was there for the second time. This time, he had come to India with the hope of finding a way to go to Europe to find his child, whose name he repeated tens of times every single day. He tried every avenue he could think of, but by 1998 he still had not found a way ahead. When he ran out of money, he stayed with us for some time during Mona's pregnancy before deciding to return to Iran. The Iranian Embassy in Delhi helped him with his ticket and other minor expenses to get him back home but before he left, Shahrooz gave me two phone numbers, saying each of them belonged to an embassy employee who, in his opinion, was sympathetic.

By the time I have the numbers in my hand, my mind is made up. I leave for a public phone in the market, planning to confess my refugee status to the embassy and ask for help with repatriation. I call both numbers and the phones ring and ring with no answer. Hanging up, I light a cigarette and walk around near the phone booth for a few minutes, beginning to doubt my decision. However, we can no longer continue like we are, and losing our child is a realistic fear. I finish my cigarette and dial the numbers a second time. Again, there is no answer. Could it be a holiday? No, I make a mental check; it is a workday. Why aren't they answering then?

Putting into action our decision to contact the
Iranian Embassy.

Returning home, I comment, "Guess what? Nobody answered the phone; I called twice and there was no answer either time."

"Maybe we aren't meant to return to Iran," Mona prophesies.

"Ghorban' gives the idea of sacrifice. In daily conversation, this word shows a kind of respect; a close equivalent is 'sir', 'master' or' your majesty'.

²Pankeh or fan was the first object Sroosh identified by name. Every time he heard the word pankeh from Amu's lips, he would glance up at the ceiling.

~ * ~

Westward ho

On the same afternoon that I try to contact the Iranian embassy, my landlady calls up from the first floor saying a friend wants to meet with me. I head down the stairs and there is Arsalan, an Iranian refugee who arrived in India almost at the same time I got to Delhi. Living alone on the other side of town, he has never visited me before, but we do meet at the UN bank once a month when it is time to collect our payment.

At the bottom of the stairs, I welcome him.

"I was just passing by," he says with a smile, "and I remembered you. I knew you lived somewhere around here, but I was not sure where, so I asked some people in the alley and found your place through them."

I invite him in and we walk upstairs to my room. Arsalan spends some time with Sroosh while we are catching up on acquaintances and events.

"Actually," I admit at one point, "we've been thinking of going back to Iran."

"Whatever for?"

I give him a detailed story of my long-term poverty in Delhi and he listens patiently until I have finished.

"Don't decide too hastily. You have done all the hard work already. Now, just wait for the UN to find you a country."

I explain to him how terribly we are suffering.

"Give me a day or two," he boasts, "I will find you a job."

"I have jobs teaching English," I answer. "But about once a month I get sick from riding in those hot crowded buses, and can't continue until I recuperate, so I lose that income."

"You just give me one day, ok?" he repeats, and soon is gone.

Before nightfall, Arsalan calls to me from down in the alley; from the terrace, I invite him up.

As soon as he gets to our room, he grins and states, "I found it. I got you a job."

Thinking he is kidding, I ask, "How could you find me a job so fast?"

"I have an Afghan friend who runs a school, very close to your house, with many English classes for Afghan refugees. It is all private and students pay him directly. So, you can work with him as an English teacher. He will tell you how much he is willing to pay each month. For sure, it will be much better and easier since you will not have to travel around Delhi every day."

Later that same night, Arsalan comes to our place for the third time in one day; this time, Abdo, the Afghan who runs the school, is with him.

We discuss the details of my position in his school and as a test of my ability, he gives me an assignment; I am to write out a graduation certificate and bring it with me on the first day of my employment.

"How soon can you start?" Abdo asks.

"The sooner, the better!" I answer with relief and renewed hope.

"Ok, I'll see you tomorrow, then," he concludes as the two of them get up to leave.

Afterwards, knowing that Balooch's children have the kind of certificate I think the professor wants, I go to their house and copy it.

The next day when I present this paper to Abdo, he sneers and says, "What is this?"

"The certificate you requested."

"This is nothing, it's useless, it's too simple, anyone could do this."

"But this is a common form of certificate given out by language schools."

"I meant something more well- organized and professional looking."

The dissatisfaction in his voice surprises me; obviously, his expectation was different from mine.

* * *

The school has several levels and there are Afghan refugees of all ages attending classes throughout the day, a couple of Iranians scattered among them. The only teacher is Abdo, who teaches classes straight through from early morning until late in the evening. Although his English vocabulary is extensive, he has no academic education and his teaching methods are old-fashioned and outdated; he often uses force against the students the way I remember the mullah treating my brothers. Once I start giving classes, seeing the contrast between the methods of Abdo, whom they call 'the mad master', and my own teaching style, many of the students come and ask me to teach them at their homes. But because I feel I owe Abdo my loyalty, I decline.

Every now and then, on different occasions and for different reasons, Mr. Abdo asks for a copy of my university diploma. Thinking back to his original request when he first came to my house, and remembering his reaction to my assignment, I begin to suspect he is planning to make a copy of my original documents and forge his name onto them. Each time he brings up the subject, I make an excuse and avoid meeting his demands. He soon becomes less friendly and often keeps me past my contract time so that I am unable to get to my afternoon classes.

At the end of a month, he calls me to his office and gives me my paycheck. "This is your salary," he says, "and today is the last day of our contract. I will certainly let you know if I need a teacher again."

We say goodbye and I leave the school.

It is almost evening by the time I approach the Bhogal market. I stop to adjust the lid of my tea thermos, which has worked loose and is about to fall, when a voice suddenly calls my name. "Hassan Agha! Hassan Agha!"

I turn at the sound and am looking into a juice bar at Amu, sitting and sipping a fruit drink. He looks much healthier than the last time I saw him.

"Dr. Sardar Ji says," he tells me as I walk at a fast clip to where he is perched on a stool, "that I should drink a lot of natural juice."

Before I can get there, he has called the waiter and ordered a juice for me.

"I thought you had forgotten us, Amu."

"Why?"

"It has been ages since we've had any news from you."

"It's only been a few months."

"Yes, Amu. But to me, it was centuries."

We talk about Manali as we sip our drinks.

"Now, on your feet, let's go see Ahmad," he says in his usual commanding tone. On the way to my house, I bring him up to date on all the current news. Mona meets us by the doorway to our room.

"Where is Ahmad?" Amu asks loudly.

Our child, remembering this voice, begins to kick his legs and wave his hands rapidly as Amu reaches out to pick him up.

"You are Ahmad, ok?" He tells Sroosh.

We all sit down on the floor, Amu bringing Sroosh in his arms.

"So, did you have enough time to think?"

"About what, Amu?"

"Do you want to go to Iran or to Canada?"

"I don't really know, Amu," I answer pensively.

"Maybe you'd like to stay in India forever?"

"No, Amu, but I have no idea how I would travel to Canada with a wife and child."

"On the contrary, it will be easier if they are with you," he judges.

Mona joins Amu in trying to convince me. While we review the possible risks and rewards of the proposition, Amu stands up and says, "Ahmad and I will take a stroll on the rooftop. I want to show him your neighbor's doves from there."

He takes Sroosh and leaves.

"Why are you so worried?" Mona asks me. "Are you concerned about Sroosh? I assure you that nothing worse than this life can happen to us on the way. Thousands of people take risks and find a better life. At least we can try. If we go back to Iran and you tell your friends that you let such an excellent opportunity pass you by, they will certainly think you made it up.

Let's do it; we have nothing to lose. Besides, we have the UNHCR refugee certificate. If we get arrested on the way, this paper may help."

After weighing the pros and cons of this venture, I finally agree to risk it. "All right, let's test our fortune and head west."

We call Amu down and tell him that we will make a try at getting to Canada. Hearing this, he puts Sroosh in his crib, opens his bag and takes out a strange-looking object with straps.

"What is this, Amu?"

"Ahmad cannot walk, and you have a long trip ahead. You need to carry him on your chest kangaroo style with the help of this baby pouch."

We are amazed that Amu has anticipated our answer even before we knew it ourselves.

"I was sure you would agree eventually," he continues, "so, I got this for Ahmad awhile back. What you need to do now is supply me with a few passport photos; agreed?"

"Upon my eyes¹, Amu."

* * *

Not too long after that, Amu brings us two Italian passports. Excited, we thumb through them. I love the way our pictures look in the documents. "Look at me! Can you believe it?"

Without answering my question, Mona, looking at her own photo, exclaims, "Look at this! I am Silvia now. Talk to me in Italian!"

"Good? Happy now?"

"Yes, Amu. They are beautiful."

"Now do you think you can get to Canada with a wife and child?"

"I think so, Amu."

"What does 'I think so' mean? Look at these! Nobody can ever say you do not look Italian," Amu adds, pointing at Sroosh's image next to his mother's. The halo of his long dark-blonde hair around his light skin makes him look European.

"The people who made up the passports said the name given the baby is from a famous Italian soccer player," Amu explains.

I look at Sroosh's new name again. It is Roberto.

"Yes, Amu," I agree, "Roberto Baggio is a famous player."

"Ahmad is a football player, yes?" Amu asks Sroosh.

We laugh as Sroosh kicks his legs and waves his arms again.

"Now, sit down and practice these signatures. You want to make them look exactly as they do here."

Seeing the backward-slanted handwriting in front of me, the seriousness of what we are proposing suddenly dawns. Stories of failed attempts parade through my mind.

"Listen, Amu, I have not been out of India since I arrived here; what if I can't make this journey alone?"

"I will go with you as far as Nepal," he assures me. "I need to meet one of my old friends there. But from Nepal, you must continue your journey alone. It should not be difficult. As you know, millions of people have traveled like you. Many of them did not even know English. Why are you worried then? This Ahmad is your green card."

Then, he turns to Ahmad and calls him with a louder tone, "Yes?"

Sroosh moves, startled out of his daydreams. Mona leaves to brew tea and Amu continues to encourage me with mental pictures of a brighter future.

A few weeks later, Amu gives me money and sends me to the Chinese embassy in New Delhi to apply for visas. After filling them out, I hand over the forms, along with the two Italian passports, to a young man working behind the window. While he checks everything, my heart calls out silently, hoping my features don't give away the panic I feel, 'please God, please God, please, God'. Finally, his eyes lift from the papers and he asks for the fees. With a big smile of relief, I reach into my pocket for my money, and count it out in front of him. I am short fifty dollars!

"I'm really sorry, it seems I don't have enough cash with me," I stammer. "Can I come back later?"

"No problem," he answers, giving the documents back to me.

I leave to find Amu. In an hour or so, with more money in my pocket, I arrive at the embassy in a rickshaw, praying all the way that the same fellow will still be there so I won't have to worry about answering any more questions. Thank God, my prayer is answered; he is there, I give him the money and the documents, and he tells me I can collect them in a few days.

On the day when I return to the embassy, I find myself standing in line behind several Hindustani people. My face is sunburned from the hot summer weather and people around me mention how much I look like the Kashmiris. To keep a low profile, I remain silent and pretend that I do not understand what they are saying.

It is then I notice that standing a ways in front of me is an Iranian woman whom I know from Tourist Camp. I have a sudden rush of blood to my face and my heart is pounding loud enough for her to hear it. I turn my back on her and busy myself reading some papers I am carrying. When she gets to the window, she asks for a Chinese visa.

"Sorry, Madame," a voice comes from inside the window. "To get that visa, you need to apply at the Chinese embassy in Tehran."

"But I am already here! It will cost me a lot to go back to Iran to apply. If possible, please."

"I am really sorry, Madame. This is the regulation. There is nothing I can do."

She walks away in frustration and soon it is my turn to talk to the embassy people. The young man smiles respectfully and hands me the passports. My eyes fly to the beautiful Chinese visa on each document and I smile, saying to myself, 'Madame, if you want to get a visa for China, you need to be Italian'!

* * *

The next step is to apply for tourist visas at the embassy of Nepal. Borrowing from the encouragement I have received from my experience at the Chinese embassy, everything goes without a hitch.

We are now ready for a long, long journey into our uncertain future.

––––––––––––––––––––––––––––––––

¹Literally, this means my eyes are yours as a guarantee, if I don't do this, you can take them; figuratively, it is a very common way of saying yes when you are asked to do something.

If you are going through Hell, keep going!
.............................Winston Churchill

Ten

Border crossings

By late September 1999, Sroosh is almost nine months old and we are preparing for a better life in another country.

Mona begins to clean the room as if we are just settling down, washing all the old clothes, bed sheets, woven mats and the military blanket we got in Bhogal's market and served as our carpet, dusting the window, wiping down the doors and walls, and tenderly setting the kitchen stuff we are leaving behind, in boxes.

"What are you doing?" I ask her. "Are you crazy? We are leaving this place forever; we don't need these things any more. The landlady will take care of everything once we evacuate."

"Now that I know I am leaving," she explains, her voice choking, "this place has become sacred as if I was born again here. Each part of this room is alive for me. We witnessed a spiritual awakening on that tiny terrace which helped us survive and draw closer to one another in spite of life's cruelty. Our very own God's voice was born here in this humble home. You know? I have always felt blessed in this room and I miss it already. I know we have gone through lots of challenges here. Do you remember how many times we were hungry and Shadi brought us food, and we had lunch or dinner together? Look at that jar of drinking water; without a refrigerator we wrapped it in wet cloth to keep it cool like our ancestors used to do. How can I forget this snowy old black and white TV or this radio and tape player? Can you imagine? We will not be taking showers with cold water any more. We will no longer be bathing in those wash pans on our terrace in the dark. How can I forget these village posters we put up? Look at all the white lines on the walls, drawn with a piece of special chalk to prevent little lizards from coming into our room. Still some lizards ignored the chalk and crossed those lines to come in anyway. Do you remember how many times we sat and watched them chasing each other up and down the walls?"

"Do you really feel nostalgic about this room or do you just wish to stay here so you can pour more garbage on the landlady through those grills?" I ask her sarcastically and we both giggle.

Mona and Sroosh on a cycle rickshaw in Bhogal market

On the afternoon of our final day in Delhi, Mona and I visit the Afghan family one last time, sick with the knowledge that we cannot tell them about our upcoming trip. Lately, because we have been under pretty intense pressure with getting ready to leave, we've quit visiting them regularly and their kids, as well as the landlady's grandchildren, both feel neglected. Some of our Hindustani neighbors surmise that we do not like spending time with their kids now that we have one of our own, but the reality is we are concerned about accidentally giving away our secret.

After a visit of several hours with Shadi, her mother and the children, I begin to wind up our conversation, saying, "We'd better go now."

"Not yet. I just brewed fresh tea. One more tea," Shadi says, teapot in hand.

"You are very kind. I hope God will give you good health and a new country in which to raise your children with a bright future. We have lived close to each other like real family, and I really thank you for your generosity with us. If we have given you any trouble, I am sorry."

Suddenly, as Shadi is pouring us tea, I notice a sort of awareness dawn on her face and she holds the teapot motionless for a few seconds. The moment passes, and I say, "When do you think Balooch will be back?"

With a sigh, she says, "I am not sure."

We drink our tea in silence and then bid each other farewell.

Our Afghan friends

* * *

Hearing we are leaving, the landlady and her family purchase honey cakes and candies and invite us downstairs to have a goodbye snack with them. We share these treats and they make us promise to come to their house if at any time we return to Delhi.

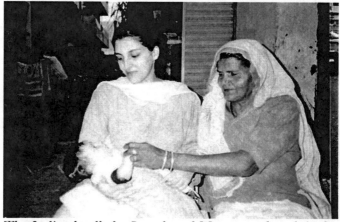

The Indian landlady, Sroosh and Mona on a bench in the alley outside the main entrance to the house

No sooner do we get back to our room, when Amu calls to us from the alley and joins us for a cup of tea in farewell to the house. Seeing all my books on the floor along with our bags, he says, "Why are these sitting here? It's a long journey and you cannot take a lot of heavy books with you. Besides, you will not have free time in Canada to read poetry. You will have to work there. Your long vacation is over, Mr."

What he says sounds reasonable. I leave all my books in India, including Rumi and Hafez, to head out for a new life in the West.

As evening approaches, we find ourselves in a train that is taking us to the India -Nepal border. The journey is underway. Along the route to the frontier, a blur of vast rice lands and vegetable gardens have old, gnarled trees marking the boundaries between them. How this country reminds me of my province! The rhythmic sound of the train wheels traveling on the rails and the greenery of the landscape, lull me into a dream-like state.

Child vendors passing back and forth through the train, calling out, 'tea-tea-tea', and 'coffee-coffee-coffee-coffee,' take me out of my reverie. Once in awhile we order tea and peanuts.

When the long, crowded train eventually reaches its final destination and the tracks go no further, we board one of the private taxis, drivers calling 'border? border? border?' and head towards Nepal.

"That's the border," the driver finally tells us, continuing, "from this point on, you need a cycle rickshaw."

Before we can unload our luggage from the taxi, a swarm of cycle drivers surrounds us; two of them take charge and the others scatter. Our luggage is transferred to the new mode of transportation and in no time we are at the border. The drivers stop short of the frontier and point us to the customs office we need to go through before we can exit India.

Amu sends me in first. Accompanied by my rickshaw driver, I walk into a small, quiet room where a lone officer sits at a table. From a bigger room behind him, I can hear several voices.

"Hello."

"Hello. Documents, please."

After checking them, he puts the documents on the table.

"Where is your luggage?" he asks me, his English Hindi-accented.

"In the rickshaw."

Turning to the driver, he asks, "yes or no?"

"Ha, Ji," the driver confirms.

"Traveling alone?"

"No, my wife and child are with me."

Again, the officer confirms with the driver and sends him for them, grabbing the stamp.

"Actually, my son was born here in your beautiful country," I mention in an attempt to act natural.

His stamp hits my passport with a 'whomp'!

"All the best," he says, handing me my document. "I hope one day when your child is grown, he can come back to India."

"Thank you. I can't wait to see that day."

Outside, I face Mona who, holding Sroosh in her arms, is heading in.

"A piece of cake," I whisper to her as we cross paths.

She goes in and suddenly, a deep tremor of fear passes throughout my body. Until now, I have felt I am dreaming or playing a part in a movie, but suddenly it hits me that what I am doing is a reality. In the several movies I saw during my childhood, people traveling on fake documents always made me tense with fright. Now we are doing what those people did in the movies, but this time it isn't make believe and fear has turned my legs to water; my heart into a vacuum. My brain is filled with a loud buzzing and everything I see is out of focus. I am still overwhelmed with panic when Amu brings me back to the present.

"Did I not tell you it would be easy?" he asks from on his cycle.

"Yes, Amu. More than easy, completely painless!"

Before I can light a cigarette, Mona is back, all smiles. When it is Amu's turn, he comes back even faster.

We cross the border on our rickshaws and I don't dare to look back. Any voice I hear, my imagination thinks is somebody calling after me. Riding the waves of my nervousness, I can vaguely hear Mona's voice in the background but the only answer I can summon is a nod or a single word of encouragement.

"We just left India," she tells me.

"Hanh? Oh, yes. We did."

"Are you ok?"

"Couldn't be better," I answer distractedly.

The rickshaws stop at Nepal customs no more than a few feet from the Indian border, and I find myself in a similar small room with a few friendly-looking customs people who, in contrast to the officer on the Indian side, are very relaxed and assume our papers are in order. Walking to the desk, I hand over my documents.

"Italy!" he exclaims. "Beautiful country."

"Thank you."

"Staying long here?"

"I wish I could; unfortunately not this time."

"Pity! Nepal has a lot of tourist attractions."

"Yes, I know. I will certainly be back again."

Once the officer and his colleagues find out I am Italian, they all want to talk to me about Italy. I, on the other hand, keep my answers short and ask about the best way to spend the week I have in Katmandu.

After this rather lengthy exchange of pleasantries, I am feeling more relaxed and hope that by being talkative I can control the direction of the conversation. Finally, I thank them for receiving me so warmly, and leave the room. I have hardly walked a few steps when one of them calls me back. A sudden eruption of terror replaces my newly gained calm. My eyes fly to a row of trees lining a nearby river and the thought of fleeing flashes through my mind. Even while I am contemplating this idea, I catch sight of Mona and Sroosh in the rickshaw waiting for me. Their presence brings me to the reality that there are three of us involved in this venture and I face back to the officers again.

"Yes, please," I say in a deadpan voice.

"Your passport. You've forgotten it," the one sitting at the table says, smiling.

"I did?" I reply, trying my utmost to keep breathing evenly. "Oh, maybe it is because of my haste to visit Katmandu. I have heard it is a real paradise," I add, taking it from his hand.

"Thank you," I repeat.

"By the way, how do you say 'thank you' in Italian?"

This phrase is not in my list of vocabulary; 'ciao' and 'bonjorno' are the only two Italian words I learned before our departure. "Gracias," I reply, searching my mind for a word and coming up with the Spanish.

Waving my passport to them, "ciao", I say.

"What did he say?" one of the officers asks his friends in Urdu.

"He said 'bye' to us in his mother tongue," answers his colleague, proud to know Italian.

Now, Mona and Amu take their turns getting a visa stamp.

What a tremendous relief we feel! We have crossed two borders without any problems and have only three more to go. Our cycles pass among the crowd of noisy bus conductors who are calling for Katmandu passengers. However, believing we have been traveling long enough for one day, and worried that his Ahmad might be harmed, Amu suggests we take a short break in a border hotel to shower and get a little rest.

~ * ~

Katmandu

Our bus winds up the mountainous road for hours through the middle of the night. Then, it descends switchbacks for about the same amount of time before the conductor announces the Katmandu station. It is still dark the next morning when we haggle over the price of a hotel with the men who have entered the bus earlier; we settle for one in the market area.

Leaving the hotel by the light of day, we see the whole city is surrounded by soaring snow-clad mountain ranges. Katmandu, at 4,500 feet, is a basin whose bottom is carpeted with deeply green trees and grass and whose sides are the giant peaks. We walk through a small street market, cross an open field where vendors with their baskets are selling a locally-grown short and fat cucumber which, when you order it, the seller cuts in pieces and sprinkles with spices, descend a hill to enter a massive, crowded bazaar resembling an ant colony, covered by woven mats and plastic tarps. Cloying scents of spices, vegetables and new cloth mingle pleasantly. Passing through the melee we climb a bit to an area of temples, seedy old wooden houses with balconies, and stone and brick monuments where foreigners wander with cow horns hanging from their necks or a huge earring in one ear, and dressed in weird tourist garb.

A wide variety of restaurants populates this area; Mona, Amu and I go from one to another, window shopping.

"Come take a look at this!" Amu calls us, pointing to a large steak sizzling on a wooden plate. "They cook meat on a slab of wood!"

"Ah, Amu, it looks delicious."

"Let's go in then," he commands.

We enter and are surrounded by a huge crowd of foreigners. Once we are seated, Amu orders tea along with our meal. The waiter brings cups and a pot full of fragrant milk tea hinting of the freshness of the green Himalayan countryside. Ahmad perks up immediately after drinking some of it and starts playing. He insists on sitting on the table and trying to capture the attention of foreigners with his little-boy charm. He claps his hands and calls out to people over and over, and refuses to be satisfied until they notice him and wave back.

"You are traveling illegally and you want to make friends along the way? Yes?" Amu says to him.

* * *

During our stay in Katmandu, Amu continues to listen to the BBC, VOA and Radio Israel through a small hand-held radio; as a result, he never misses any of the news coming out of Iran.

"Why do you listen to these radio stations so much of the time?" I ask him.

"Because these broadcasts predict what is going to happen next," he answers, "and I'm waiting to hear when the son of the Shah will come to power in Iran."

"Do you think he will ever come back?"

"If Mr. Blair agrees, he will."

It is Amu's wish to see our country ruled by someone, like the heir to the Pahlavi throne, who can reestablish order. Whatever happens around the world, Great Britain is blamed; Amu's idea is that if Great Britain wants peace in an area, there will be peace there, and if it isn't their wish, an area will never experience peace.

* * *

The day comes when we have to say goodbye to this stunning paradise nestled among tall, perpetually glacier-clad peaks. We all have enjoyed our last few days sightseeing and shopping together while waiting for our airline tickets. After successfully crossing two borders with Amu, both Mona and I feel energetic, secure, and hopeful about our future as long as he is around. How hard it will be to take leave of such a great traveling companion and to continue on alone!

Amu, Mona with Ahmad in her arms and I are standing together at dusk outside our hotel under a gentle, continuous and quietly falling rain. Our tears mingle with the drip of the skies as we embrace Amu and say our farewells.

"Do you want to go or not?" he shouts, pulling himself back a bit. Then, he turns his back to us and, with a move of his hand, motions us to go.

As our taxi heads for the airport, we turn to see Amu standing in the rain, watching. In our hands we have our tickets and the two thousand dollars which this selfless friend just gave us the night before.

The airport is filled with people. Threading our way through them, we find our gate, look for the necessary forms, fill them out and put our signatures on them. We then grab our luggage and walk to the customs check. The journey so far has taught us that Sroosh has a positive effect on the minds of the guards, so plopping him at the top of our luggage, we walk to the customs officer.

"Look at this; what a charismatic child!" he exclaims. "Boy or girl?"

"Boy," I reply.

"Maybe one day he will become the President of Italy," he says with a smile.

"Wow! Do you think so?" I exclaim in a loud voice, "really?"

"Yes, why not? I have studied psychology."

'Thank God you didn't study sociology,' I think to myself with a smile, saying nothing.

* * *

An hour or so later, we are in the plane flying from Katmandu to Shanghai.

~ * ~

Into the mouth of the Dragon

Early on the morning of October 3, 1999, we pass the customs gate of Shanghai airport and walk into a big exit hall. It is very easy to enter China and I hope leaving will be the same.

Since we have no Chinese currency, we look around inside the airport for a bank or a money exchange booth. The small bank is closed and there is a young Chinese man by the door, who asks if he can help.

"We would like to exchange some dollars."

"As you see the bank is closed," he tells us in good English. "I work in this airport and that is my office," he adds, "I can exchange your money if you are in a hurry."

We follow him into his office, a small room containing only one chair and a folding table. Showing us the list of exchange rates in a newspaper, he explains, "this is the rate today at the bank, but I can't pay you that much."

One American dollar is around 8.7 Chinese Yuan; he offers to pay us 7.7.

"It is very difficult for you to exchange your money outside," the man assures us, "I have given you a fair price."

All my previous information about China being a very restricted country tells me that he is right. We exchange one thousand dollars, then leave to look for a taxi. Two young men rush up to us saying, taxi, taxi, taxi and adding in broken English, or Chinglish as it's called, "Hello, nice to meet you! Where are you from?"

"Italy."

"Do you want taxi?"

"Yes."

"Where are you going?"

"Shanghai train station. We are going to Beijing."

"Ok, no problem."

"How much?" I ask.

"One hundred fifty Yuan."

"No, it's too expensive."

"It's far," they both jump in, trying to convince us.

"No, that is too much."

"Ok, you say, you say."

"I don't know."

"Ok, ok. One hundred Yuan. Now ok?"

I agree, and pelting us with questions, they help us with our luggage to the outskirts of the airport where there are no taxis or people.

"Where is your taxi?"

"There," they reply but we see nothing.

We are about to change our minds when they point out an old car and insist it is an official airport taxi.

"Maybe they are dangerous," Mona whispers to me.

"They are too young to be a danger," I answer. "They are just curious, which is natural since we are foreigners and they want to find out about us. Take it easy."

A bit later, we arrive at the train station.

"For sure taxis are expensive in China," Mona comments, "it was not far."

The car drops us near the station and the two young men ask for two hundred Yuan.

Why?" I ask in surprise.

"This one hundred Yuan for me," the driver says, pointing to the money I just gave him, "but another this for government."

"Why government?" I say, mimicking his English structure.

"Because highway, highway, you know – highway."

"But you didn't pay any toll on the way."

"No problem. I give to government every day."

They keep smiling and insisting that they have to pay one hundred yuan to the government for using the highway.

"Highway tax is also very expensive here," I tell Mona.

We pay them the money and they walk us to the main gate of the train station, carrying our luggage and opening doors along the way[1]. Thousands of Chinese are milling in and around the station;

the country is celebrating the fiftieth anniversary of Communism, and multitudes of people are taking advantage of their national holidays to do some traveling.

We arrived in Beijing as Italians during the 50th anniversary of Communism

Except for those few persons whom we meet upon our arrival, the majority of the Chinese do not speak English. I use a lot of body language and create the sound of trains, trying to make people understand that we need tickets to Beijing, while they watch us in confusion and amusement. While I am mimicking a train and making a fool of myself in a crowd outside the station, a small group of teenagers approaches us. They are learning English, love to talk to foreigners, and volunteer to help. One of them looks like Jackie Chan; I do my best to explain to them but they have no idea such a famous movie star exists.

Using clipped words such as 'no', 'not this one', 'another place', they make me understand that I need to go to a different office for my tickets. Leaving Mona and Sroosh behind to rest, I let the teenagers lead me to the right office which turns out to be small, quiet and luxurious. My young companions chatter to the ladies at the window, who turn to me and in English tell me there are no coach seats and I will have to purchase first-class tickets at a cost of five hundred Yuan apiece.

Before the students leave, they show me a large, comfortable waiting room with rows of shops around a raised stage in the center where a woman is playing a piano.

"Wait here," they say, indicating the chairs, benches and sofas situated around the hall. I wish them well for their kindness before returning to Mona. "Even train tickets are very expensive in this country," are my first words to her.

* * *

Inside the hall, crowds of people gather around Sroosh, wanting to hold him and to have their pictures taken with him. Many of them cannot believe he is a boy. One elderly woman actually pulls Sroosh's pants down to make sure. At this, everybody including us, bursts into loud laughter.

Sroosh before his first haircut

Gradually, they go back to their seats and we sit down close to a Chinese man who begins speaking English to us.

"Where are you from?"

"Italy."

"No kidding!" he exclaims loudly, "I love Italy. I have been there three times. Italy is beautiful. Which city?"

"Firenze. It is very small compared with Shanghai."

"I have been to Firenze. I have been there and to many other places."

"Great! What did you think of my country?"

"It is like a paradise," he answers. "But I have a question."

"Actually, I have not been there for quite some time," I admit, smiling. "So, my information may not be updated."

"No," he interrupts me, "just on the contrary. My question is about the past. Why is it that streets are so narrow in Italy?"

I smile a few moments, trying to find a good answer.

"You know?" I begin to explain. "Italy is a very ancient country. Do you remember the Roman Empire? The whole country is historical and we don't want to break down the old walls for new cars."

He laughs and praises the people of 'my country' for having such great respect for their past. Obviously, he is eager to continue talking about Italy, but worried he will find me out if I talk too much, I apologize and tell him that we need to go buy something to eat before our departure.

I walk Mona and Sroosh towards the exit gate of the hall, cursing my wretched luck. From among such a huge population of travelers, I have to sit next to somebody who has visited Italy three times! Mona is laughing as we leave the building. I find her a place to wait for me while I go off to get some fruit.

It is hard for me to communicate with the local shopkeepers. Many of them will not even try; as soon as they face a foreigner at the door, they feel frustrated and give up without attempting to understand. As a result I hear, 'ni hao' and 'mei yo', phrases I later learn mean 'hello' and 'we don't have it', several times in almost every store I enter. Once, inside a small grocery store, a man says 'ni hao' then answers 'mei yo' when I ask a question.

"One coke, please."

"Mei yo," the owner says.

"What mei yo? Over there, over there."

He opens a small gate and lets me make a selection. I show the bottle to him and say, "Coke".

He answers, "ke-luh."

I hold up the bottle to him and say, "English, Coke."

He repeats after me, "ko-kuh."

"Yes. Ok. Good," I smile. "Coke."

"Ko-kuh."

With the use of body language, I finally manage to buy fruit and snacks to have on the way and return to find Mona sitting alone under a tree.

"Where is Sroosh?"

"Don't worry, he is enjoying himself. That woman who runs the store over there asked for Sroosh and I felt reluctant to say no to her."

I walk over to where some twenty people have formed a circle with Sroosh in the middle. A young woman is holding him in her arms with obvious enjoyment. She has opened a Coke and Sroosh, licking the other end of a straw she has put in it, tries to pull the liquid out of the bottle. People are all laughing and Sroosh, who loves getting attention, is deeply enjoying being cradled in the woman's arms. He finally figures out how to suck the Coke up through the straw and everybody begins to clap for him. When they find out I am his father, people give me thumbs up indicating they like my child.

* * *

By eight the same evening, we are inside a train as comfortable as a hotel room, heading for the dragon's lair.

'It wasn't until months later that we found out there was no such thing as a highway toll and the going taxi fare was several times less than what we had paid.

~ * ~

Dragons breathe fire!

We arrive at the Beijing railway station early the next morning. Across a large yard and a short way down a road, stand a restaurant and a building with a sign reading 'international flight tickets' so we decide to buy our tickets to Canada before hunting for a hotel. In this small office, I say, "We need to book flights to Vancouver, in Canada." Several employees look at us blankly, not understanding one single word.

"Ca – na – da," I say, separating it into syllables.

A woman repeats, "Cha na da."

"Canada," I say again, putting a map of the world in front of her, pointing out the country.

"Ye suh," she confirms, "Cha na da."

Pointing at Mona, Sroosh and myself, I say, 'Tickets, tickets, Canada, Beijing to Canada."

"Ok."

On the map I single out Vancouver, Canada, and say, "Beijing to Vancouver, how much?"

In Chinese, she says something I don't understand, so she calls a young man and talks to him awhile. Then, looking at me, the girl points to the man and says, 'go, go', meaning follow him. He takes us by taxi to an Air China office.

Like Shanghai, Beijing is very crowded with travelers and there are no available flights for about ten days. We book our tickets for the first available flight and check into a nearby hotel where the workers and the managers are very friendly. Cautious about people finding out we are traveling illegally, we tend to avoid the millions of personal questions posed. Watching as housekeeping checks every single wastebasket in each room before emptying them into their large black containers, we begin to think that security issues are very serious in this country.

The child of the only foreigners in the hotel, our son Sroosh, whom the Chinese call Lo beto, becomes very popular among the personnel. Everybody who works in the hotel knows our son; the receptionists, when they see us, run and pull him out of our arms for a hug or offer a toy to entice him to come to them, and maids come and take him to the lobby or hallway to play until he gets hungry or fussy.

There is a small Chinese restaurant close by where we decide to have our meals. The woman, who is the cook and manager, uses a lot of local sauces and condiments in her dishes, creating aromas we can't stomach in the beginning. We can smell those sauces coming from the pores of her skin whenever she passes by our table; in fact, the whole restaurant has the same smell and I'm sure there is no way to get rid of it. In vain, we try to make her understand that we prefer our food without the addition of the spices[1].

For the next few days, we eat at this restaurant a couple times, then try other restaurants, but their food is prepared the same way, only more expensive, so we return to the first one. Then one day, while strolling through streets close to the Beijing railway station, we see a scattering of Xingjiani restaurants. Xingjian, with its dominant Moslem population, is a province in China; it borders Pakistan and is similar to Iran in both cuisine and culture. After days of picking at the Chinese food, Mona and I decide to eat a substantial lunch in one of these localities. A few are preparing kabobs outside and we choose one of them. A Xingjiani family, who works together and runs the establishment, welcomes us warmly and shows us to a table. Very few other customers are there so early in the afternoon.

"Moslem?" The father of the family asks me.

"Yes."

"Afghan?"

"No."

"Turkey?"

"No."

"Iran?"

"Yes."

"Name?"

"Hassan."

He turns to his family and exclaims, "I told you they were Moslem!"

They speak Turkish; we communicate with the help of just a few Turkish phrases I still remember from the mother-in-law of my aunt in Tehran, who was from the Turk tribe. The head of the family explains how their longtime friendship with some Afghans has made them familiar with our culture and I thank God this man does not work at airport customs.

"Lunch?" he asks, bringing his hand to his mouth in a gesture of eating.

I nod my head yes and they begin to set a table for us. With no idea what to order, we try our best to make them understand that we need good wholesome food. We are still talking to the owner when Tore jaan, the son of the family, brings us our lunch, asking if I want a beer. Although I want one, I am afraid they will be offended if I say yes, since they know me as a Moslem and I do not want to show them any kind of disrespect. To my surprise, he brings me a bottle of beer and puts it on our table as if it's no big deal.

Our new Xingjiani friends show their amazement that two such skinny people can eat so much.

"Hassan," the father calls to me from where he is sitting with his family and a young doctor friend of theirs. He gestures with his hands in the air to ask me how anyone can eat that much food without getting fat, then pats his own protruding stomach in comparison with mine to the sound of the laughter of his family and their friend.

Mona and I eat so much for lunch that we don't feel hungry again for the next two days; the meal is so memorable that we go back for either lunch or dinner quite often between then and the day of our flight.

On the morning of October 12th, Mona and I pack, say goodbye to the hotel staff and leave for Beijing Capital Airport. After paying the exit fees, we sit with our luggage at our feet, filling out customs declarations. It is our final border and we seem to be more nervous. The more we check, the more we doubt our signatures. We pick up two new forms, fill them afresh, put our signatures on them and join the passengers who have lined up under a sign with one 'lovely' word on it: Vancouver.

The morning of October 12, 1999 – packed for Beijing Capital Airport

327

Soon Mona and I are standing in front of a customs official who is checking documents. We greet him and hand over our papers, sitting Roberto, like before, at the top of our luggage. This official is not interested in looking at a toddler; he keeps his eyes on our passports. We wait in silence until he finishes his job and returns them to us.

"Have a good journey," he says.

We thank him and put our bags on the security rail, which will take them to the plane, then start walking away towards the passengers' lounge.

"You see how easy it was?" I say to Mona triumphantly. "I told you everything would be ok."

Before we have taken more than a few steps, from the second floor a man dressed in a white uniform, whom we have seen looking at passengers since we arrived, comes to the ground floor and calls to the customs officer from a short distance away.

Starting from the time we lined up, I remember noticing how very carefully this man was scanning the crowd from upstairs. He says something to the customs officer who then stops the luggage carousel and reverses it, calling us back to his table.

"I am sorry," he says, "May I see your papers once more, please?"

"Yes, of course," I reply, handing our documents to him.

He in turn takes them to the senior officer who, at a distance of about ten meters away, looks at us and then looks at our papers carefully. The two exchange a few words before the man in white, our passports in his hands, turns and walks to a small room behind the checkpoint. Mona and I watch in silence, our hearts in our throats. A long agonizing five minutes pass before he returns our passports to the customs official, gives him an order and walks away.

"Excuse me," the customs officer tells us, "your tickets are not confirmed. I am afraid I cannot let you board until you confirm them."

"But they are confirmed. I got them from Air China. You can call them."

"No, that is not my job. You need to do that. I suggest you not waste your time here."

"Where can I confirm them?"

"From the same place you got them."

"But that is a long way from here, and I have less than two hours."

"I am sorry," says the man, "it's not my problem. Unfortunately, I cannot do anything."

I leave Mona and Sroosh there and run out of the airport. There are many people standing in the airport taxi line. With no time to waste, I run to the front, trying to get a taxi. A young police officer controlling traffic, says, "Line please, line please."

"No time no time no time!" I yell repeatedly, tapping my left wrist with a finger to make him understand that I am talking about time.

He gives in and I jump into a taxi.

"Faster! Faster!" I urge as we rush along the highway. I begin to review in my mind the events of us being spotted, when suddenly it occurs to me that the officer deceived me and I could have confirmed the tickets right there in the airport. By now, the car is dropping me at the Air China office and I run inside the building. An employee checks the system; the tickets have already been confirmed. Like I suspected, it was a ruse to get rid of me. I fly out of the building and run all the way back to the main road to grab a taxi.

When I arrive at the airport, the crowd in the hall has thinned out and I walk in to see Mona sitting on the floor under a huge cement pillar, watching motionless and mute as Sroosh plays on her lap. When I get to them she bursts into tears. "You are late," she tells me deadpan. "The flight has left."

Our last hope flies away with that plane. We have missed the flight and are left with not much money in our pockets. How will we go on? How did this happen? What will we do now?

With no definite plan in mind, we return to the customs checkpoint, but now, nobody is there. Seeing an officer coming out of a room, we peek inside it and there is the officer we dealt with, sitting with his head down, drinking tea and smoking a cigarette.

"You lied to me," I accuse him. "You said my tickets were not confirmed. This was not true; Air China just told me that everything was in order. Why did you do that? What is your name? I want to make a complaint to authorities."

He remains polite but says little. The more I talk to him and the louder my voice becomes, the less he says. His lack of reaction makes me desperate. I do not know what we will do if we leave the airport; maybe if I hit him on the head it will make him angry enough to take action. Even if we are put in jail, at least we will have a roof over our heads. Our condition is miserable; no way ahead and all the bridges burned behind. What else can we do with so little money left? I am so despondent that I do not have the energy to fight.

Holding onto our documents, we trudge out of the room and wander over to where our luggage is waiting for us in the middle of the silent hall. Bags in hand, and without a word spoken, we drag our tired bodies from the airport and with no goal in mind find ourselves in line with a few people waiting for taxis.

"Where are we going?" Mona sighs.

"Back to the same hotel, I guess."

"But we just said goodbye to all of them."

"It can't be helped; we have no other way. That's the only place we know."

----

[1]Once accustomed to it, we learned to love food prepared this way.

~ * ~

'If you need something, get up and walk'

Four hours after leaving it, we return to a puzzled staff at our old hotel and spend a long, confused, disoriented and wakeful night. Hopeless, we can't figure out what our next step should be; we can't leave here and we haven't prepared ourselves for the eventuality of living here, either. In such a vast country, with 1.3 billion people, all of a sudden we feel alone and lonely, frightened and desperate.

No money, no documents, no friends, not speaking the language, not even daring go to a supermarket to shop, I am afraid anybody who looks at me knows my illegal status. Confidence gone, a deep cold dread occupies every single fiber of my body.

After a few days, Mona and I discuss the possibility of returning to India by way of Tibet and Nepal, so we travel by train to Chengdu in Sichuan province. On the 32-hour trip, because of Sroosh we make friends with people who quiz us about Italy and ask us how to say many things. Among them, there is a young Chinese man who speaks a little English and is very eager to learn Italian. He pulls out a paper and pencil and bombards me with words for translation along the way. Not knowing Italian, I give him these words in French or if I don't know the French, in Farsi or in my local Gilaki dialect. Shamefully, I watch as he carefully takes notes of these words. If, as we are traveling, he sees pigs in a field, he asks, 'What is pig?' I don't know pig in French, so say the Farsi word, 'khuk', but try to give it an Italian accent by adding a syllable so it sounds like 'khukah.' If it happens to be a bull, I say 'kalgeh'. 'Train,' he says, and I answer, 'Tranno'. 'Bus,' he wants to know, and I say, 'L'tobusso'.

A couple who are our neighbors on the train know a few words of English, so I ask them where to stay cheaply in Chengdu. Since Chengdu is their destination as well, they offer to help us, but even with their help, we cannot find a cheap place which takes foreigners. What we do find is a bigger hotel with a lot of tourists.

"Lhasa? Are you crazy?" Everybody says. "This child will die at that altitude!"

What should we do, then? With our few remaining dollars melting, we decide to call my brother Davood for help. He is not home so I leave him a message to call this number in China and ask for a Mr. Baldini. Within a few hours the phone rings and I pick up, immediately recognizing Davood's voice.

"Hello," he says politely. "May I talk to Mr. Baldini, please?"

"Hello, Davood, this is me, Hassan," I bleat.

He pauses for quite some time as if he can't believe what he is hearing.

"Hassan?" he repeats after me with uncertainty, then angrily, "what the Hell are you doing in a dangerous country like China?" he shouts. "They may kill you."

"No, that is not true," I interrupt him. "The people are very warm and friendly here even though cheating foreigners is in their blood."

"How did you end up in China?"

"Well, it is a long story," I stammer. "Trying to reach Canada, we got caught here."

"How could you do that without telling me first?" he squeaks in a voice hoarse with fury.

"Listen, this trip was not pre-planned," I lie. "I never thought of the consequences of what I was doing."

"You have not changed at all. That's how you went to India and this is how you planned to come to Canada".

"Ok, Davood. The past is past."

"You are always like this," he says, raising his voice further. "You never think before doing anything. When are you going to learn to think first, then act?"

"You are right, but I need your help."

"What can I do for you now?"

"I need a little money."

"Listen," he wonders, "how did you get there?"

"A man called Amu helped us."

"Legally, he is responsible for you, then," Davood judges.

"There is no legality here, Davood. He was not a travel agent. He was someone I know. A friend."

"You mean a smuggler?"

"You could call him that."

"How much did you pay him?"

"Actually, we didn't pay him anything; he paid for our trip."

"Why would he do that?"

"I don't know, Davood. I can't explain it. Sometimes things happen which can't be explained. What I do know is that he is my friend and he did all this just to help."

"What can I do now?" he eventually says with a sigh and in a warmer tone.

"I need money."

"How can I send it to you?"

"I will let you know as soon as I find a way."

* * *

On Amu's premise that if you want something, don't sit at home but get up and go after it, I start walking around the hotel area searching for a foreign tourist to ask how to receive money in China. After talking to several people with no results, one morning in the hotel restaurant I see a young man sitting quietly and ask him for permission to sit. We exchange a simple greeting and introductions; he tells me his name is Justin and he is American. "What about you?" he queries.

"Actually," I begin, "this is a very long story. Originally, I am from Iran, but because of conditions in my home country, I fled to India and eventually became a refugee. After my wife joined me and my child was born, conditions there were tough. Through a friend, we decided to test our fortune by going to Canada. In Beijing airport, our fake documents were discovered, but we weren't arrested; they just didn't let us fly out."

"So you are not traveling with your Iranian passports?" he confirms.

"No."

"Which country then?"

"Italy."

"So you are Italian?"

"In this hotel, yes. My Italian name is Baldini, but my real name is Hassan."

"Interesting. I haven't been in a similar situation so can't know how it feels to live like this, on the run. How can I help you, Hassan?"

"We are trapped in China and don't know what to do; what I urgently need now is to find a place where I can have money sent to me from my brother, preferably some place I don't need documents. Because I don't speak Chinese and don't know how to use the internet, I was wondering if you could help me find out this information."

"You mean you want to have money sent from Canada to Chengdu?"

"Exactly."

"I leave for Taipei tomorrow but I have the whole day today; except for a few minor errands, I can spend it with you."

Justin tells me a little about himself while he finishes breakfast and then we walk off together to find an internet café. He studied mandarin for three years before arriving in China, and is working in Taipei teaching English and translating documents in a temple. In the internet café we find, he looks up addresses of banks and Western Union. After an exhaustive search online, he finally finds a couple of offices through which I can receive money. Before we split up, he invites us to have dinner with him that evening.

Over dinner, Mona and I ask him how to order the dishes we are eating and a few others besides, and he jots the names down on paper; we carry that torn, wrinkled scrap of paper with us until it completely disintegrates.

We talk late into the evening, enjoying an exchange of opinions and ideas about languages, customs, religions and the relationship between our separate countries. I am surprised to hear how thoroughly he has studied religion, and as a Buddhist, how very open he is to different cultures and beliefs.

The next morning early, Justin comes to our room carrying a camera and asking to get some pictures of us together. Before he leaves, he puts an envelope on the table and says, "I thought it might take you awhile to receive money from Canada so I want you to keep this just in case, inside are two hundred dollars in Chinese Yuan. Since your documents are not legal and you probably can't use a bank, I have already changed the money for you."

This is such a kind and generous gesture that I feel ashamed and look around for something to give him in return. From my bag, I take out Mona's and my wedding rings and put them on the table in front of him.

"Listen, Justin. I have nothing else to give you in return, so, please accept these as a token. They will help you remember us in the future."

Laughing, he says he cannot accept our rings as a gift. "I have your pictures," he adds. "I can look at them whenever I want to remember you. By the way, here is my business card, and it has my parent's address in the USA. You may ask your brother to send the money to my parents later if you wish. And if you ever get to the US, I'll see what I can do to find you a teaching position."

We embrace each other for the first and last time and then he is gone.

A farewell picture of Justin, Sroosh and me - Sichuan
province, China

* * *

When the money from Davood comes, against all advice, we
still try to buy tickets to Lhasa, but find out we are unable to enter
Tibet except with a tour group, so return to Beijing and check into
the same hotel.

~ * ~

Gone with the wind

A few days pass and no other ideas of how to go on occur;
the expiration on the visa is counting down and the money my
brother sent is dwindling.

Suddenly I remember how in India every week Roberto
would hunt different people at his church to ask for financial help.
"Maybe a church will help us," I begin to think.

Mona agrees with the plan; through the Beijing Guidebook,
we search the list of churches and choose one to visit. On Sunday

morning, we are sitting among the congregation. At the end of the service, we ask how we can find the pastor. A 'sister' takes us to the other side of the auditorium where there are a few offices and a garden.

"Pastor Christopher, these people want to meet you," the sister tells him, leaving us in private.

"What can I do for you?"

"My name is Hassan and this is my wife and child. We are Iranian refugees. Trying to get to Canada, we got caught in the Beijing airport and are now trapped in China. We are running out of money and wonder if it is possible for your church to give us a bit of support."

"What did you have in mind?"

"A little financial support, if possible."

"Are you Christian?"

"Well," I hedge, "we are Iranians, and, ..."

"Oh, you are Moslem," he interrupts.

"Well, I can explain. But in the meantime we need help urgently."

"As you see, this is a very small church and we cannot do much. Why don't you go to the Iranian embassy for help?"

"As refugees, we can't do that."

"Or you may contact other organizations for assistance."

"We are new in this city and are not familiar with anything. If you can, please help us out with a little money."

A few people who are waiting for the pastor interrupt our conversation to call to him.

"I am sorry; I have to go," he tells us.

"May I have your phone number to contact you later?"

"Sure, but I don't have my business card with me right now."

"Any contact number would be appreciated," I persist.

He starts searching his pockets; emptying one of them, he pulls out a handful of cards. Grinning and handing me one, he says, "I am sorry. I didn't remember these cards were still in my pocket."

"When can I call you?"

"Tomorrow around noon."

The next day I dial that number a few times but the phone rings and rings and rings with no answer. I know he is not going to help so I flush his card down the toilet.

* * *

Every few days, we go to the airport to try to convince the customs officials to let us leave China. We enter the hall and walk directly to 'our' officer or, if he is not there, we go to the break room and find him with his senior officer who usually walks away when he sees us. We start complaining again.

"What should we do now?" I ask in a pleading tone, but he says nothing. "We missed our flights," I continue, "because you told me our tickets were not confirmed. Either reimburse me the price of the tickets, or let us fly."

Still he remains silent. "What's your name? I want to lodge a complaint against you."

He stands and walks away, Mona and I sticking to him like ticks on a dog for a while before we decide he isn't going to respond, and we leave.

Some twenty days pass this way and finally the senior officer agrees to talk to us. "You cannot travel to Canada on these passports," he says.

"Why not?"

"Are you Italian?"

"Of course."

He gives me an English paper and asks me to translate it into Italian.

"What is your point?" I object, "Italian passport holders do not have to answer such questions."

"Italians no, but you do."

"Call my embassy and talk to them."

"No, I cannot do that."

"What should I do then?"

"There is only one way I can let you fly from this airport and that is if you have tickets for Italy issued by Italian airlines."

"What about these? I already have tickets to Canada. You are responsible for the loss and you must cover it. Besides, I am traveling to Canada, not to Italy. You cannot decide my destination. I am free to travel."

For days we bargain back and forth without coming to an understanding; they are polite but adamant, neither detaining us nor setting us free.

"Why don't you arrest us then, if you think our passports are not real?"

"That's not my job," he answers.

"Please tell me what else I can do."

"There is one more option for you."

"What?"

"Call this number and talk to them. If they agree, you can fly."

"What is this number?"

"It belongs to Mr. Tom C in the Canadian embassy."

"Why would I talk to him? I am not Canadian."

"But you are traveling to Canada. You need their permission."

"Italian passport holders do not need visas for Canada," I repeat.

"But your passports do need visas."

With the hope of our using the Italian passports fading, we call the Canadian embassy and ask if an Italian needs a visa to travel to Canada.

"You mean, a native Italian?" asks Mr. C.

"Yes," I reply.

"No. Italian nationals do not need visas for Canada."

"But they are asking me to get visas from your embassy," I explain.

"I don't know about that, but I repeat that native Italians do not need visas."

Then I pass the phone to the customs officer who begins to explain that our passports are suspect and he won't let us fly unless they are confirmed by the embassy. The officer hangs up and gives me a piece of paper. "Go to this address," he tells me, "and talk to Mr. Tom C."

There is no other way except to visit Mr. C. We leave the room, and on the way out come face to face with 'our' officer. "You haven't told me your name," I insist. He turns his face from us and walks away. I tell Mona, "I think I am going to be in this man's nightmares." Mona laughs as she bundles up Sroosh against the very cold wind, and we go directly from the airport to the Canadian embassy. The guards let us in and at the window inside the hall, a shrewish old woman mutters, "Yes?"

"I just talked to Mr. Tom C on the phone and he told me to come here."

"Where are you from?"

"Italy," I answer, handing her our documents.

She scans through our documents and takes a cold look at us. "Are you Italian?" she asks.

"Well," I stutter, "I need to see Mr. Tom C, please. I just talked to him on the phone."

"The answer to my question is 'yes' or 'no'," she says icily, then leafing through our passports and flight tickets, she repeats, "Are you Italian."

"Yes."

She picks up the phone. "Tom? There is a man here who says he is Italian. He wants to see you."

They exchange a couple more words and she puts the receiver back in its cradle saying 'wait', and leaves the window with our documents in her hands. When a young man appears in her place, he points us to a room, then telling Mona to remain behind with a crying Sroosh, he disappears as well. The tiny space he sends me to reminds me of a vertical grave and makes it hard for me to catch my breath. It has its own window behind which the same young man, who turns out to be Mr. C, appears. Introducing himself with a smile on his face, he greets me calmly and says gently, "Are you Italian?"

"To be honest, no."

"Where are you from then?"

"Iran."

Smiling, he says, "Ok. Do you want to tell me the story?"

"My name is Hassan, I am married and have a child, a boy. I come from a dissident family and two of my brothers were executed under Khomeini because of their political activities, one in prison and the other in an ambush. Two others were imprisoned for about 4 years. One of them, on his release, relocated to Canada in the eighties and is now a Canadian citizen. Being the youngest and facing the aftershocks of the post-revolutionary turmoil, one of which was being unemployable, I left my homeland and sought asylum in India, eventually becoming a refugee. Two years after leaving Iran, my wife, with whom I had only a short time after our marriage, joined me. The birth of our child in Delhi caused us severe financial straits and seeing how long other refugees had been waiting in vain for resettlement, we gave up and decided to repatriate. Before we could act, an old friend volunteered to send us to my brother in Canada. Through his help, we entered China but when trying to leave for Canada, we were stopped at the airport. Today, the customs officials gave me your number, you asked me to come, and here I am. Please," I beg, "please let me fly to Canada. For God's sake, let us go."

"You mean I should give you a letter that says you are Italian?" he asks gleefully.

"I don't know anymore. I just know I need help out of our current chaos."

As he begins talking about the risks of traveling with a baby on fake passports, the long waiting lists of asylum seekers in Canada and the role of UNHCR in protecting refugees, Sroosh's loud cry draws my attention. He has been restless from the time we arrived at the embassy and has cried nonstop. Suddenly he begins to speak, "Mama! Mama!"

Upon hearing my child say his very first words while I have been brought to my knees here in the Canadian embassy by our miserable predicament, I burst into tears. The officer waits silently for me to compose myself. Abruptly he stands and leaves, asking me to wait. Moments later, he appears again, saying, "I have good news for you although it may not be what you expect."

He shows me a paper and begins to explain. "Here are two addresses; one is for the Iranian embassy in Beijing. I'm not saying you should go there. However, it is a possibility and you would do well to keep this address with you. The other one is the UNHCR office. Both of them are very close to this building. I hope they can help you."

"But I ran away from the UNHCR office in India," I lament.

"You have already tried the Indian office. Try this one as well. It may be that they are different, eh?"

"Ok. Can I get my documents back, please?"

"No, I told you," he begins again, "these are not your documents. I understand you have spent a lot on these papers and tickets but there is no way I can return them since they do not belong to you."

I leave the room without protest. No sooner do I walk away than I realize what a relief it is to be freed from fake IDs and the burden of deception killing us from inside.

"What happened?" Mona asks, her face tired and dark circles around her eyes. Sroosh has been driving her wild with his fussing and she is just barely hanging onto a shred of sanity.

"He said you will have to go see Vinira again," I joke.

"They are sending us back to India?" she asks in happy surprise.

"No, but we may need to apply for a refugee certificate in Beijing."

* * *

Around the corner on a riverbank, somewhere in between the Canadian embassy on one side and the Iranian embassy on the other, we see the Ta Yuan Diplomatic Office Building with flags flying from the courtyard, one of which belongs to the United Nations High Commissioner for Refugees.

Victory is sweetest when you've known defeat
...................................Malcolm Forbes

Eleven

Born again

Unlike the Indian office, which looks like our hometown's Islamic Revolutionary Guards base from outside, the UNHCR in Beijing is housed inside a diplomatic building. Here, without an invitation, we are allowed to walk into a quiet office with no sign of refugees. At the door, a smiling young Chinese woman, her hand out in welcome, hurries to us as if she is receiving friends. Introducing herself as Wang, she asks, "What can I do for you?"

Unsettled by her warm reception, I wonder if we are at the wrong place. "Excuse me," I begin in an uncertain tone, "we are looking for the UNHCR office."

"This is the UNHCR office," she states. At the look of doubt and confusion on my face, she points to the logo on the wall, "You see?" she adds, reaching with her hands for Sroosh to cuddle him and coo to him.

Sroosh in her arms, she invites us to a meeting room. "Can I bring you water or tea?" she asks.

With such a warm and personal welcome, I feel embarrassed to tell her that I am a refugee. "Well, how can I begin?" I stammer. "Actually we are refugees."

"Ok," she adds, smiling. "And helping refugees is our job."

Mrs. Wang takes notes while I hand over the original copy of our India refugee certificate and give her a resume of our case, including the story about the Canadian embassy and our Italian documents. She then leaves us in the meeting room for a few minutes and when she comes back, she is accompanied by a tall young man. "This is Mr. Lam Naijit," she introduces him. "He is from Malaysia and is the UN Protection Officer here."

Mr. Lam continues with more questions and Mrs. Wang records my answers on paper. When we get to the end of the interview, Mr. Lam sends us back to our hotel and tells us to stay there until, in compliance with regulations, he can talk to the Beijing Security Bureau about us and decide on further action.

"What does the Beijing Security Bureau have to do with refugees?" I want to know.

"When a new asylum seeker arrives, this is the rule. We have to report it to the Chinese police," Mrs. Wang explains in a polite, lady-like manner.

"What happens then?" I ask.

"An asylum seeker spends some time in a Chinese prison where he is questioned. If the police are satisfied with the answers, he is then returned to us here and we can start processing a case for asylum seeking. Otherwise; that is, if the police are not satisfied with his answers, they will deport him."

"How long does their process take?"

"It depends," Mr. Lam chimes in. "It could be anywhere from a few weeks to several months. For example, before you, we had another family here. The police took the father to prison where he was kept for a month or so. But the mother was not detained because she had a baby to care for. So I don't think they will detain your wife."

"What happened to them?"

"We were able to resettle them within a short period of time. In another case, a couple was sent directly from prison to their resettlement country. However, you need to understand, I cannot offer you a general rule since each case is handled differently. So, we are not promising anything. But we do promise to do our best to help you and your family, since you are already refugees. In the meantime, we will ask the UNHCR in India to send us your documents."

Visiting this office brings such relief that Mona and I immediately forget all the pain and tension of the previous month. On the way home, we pick up a bottle of wine to celebrate the occasion. That night we go to bed feeling born again.

* * *

Beijing is cold and we do not have suitable clothes. Almost everybody, particularly the elders we meet in the streets, tells us by way of gestures that our child ought to be wearing something warmer, shoes, a sweater and a jacket. We have come from a country that is so hot children nearly always go barefoot and hardly ever wear much clothing. Sroosh did not even own shoes when we arrived in China. Going through such tense times in Beijing, in the beginning we were not aware of the cold wind so we never thought about what the weather might be doing to Sroosh; he comes down with a fever. We call Mrs. Wang at the office and she advises us to take the child to a hospital near our hotel, saying the office will reimburse the expense.

After a week of medication, Sroosh's face is still red with fever; having no appetite and shivering with chills, he weakly points to his clothing hanging from a peg, saying, "unh, unh."

"This boy feels cold!" Mona says. We dress him in his heavy sweater and he settles down, relieved.

"You see? He understands more than we do."

"That's my boy!" I boast. "If he doesn't become somebody in life, then no child will."

"Put aside your bragging for another day; this poor child is burning with fever and we have to do something now."

We decide it is time to ask our Xingjiani friends for help. Having eaten at their restaurant often, we have become good friends with them and with their eye surgeon friend. Sometimes we are invited to join them in their evening meals; the father, the doctor and I drinking and laughing and joking while the mother, daughter and Mona with Sroosh sit off in a corner, chatting. This time, as in the past, the Xingjiani family receives us warmly and, hearing about Sroosh's illness, asks us to wait for their friend, who is expected for lunch.

Our Xingjiani friends

When the doctor arrives, he examines Sroosh right there in the restaurant but is not able to determine what is wrong with him so asks us to let him take our son to one of his colleagues. We agree and he gathers Sroosh in his arms and rushes to the hospital where he works; Mona and I right behind him. In emergency, tubes are passed through Sroosh's nose down to his stomach to find out if he has aspirated a foreign object. Mona and I are afraid a bone might have become lodged since his fever started right after we ate a meal with fish. But his esophagus and airway are clear and the doctors send us to a pedo ward where a woman doctor receives us. She presses on Sroosh's chest and immediately says he has bronchopneumonia; tests prove that her initial diagnosis is correct. Sroosh needs to be hospitalized and I am sent to registration on the first floor where the cashier tells me I need to deposit three thousand Chinese yuan first. With only around 1500 Yuan left in my pocket, I can't make the deposit, so run back upstairs and ask my friend to persuade the doctor to start her treatment while I go out to hunt money. At the eye surgeon's insistence, the ward doctor begins Sroosh's treatment.

Leaving Mona and Sroosh behind, I rush out, hoping to find Mr. Lam in his office on that late Friday afternoon. The taxi drops me near the river and I hurry upstairs to the UNHCR office. It looks as if everybody has already left for home; however, the office's entrance door is still open. I step in and surprisingly see Mr. Lam in the hallway walking toward his room with a teacup in his hand. Seeing me by the door, he turns and comes forward; I begin to explain my situation to him in a rapid-fire voice. When I finish, he says, "Listen, Hassan, I didn't understand one single word you said. Calm down and come with me."

He walks me to his office, gives me a cigarette and asks me to relax. Then, he brings a cup of tea which I drink while he waits. "Now tell me what your problem is."

I tell him what happened and say that I need to deposit three thousand Yuan at the hospital registration desk before my son can be admitted. He leaves the room, returning moments later with a check in his hand.

"Take it and go to the hospital and take care of your son," he says encouragingly. "Don't worry. Your child will be fine; I will pray for him."

His words give me more comfort than the check in my hand; tears spring to my eyes. "Since my experience with the UN office in India," I begin to explain, "I have hated all human rights organizations. But you have proved me wrong. I promise you that as a result of your example, to the best of my ability, I will devote my life to helping people."

All the way back to the hospital, I can't keep my tears from falling. I have a special feeling as if somebody has bought my soul and I owe a debt I can never repay. Several times the taxi driver, puzzled, looks at me through his rear view mirror without comment.

During the four days Sroosh is in the hospital, Mrs. Wang, Mr. Lam's assistant, calls us several times to ask about his condition. She also arranges to cover our hotel and to start paying us monthly stipends just like the other refugees. I can hardly find a single similarity between the Indian human rights office and the one in China.

* * *

"Listen, Hassan," Mr. Lam tells me on the phone one day, "some people from the Beijing Security Bureau will visit you at your hotel. Make sure somebody is home at all times until then. Also, do not leave the hotel on days our office is closed, because if something were to happen, we would not be available to help. In the meantime, while we are waiting for your documents to arrive from India, I need to know more about your case. Write down every single detail of your life and leave it with your wife so that she can bring it to us if the police detain you. The more I know about your life, the better I can defend you against your probable deportation."

"What did he say?" Mona is impatient to know.

"He wants a written record of our life history, since our profile has not yet arrived from India."

This answer seems to satisfy her; before she can ask more questions I tell her I will go for take-out, then begin after dinner.

That night after she goes to bed, I start writing and continue straight through the night. When Mona wakes up the following day and sees that I am still writing, she begins to worry that something is wrong, that I am hiding something from her.

"Listen," I say, handing her the papers, "we have arrived in the middle of a battlefield and are fighting for our lives. We must be ready for whatever comes. If anything happens to me, you must be strong and fight for us on your own; this is what I want from you. There is a possibility that the police will detain me today or tomorrow, if this happens, take these papers to Mr. Lam and let him handle the situation. Under no circumstances do I want you to look back; look to the future for the sake of yourself and Sroosh."

We stay in all day Saturday; nobody comes. Sunday noon rolls around and we are still waiting for the police officers. Mona is hungry and begs me to take her to the Xingjiani restaurant. She is so insistent I decide to take the chance.

Mona and I order our lunch and when it is brought, the whole family, including the doctor, joins us. We are chatting together animatedly using our clipped phrases and body language when a young man walks in. Pointing at me, he starts shouting angrily in Chinese. The doctor and the father of the family intervene and argue with him. Even though I do not understand a word of what they say, I know the family is defending me. While this is going on, the daughter of the family, who knows a little English, begins to translate. It seems the young man has a cigarette store next door to the Xingjiani restaurant. Several months earlier, a foreigner, who introduced himself as an Italian, cheated him out of about three hundred Yuan. When he sees me enter the restaurant on this Sunday afternoon, he decides I look like that man.

There is no doubt in my mind that the young man has been cheated but I wasn't even in China when it happened. However, he is so sure I am guilty he refuses to back down. One by one, every member of the Xingjiani family leaves the table and surrounds the accuser; unable to convince him that I am Iranian not Italian, the father grabs him by the collar and kicks him out of the restaurant.

During the argument, I suddenly remember Mr. Lam's words asking me not to leave my room on days when the office is closed. I break out in a cold sweat and my heart is racing.

Urging Mona to finish her lunch, we take leave of our friends, then, thinking the shop owner might follow us to our hotel and find out about the Italian passports, we take a taxi a few blocks in another direction before returning home.

* * *

On Monday, I call Mr. Lam.

"Are you calling from prison?"

"No, I am in my hotel."

With surprise that the Beijing security forces have not detained me yet, he asks me to bring my papers to him at once.

~ * ~

What if officers smiled?

On a November morning in 1999, somebody from the Beijing Security Bureau phones, asking me to come to their office the next day and bring my family. I call Mrs. Wang for advice. She is her usual source of hope, and encourages me to be patient and honest with the Chinese police so the UN office can support us.

* * *

"Promptly at nine o'clock," I tell Mr. Lee, "we arrived here at this very building and climbed to the second floor, asking for Mr. Fu who, along with several others, appeared shortly and walked us to a small room in the basement near the underground car park. I was questioned for about three hours and my answers were recorded on paper. Although Mr. Fu had a serious demeanor when he talked, I didn't notice any sort of hostility or anger in either him or the others; they even offered me cigarettes and let me smoke as much as I wished during the long interview. At the end of the session, I apologized for entering China illegally and explained that everything I had done was to save my family. Around noon, they sent us back to the hotel to wait for their call. Several days later I was asked to come back alone."

'Almost positive this time they are going to detain me, I give Mona and Sroosh a goodbye hug, encouraging Mona to be strong and fight for our lives. When I get here, the police officers set a thick pile of paper, a pen and an ashtray in front of me on the table and tell me to quickly jot down everything I have already told them, leaving the room with a single officer to monitor me. I am still writing when they come back some three hours later. After reviewing my statements, they say I can go back home to my wife and child.

"You mean I can go back to the hotel?" I ask with a bit of surprise.

"Yes," answers Mr. Fu, "go home, sit tight and don't change rooms or hotels until we call."

* * *

'Four months or so after we arrive, our documents from the Indian office finally make it to China. Then on January 28, 2000, around eight in the morning, I get a call.

"Mr. Hassan?"

"Yes?"

"I am calling from the Beijing Security Bureau," a male voice says. "You and your family have twenty minutes to pack everything, check out, and be ready at the hotel's front door. We are sending a car for you and transferring you to another place."

"Where?"

"We will tell you later."

"But twenty minutes isn't much time," I object hesitantly. "We have lived in this hotel for so long that we have things strewn everywhere. I don't think twenty minutes will be enough."

"Ok, thirty minutes."

I hang up and wake Mona, "Quick. We have only thirty minutes to check out."

Startled, she jumps out of bed. Hurriedly and carelessly, we cram everything into our bags while I repeat what the officer told me on the phone.

"But, we have to let our office know first," Mona complains, panicky that the police are going to deport us.

"The office won't open until after nine," I explain. "Besides, how could I say no to the police?"

An hour later, I open to a knock at the door and face Mr. Fu and one of his colleagues.

"Please come in," I invite them.

Seated on a chair close to me, Mr. Fu turns and with a puzzled look, asks, "How long have you been here in this hotel?"

"About four months."

"You have lived here for four months and the hotel staff still doesn't know that you are not Italian?" he asks with surprise.

"Yes."

"What about your visa? Didn't they ever ask for your visa?"

"They did, but, as I was instructed by Mrs. Wang, I referred them to her for further information. However, nobody here knows anything about our refugee status. They still think we are Italian."

Chuckling, Mr. Fu begins, "I came to the hotel this morning asking for an Iranian Hassan. The receptionist told me that there were no Iranians here. Then I asked about a young man and woman with a little child. 'Oh, you mean that Italian family,' the receptionist told me."

We all laugh at this anecdote.

It is time to leave and Mr. Fu and his colleague help us with our luggage.

"Where are we going?" I query.

"You have a child and this room is very small for you, so we are taking you to a larger place."

Downstairs at reception, we check out. Some of the staff, who have been closer to us, start to worry when they see the officers accompany us to the police car at the gate. We assure everyone that there is no problem and promise to return and bring the pictures we have taken of us together but haven't been developed yet. Relieved, they kiss Sroosh goodbye several times and we part ways.

Moving through the flow of traffic towards the outskirts of town, Mona silently looks out her window, and I look out mine as stores, buildings and people blur before our eyes. No one talks. It seems the road will never end and the white silence is pressing on our hearts. As the car leaves the city behind and only highway ahead, finally I ask again, "Where are we going?"

"You will know soon."

"I need to talk to my office."

"You can talk to them later."

"But they asked us not to leave the hotel without their permission."

"They already know about your move."

The car turns onto the freeway where the first thing we see is a large green sign along the route that reads 'Airport'.

"I think they are taking us to the airport to deport us," says Mona in a voice choking with hopelessness.

Stifling the same fear, I tell her not to worry; everything will be all right.

Then abruptly, Mr. Fu turns back to us and begins to speak. "That is the place you will live in from today," he tells us, pointing out a hotel across the highway. "Other refugees already live here. A few of them are Iranians. The hotel is larger and will be more comfortable for your family, and your child will have a bigger space to play. Besides, things are less expensive in this area and you can get whatever you need from a nearby traditional market."

What a comforting man a police officer becomes when he delivers such a message with a smile!

We walk into the lobby of the new hotel and are warmly welcomed by a charming, middle-aged woman who takes charge of Sroosh and calls for the staff to help us with our luggage.

"This lady is the manager here," Mr. Fu introduces the woman. "You can ask her for whatever you need."

* * *

After all the tension, we eventually settle down in our new quarters. The hotel has a courtyard where we meet other refugees and through them, we come to know some of the surrounding neighborhoods of Beijing.

There is nothing much for us to do now but watch TV and wait for our resettlement. Watching Chinese TV stations, I finally realize why those teenagers in the Shanghai train station did not know Jackie Chan. All TV, including what actors read from a book or a newspaper, for example, has Chinese subscript covering the original language. Therefore, the majority of local people have no idea what the stage names of their stars, such as Bruce Lee and Jackie Chan, are. In addition, they do not know universal words like 'taxi', 'basketball', 'football', or 'ok'.

Jackie Chan is Cheng Long in Chinese, which means 'Chan the Dragon', Bruce Lee is Li Xiao Long or 'Li the Little Dragon', while 'ok' has three or four equivalents[1].

Do in Rome as the Romans do!

'These days, with a huge tendency among the younger generations to learn this language, English has already surpassed Russian in popularity.

~ * ~

Hassan's new toy

"Why did you protest then?" asks Mr. Lee.

'Shortly after we arrive in the Beijing UNHCR office, Mr. Lam submits our case to Sweden for resettlement. About the same time as we move to our second hotel, Sweden rejects us.

Two weeks or so later, a Swedish national, suddenly and without notice, replaces our protection officer. When Mr. Lam steps out of the office, new regulations step in. Anaya, the new protection officer, right away has a security door installed at the front of the UNHCR office, and refugees have to be checked with a wand before entering the meeting room. Next, she changes the payment method. Mr. Lam distributed our monthly payments in cash at the office on the first of every month, but after Anaya takes over, the office becomes more formal and institutionalized. Now, we have to call, sometimes several times, to make an appointment to go in, get our payment in the form of a check, and go to a Chinese bank to exchange it for cash.

She begins a campaign to reduce the UN expenses by cutting down the amount of our payments, replacing our former hospital with a cheaper one, and refusing funds for such things as circumcision for boys.

While Mr. Lam was in office, he had a contract with one of the best hospitals in Beijing, one used by ambassadors, diplomats and government personnel. Knowing the refugees didn't speak Chinese, the UN office had chosen it for its English speaking employees. He issued in advance signed, blank checks, which we took with us when we went to the doctor or hospital; no limit was imposed on these checks.

After my second son is born, I talk to Anaya about circumcision for both boys. She says she has to inquire at the office in Geneva; months pass and I don't hear anything from her. I persist until she finally says the procedure was denied coverage.

She makes the decision that since the refugee case supports only me, I am the only one who will get the full allotment; my wife's will be cut in half. With each new restrictive measure, I am the first victim, since other refugees, most of whom are single, don't feel the stringency of the cuts.

* * *

In 2001, our second boy is born; his name is Darius after my oldest brother. Compared with Sroosh, Darius is dark skinned with very straight, black hair and two large, dark eyes in his round face. The Chinese nickname him 'Da Yanjin', which means 'Big-Eyed'.

I call my parents in Iran to give them the news. As soon as my father starts to speak, I know he is trying to hide something from me; his usual sense of humor[1] is absent.

"Where is mom?" I ask in alarm.

"She is not home."

"What do you mean she is not home? She can't go anywhere. Besides, it is already late; where would she go at this time of night?"

"To tell you the truth, your mother has left me forever. She died last week. I didn't want to disturb your life by this news so I asked Mirza not to tell you anything about it."

The news hits me hard and I remain speechless for moments.

"Listen, Hassan jaan," my father begins in a gentle tone, "this is how life is; each person has a destiny to fulfil. Look at your wife; she has lost both her parents since you two have been in China. Can she bring her parents back to this world by grief? I beg you not to keep your mind occupied with family or with the problems at home; don't let such losses take you down. If someone tells you tomorrow that your father is also dead, say, 'may God bless his soul' and go back to your work. I will be delighted if you go on with your life. Parents are like cicadas, my child. They must sacrifice themselves so that from inside their old, dried shells, new children can come out to fly and sing. If you want people to hear your voice, forget about the old shells and start flying."

This man is doing his best to bolster my spirits, but I can feel his message is as much for himself as it is for me. After so many years together, suddenly he is left with only an old house; his children gone, his life-companion, who for five decades suffered the brunt of his anger without complaint, now absent. Although physically disabled since the episode in the rice field, my mother wasn't one to complain about her life. She was always the backbone of our family. In contrast to my father, she never beat us no matter how many problems we created. Beggars never went from our house empty-handed. She encouraged our neighbors when they mourned, and shared the joy of their successes. I can't imagine how my father will survive without her.

* * *

While we were in our first hotel, Mr. Lam was paying me about 7500 Yuan every two weeks, half of which was for our rent. When, right after a payment, we were moved to our new hotel where our rent would be paid directly to the manager by the office, I was allowed to keep this 7500 Yuan as an emergency fund. I use some of it to buy us warm clothing, and still have about 5000 cash left.

One day while I am sitting in the lobby of my hotel, an Iranian refugee, on his way out the door, sees me and changes direction to walk over and say hello. After a few minutes of shooting the breeze, "Are you free?" he asks.

"All we have here is free time. Why?"

"I'm going to buy a computer and if you aren't busy, we can go together."

We discuss how computer technology is changing our lives. While we talk, the idea of buying a computer for myself comes to me. "How much does a computer cost, by the way?'

"Depends. From about three to 20 or 30 thousand."

"What is the difference, then?"

"The distinction is in their power and capacity. A computer costing 20 thousand has better hardware."

"What is hardware?"

Smiling, "You're kidding me," he says.

"No, I'm serious. Well, to be frank, I've heard the terms hardware and software, but have no idea how they function."

"Hardware consists of the body of a computer," he explains, "and software is the program put into its brain."

"Is it difficult to learn?"

"No, it's exciting."

"If I buy a 4000 Yuan computer, will it work as well as a more expensive one?"

"Yes, why not? The system works the same way. For you as a beginner, it should meet your demands."

"OK, maybe I'll buy one, then." Saying this, I ask him to wait while I talk to Mona and get the money.

"I'm going out to buy a computer," I tell Mona as I walk in the door.

"Computer?" She asks with surprise.

"Umh humh."

"Do you know how to use it?"

"Reza says computers have a Help menu which, like a teacher, mentors you."

"But I once took a computer class in Iran and was given hundreds of pages to memorize. I hated that class and quit."

"Reza says you can learn about the computer in a few days just by playing with it; no memorizing necessary."

"So you're sure you can handle it?"

"Absolutely."

She puts her bag in my hand, saying, "Take what you need."

I take all five thousand Yuan and walk out; the computer I choose costs me 4700 Yuan.

My friend and I haul the components to my living quarters and he sets it up, turns on the power and leaves me alone with my new toy. I begin to click buttons and icons and keep this up until late into the night. When I have had enough and want to go to bed, I realize nobody has mentioned anything about turning it off. I look for a Shut Down icon on the screen but do not find it. Finally, I just unplug the cord from the electrical outlet and the screen goes blank. The next day when I plug it in and hit the power button again, an Error! message flashes onto the screen.

Several times, I cause the computer to malfunction before, following the guidelines of the Window's Help menu, I manage to conquer this new technology.

* * *

In March 2001, after a lot of persistence on our part without result, from an outside source we bring pressure on the UN office for resettlement. Displeased with our effort, Anaya calls me in, "Look, Hassan," she says miffed, "I know my job. I will help you if there is any way to do so. I do respect my colleagues, but you must understand that the person with whom you shared your life story is a retired UNHCR officer. She may not be aware of the updated immigration system. So, please, don't keep pushing me."

"In '99, when I first came to this office, I was told that I would be here only a short time. A year and a half later, and we are still not resettled."

"But your case was submitted to Sweden and you were rejected."

"There are many other countries besides Sweden which accept refugees."

"We are working on it, we are working on it."

Still annoyed with our interference, Anaya grudgingly agrees to submit our case to Canada.

* * *

While waiting for our interview with the Canadian embassy, we come to know a young Canadian named Paul who is teaching English in Beijing. In addition, Paul offers internet guitar lessons.

This becomes a source of inspiration for me and I start getting acquainted with the internet and cyber life. An idea pops into my head that I could teach Persian online; share the language of Ferdowsi, Rumi and Hafez with others. I mention my idea to Paul who searches the internet and, seeing nobody else is doing that, he agrees it is a good idea and offers to help me with a webpage if I decide to go ahead with the plan.

I put a magazine in front of me and start practicing typing to learn the computer keyboard. Then I realize I could be writing lesson plans instead of copying someone else's words. So, I start writing lessons, but soon figure out I can't write in Farsi and in any case, Paul can't read in Farsi either, so he can't help me. I go online, download and install programs. I play them and they don't work, so I hunt others and install them with still no success. During this time, I crash the computer frequently; it takes me about four months to find a Farsi alphabet that works for me and doesn't cause computer meltdown. But in spite of the difficulties it presents, I find this work to be pleasant rather than tedious. The more I work, the more I enjoy it. Sometimes, I spend more than fifteen hours at a time on my computer and will still continue if Mona doesn't interrupt me. Once several lessons are ready, I call Paul, hoping he will put them online immediately.

Paul and Sroosh having a common birthday party. Since they were born on the same day, every year we got together at our place to celebrate this occasion. Our Mongolian friends are also in this picture – they played the role of real grandparents for my children during our stay in China

"Now we go to the internet," he says, showing me a CD. "But before you can become a webmaster, you need to learn another program. This CD is Dreamweaver, used to develop web pages. It is an older version I bought in Canada and don't use anymore. But, it will do for at least a couple of years."

He installs the program on my computer and opens it. "This is the Help menu," he explains. "And this one is the Tutorial. All you need to do is to follow them very carefully. Be patient and start studying as of now."

After several months of familiarizing myself with the program and working on the presentation, my website is ready offline. Paul comes back to upload it.

"Do you have a credit card?" he asks.

"Are you kidding? I am a refugee. I have no ID; I only exist inside the UNHCR office. All I have is this computer and I have put all my hopes in it. What would I do with a credit card?"

"Well, you may not need one, but your webhost does."

"Isn't internet free?"

"Watching is free, but you need to pay to own a website."

"What's the fee?"

"The fee covers the web hosting and domain name, about one hundred to one hundred fifty dollars per year."

"What is a domain?"

"Domain is the name of your website. You have to register the name so no one else can use it. But don't worry, I will find a free web hosting service for you. In the meantime, focus on Dreamweaver and work a little longer to refine the layout of your pages."

In October 2001, when Paul uploads my website to a free webhost service, we notice that free hosting websites don't load in China so he adds my new webpage to his guitar lesson site and I become a webmaster. Now every week, I update my website and email it to Paul, who downloads the files and uploads them to his own server. Not too long after that, he purchases both my domain and webhost, and easypersian.com goes online.

I begin to present the language of my country with an approach avoiding the negative methods of some of my past teachers. By the time my website is a few months old, thousands of students from across the globe have visited it, giving me renewed hope and inspiration. After years of feeling worthless, suddenly people all over the world, through their comments on my website, give me the courage to believe in myself once again.

For the past few months, my website has averaged two and a half million hits per month from 114 countries. Classes were - and still are - absolutely free. A couple of educational CDs I have made are available for purchase to my online students and provide a limited source of income. These, plus a few donations have enabled me to keep the website – and my life – going.

Our hotel is located near two well-known universities and most of its occupants are students. Feeling embarrassed about letting others know their conditions, in order to save face, refugees choose various occupations for themselves: businessman, import export manager, oil industry engineer; I choose professor. In addition to teaching Persian online, I find several Chinese students in the hotel and in neighboring areas and teach them English. In the beginning, since my students are mainly my friends or neighbors, I don't have the nerve to ask them to pay for classes. To show their gratitude for the lessons, they bring us gifts such as tea, toys for the children, seasonal fruit, and even cigarettes. These classes are very beneficial for me as well, teaching me many things about the Chinese language and culture.

Mona learns how to prepare several tasty Chinese dishes from a couple of women who work in our hotel. Most of the hotel employees love playing with our children, giving Mona more opportunity to learn the Chinese language, and her skills soon surpass mine.

* * *

Very pleased to learn that we are going to be resettled in Canada, Paul brings us several Canadian magazines and tour books to give us a head start at learning about his country; I eagerly devour all of them. He is a good source of knowledge about Canada, just as he has been for online activities, giving me ideas and letting me ferret out the details for myself. I memorize pages and pages of information about Canada and get ready for the interview coming up in November.

On September 11 of that year, a man appears who turns world order upside down and makes our resettlement an impossibility.

The day of our interview, Mona and I stand in line at the Canadian embassy waiting our turn to enter. This time, we are not Italian. When we get to the lobby, there is an elderly lady at the information window who looks very much like the one I saw the last time I was here.

"Name."

"Hassan."

"Nationality."

"Iranian."

"Married?"

"Yes."

"Why are you late?"

"Sorry, we got caught in traffic."

"That's not a good answer."

"Actually, we have two little children whom we were asked not to bring to the interview. We left the baby with our neighbors', but since we did not have anybody to take care of the older one, I took him to a kindergarten nearby. It was early in the morning, and the school was not open yet. I had to wait until one of the teachers arrived; that's why we are a few minutes late."

Sroosh among his friends and teachers in kindergarten

"Are you his wife?" She asks Mona.

"Yes."

"Can you speak English?"

"A little."

We are told to wait for the interviewer; half an hour later, a young woman approaches us in the lobby. We exchange a couple of pleasantries and she guides us to a small room, then leaves to appear at the other side of the window a few seconds later. We greet each other again and she asks Mona a few simple questions to establish her English ability. Fortunately, Mona communicates with her without any problems. She is then asked to leave the room while I am interviewed.

Finally, after more than three hours, when all the questions have been asked and answered, we are told to go home to wait for their decision.

"How long will it take?" I ask the interviewer.

"It would be stupid if I said you will get the results by the end of the month," she answers, "but for sure, by the end of the year you will hear from us."

"What do you think about my chances?"

"Personally I have no problems with it. However I have my boss, you know? I need to talk to him and this will take some time."

I thank her and leave the room, certain that our refugee life is over.

The year 2002 rolls around and still we have heard nothing. For several months each time we see a mailman in the hotel yard, we think he has a letter for us, and each time the phone rings we are sure it is from the embassy. Then, finally in late June, a letter comes that plunges our spirits into despair. The letter reads,

"Dear Mr. Hassan,

This refers to your application for permanent residence in Canada as a Convention Refugee seeking resettlement and to your interview in Beijing on 15 November 2001. You were interviewed in English. At no point in time over the course of the interview did you indicate that you were unable to understand or had a difficulty with the English language.

After an assessment of the information submitted I must inform you that I have determined you do not meet the requirements for immigration to Canada as a Convention Refugee seeking resettlement because you have failed to establish a credible and well-founded fear of persecution. In addition, you have failed to satisfy me of your ability to establish successfully in Canada."

In support of their verdict, the Acts and Rules of Canada's Immigration are included in the letter.

We appeal but to no avail. Rejection from a country like Canada, which has been awarded the Nobel Prize for Peace, ruins our hopes. Our two-year wait has come to nothing. For months, we feel broken and unable to overcome the pain.

'In spite of his lack of education and a life of hardship, my father, even though illiterate, has always amazed me with his sharp banter and our house was a common meeting ground for neighbors to visit and chat. He told us he had missed out on school because at a young age his parents had been lost, and he took on the role of father for his four brothers and a sister. His attempt at adult education ended abruptly.

²This Mongolian family has been living in our neighborhood for the past seven years. They care for our children as if they are actually grandparents and our children treat them as such.

~ * ~

Love is what matters

To overcome our disillusionment, an old acquaintance advises us to seek new friends through a church. With this idea in mind, I start skimming through the Bible online, reading parts of it to Mona, until we have a fairly good understanding of this Book and it attracts us; we decide to give church a go.

Church is so totally different from the services in a mosque, where crying is the predominant emotion, that Mona and I feel exhilarated from our very first visit. Instead of women covered in chador and relegated to the second floor, ladies here are wearing expensive, chic, and often sexy outfits. The giant auditorium, which my village mullah would probably call a religious disco, is completely full of people. At the host's instruction, stewards move from side to side of the audience and hand mikes to newcomers so they can introduce themselves and tell where they are from. I

362

am one of them. Then the mikes move to those who are saying goodbye, as it is their last time to be in the service. Live music starts and an offering is taken. People stand to sing; two or three thousand voices are raised in unison. We join in the singing, reading the hymns from a huge screen projecting the words. A pastor speaks for half an hour or so, and the service is over; the members, now knowing we are from Iran, come up one by one and welcome us warmly to their fellowship.

By the time we have been attending for some weeks and know a few people, we join a home group for Bible study classes. After months of study through both home group classes and with a Bible teacher, I am put in charge of the young adults in our home group and teach them Biblical verses and books on Christianity. Eventually I become a Sunday school teacher and, with the help of a couple other teachers, I begin to teach Bible lessons to a class of foreign teenagers. Sometimes, there are more than twenty students in our classes, most of whom grew up in religious families and already know a lot more Bible verses than I do. Being young, they often have strange questions about the deity of Jesus, or about Heaven or Hell, questions which have passed through my mind as well. In order to give answers loyal to the teachings of the church, I present these questions to my teachers, but their explanations expand my confusion by creating new questions. In the end, they say we have to believe simply because the Bible says so.

I begin to notice a conspicuous kinship between these teachers and those mullahs whom I have rejected in my own country. Both believe we need to put our faith in our messenger in order to be saved, both focus on good works, and both pass by the stretched-out hands of the needy around them to fill the coffers of their holy temples. Neither one can answer why God would send a good person to Hell merely because he does not know Jesus or Mohammad as his Savior, nor can they tell me the fate of those countless millions of people who came before them. The conclusion is simple: a church is the other face of a mosque; from outward appearances, the difference is vast, but at the core both ask you to turn off your brain and follow their tenets like a sheep. When as a child I asked the mullahs if I would go to Heaven if I believed in Mohammad, they said, 'no, you have to also do good deeds and be righteous.' Here, when I ask if believing in Jesus means I will go to Heaven, they say the same thing: 'no, you have to also do good works.' So I think to myself, 'it seems that all religions expect you to do good deeds if you want to earn a way to Heaven, but none can agree in what name you need to place your faith. How should I choose which name to believe in? Why would a God who loves me condemn me to burn in Hell for eternity because I don't know how to make that choice? If God, who loves everybody equally, is not willing to hear my voice when I talk to him directly, then will He be willing to hear me through an intermediary?'

I notice that people of different nations describe God in their own language and wonder if animals could paint, would a vulture paint God in the form of a vulture, and a wolf paint God in the form of a wolf? Would God look like a fish if a fish painted Him? What would their messengers look like?

A little girl named Sarah came home from school one wintery day and said to her dad, 'Dad, my teacher said the robins cannot find food because the grass is frozen. Will you please put out some food for the robins today so they won't starve?' This is a very poignant story but has a flaw. What happens if, instead of a robin, a crow or a cat finds the food? Sarah will probably shoo them away because in her childish brain she is waiting for a robin. The same thing is happening in the world of religion. Instead of opening the eyes of their followers to the outside world, the leaders of religions sacrifice universal values to focus on a particular religious flag.

Mona and I explore the Bible on our own and realize there is a huge difference between the Book's teachings and the words of our instructors. We begin to feel that teaching religious dogma to children might be a form of child abuse and I withdraw from teaching classes at church. Together we come to the obvious conclusion that no religion can save a human being. If you are thirsty for water, forget about the shape of cups. What matters is love, and love cannot be enforced by rules, moralities, or formalities. We attend church less and less often and finally withdraw completely from all religious congregations.

~ * ~

Friends in need are friends indeed

In 2003, our third child is born, a beautiful little girl with curly red hair, whom we name Hanna.

"She is like a doll," says Mr. Lee to his colleagues.

"Yes; I saw his children yesterday," answers one of his friends, "and we have pictures of them. How fortunate you are to have three beautiful children!" he adds, turning to me.

Beaming with pride, I thank them, after which Mr. Lee asks me to continue.

'Around this time, Anaya, the Swedish protection officer, leaves the office and soon after that, we hear she has unexpectedly died of cancer. She is replaced by Mr. Choocain, who right away decrees that the office should pay two hundred Yuan extra to my newly born daughter; a decision which gives me hope that he will be sympathetic and friendly towards us and other refugees. Before Hanna was born, Anaya reduced our monthly payments from 3600 to 2400 Yuan; earmarking 1200 Yuan for me, while my wife and the kids got 600 and 300 respectively.

As is common when a new protection officer steps in, we meet with Mr. Choocain to get to know each other. He is calm, friendly and seems very experienced in his job. After four years of dealing with Anaya, we feel we are now able to communicate with Mr. Choocain in the same way we did with Mr. Lam. This new protection officer decides to move us to an apartment. My family has lived in a hotel room since October 1999, and a new residence, located in a very good neighborhood, gives us an idea of how it would be to resettle in a new country; we are grateful and respect Mr. Choocain for his decisions.

I mention I want to have my boys circumcised and he says, 'OK, take them to the hospital and have it done'. When I need a couple minor surgeries, the office pays the bills without a hassle. In addition to financial support, Mr. Choocain values us as human beings, is considerate and always makes himself available, and as a result, Mona and I feel close to him.

Following the rule that refugees have to inform the UN office about any changes in their life conditions, during one of my meetings with Mr. Choocain, I tell him about my conversion to Christianity and go beyond this to explain how I have since come to feel about different faith systems, and the way they are politicized to be used as weapons in the hands of governments. I share my opinions with him that messengers are like policemen in the street; they are not there to bring attention to themselves, but to point out the way we should go, and we can't stop to thank them without bringing disorder. In the same way that policemen are not the final destination, messengers also are not the destination. Focusing on them brings division. "Maybe this is not important to you but to us it's a new revelation," I finish.

"To me, everything is important," he answers.

* * *

As the months pass, Mr. Choocain begins to withdraw from us and we start receiving new regulations from the UNHCR office. According to the new rules, whenever we meet with the protection officer or other senior official, we have to go into an isolated room and speak through a window. Monthly payments are reduced again and my children now receive only 250 Yuan per month, hardly enough for feeding a cat in Beijing. The UN contract with a local hospital is cancelled and we have to pay our hospital fees from our own pockets then submit the bills, which they promise will be reimbursed immediately; although it now becomes our responsibility to pay the first twenty percent. In the beginning, the bills are paid in a timely manner but soon payments are postponed for longer and longer periods of time. To talk to a person in the office becomes more difficult; the personnel don't answer phone calls and we have to call over and over for days and even weeks in order to ask them what to do about our problems, and when we finally do reach somebody, the stock answer to our questions is 'I don't know'.

Within a period of several months, a Chinese model of the Indian office has been established here under Mr. Choocain. The prices of commodities increase several times over while we are receiving less and less money. At the same time, both the UNHCR office and the Chinese government forbid us holding a job in this country.

"We already have a huge population who need employment so we can't offer jobs to refugees," intervenes Mr. Lee.

"I understand, but what do you expect me to do with three children?" I object.

They don't say anything and I continue. 'We arrange a meeting with Mr. Choocain with the hope of improving our conditions'.

"How can we survive on so little money?" I ask him once after I have talked with him a few times on this issue without changing his mind. "I have three children whose expenses increase every day."

"You should have thought about this before deciding to have them," he quips.

"To have children is my personal right," I reply. "I am talking to a human rights protection officer who is here because of my plight. You are supposed to defend my rights."

"I'd love to, but we have no budget for doing so. China has the highest rate of expenses of all UN offices. We have to bring them down."

"What are we supposed to do then?"

"There are a lot of refugees who live in tents in deserts," he says very seriously. "You are living in a house in a very good district, but you are complaining?"

"I appreciate the house, but when you are hungry, you cannot enjoy the house even if it is a palace. My children have daily needs. They do not know what it means to be a refugee. My oldest child became the top student in his class but I didn't have 100 Yuan to buy him a bicycle as I had promised him."

"I understand how you feel. But you must realize your condition; you are a refugee."

"I might be able to handle it if this condition were temporary. But I have been a refugee for over nine years. How long can I wait?"

"All refugees are equal."

"But I am more equal," I answer, smiling. "No refugees have lived this long here. I am a long-term refugee."

"We are paying you according to the fees set by the local system," he explains. "Ordinary Chinese laborers get four hundred Yuan a month while I am paying your wife six hundred."

"Who works for four hundred Yuan in Beijing in 2006?" I almost yell. "Even unskilled laborers demand one thousand Yuan now."

"No, that is not true; I know that dish washers in a restaurant get only four hundred Yuan a month."

Mr. Lee raises his eyebrows in surprise, "he means in Beijing?" he asks.

"He said so. Then he wanted me to explain how I could own a cell phone when I had problems feeding my children."

'Putting my phone on the table in front of him, I say, "Look at this; it's worth less than one hundred Yuan. Besides, when I bought it a few years ago I didn't have the financial problems I have now."

"How much do you pay in monthly fees?" Mr. Choocain asks me.

"It depends, maybe around 50 Yuan."

"Whom do you call?"

"I have been living in this country for such a long time that naturally I have many friends. This is a big city, not a desert full of tents, and to have a cell phone is part of the culture here."

"As I said, I would like to help, but we have no budget. If this lack-of-budget condition continues, we will have to take your child out of his school."

Our long discussions with Mr. Choocain bring us nothing. In fact, he does cancel my child's school bus and lunch fees. All of a sudden, I find myself facing a situation similar to what we endured in India. We live in a good house among good neighbors but we are starving. The 2250 yuan I receive from the office every month for a five-member family has to pay for food, clothing, electricity, water, gas, co-pay of hospital bills, school bus service, Chinese language support for my kids and all the little unexpected expenses which pop up. The office payment lasts about ten days and I have to look for other sources of income to survive the twenty days left in the month. In desperation, one day Mona and I take the children to the office and tell Mr. Choocain we cannot care for them and want them put into an orphanage until we are in better circumstances.

"That's no business of ours," he says, turning to walk away. Hopeless, my wife grabs his hands and starts kissing them, begging him to help us.

"Ok," he says with a sigh, "bring me an itemized list of your daily expenses; let me see what I can do."

For a couple of weeks we work on compiling a list to present to our UN protection officer, covering everything from pumice stone to carrots and cucumbers. Then suddenly one day, I look at it and feel ashamed for myself and for my family.

"What are we doing?" I ask Mona. "If he wanted to help, he would have done so without asking for a list. I will not ask this man for help at the expense of degrading ourselves. This list is beneath our dignity."

How can I force myself to report to my human rights agent the number of sanitary napkins my wife uses each month, or the amount of tissue we flush down the toilet? What right does he have to stick his nose into our privacy? I have never been so wretched in my entire life. Throwing the list into the trash, I contact one of my American friends who was once my Bible teacher and with whom I still keep in touch in spite of my withdrawal from the church. He has been a friend in need[1] more than once; in fact, he has begged me to give him the honor of helping us when difficulties arise, without expecting anything from me in return. Several times when I least expect him, he has mysteriously shown up and saved me from desperate straits. This time when I contact him, he is more than happy to loan me money which he knows I cannot repay, and advises me not to waste my time with such list-making projects.

----

[1]Another friend who has been a source of support to me during the past few years is Christine in Switzerland whom I came to know through the online Easy Persian classes. At times when I have totally lost hope, she has offered financial backing.

I know not what comes up after I die,
And want not to know what the Potter will make of my clay
on high,
My throat, like a whistle on a child's lips, I desire to see,
Who, restive and bold, blows into it to awaken thee
....Ali Shariati

Twelve

Victims of world politics

Sometime during the year 2006, I dream I am wandering around the track of a huge soccer stadium where thousands and thousands of people fill the bleachers and spill out onto the field, when I come face to face with US President George W. Bush. 'What a great opportunity,' I tell myself, 'being near such a prominent figure is!' Without much thought, and with my head full of the data surrounding my refugee status, I start to speak. "Mr. President," I call to him, "I was born in Iran; a country you have called an axis of evil. My parents called me Hassan; an Islamic name – a religion you have associated with terrorism. My father's name is Islam, a name you surely don't like. When I was a young boy in primary school, my brothers, who were my heroes, supported the Mojahedin organization and I followed them for a few years. About three decades later, your White House blacklisted this organization. After I graduated from the university, I was arbitrarily sent for my mandatory military service to the Islamic Republic Guards, another group you added to the list of terrorists. Now, no country wants me for fear I might be dangerous. Please tell me what I should do."

Finishing my statements, I raise my head to look at the president but he has disappeared as if he had never been there. I search for him in the crowd and finally spot him tucked in behind people on the highest row of bleachers farthest from the center of the field. Before I can get to where he is sitting, to talk to him again, I wake up.

* * *

"Why have you not been resettled during all these years?" Mr. Lee wants to know. "When you were rejected by Canada, did your office ever submit your case to any other country for resettlement?"

'During the Clinton administration, Mohammad Khatami, considered a less conservative politician, came into power in Iran, and America, in a gesture which was believed to be one of goodwill with Iran, and as a political maneuver, put the Mojahedin organization on the list of terrorists.

After September 11, 2001, the word terrorist explodes on the world and its direct and indirect aftershocks cause the foundations of various political groups and organizations across the globe, including the Mojahedin, to tremble. The war on terror suddenly dominates the world and governments start using this term against their oppositions.

In 2003, the US invades Iraq where the military branch of the Mojahedin organization is based. The members of this organization surrender themselves to the US forces without resistance and their leader, Mr. Masood Rajavi, disappears like smoke into the atmosphere.

According to news reports, the US government, who wants Al Qaeda members, and the Iranian government, who wants Mojahedin members, negotiate for an exchange. For unpublished reasons, this bargain fails. The White House decides to detain the more than three thousand Mojahedin members inside Iraq until the United Nations High Commissioner for Refugees can relocate them in other countries. That is why the destiny of the this organization remains unclear in the paradoxes of our new world order; the military part of it is considered illegal, its political part is legal, putting countries in a quandary about giving asylum to its ex-members or supporters.

* * *

During the three-year period between 2003 and 2006, once in a while we put pressure to bear on him and Mr. Choocain claims he has submitted our case for resettlement to countries such as, but not limited to, Norway, Holland, USA, Iceland, and the Ukraine. For each claim he makes, we wind up waiting four to six months, sometimes longer, before at our insistence, he finally tells us that we have been rejected. For example, to give us enough patience for a six-month wait, he says by June or July, Denmark will start accepting some refugees and I will submit your case then.

Frustrated, I go to the Australian Embassy to see about the possibility of applying for resettlement; I tell them about my case and condition and they say, 'OK, fill out these forms and you can apply'. Happy with the news, forms in hand, I hurry back to the UN office to talk to Mr. Choocain.

"Don't apply by yourself," he advises me, "because if you do and are rejected, you will ruin your chance for Australia."

"Do it for me, then," I plead.

"Let's wait on Denmark's decision," he answers. "We cannot apply to two counties at the same time because if one country accepts your case, the other one will have to cancel your process and if this happens, we will lose our credibility. So let's try one at a time."

Six months later, when we contact him, he tells us the Danish government has changed its mind and will not be accepting any refugees this year.

In 2006, when the UN High Commissioner for Refugees visits Beijing, he decides to meet with some refugees here during his trip and I am chosen by the office to represent the long-term dwellers in this city.

"I have been under the protection of UNHCR since 1997," I tell him in the meeting. "I have three children who were born since then, one in India and two here in China. I am not allowed to work, to study, or even to travel in China. I am not permitted to sleep away from home for even a single night without prior permission from the Chinese government. Both our human rights office and the Chinese government have asked us to sit tight here until the UN finds us a country for resettlement. But, how long can I wait?"

"He belongs to the Mojahedin organization," Mr. Choocain interrupts me. "His organization is on the list and no country is willing to accept them."

"I ran away from Iran because of the problems my family had with the Khomeini regime," I protest. "On the other hand, the so-called free world, which claims to be against the very same regime, is not willing to back us. We are double-crossed because of political games. The Khomeini regime doesn't want me because I am from a dissident family and the world doesn't give me shelter because I am from Iran and countries think I am a terrorist. To me, both Khomeini's regime, known to be anti freedom, and the free world which defends freedom have one thing in common: neither one wants me!"

Turning to Choocain, I continue, "What can I expect from others when you as my human rights protection officer call me a terrorist? Why would this human rights organization support me for almost ten years then, if I am a terrorist? How is it that the political section of the Mojahedin organization is legally active in the USA and other countries up to this very day while I, who just supported this group for a short period of time at a very young age, am being denied a normal life? Why should my family be the victim of such political games?"

"No I am not saying you are a terrorist," Mr. Choocain jumps in, "I just mentioned what countries say your situation is; I don't make world policy."

"This organization has decided that I am eligible to be a refugee," I stop him, "so it is your responsibility to defend your decision against countries."

I am still talking about the conditions of other long-term refugees when Mr. Choocain and his boss cut short my story. "The commissioner has very limited time," they say. "So please, make it short and let other refugees speak as well."

Although he does not promise to break the wicked curse put on my family, Mr. Antonio Guterres, the High Commissioner, sympathizes with me and asks for my continued patience until the UN can find a solution for us. At the end of the meeting, he calls me back and holding my hands in his, he promises not to forget our cases after returning to the UN Headquarters in Geneva.

~ ∗ ~

My longest day—Two

Although visiting with the UN High Commissioner for Refugees was an honor for me, it gives Mr. Choocain an excuse to avoid his responsibilities in our resettlement. Any time I ask him about our status, he brings up the High Commissioner, saying, "The highest level of the UNHCR organization in Geneva is personally taking care of your case. If he can't do anything for you, what can I do? You must wait."

"How can we wait longer in this miserable condition? At least pay us enough so we can wait without starving."

"We have many refugees living in tents without water. Their condition makes yours look like a paradise. If there is anybody who needs immediate help, they do."

"I do sympathize with them. However, you were sent here to take care of refugees in China. If you are worried about others, why not ask to be reassigned to an area where you can be of some help to them?"

* * *

In parallel with the frustration we feel with the delay in resettlement, our already wretched financial condition continues to deteriorate. To survive, I seek more and more students in my neighborhood since I am not officially allowed to work. Like in India, I teach my students English in their homes.

At the same time, I establish online classes for a small fee to those interested in learning more advanced Persian. But since I have no identification card and without it, am not allowed a credit card, I am fully dependent on Paul to collect my earnings. When he leaves China, my source for collection from my internet work goes with him; I cancel my new classes.

Although teaching gives me much needed self-confidence in one way, it imposes a duality on my personality in another. When I visit my UNHCR office, the respect I have garnered from students all throughout the world, who visit my website and value my opinions on language, cultural and social issues, evaporates and I feel as if I am a nobody. I am kept waiting outside, ignored and slighted, for long periods, like a slave awaiting his owner's bidding or a puppet who can't dance until someone pulls his strings.

* * *

Meanwhile, we continue to apply pressure on Choocain to find us a country, saying, "If you don't have the budget to support us, find us a way to leave."

"It's out of my hands; we cannot force any country to accept you," he answers. "I have already submitted your case to many countries who don't want you. What else can I do?"

By now, knowing he has said the same thing to three other refugees who arrived in China a short time after I did, I talk to them and together we arrange for a group meeting with him.

"Let us see for ourselves the rejection letters you have received from those countries," we demand.

"Why don't you trust me? Take my word for it."

"We just need to see written proof."

"You must believe me."

"It is not a matter of believing you or not," we tell him, "an official process has official papers¹. This is about our life; it is our right to know what's happening."

Thwarted by Mr. Choocain's refusal to meet our demands, together we write some slogans on a wide piece of cloth and stage a demonstration outside the guarded door of the UN office on the second floor. Our silent and peaceful protest lasts for more than two weeks during which time Mr. Choocain and his assistants counsel us severely on different occasions to go home, threatening they will contact the UN Headquarters in Geneva to cancel our resettlement process forever if we do not stop.

We continue to sit there in silence, writing letters to various human rights organizations around the world, including the UNHCR in Geneva and Amnesty International, until Choocain agrees to another meeting. During the so-called meeting, he warns us that in no uncertain terms he will cancel our cases if he sees us in the office the following morning. When we refuse to budge from our position, he calls you at the Beijing Security Bureau, as well as the building's security forces, who immediately arrive and surround us as if we were criminals. Your guards check all our bags and, seizing our posters, make us promise not to enter the building without prior arrangements with the UN office.

Our protest ends this way and I decide to take action on my own. Yesterday, my wife and I wrote phrases like 'I want my ID' and 'I am a refugee' on pieces of cloth, some of which we pinned on our children's T-shirts, and holding a couple others over our heads, we protested in the street outside the UNHCR building.

"Before launching the protest, I wrote a letter to you asking for your permission," I explain to Mr. Lee.

"I never gave you permission," he objects.

"I know, but we had no other choice. Our rights and the rights of our children are being abused in this country and all we did was to try to bring attention on the office."

"You have problems with your office, not with China, and you'd do better to solve your problems inside your office," says Mr. Lee. "What happened then?"

'A few minutes after we gather outside the UNHCR, the building's security forces appear and ask us to leave. We tell them that this time we are not going anywhere. Then they notify you, and you come right over with your colleagues who take pictures of us with our posters before confiscating them.

"Since you have been very friendly to me and to my family during all these years, I apologize that, to defend the rights of my family, I had to take such an action."

"But you ought to know that protests are illegal in China."

"What am I doing that is illegal? Defending the rights of a family?"

Smiling gently, Mr. Lee says, "No. To have a public demonstration is illegal in this country and you have to obey the law if you want to continue living here."

"This is not law; this is force."

Smiling again, he says, "You can interpret it that way."

"But I am not demonstrating against the government of China. I have problems with the UNHCR office."

"We don't like any kind of troubles here, Hassan. Solve your office problems inside your office."

"I tried that before, but you and your friends seized our writings and sent us home."

"Hassan," Mr. Lee starts with a sympathizing gesture, "We all love your family. We do not enjoy questioning you here all day long. Let me tell you something. The four of you single protestors who were sitting in the hall outside the UN office last time, looked like a gang when we arrived."

"But in the beginning, my family was with us too," I reply. "Unfortunately, my children got sick during the first days of our protest and could not come with me anymore."

"Your actions have made the Chinese government very angry, Hassan. We don't like any kind of trouble here. You must understand this. We all want to solve your problem. But you must realize that you cannot have a public demonstration in China for any reason whatsoever unless you have prior permission."

"But I did let you know beforehand."

"I know, but did I ever say yes to you?"

* * *

It is almost evening and I am too tired to keep arguing so I remain silent. Mr. Lee asks for a written guarantee that I will never again make any kind of trouble for the government of China. "Otherwise," he warns, "you may face deportation or imprisonment."

I sign the paper and Mr. Lee ushers me out, sympathizing with me along the way. "I understand you are disappointed," he explains, his voice kind. "But we have our own responsibility as well. What makes us happy is to see all refugees leave China with good memories. We want you to remember us with love not hatred."

There are not many people left in the hall as I exit the building. My head pounding, I sit off in a corner, lighting yet another cigarette, trying to remember where I left my bicycle. Once I finally locate it near the gate, I force myself onto the saddle, asking a young guard for the time. It is almost five-thirty and I am still an hour's ride from home.

----

[1]Except for Canada and Sweden, I was never given any written proof to confirm Mr. Choocain's claims.

~ * ~

Tomorrow is a different day; smile!

Later that very same night, I receive a phone call.

"Hello, Mr. Hassan?" a warm, well-modulated voice asks in Persian.

"Yes, go ahead, please."

"My name is Niusha Boghrati from Radio Free Europe/Radio Liberty. I work for Radio Farda, the Persian section of this radio broadcast. Our office is based in Prague, in the Czech Republic. Have you ever heard of this radio station?"

"I think so," I answer, "but to be honest, I have not been a big fan of Persian media during the past few years."

"As you may or may not know, World Refugee Day is approaching and we are preparing a program for this occasion. Your friend Sam in Sweden gave me your phone number."

Sam is one of my old friends from university days. Like many others who could not convince themselves to adapt to conditions in Iran, he went west to find a new life, and stopped when he got to Sweden.

"Do you remember him?" Mr. Boghrati asks me.

"Yes, of course."

"We are interviewing some refugees for our program, and I think it would be very interesting for our listeners to know that an Iranian refugee has been living in China for such a long time."

Even though I am having trouble focusing on my words and sentences after the day-long tension at the Beijing Security Bureau, I agree to take part in the interview.

* * *

A few days after the interview, I receive a phone call from another professional-sounding voice.

"Hello, Mr. Hassan?"

"Yes, speaking."

"This is Gorgin, from Radio Farda. Your name and telephone number were given to me by Mr. Boghrati, who spoke very highly of your language abilities. I was wondering if you would be interested in being our reporter in China."

Even as he outlines the job, my mind begins to focus on possible problems; for a person who has just signed a paper at the

Beijing Security Bureau, agreeing not to make any troubles in this country, will reporting bring the attention of the police on me?

Mr. Gorgin finishes the job description and asks, "So, what do you think? Are you interested?"

His question brings me back to the present.

"Yes," I blurt. "I certainly am interested."

"Ok," he says. "To test your ability, I want you to prepare a report on your own; I will call you back to record it."

I choose 'explosion in a coal mine in China kills 54 in a neighboring mine' and summarize it into a two-minute blurb. From that day on, Mr. Gorgin becomes my boss at Radio Farda.

In the beginning was light, And the light gave life to the earth,
And the earth hosted man. But man in his folly was selfish,
And blood was shed, Thus tension replaced peace.
....Hassan H Faramarz

Epilogue

Here is my flag

As is the case with emperors who come and go, Mr. Choocain leaves the UN office in 2007, as do several of his colleagues. To our deep surprise and joy, after nearly a seven-year absence, the very same Mr. Lam, whom I remember from his original kindness to us, returns as the protection officer, replacing Mr. Choocain.

* * *

February of 2008, the historical year of Beijing Olympics - we are still here.

Our UN office these days is divided into two parts: in the resettlement division under Mr. Lam, at the insistence of the Chinese government that foreigners must leave the country before the Olympic games start, refugees are being resettled one by one or in groups and are happy to be done with years of passivity. The atmosphere has changed; medical exams, interviews, fingerprinting and embassy visits for visas are in the air. But there is another section; the financial department apparently operates independently from resettlement. Many of the staff are young newcomers led by a program officer who is so difficult to deal with that we have already started saying, 'God bless Choocain'! The

UN office is flooded with new regulations issued by employees who had hardly graduated from kindergarten when I started my life as a refugee.

For the past four months, our medical bills have not been reimbursed, the reason given being 'fraud investigation'. Under extreme financial pressure, I have developed a heart problem, two of my teeth are broken and I can't afford to fix them, my eyes hurt and I often have headaches, my wife and I are suffering from a chronic infection, two of my children have been coughing for a couple of months, another needs a long-delayed vaccination. We can do nothing to solve any of these problems because our 'invisible program officer' – as we refugees say, since we have never seen him/her – insists that there is no budget.

My children have been taken out of school and are idle, because, according to the staff, the program officer says since we may be leaving China soon the UN office doesn't want to pay for this semester.

Under these bitter conditions, worry replaces peace in our home; the dark presence of poverty terrifies us. With each successive visit to the office, I come home feeling anxious, confused and hopeless and for days I am ill. Unable to function, I waste hours playing computer games and accomplish nothing. No longer financially able to socialize, Mona and I begin to withdraw from everybody, including our neighbors with whom we have established close friendships.

One day, while our children are still suffering from a long-term flu and we have no money to take them to a hospital, Mona begins to complain. "The children are still coughing," she tells me in a powerless whimper. "We have to do something."

"What can we do?" I answer, deadpan, looking at our children who, like three little cats, have crept under a blanket on the sofa, and are busy watching television. "You are witness to how many times I have fought with the UN office. I have done all I can. No more power left in me. The office is strong and we are weak."

"But these are your children," she raises her voice. "So what if the human rights organization does not care what happens to us! Let them all go to Hell! But I will fight for the rights of my kids."

Saying this, she stands up, walks to the other room, and in a minute, returns, dressed to go out.

"Where are you going?"

"Last night, I learned a new lesson," she begins. "You want to know what it is?"

"Sure."

"Do you remember the three red fish in that jar?" she asks, pointing to the little glass bowl on the table, which now has only one fish.

"Yes, I do."

"I found my answer in the jar."

"Well?"

"After I changed the water last night and put food for the fish, I watched it for awhile and noticed it had no more swollen spots on its skin. The fish has recovered and is eating food again. When they were three, this poor fish always felt unhappy and we were always too busy with office problems to buy a separate jar for it. I think the other two, who were younger, weren't friendly with this one, and that's why all three of them seemed very weak and dejected. Two eventually died, but this one survived. Do you know why?"

"No."

"Because this fish was simply stronger than the other two, it defied death. From that, I learned the weak die sooner. I don't want to die, I want to survive."

"Don't be so worried; nobody is dying."

"I am. You just can't see my pain."

"What do you plan to do?"

"This damned office never frees my mind so I can focus on my life. If I had taken the time to separate these fish from one another, none of them would have died."

"The difference is we cannot separate ourselves from this UN office," I say ironically. "They are the ones who will decide when to put us in a new jar."

"Maybe not, but I certainly can separate myself from you."

"What do you mean?" I ask, smiling in disbelief.

"Together, we have been refugees for almost a decade. During this time, you have almost always represented this family in the UN office by yourself because the case is yours. But from here on out, this is no longer only your case. Today, I am going to the office to start a new case, the case of my children."

"Please, don't make the condition worse than it is. You know, due to the upcoming Olympics, the Chinese government and the office are very sensitive these days. Many asylum seekers and some refugees have already been deported. Besides, the office has told us that they have submitted our case to Ireland."

"I don't trust them anymore; I think these people in the office are trying to distract us from our financial woes by dangling this so-called resettlement in front of our noses. Do you remember how many times Choocain lied to us?"

"But this time is different; I trust Mr. Lam. It is not a good time to take such a risk. Please be patient."

"Just on the contrary, now is exactly the right time to take action. These people, because of the Olympics, want to save face in front of the whole world, right?"

"Right."

"Today I am going to tell them if they don't deal with us now, I will take my children to the stadiums during the Olympic Games and will shout in front of people and the world's media that the rights of my children are being abused in this country. If necessary, I will kill myself to save my children."

"Please, Mona. Don't do that. You are angry now and may do something to make things worse than they are."

"Don't you even try to stop me!" she shouts, tears running down her cheeks. "If anybody calls you from the office today and asks you to intervene, you just tell them your wife has gone crazy and you can't control her any longer."

My children and I watch her in silence as she turns and walks out.

Hardly an hour has passed when the phone rings.

"Hello, Mr. Hassan?"

Recognizing the voice to be Mr. Chen, I answer in a cold tone, "Yes?"

"This is Chen from the UNHCR," he tells me in a very soft voice. "Mrs. Hassan is here, very distraught and crying uncontrollably. Please note that these days the Chinese government is very sensitive and may not be tolerable of disorder. Her presence at the office in such an excitable condition may cause the police to take negative action. As you know, many have been deported recently."

"What do you expect me to do?" I ask, cold and serious. "Do you want me to say shut up to a mother who is crying in an effort to save her children? Why don't you solve this problem? Who has created this condition for us? Do you think I enjoy seeing my wife coming to your office in this manner? When we want resettlement, you say it is out of your control. Now, we are not talking about resettlement, we are demanding the money that is rightfully ours. For the past three or four months, under so-called 'fraud investigation', you have stopped reimbursing our hospital bills. This office owes me about eight thousand yuan, which I borrowed from people to spend on my children's hospital expenses. You asked for our patience and cooperation, and we did cooperate. Now after this long period, the office tells me that bills submitted during the past four months will not ever be reimbursed. Why not?"

"That is the program officer's decision. I don't know about it."

"Who is this program officer? Why is it that this person hides himself from me? All I hear from this person are messages passed to me through the staff who themselves have no clear answer to my questions. What's happening in that office? Why is it that nobody knows anything? Who else can solve my problem? You tell me what I should do."

"We are modernizing our computer systems and this process takes time."

"As far as I know, the computer was invented to speed up processes, not to slow them down."

"Listen, your wife's presence in this condition will help neither your family nor the office."

"Give her the rights of her children and I promise she will immediately leave your office. I have kept her quiet for the past nine years, but I can't do it any longer. In fact, in support of my wife, I am sitting here writing a letter to the offices of President Hu Jintao, Prime Minister Wen Jiabao and the Chinese Foreign Ministry, copies of which I will send to all major media of the world to let them know what is happening to my family."

"Please, you are just making things more complicated."

As we talk, I feel a slow, cold pain spreading through my chest, drops of sweat flow down my forehead and my body starts to go numb. Our 20-minute-long discussion ends with no consensus.

"Dad, we won't have money later?" Sroosh, whom I thought was watching television, asks me in Chinese as I hang up.

"Why?"

"Because you just fought with your office."

"So?"

"I think they will not help us anymore."

"How do you know it was from my office?"

"I just know."

"If they don't give us money, we can't go to school?" Darius jumps in.

"Baba," Sarah joins her brothers, "when I grow older, I will work to give you money."

Embracing all of them, I say, "You don't have to worry about these things. Mommy and I will take care of everything. If you want to make me happy, read a lot of books. Do you know why?"

"No, why?" they answer.

"Because if you read a lot of books, you will know a lot of things and you will find a lot of jobs. And when you have a lot of jobs, you will have a lot of money, right?"

"Then we can buy a house?" Sarah asks.

"Of course, we can."

"I want to buy a jeep like the one our Mongolian grandma's friend has," Darius explains. "And a dog and a horse."

* * *

Mona returns home in the afternoon, smug. "In the beginning," she begins at the door where I go to welcome her, "these stupid people sent me to a room to talk to a woman. Believing she was the program officer, I gave her all the details about our life condition and she listened very patiently. When I finished talking, she said she had no idea what to do."

"Who are you then?" I asked her.

"I am working for this office as a psychiatrist."

"A psychiatrist? You think I am mad?"

"No, don't think that way. You were angry and I was called in to help you."

"Give me my money," I shouted. "I don't want your help. Your presence here is bothering me."

"Saying this, I left the room and, right in front of the security door, I began to shout afresh, this time louder. A couple of reporters, who had come to the office to write an article on the deportation of some refugees, watched me in silence without even asking what was wrong with me. I kept shouting until a woman came who introduced herself as the program officer. She took me to the common interview room which I hate, and insisting that the office had run out of budget, she eventually promised to try to reimburse two thousand out of eight. At first, I didn't want to accept it, but knowing we really need that money, I finally agreed. Something is better than nothing, isn't it?"

"Well, well," I begin to praise her. "Look at my lion-hearted wife! I have had such a hero in my house all this time, but didn't know it myself! I am really proud of you."

Hearing Mona's voice in the hallway, the children leave the television and run to embrace her.

"Mommy is back!" they exclaim, throwing themselves all over their mother. "What happened, mommy?"

"Everything is fine now," she tells them.

"Listen, kids," I say happily. "Mommy defeated the office!"

"Yeah!" together, we shout, our fists in the air.

"Mom-my," I coach the children. "Mo-mmy, come on, mom-my, everybody, mom-my. Mom-my, mom-my, mom-my!" we chant.

* * *

Some time before April 2008, together with my family, I am watching television when the phone rings.

"Hello?" I answer.

"Hello, Mr. Hassan?"

"Yes?"

"This is Peter from UNHCR. How are you doing?"

"Not dead yet."

"How is your family doing?"

"Not bad," I answer curtly.

"I have good news for you, sir," he says in a warm tone.

"Does UNHCR ever give good news to people?"

"Of course, we do," he emphasizes.

"Why is it that I have never received any?"

"Today, you will receive some. The people of Ireland have decided that you can live in their country."

Pausing in silence for a moment, "No," I say, disbelieving.

"Yes!" Peter answers crisply, his voice happy.

"No," I repeat with the same tone.

"Yes!"

"Yes!" I suddenly shout. "Really?"

"More than really!"

"Yeeeeees!" I cry out again. "Honestly?"

"Unhuum!"

"No joking?"

"No, I am very serious."

"Wow! Thank you Peter, thank you very much."

"You are very welcome. We are just sorry that you had to wait so long for this."

"What do I do now?"

"All you need do is to bring your family to the office next week, and we will help you with the forms and other necessary paperwork."

* * *

The day we submit the final papers to the UN personnel in the small interview room, we ask if it is possible to see Mr. Lam one last time. In seconds, he walks into the room and, with the same familiar smile on his face, holds out his hand to shake ours. His usual warm presence is still comforting.

"Years ago, you saved my child," I begin, holding his hand in mine, "and today, after all this time, you have come back to save my family. Please allow me to kiss your hand."

Before he can say anything, I bow down and kiss his hand.

"To tell the truth, this was teamwork and I played a very small role in it. I am really sorry to see you again all these years later," Mr. Lam tells us, then laughs. "I don't mean I don't want to see you, I mean I was shocked and sorry to see you still in this refugee condition when I returned from Iran."

"Were you in Iran?"

"Yes. I left Beijing for Tehran."

"No kidding! How did you find Iran?"

"Ah, Iran is a great country. People are very friendly and hospitable. I even learned the name of my favorite food: ghormeh sabzi!"

"Mr. Lam, thank you very much for everything you have done for my family. I want you to know that with the help of a friend, I am writing my life history in the form of a memoir. In this book, I talk about my life in Iran, India and here in China, doing my best to reflect honestly what life has placed in my path. Included are stories about the condition of refugees in the two countries I have lived in, and the good and the bad people I have encountered on this long journey."

"I hope my name is not among the bad people," Mr. Lam says, smiling.

"Actually, the hero of my book is a person who is my symbol of peace and humanity, and this person is Mr. Lam. I would appreciate it if you kindly let me have the honor to mention you in my book."

"Ah, the honor is mine," he replies. "Is it in English?"

"Yes, indeed."

"I hope this book sells millions; I can't wait to receive my own personal signed copy!"

Mr. Lam sandwiched between Mona and me in the UNHCR office five days before we left China

The end

CPSIA information can be obtained at www.ICGtesting.com
Printed in the USA
LVOW12s0757260514

387280LV00020B/1155/P